Preparing for
Microsoft Office Specialist Certification
Microsoft Word 2000

Series Authors
Patty Winter
Rick Winter

Authors
Elaine Betts
Rebecca Fiala
Faithe Wempen
Patty Winter

Acknowledgements

About the authors:

Patty Winter and **Rick Winter** have each trained over 3,000 students on personal computers during the last eleven years. Rick is a Microsoft Office Specialist Master for Office 97, Microsoft Certified Trainer, and former president of Information Systems Trainers.

Elaine Betts is a Certified Technical Trainer who, during the past three years, has authored all or portions of six computer-related books covering graphics, desktop publishing, Web graphics, databases, and word processing. She is also a certified teacher of English at the Secondary level. You can learn more about her and contact her at www.ebetts.com.

Faithe Wempen owns and operates Your Computer Friend, a computer training and troubleshooting business in Indianapolis that specializes in helping individuals and small businesses with their PCs. Her writing credits include over 40 computer books, as well as training manuals, OEM documentation, and magazine articles.

Contributing Author: **Rebecca Fiala**

Project Managers	Technical Editors	Copy Editors	Layout and Design
Kathy Berkemeyer	Cheryl Brumbaugh	Kristen Cassareau	Jeff Grisenthwaite
Jeff Grisenthwaite	Rebecca J. Fiala	Nicole Sulgit	Maria Kardesheva
	Jeff Grisenthwaite		Bethany Stubbe
	Marty Mechtenberg		

First DDC Training Services Printing
10 9 8 7 6 5 4 3 2 1
Printed in the United States of America

ISBN: 1-58577-024-8
Catalog number: EP4

TABLE OF CONTENTS

INTRODUCTION

SECTION A

SECTION B

SECTION C

MICROSOFT OFFICE SPECIALIST INDEX

INDEX

ON THE CD-ROM

The following lessons can be found in the **WORDCert** folder on the CD-ROM. See the **To open a PDF file** procedure in the Introduction for help on opening and printing these lessons.

INTRODUCTION

Welcome to *Preparing for Microsoft Office Specialist Certification for Microsoft Word 2000*. This book is designed to provide you with exciting and informative instruction that will prepare you to take both the Core and Expert level Microsoft Office Specialist exams. This material, and your determination to master it, should provide you with the tools you need to achieve certification and be productive with the software.

Who Should Use This Book?

This book is designed for users who want to take either of the Microsoft Word 2000 Microsoft Office Specialist exams, as well as those who want to master the powerful features of Word. To get the most out of this book, you should be familiar with basic Windows features, including the mouse, menus, dialog boxes, the parts of a window, and the Help feature. An overview of this information is available in **Appendix A: Getting Help** and **Appendix B: Windows Features** located in the **WORDCert** folder on the CD-ROM on the back inside cover of this book.

How to Use This Book

The *Preparing for Microsoft Office Specialist Certification for Microsoft Word 2000* consists of three sections; each section contains a number of lessons. In each lesson you'll learn how to perform several tasks. First you'll find out why you would perform the task, then you'll get a general procedure for accomplishing the task, and then you'll have the opportunity to practice what you've learned with a Practice Exercise.

WALK, RUN, FLY AND FINAL EXERCISES

At the end of each lesson, you'll be able to take three challenge exercises designed to reinforce and test your skills. All of these exercises are on the CD-ROM in the **WORDCert\Word A, WORDCert\Word B,** or **WORDCert\Word C** folders.

Walk This exercise reviews each of the tasks covered in the lesson, with complete step-by-step instructions to help you.

Run This exercise is similar to the Walk exercise, in that it also reviews each of the lesson's tasks. However, the Run exercise is a bit more difficult because it tells you **what** to do, but not specifically **how** to do it.

Fly This exercise presents the biggest challenge by including not only tasks covered in the lesson, but also related, more advanced tasks.

At the end of each section, you can take a **Final Exercise**. This ties the entire section together and provides excellent practice for Microsoft Office Specialist tests. The Final Exercises are located on the CD-ROM in the **WORDCert\Word A, WORDCert\Word B,** or **WORDCert\Word C** folders.

DDC TESTING CENTER SOFTWARE
Included on the CD-ROM that ships with this book is DDC Testing Center software that will provide a realistic assessment of your skills. This software is similar to the testing environment of the actual Microsoft Office Specialist exam. A detailed report will display after the test. You can then do additional study using the book to improve your skills and better prepare for the Microsoft Office Specialist exam. You may only install DDC Testing Center on one computer. See the End-User License Agreement (EULA) on the CD-ROM for further information. You can take up to three tests. Additional practice tests are available from DDC. You may want to take a practice test before you begin the lessons in this book so you can get an idea of the areas where you need to focus.

About the Microsoft Office Specialist Exams
Microsoft Office Specialist is a certification program sponsored by Microsoft to help you prove your ability to use Office programs. Microsoft Office Specialist offers two levels of certification exams, **Core** and **Expert**. All the Microsoft Office Specialist exam objectives for both levels are covered in the three sections of this book.

Sections A & B work in combination to cover all of the objectives on the Microsoft Office Specialist Core exam. Section C covers all of the Expert objectives that were not covered in Sections A & B. After you complete this book, you will be well prepared to take the Expert level Microsoft Office Specialist exam for Microsoft Word 2000.

Since each lesson is self-contained, you can identify the skills you need to work on and target the lessons that cover those features. At the end of the book, you will find an index of the Microsoft Office Specialist objectives and where they are covered.

Learn more about Microsoft Office Specialist certification at **www.certiport.com**.

Test-Taking Tips:
- Read instructions and test questions carefully. After completing each question, read over the question again to make sure you performed all the tasks exactly as asked.
- A timer is available if you want to see how much time remains. If a small clock icon displays on the title bar, double-click it to activate a digital timer. If the timer is distracting, double-click it to hide it.
- Errant keystrokes or mouse clicks will not count against your score as long as you achieve the correct end result.
- Remember that the overall test is timed.
- You can use menu commands, toolbar buttons, or shortcut keys.
- A Reset option is available if you want to start a task over; it does NOT let you return to a question. Reset will only work for the task that is currently on-screen.
- Microsoft Office Help is available during the Microsoft Office Specialist exam. Using it will not detract from your score, but be aware of how much time is remaining as you use Help.
- Save your Results Page that prints at the end of the exam. It is your confirmation that you passed the exam.

BEFORE YOU BEGIN

All folders and files for this book are stored in a folder named
WORDCert on the CD-ROM inside the back cover of this book.
Additional folders on the CD-ROM will not be used for this course.

How to Use the Practice Files

A number of practice files are provided on the CD-ROM for use with exercises in the
book. Whenever you need to use a practice file, the book will tell you to open a
specific file from the **WORDCert\Word A, WORDCert\Word B,** or **WORDCert\Word C**
folder. The backslash between the folder names indicates that the section folders are
located within the **WORDCert** folder. A folder symbol 🗁 in the book identifies all files
from the **WORDCert** folder, so you'll always know where to find them.

How to open a practice file:

1   Insert the CD-ROM into your CD-ROM drive.

2   Click the **Start** button on the Windows taskbar, point to
     Programs, and choose **Microsoft Word.**

3   In Word, click the **Open** button on the Standard toolbar.

4   Click the arrow on the **Look in** box and select your CD-ROM drive.

5   In the list below the **Look in** box, locate and double-click
     the **WORDCert** folder.

6   Double-click on a section folder to open it.

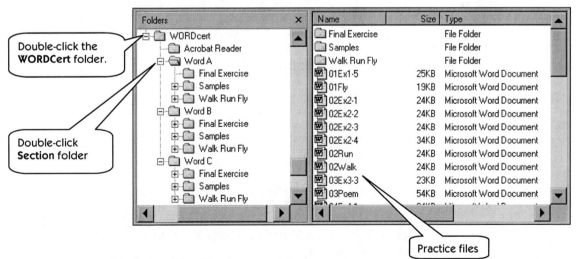

7   Select the file you want to open.

8   Choose **Open.**

After you open a practice file, you will usually be asked to save it under a new name.
A disk icon 🖫 identifies all saving instructions, so you'll always know when to rename
a file. You'll learn how to save and name a file in Lesson 1.

How to Use the Sample Exercise Solutions

Sample solutions are provided for many of the practice exercises. Inside each of the section folders on the CD-ROM, you will find a **Samples** folder. At the end of an exercise, when there is a sample available, there will be an explanation on where to find the sample solution. For example:

A completed example of 06Table is available in the **WORDCert\Word A\Samples** folder.

Solutions for Practice Exercises are provided in Word file format. To open these solutions, follow the steps on the previous page for **How to open a practice file** (double-click the **Samples** folder after step 6 to open it).

Solutions for the wrap-up exercises (called **Walk, Run,** and **Fly** exercises), are provided in Adobe PDF (Portable Document Format) format. You can view or print these PDF files using Adobe® Acrobat® Reader. Adobe Acrobat Reader 4.0 is included in the **WORDCert\Acrobat Reader** folder on the CD-ROM; install it on your computer if you do not already have Acrobat Reader.

 CAUTION: If you already have any version of Adobe Acrobat Reader installed on your system, **you must first uninstall it before you install Acrobat Reader 4.0**. To uninstall, you can use the uninstall option in the **Adobe Acrobat** folder in your **Start** menu or **Add/Remove Programs** in the **Control Panel.**

To install Acrobat Reader:

1   Insert the DDC CD-ROM in your CD-ROM drive.

 2   Double-click **My Computer,** located on the Windows desktop.

 3   Double-click on the CD-ROM drive to open it.

4   Double-click the **WORDCert** folder and then double-click the **Acrobat Reader** folder on the CD-ROM.

5   Double-click the **setup** icon.

6   Follow the prompts to install **Acrobat Reader 4.0.**

To open a PDF file:

1   Insert the DDC CD-ROM in your CD-ROM drive.

2   In Windows Explorer, double-click the **WORDCert** folder and then double-click the **Word A, Word B,** or **Word C** folder. Then click the **Samples** folder.

3   Double-click the desired PDF file.

Adobe Acrobat Reader will start and the file will open for viewing and/or printing.

LESSON 1: CREATE SIMPLE LETTERS

Microsoft Word helps you produce many different kinds of documents, such as letters, memos, and tables. Most of us need to create letters. When you know how to create a business letter in Word, it's only a short jump to creating bigger and more complex documents. This lesson will introduce everything you need to produce a letter. The remaining lessons in this section will explain in detail some of the topics introduced here. This is intended to give you a jumpstart on word processing.

In this lesson, you will learn to:

> Start and Exit Microsoft Word

> Understand the basics of typing in a word-processing program

> Use the Office Assistant

> Save your work and print your letter

You will have an opportunity to practice these skills in the Practice Exercises and the Exercises at the end of the lesson.

Parts of a Letter

Business letters have several parts: the **date line**, which identifies when the letter originated; an **address block** that tells where the letter is going; a **salutation** or greeting, to the recipient; the **body** of the letter; and the **closing**, complete with a **signature block** and often a notation of who typed the letter. (See Figure 1.1.)

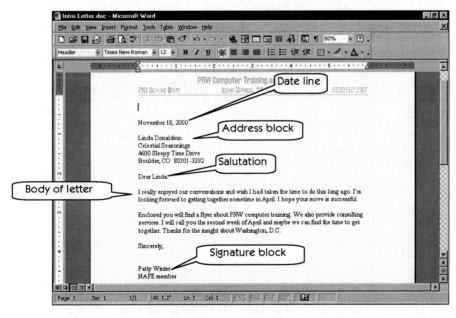

Figure 1.1. This shows the different elements in a completed letter.

Start Word

Before you can do anything in Word, your computer must be booted up, and the Word application must be open and running. (If you're still a novice in the world of computers, you can refer to Appendix B on the CD-ROM for help using Windows.) After your computer is on and Windows is running, starting Word is simple.

 TIP: If you installed Microsoft Office in a group folder, you will need to select the Microsoft Office folder from the **Programs** menu and then choose **Microsoft Word**.

Open Microsoft Word:

 1   On the taskbar, click the **Start** button.

2   On the **Start** menu, choose **Programs**.

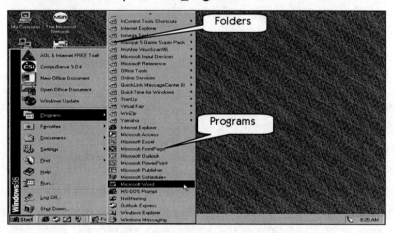

Figure 1.2.   The Start>Programs menu.

3   On the **Programs** menu, choose **Microsoft Word**.

The Microsoft Word window is displayed, as shown below.

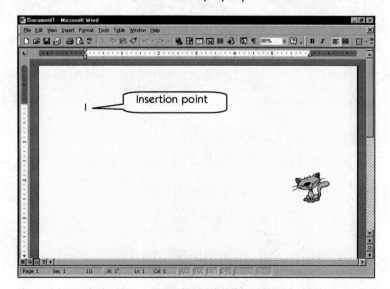

Figure 1.3.   A blank document window in Microsoft Word 2000. The insertion point is identified by a flashing vertical bar.

NOTE: One new feature of Word 2000 that differs from Word 97 is the positioning of the Standard and Formatting toolbars. They now appear side by side, in a single row along the top of the workspace. If you prefer the "old look," choose **View**, **Toolbars**, **Customize**, and click the **Options** tab. Deselect the **Standard and Formatting toolbars share one row** check box.
Then choose **Close**.

Practice Exercise 1-1

Start Microsoft Word

 1 Click the **Start** button on the taskbar.

2 Choose **Programs** on the **Start** menu.

3 Choose **Microsoft Word** on the **Programs** menu.

By default, when you start Word 2000, a blank document opens along with the application, and you're ready to begin creating any sort of document you need.

 NOTE: Each time you create a new document using the **New Blank Document** command, Microsoft Word uses the Normal template (NORMAL.DOT). This template provides basic settings for margins, tabs, styles, and paper size that you can use every time you create the same type of document in order to make your documents look consistent.

Enter Text

At the top of a blank document you will see a blinking **insertion point**, as shown in Figure 1.3. Once you begin typing, the insertion point will move to the right.

Unlike older-model typewriters, Word has a feature called **word wrap** that eliminates the task of manually starting a new line of text when you've reached the end of a line. Simply continue typing, and, when you reach the end of the line, the insertion point automatically moves down one line to the left margin.

When you want to begin a new paragraph, whether you're at the end of a line or before the line has reached the right margin, press the **Enter** key.

As you type, use the following keys:

- Press **Enter** for
    - Short lines (date lines, titles, addresses)
    - End of paragraphs
    - Blank lines

- To remove a paragraph break created when you pressed the **Enter** key:

  - Position the insertion point in front of the first word you typed after pressing **Enter** and press **Backspace,**
OR

  - Position the insertion point at the end of the original line, in front of the paragraph symbol (¶), and press **Delete.**

The text you type includes letters, numbers, and spaces. Some words need to be capitalized. Sometimes you need to type special characters, such as the dollar sign ($). To accomplish these feats of typing excellence, use:

- **Shift** + a letter to create a capital letter.
- **Shift** + a number key to create the character shown at the top of the number key.

Use these keys as you type and edit text:

- To type text in all caps, press the **Caps Lock** key before you begin typing.
- To use the numbers on the keypad on the right side of your keyboard, press the **Num Lock** key.
- To correct a mistake to the *left* of the insertion point, press **Backspace**.
- To correct a mistake to the *right* of the insertion point, press **Delete**.

 TIP: Use **Ctrl+Backspace** to delete one word at a time to the left of the insertion point. **Ctrl+Delete** deletes one word at a time to the right of the insertion point.

NONPRINTING CHARACTERS — SHOW/HIDE ¶

As you type, you may see mysterious characters at the end of paragraphs or where you have used the **Tab** key, and tiny dots between words. These characters appear onscreen but don't print. In this case, what you see is **not** what you get. These are nonprinting characters, Word's version of road signs that help you by indicating where you pressed the **Enter** key at the end of paragraphs, pressed the **Tab** key to indent a line, pressed the spacebar between words, and created a line break.

Some nonprinting characters include:

- A **hard return** ¶ created by pressing the **Enter** key, indicating the end of a paragraph
- A **soft return** ↵ (or line break) created by holding down the **Shift** key as you press the **Enter** key

- A **space** · created by pressing the **spacebar**, indicating a separation of letters, numbers, or words
- A **tab** → created by pressing the **Tab** key

None of these characters appears in the final printout of your document. They serve only as a means of alerting you to the existence of double spaces between words, to excessive use of the **Enter** key to create space between paragraphs, and to places in the text where you have used a **Tab** or a soft return.

 Most people display these nonprinting characters while typing but then prefer to hide them at some times, for example, to give a clear view of the text as they revise content or when viewing their documents in Print Layout view.

 NOTE: If you are familiar with WordPerfect, **Show/Hide ¶** is similar to Reveal Codes.

Turn nonprinting characters on or off:

 • Click the **Show/Hide ¶** button on the Standard toolbar.

 • Click the **Show/Hide ¶** button again to toggle nonprinting characters from off to on, and vice versa.

Exit Word

When you finish working with Word, you can either exit the program or leave it running in case you need it again later. You can have several programs running at once in Windows, and you can switch among them using the taskbar. (You'll see how to do this in the next lesson.)

If you have a lot of programs running at once, the performance of the computer may diminish. The applications may run more slowly or, in a worst-case situation, will lock up. Most people prefer to exit a program when they are finished using it.

Exit Word:

1 Choose the **File** menu.

2 Choose E**x**it.

If you have a file open and not saved (even if all you did was press the spacebar in a blank document), you will see a message from Word asking if you would like to save the file.

3 At this point you choose **Yes** or **No** depending on the file:

- If you have not created anything you need to save, choose **No**.
- On the other hand, if you need to save what you created, choose **Yes**. (Follow the instructions for saving that appear later in this lesson.)

Practice Exercise 1-2

Create Your First Letter

1   If necessary, start Microsoft Word (**Start>Programs>Microsoft Word**) and open a new, blank document.

 TIP: As you are typing, use **Backspace** to correct mistakes to the left of the insertion point, and press **Delete** to correct mistakes to the right of the insertion point.

2   Type today's date.

 TIP: After you type the month and a space, you may see a ScreenTip displaying the current date. You can press **Enter** when you see the date; Word will automatically enter it.

3   Press **Enter** three times.

4   Type the following text (press **Enter** at the end of each line):

Fred Jorgenson
ABC Merchandise
PO Box 1622
Colorado Springs, CO 80354

5   Press **Enter** twice.

6   Type Dear Fred: and press **Enter** twice.

 7   Click the **Show/Hide ¶** button on the Standard toolbar to display nonprinting characters.

 TIP: The keyboard shortcut to toggle the display of nonprinting characters on and off is **Ctrl+Shift+8** (the 8 on the number row above the letters, not the 8 on the keypad).

8   Type the following text (do not press **Enter** at the end of the lines; let word wrap do the work for you):

Thank you for your time on the phone today. As promised here is a letter stating who we are and what we do. Please keep this for future reference, and give us a call when you have a need.

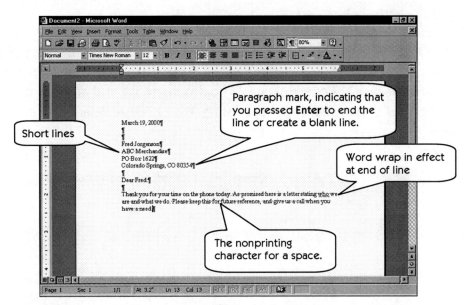

Figure 1.4. The way your first letter will look.

 NOTE: If you see any red or green wavy lines, Word is trying to tell you that you may have a spelling or grammar error. If you have any errors, leave them for now; later in this section you will learn how to correct errors.

9 Choose **File>Exit** to exit and close Word.

10 Word will display a message asking if you would like to save changes to the document you were working on. Choose **No** to exit Word without saving the document. (Saving documents is covered in detail in Lesson 3.)

11 Click the **Start** button and choose **Programs>Microsoft Word** to start Word again.

Office Assistant

The Office Assistant is a clever device Microsoft added to the Office applications for helping you through document creation. As you are typing in Word, the Office Assistant takes note of the shape of your paragraphs and makes a calculated guess as to the kind of document you're creating. The Office Assistant may display a message telling you that it looks like you're writing a letter. Figure 1.5 shows the Office Assistant at work.

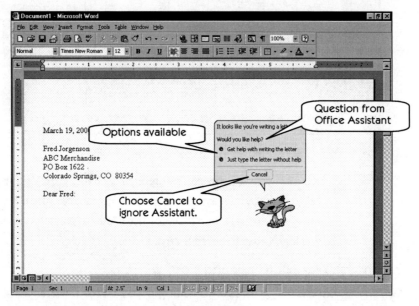

Figure 1.5.   The Office Assistant is waiting to help.

If, in fact, you are writing a letter and you do want help from the Office Assistant, choose the **Get help with writing the letter** option.

 NOTE: If the Office Assistant does not show up automatically, choose **Help>Show the Office Assistant**. Then, to use the Letter Wizard to get help writing the letter, choose **Tools>Letter Wizard** (see Figure 1.6).

As the Office Assistant guides you through the process of creating a letter, the Letter Wizard opens and steps you through the process of creating a business letter. If you use the **Tools>Letter Wizard** command to create a letter without using the Office Assistant, you will move through the Letter Wizard dialog box by selecting the tab you need (the navigation buttons **Back**, **Next**, and **Finish** are not displayed in Figure 1.6).

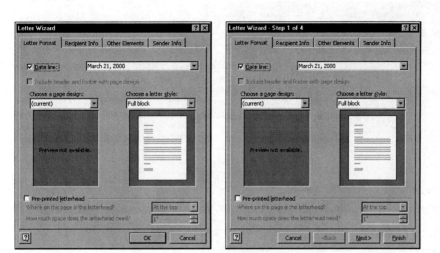

Figure 1.6. Letter Wizard on the left; Letter Wizard with the help of the Office Assistant on the right. The **Letter Format** tab is shown in both dialog boxes.

Navigate through the **Letter Wizard** dialog box and select options that you want to use. Figures 1.7 through 1.10 show the contents of the four tabs that appear in the dialog box. If you are using the Office Assistant, you can use the navigation buttons on the bottom of the dialog box, or use the tabs at the top of the dialog box to see all the options.

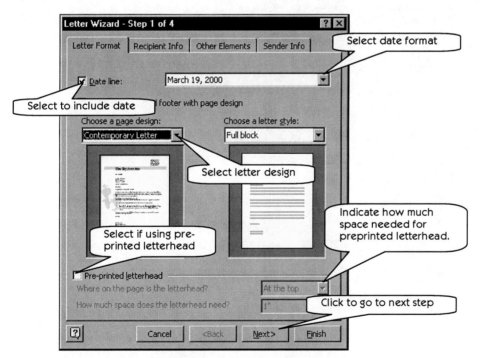

Figure 1.7. Step one, the **Letter Format** tab, gives you options to define the general appearance and style of your letter.

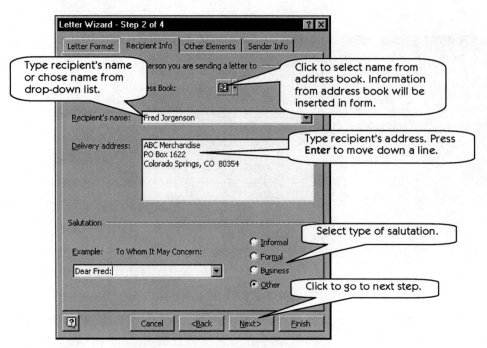

Figure 1.8.   Step two, the **Recipient Info** tab, gathers
                   information about the letter recipient .

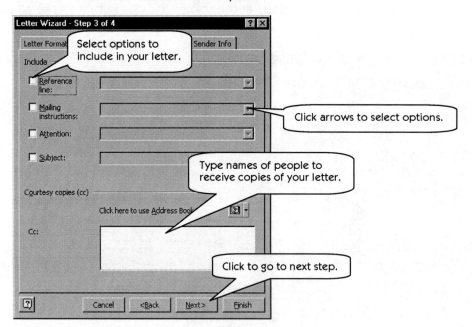

Figure 1.9.   Step three, the **Other Elements** tab,
                   gathers information about other elements
                   for your letter.

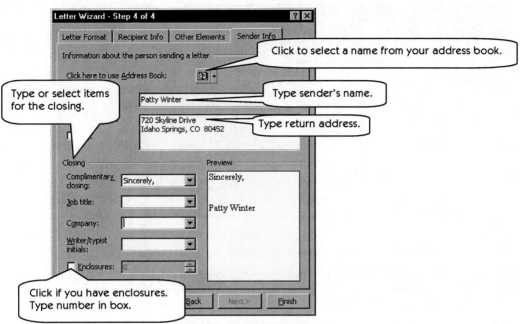

Figure 1.10.   Step four, the **Sender Info** tab, gathers
information about the sender of the letter.

When you finish completing the necessary fields on the different **Letter Wizard** tabs, do
one of the following:

- Choose **Finish** (if you began the process using the Office
  Assistant)

- Choose **OK** (if you began the process using the **Tools>Letter
  Wizard** command)

If you've used the Letter Wizard, your document will then be displayed with
placeholder instructions for the options you chose. For instance, **Type your text here.**
is already selected (as you can see in Figure 1.11), and all you need to do is type the
body of your letter. You can also use the Office Assistant to create an envelope for
your letter, make a mailing label, or run the Letter Wizard again if you overlooked
something the first time through.

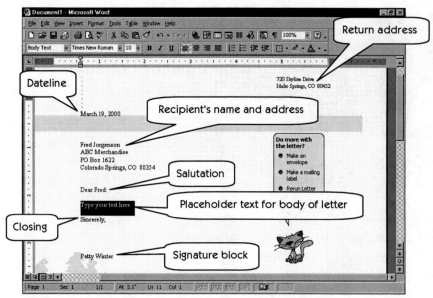

Figure 1.11.   Begin typing the body of the letter.

To replace the placeholder instructions, if necessary, drag to select the instructions and start right in typing your own words. The placeholder text is automatically deleted as you begin to type.

Create an envelope to go with your letter:

- Choose the **Make an envelope** option from the Office Assistant.
- If the Office Assistant is no longer displayed, place the insertion point anywhere in the recipient's address and choose **Tools>Envelopes and Labels** to display the **Envelopes and Labels** dialog box (see Figure 1.12).

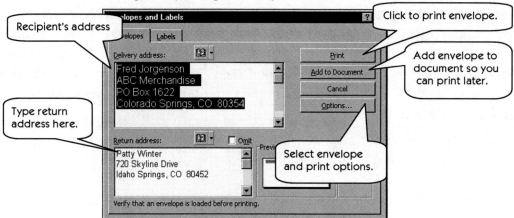

Figure 1.12.   The **Envelopes and Labels** dialog box is displayed.

    NOTE: If you added a return address to the envelope, note that when you choose to print or add the envelope to your document, Microsoft Word will ask if you want to save the new return address as the default. Choose **Yes** if this is the most common return address you will be using.

Practice Exercise 1-3

Type a Letter Using the Office Assistant Help

1   Start Microsoft Word and open a new, blank document if necessary.

2   Begin typing today's date.

3   When the ScreenTip appears after the month, press **Enter** three times.

4   Type Dear Joan, and press **Enter**.
    The Office Assistant will ask if you would like help.

5   Choose the **Get help with writing the letter** option.
    Step 1, the **Letter Format** tab of the Letter Wizard, is displayed.

6   Make the following changes:

- On the **Letter Format** tab:
  - Go to **Choose a page design**; select **Contemporary Letter**.
- Choose **Next>** to move through the Wizard's dialog boxes.
- On the **Recipient Info** tab:
  - Type the following name in the **Recipient's name** box:

    Joan Vieweg

  - Type the following address in the **Delivery address** box:

    PO Box 348
    Idaho Springs, CO 80452

  - In the Salutation area, if necessary, select **Formal**.
- On the **Sender Info** tab:
  - In **Sender's name**, type your name.
  - In **Return address**, type your address.
  - In **Complimentary closing**, type or select Sincerely, .

7   From the **Sender Info** tab, choose **Finish** or **OK** to display your letter with all the elements you selected.

8   Type the following text to replace the text placeholder:

    Thank you for your interest in our organization. We are happy to serve your needs and hope that you find the following Web locations useful.

9   Press **Enter** and then type the following three lines, pressing **Enter** at the end of each line.

    To purchase books use: www.amazon.com
    To purchase music use: www.cdnow.com
    To check the weather use: www.weather.com

10 Choose the **Make an envelope** option from the Office Assistant. Make any changes to the delivery and return addresses, if needed. Then choose **Add to Document**.

 NOTE: The Office Assistant asks if you want to save the new return address as the default return address. Choose **No**.

 TIP: If the Office Assistant does not ask if you would like to make an envelope, position the insertion point anywhere in the recipient's address and choose **Tools>Envelopes and Labels** to display the **Envelopes and Labels** dialog box.

11 Leave the document open and continue with this lesson. Compare your document to that shown in Figure 1.13.

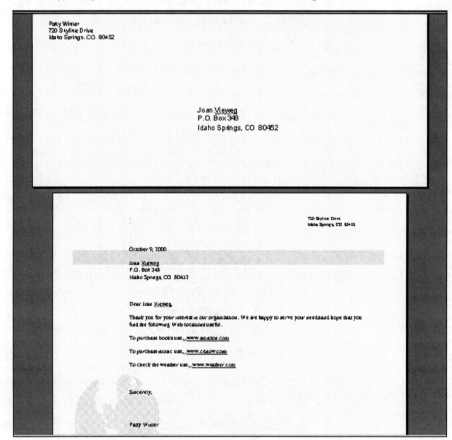

Figure 1.13. The letter and envelope you have created.

 NOTE: Notice that your envelope appears before the letter. If you want to print both the envelope and the letter, you need to feed the envelope first and then choose the **Print** command.

There, you've done it: you've typed your first complete letter. CONGRATULATIONS!

Save

Save, Save, Save! Those are the watchwords of all tasks in computing. Without saving your work, you run the risk of losing it all. As you create a document on screen, you see all the information you type, but your computer has no permanent record of your information. A single interruption of power to your computer causes all unsaved information to disappear into the ozone!

Using **File>Save** stores the information on a disk. The disk you choose for storage could be your computer's hard disk, a floppy disk you insert into the floppy disk drive, a network drive, or a Zip, Jazz, or SyQuest cartridge. (More detailed instructions and options on saving will be covered in Lesson 3.)

Save a document:

1   Choose **File>Save** from the menu bar. The first time you save a document, the **Save As** dialog box opens (see Figure 1.14).

The button to the left of step 1 indicates that you can use a toolbar button instead of the menu command to complete the step. You'll see buttons like this throughout the book when there's a toolbar alternative.

 TIP: The keyboard shortcut for the **Save** command is **Ctrl+S**.

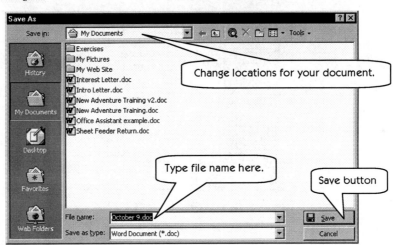

Figure 1.14.   The **Save As** dialog box offers many options for saving your document.

2   In the **File name** box, type the document name. The name that you type replaces the name that Word suggests automatically.

3   Open the drive and folder to save the document in:

*   Click the **Save in** arrow and select a location.

*   Double-click a folder to open it.

4   Choose **Save**.

The document is now stored on the disk media you specified so you can open it later. Saving a document does not close that document.

Practice Exercise 1-4

Save Your Document

1   With the letter you created in Practice Exercise 1-3 still open, choose **File>Save** from the menu bar.

2   In the **File name** box, type O1Letter .

3   Notice the folder next to **Save in** is called **My Documents**.

   NOTE: When Microsoft Word is installed, the default location for document files is **My Documents**. If, however, another default storage location has been specified, the name of that folder will be displayed in the **Save in** box.

4   Choose **Save**.

5   Exit Word (save changes if prompted).

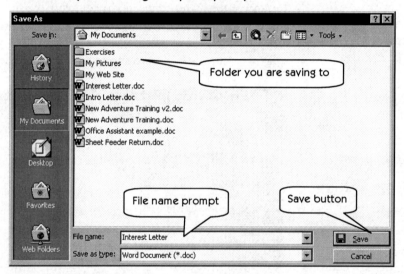

Figure 1.15.   The **Save As** dialog box is displayed.

Print, Save As, and Open

After you have created a document, you may want or need to print it. There are several ways to execute the **Print** command. You can use a menu command, a toolbar button, or a keyboard shortcut. In this lesson, you'll learn how to use the **Print** button on the Standard toolbar. (Printing options are covered in detail in Lesson 7.)

Print the document:

1   As always, you should save the document first.

2   Click the **Print** button on the Standard toolbar.

SAVE AS AND OPEN

While you are working with documents, you may need to save a document you have already created with a different name and open a document you created earlier. In this exercise, you will quickly learn how to use these commands. The detail and understanding of the **Save As** and **Open** commands are covered in Lesson 3.

Use File>Save As to create a copy of a document:

1 Choose **File>Save As** from the menu bar.

 TIP: The keyboard shortcut for the **Save As** command is **F12**.

The **Save As** dialog box is displayed just as it is when you use the **Save** command for the first time (see Figure 1.14).

2 In the **File name** box, type a name for the document copy.

3 Choose **Save** to save the document with the new name.

Use File>Open to open an existing document:

 1 Choose **File>Open** from the menu bar.

 TIP: The keyboard shortcut for the **Open** command is **Ctrl+O**.

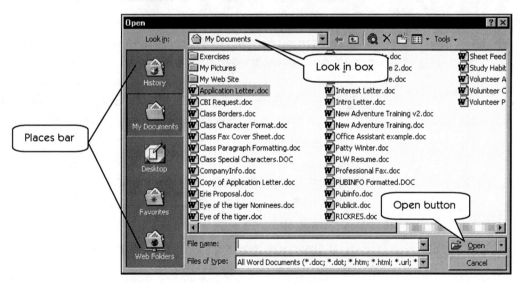

Figure 1.16.   The **Open** dialog box makes finding files easy.

2   Open the drive and folder where the document is stored:

- Click the **Look in** arrow and select a location.

- Double-click a folder to open it.

3   Select the file to open by clicking the file name in the list of files. Use the scroll bar, if necessary, to see more file names.

4   Choose **Open** to open the document.

Practice Exercise 1-5

Use Open, Save **As**, and Print

1   Start Word.

2   Open **01Ex1-5** from the **WORDCert\Word A** folder:

> NOTE: The folder symbol (📁) tells you that 📁**01Ex1-5** is a practice file provided in the **WORDCert\Word A** folder on the CD-ROM inside the back cover of this book. (The backslash indicates that **Word A** is a folder located within the **WORDCert** folder—so you'll need to open the **WORDCert** folder before you can open the **Word A** folder.)
>
> You'll be asked to open practice files like this throughout this book. See the Introduction for more information.

- Choose **File>Open** from the menu bar.

- Click the arrow on the **Look in** box and select your CD-ROM drive from the list that appears.

  > TIP: Check with your instructor or network administrator to find out if the **WORDCert** folder has been copied from the CD-ROM to another location. If it has, you may want to select a different drive from the **Look in** list.

- In the list of folders below the **Look in** box, double-click the **WORDCert** folder. Then double-click the **Word A** folder.

- Click **01Ex1-5** and choose **Open** to open the document.

3   Save the document with a different name:

- Choose **File>Save As** to display the **Save As** dialog box.

- In the **File name** box, type 01Print .

- Choose **Save** to create a second identical document with the new name 🖫**01Print**.

  > TIP: You'll see a disk icon (🖫), as in the step above, throughout the book whenever you need to save and name a file.

4   Click the **Print** button on the Standard toolbar.

5   Exit Word (save changes if prompted).

LESSON 2: UNDERSTAND WORD ELEMENTS

Before you can do very much in Microsoft Word, it's important to understand the different elements of the Word window (see Figure 2.1). It's a little like moving to a new city and learning where the grocery store and ATM machines are located. Life goes much more smoothly and a lot faster when you recognize your surroundings. This lesson concentrates on Word elements, but you may also refer to Appendix B on the CD-ROM that came with this book for helpful information about common Windows elements.

In this lesson, you will learn to:

> Identify and use the elements of Word windows, including the menu, rulers, scroll bars, and status bar

> Identify and use the buttons available on the Standard and Formatting toolbars

> Use the mouse to position the insertion point and initiate commands

> Use the keyboard to enter text and initiate commands

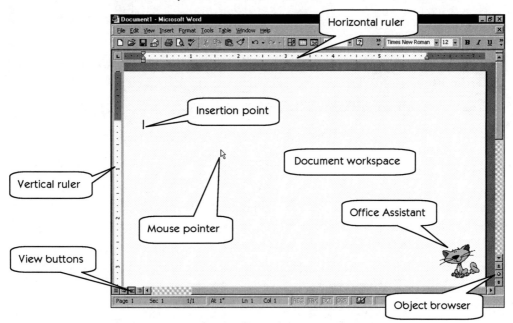

Figure 2.1.   The Microsoft Word window.

Once you understand the Word window and elements built into the application, Microsoft Word may indeed become one of your favorite tools.

Window

In general terms, the window is everything you see onscreen when you open Word. At the top of the window you see the name of the document followed by the name of the application you have open and active at the moment. That's called the **title bar**. Below that you'll find the menu bar, toolbars, and a document page with scroll bars for moving vertically and horizontally within the document. The white space for the document page is commonly referred to as the **workspace** (see Figure 2.2). At the bottom of the Word window you see the **status bar**, a very useful device for determining where you are in long documents and containing other information relating to the open document.

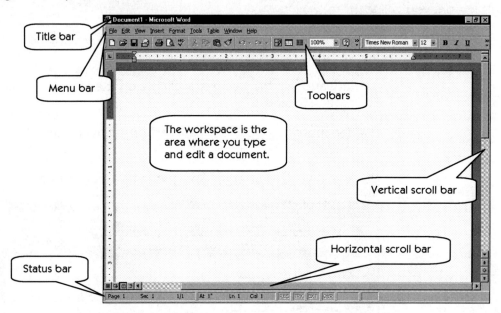

Figure 2.2. The Microsoft Word Window and workspace.

While you work in Word, you are viewing the application and document windows. The button controls for the application window appear in the upper-right corner of the window (see Figure 2.3). One control minimizes, or shrinks, the window, another restores or maximizes it, and the third one closes the window.

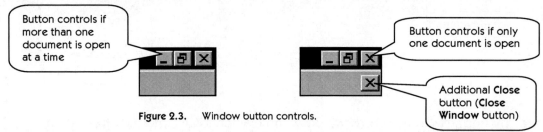

Figure 2.3. Window button controls.

If you have only one document window open, you will see an additional **Close** button on the right end of the menu bar. This **Close** button (called the **Close Window** button) allows you to close the document while leaving the application window open.

If you are using Windows 98 and you click the **Minimize** button, you minimize the active document window. The same is true if you click the **Close** button; you are closing the active document window.

If you want to close all open document windows, hold down the **Shift** key while you choose **File**>**Close All** from the menu bar.

MENUS

The menu bar at the top of the Word window holds all the commands you could possibly need to use while you are in Word. When you first start Word, the menus display basic commands. As you work with Word the commands that you use most often are stored and displayed on the menu. This is the **personalized menus** or **short version** of the full menus. The same works for the toolbars as explained later in this lesson.

The menu bar is similar to a menu used in a restaurant. All similar items are grouped together in sections on the menu bar (see Figure 2.4). For example, if you are interested in the view you have of a document, you would go to the **View** menu to see the commands that are available. If you need to format something, you would open the **Format** menu for commands that might be helpful.

File Edit View Insert Format Tools Table Window Help

Figure 2.4.   The menu bar groups similar commands together.

You can access menu bar commands using either the mouse or the keyboard. Both of these options are covered later in this lesson. When you display a menu, you will see the most common commands first. If you wait a few seconds, the rest of the commands for the menu will be displayed. Microsoft allows you to "teach" the program which commands should be displayed in the short version of the menu. Each time you access the menus, the commands that you use most often will be remembered by the program and displayed first. If you leave the menu open or point to the **expand arrows** on the bottom of the menu, the menu expands, displaying all the commands available. You can also choose to double-click the menu to display the full menu. Look at two different versions of the **Format** menu shown in Figure 2.5.

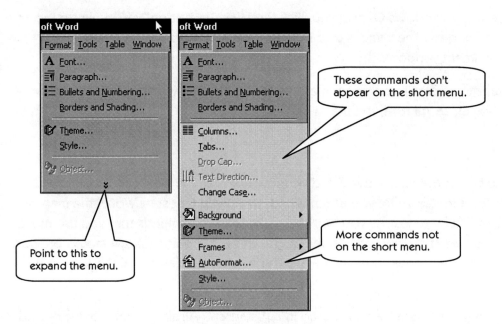

Figure 2.5.   Both versions of the **Format** menu: the short menu
                    is on the left; the expanded menu is on the right.

RULERS

Rulers along the top and left side of your document give you a sense of the placement
of various parts of your document. For instance, you can see how much of the printed
page is taken up by the header and the footer (i.e., the area at the top and bottom of
each page for optional text). You can also see where text within the document is
horizontally and vertically positioned.

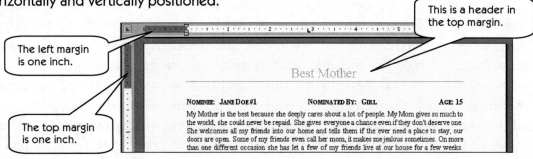

Figure 2.6.   Rulers give you a sense of where text is positioned on the page.

Only the horizontal ruler is visible in Normal view, but Print Layout view
displays the vertical ruler as well. You can choose **View>Ruler** from the
menu bar, while you're in either Normal or Print Layout view, to show the
rulers.

TIP: To switch from Normal view to Print Layout view, click the **Print Layout View** button
located at the lower-left corner of your document window. To switch from Print Layout
view to Normal view, click the **Normal View** button.

Change Page Margins Using Rulers

The rulers are adjustable. You can increase or decrease the amount of space dedicated to the header and footer, and adjust the width of space allotted to margins in the body of your document. The white portion of the ruler indicates the space allotted for text and graphics.

To change the space allotted for margins:

 1 Click the **Print Layout View** button.

2 Move your pointer over the intersection of dark gray and white on either ruler:

- Use the horizontal ruler to change the left and right margins.

- Use the vertical ruler to change the top and bottom margins.

    The pointer changes to a double-headed arrow.

     CAUTION: When you point to the left of the horizontal ruler to change the left margin, wait for the ScreenTip to make sure you are on the margin marker and not on one of the indent markers. If you need to, move the mouse just a tiny bit to get the *Left Margin* ScreenTip.

3 Press the mouse button and drag:

- Right or left on the horizontal ruler to change the left and right margins.

- Up or down on the vertical ruler to change the top and bottom margins.

    As you drag, a dotted line spans the document to give you a clear sense of how changes affect your document. Any text within the document or the header/footer is also repositioned as you reposition the ruler margin.

     NOTE: In addition to margin settings, the horizontal ruler at the top of your document window is used to position tabs and indents in text. (For more about tabs, see Lesson 6.)

VIEWS

There is no "right way" to view your document. It's purely a matter of your own work style and the demands of each document. As you develop your work skills, you'll find that you can view your document in several different ways. For instance, there is an Outline view, as shown in Figure 2.7. Some folks prefer to begin a complex document, one with many thought kernels, in Outline view. Others like to view their documents in Print Layout view to see just how the document will look when it's printed (see Figure 2.8). Others are perfectly content using Normal view to develop the document content in a continuous stream, and then later switch to other views when their thoughts are safely written down.

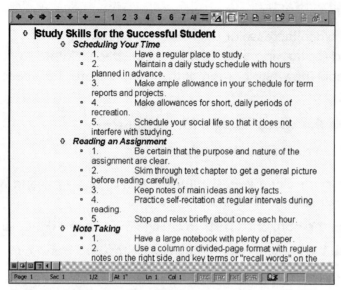

Figure 2.7. A document in Outline view.

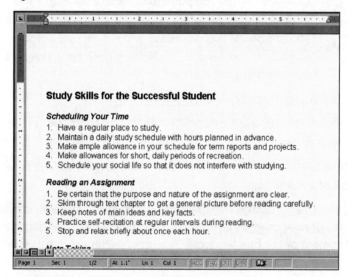

Figure 2.8. The same document in Print Layout view.

You can use either the **View** menu to change views or the view buttons at the left side of the horizontal scroll bar (see Figure 2.9). For this lesson, it's probably easier to use the view buttons, because you will only use two of the four available views: Normal and Print Layout.

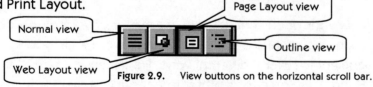

Figure 2.9. View buttons on the horizontal scroll bar.

To change your view:

• Choose **View>Print Layout View** from the menu bar.

• Choose **View>Normal View** from the menu bar.

SCROLL BARS

No matter what size monitor you use, the odds are good that you can't see all of your document onscreen at one time when you are viewing and working at a 100% or greater Zoom view. To see the parts above or below, or to the right or left, of what's currently visible on your screen, use the scroll bars (see Figure 2.10). Scroll up or down using the vertical scroll bar at the right of the workspace. Use the horizontal scroll bar at the bottom of the workspace to move right or left in your document.

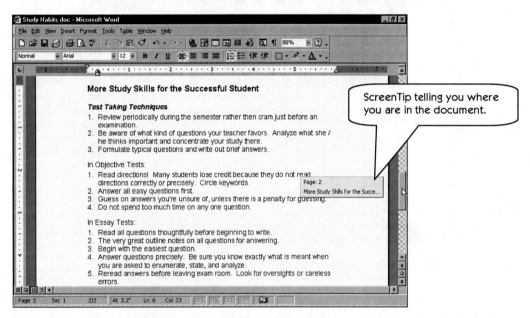

Figure 2.10.   Use the scroll bars to view any part of the document.

Use the vertical scroll bar to move the document:

* Click the up arrow to move the document upward, one line at a time.

* Click the down arrow to move the document downward, one line at a time.

* Click above the scroll box to move up one window at a time.

* Click below the scroll box to move down one window at a time.

* Click and drag the scroll box to move greater distances. Notice that, as you drag the scroll box, a ScreenTip indicates which page you are currently on.

Object Browser

The vertical scroll bar has a button called the **Select Browse Object** button. The Object Browser lets you move about in your document by selecting different target elements to move to and view on screen.

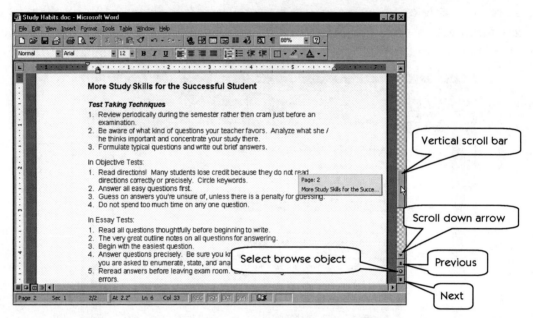

Figure 2.11.   The **Select Browse Object** button is on the bottom of the vertical scroll bar.

Look at the lower end of the vertical scroll bar. There are three buttons beneath the down scroll arrow. Between the **Previous** button and the **Next** button you see the **Select Browse Object** button, as Figure 2.11 shows. When you click this button, you display a palette of predetermined items that may be included in your document (see Figure 2.12). As you move your pointer over each button in the **Select Browse Object** palette, Word tells you the type of browse or search the button will conduct (e.g., **Browse by Comment, Go To, Find, Browse by Edits**).

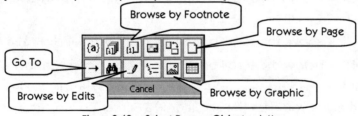

Figure 2.12.   Select Browse Object palette.

After you select a particular kind of item to browse for, Word remembers the kind of item you chose, and you can continue to find other items of the same type using the **Previous** or **Next** button.

Move in the document using the Select Browse Object button:

 1 Click the **Select Browse Object** button to display the palette.

> **TIP:** The keyboard shortcut for the **Object Browser** is **Ctrl+Alt+Home**. Then use the arrow keys to highlight the item(s) you want to browse for and press **Enter**.

2 Select the item(s) you want to use to move through the document. One of the most common items is **Browse by Page**.

3 Click the **Next** or **Previous** button to move forward or backward through the document.

> **TIP:** The keyboard shortcut for the **Next** command is **Ctrl+Page Down**; for the **Previous** command, it's **Ctrl+Page Up**.

Horizontal Scroll Bar

There are many times when it's useful to scroll horizontally in a document. For instance, you may be working on a document that's set up to be viewed at 100% or greater, and you want to read some text close to the right margin.

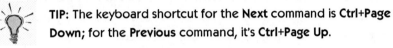

Horizontal scroll bar

Figure 2.13. The horizontal scroll bar helps you move the view of the document right and left.

View either side of the document using the horizontal scroll bar:

- Click the right scroll arrow to move the document right.

> **NOTE:** The percentage size at which you are viewing your document dictates the distance moved with each click of the scroll arrows.

- Click the left scroll arrow to move the document left.
- Click to the right of the scroll box to move right one screen width at a time.
- Click to the left of the scroll box to move left one screen width at a time.

As with the vertical scroll bar, you can also drag the scroll box to the right or left to change the portion of your document showing on screen.

Status Bar

At the lower edge of your workspace, above the taskbar, you will see the status bar, displayed in Figure 2.14. The status bar displays all sorts of useful information. It tells you exactly where the insertion point is currently located in your document.

Figure 2.14.   The status bar displays very useful information about your document.

You can even double-click on different status bar elements to invoke related commands. If you like using shortcut menus, you can also right-click on an element to display the related shortcut menu. (See **Shortcut Menus** later in this lesson.) The following table explains each element of the status bar. Figure 2.15, which appears after the table, illustrates a status bar in action.

STATUS BAR ELEMENT	WHAT IT MEANS
Page 2 Sec 1 2/7	Tells you where the insertion point is currently located. Double-click to display the **Find and Replace** dialog box with the **Go To** tab selected.
Page 2	The page the insertion point is on.
Sec 1	The section of the document the insertion point is in.
2/7	The page the insertion point is in and the total number of pages of the document.
At 1.2" Ln 1 Col 1	This area tells you where the insertion point is located in dimensions. Double-click to display the **Find and Replace** dialog box with the **Go To** tab selected.
At 1.2"	Where the insertion point is in inches vertically on the page.
Ln 1	The line number position of the insertion point vertically on the page.
Col 1	The position of the insertion point horizontally on the page (equal to one)
REC TRK EXT OVR	This section shows the status of various commands. A dimmed indicator means the command is off.
REC	Record Macro Toggle indicator. Double-click to display the **Record Macro** dialog.
TRK	**Track Changes** indicator. Double-click to turn Track Changes on or off. Keyboard shortcut: Ctrl+Shift+E.

STATUS BAR ELEMENT	WHAT IT MEANS
	Extend Selection indicator. Double-click to turn Extend Selection mode on or off. With Extend Selection on you can use the keyboard movement keys to select text. Keyboard shortcut: **F8**.
OVR	**Overtype** indicator. Double-click this button to turn Overtype mode on or off. To replace text to the right of the insertion point (rather than inserting it), you can switch to Overtype mode. The keyboard shortcut for Overtype mode is **Insert**.

CAUTION: If you are typing over information and don't want to, look at the status bar to see if **OVR** is on. If it is, you can double-click or press the **Insert** button on the keyboard to turn Overtype off.

STATUS BAR ELEMENT	WHAT IT MEANS
	Spelling and Grammar Status indicator. If the indicator is visible, at least one if not both, of the options is on. Double-click it or press **Alt+F7** to display shortcut menus for **Spelling and Grammar** commands. Right-click to display a shortcut menu for **Spelling and Grammar Options** or to **Hide Spelling Errors**. Keyboard shortcut: **F7**.

NOTE: To turn automatic Spelling and Grammar check on or off, choose **Tools>Options** and choose the **Spelling & Grammar** tab. In the Spelling area of the dialog box, select/deselect the **Check spelling as you type** check box as desired. In the Grammar area of the dialog box, select/deselect the **Check grammar as you type** check box as desired.

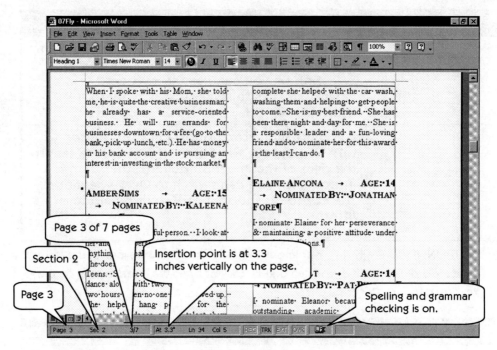

Figure 2.15.   The status bar for a seven-page document.

Practice Exercise 2-1

View a Document Using Word Elements

1 Choose **File>Open** from the menu bar, select 🗀**02Ex2-1** from the **WORDCert\Word A** folder, and then choose **Open**.

> **TIP:** Remember, **Word A** is a folder located inside the **WORDCert** folder on the CD-ROM that's on the inside back cover of the book. See the Introduction if you need help locating the folder.

2 View the workspace. Practice clicking about in the document.

3 Point to various parts of the document and click to reposition the insertion point. Watch the horizontal and vertical rulers for changes.

4 Point to the view buttons on the left side of the horizontal scroll bar. Hover the pointer over each button to see its ScreenTip.

• Click the **Normal View** button and proceed with steps 5 and 6.

5 Click on the vertical scroll bar to move different parts of the document into view.

- Click on the up and down scroll arrows.
- Click and drag the scroll box.

6 Click on the horizontal scroll bar to move different parts of the document to the right and left.

- Click on the left and right scroll arrows.
- Click and drag the scroll box.

7 Click the **Print Layout View** button and repeat steps 5 and 6.

8 Complete the following steps, using the **Select Browse Object** button to move in the document:

- Click **Browse by Page**.
- Click the **Next Page** button to move to the next page.

    NOTE: The names of the **Next** and **Previous** buttons change to reflect the browse object last accessed.

- Click the **Previous Page** button to move to the previous page.

9 Use the status bar to move the insertion point.

- Double-click the Page section of the status bar (to display the **Go To** tab of the **Find and Replace** dialog box). To close the dialog box, press the **Esc** key on the keyboard.

- Right-click the **Spelling and Grammar Status** indicator (open book) on the status bar (to view the shortcut menu). Press the **Esc** key.

10 Scroll back to the top of the document, leave the document open, and continue the lesson.

Toolbars

Toolbars offer you an alternative method for performing some of the most frequently used commands found in the Word menus and dialog boxes. Not every command found in the menus or options in dialog boxes appears on a toolbar, however. As with menus, toolbars adjust to display the most common buttons you use. This is called **personalized toolbars**. When you use Microsoft Word for the first time, the basic tools are displayed on the Standard and Formatting toolbars. As you work with the program, Word remembers the tools you use most and displays those on the toolbars.

In its wisdom, Microsoft realized that human beings have three ways of learning: verbal, hands-on, and visual. To address all three learning styles, they've made most of the Word commands accessible through the menu system, a keyboard shortcut, and a button. The method you use—the menu, keyboard, or the toolbar button—depends on your work style. Most people use a combination of all three. It makes little or no difference which method you use. They all perform the same commands. For instance, the **Cut**, **Copy**, and **Paste** buttons do exactly the same thing as the **Cut**, **Copy**, and **Paste** commands found in the **Edit** menu or the keyboard shortcuts **Ctrl+X**, **Ctrl+C**, and **Ctrl+V**.

There are many toolbars available in Word. By default, two appear when you install and start Word: the Standard toolbar and the Formatting toolbar.

Figure 2.16.   The Standard and Formatting toolbars in Word.

These two toolbars are displayed on one line, underneath the menu bar.

At the end of many toolbars is a **More Buttons** arrow (see Figure 2.16). When you display more than one toolbar on a line, you might see only the buttons that have been used most recently (the personalized toolbars). In this instance, you can click on the **More Buttons** arrow to see and use the buttons that are currently not visible (see Figure 2.17).

Figure 2.17.   More buttons for the Formatting toolbar.

If you prefer, you can display the toolbars on separate lines so you can see all the buttons for each toolbar.

Change the Standard and Formatting toolbars view:

1   Choose **View>Toolbars** from the menu bar.

2   From the **Toolbars** submenu, choose **Customize**.

3   Choose the **Options** tab, if necessary.

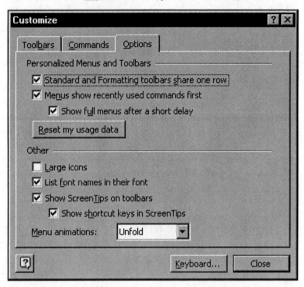

Figure 2.18.   Choose the **Options** tab to change how the toolbars are displayed.

4   Deselect the **Standard and Formatting toolbars share one row** check box. Removing the check mark turns the option off.

5   Change any of the other options. The following table explains each option.

OPTION	WHAT IT MEANS
Menus show recently used commands first	Word records the menu and toolbar choices you use and displays personalized menus and toolbars showing those commands first.
Show full menus after a short delay	If the above option is selected, this option is also available. The full menus are displayed after the personalized (short) menus are open.
Reset my usage data button	Deletes the record of menu and toolbar commands and resets the short menus personalized toolbars to the default.

OPTION	WHAT IT MEANS
Large icons	Makes toolbar buttons larger so they are easier to see.
List font names in their font	Uses the style of the font to display the font name in the Font list on the Formatting toolbar.
Show ScreenTips on toolbars	Shows onscreen descriptions of toolbar buttons when the pointer is paused over the button.
Show shortcut keys in ScreenTips	Displays the shortcut key in the ScreenTip if the above option is selected
Menu animations list	Choose how to display the menus. Choose from the following: (None), Random, Unfold, or Slide.
Keyboard button	Opens the Customize Keyboard dialog box so you can assign and remove shortcut keys.

6 Choose **Close** when you are finished.

The list of available toolbars is extensive and includes a Web toolbar, a Drawing toolbar, and a Tables and Borders toolbar, among others. For this exercise, however, you need only be concerned with the Standard and Formatting toolbars.

STANDARD TOOLBAR

The Standard toolbar, by default, is located on the left-hand side of the window, below the menu bar. Figure 2.19 displays the full Standard toolbar. It's helpful to note that each button on any toolbar has a ScreenTip (if the option is on). If you hover the pointer over any button on the toolbar you'll see a ScreenTip that tells you what the button does. Even better, you may see beside the name of the tool the keyboard shortcut for accomplishing the same command as the button does.

 NOTE: If you would like to see keyboard shortcuts with the ScreenTips, you may need to turn the option on. Choose **View>Toolbars>Customize**, choose the **Options** tab, and select the **Show shortcut keys in ScreenTips** check box.

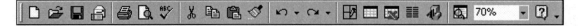

Figure 2.19. The full Standard toolbar on one row.

Preparing for Microsoft Office Specialist Certification

Buttons on the Standard toolbar perform many application tasks, such as opening a new blank document, using the clipboard, opening other applications, and accessing help. It also has buttons for document-related tasks, such as creating tables, borders, columns, and drawings. Increase or decrease the percentage view of your document onscreen using the **Zoom** list. Use the **Show/Hide ¶** button to show or hide nonprinting characters, as discussed in Lesson 1.

NOTE: Remarkably, there is one button that does not have an associated menu command. When you use **Format Painter** to copy the formatting of selected text to another location, using the toolbar button is the only way to perform this command in Word. It's one of the few commands with access limited to a button, though you'll discover a number of other commands with no corresponding button that are accessible only through menus or dialog boxes.

FORMATTING TOOLBAR

The Formatting toolbar has buttons that deal primarily with the way words and groups of words appear in your document. As you type text in a new document, the font, paragraph style, and alignment appear in the default styles selected by Microsoft. You may have other ideas for these elements.

From the Formatting toolbar, which appears in Figure 2.20, you can apply a different style to some or all of the paragraphs; change the font and font size; bold, italicize or underline words; and change the alignment of selected paragraphs from left (default) to centered, right, or justified. You can add bullets or numbers in front of each item in a list, and then increase or decrease the distance items or paragraphs are indented.

If you want to surround one or more paragraphs with a border, to emphasize certain content, there's a button to do that on the Formatting toolbar. You can even apply a yellow highlight to important words in your document, just like you did in school textbooks. For a decorative touch, select some or all of your words, and apply a color other than black to them using the **Font Color** button.

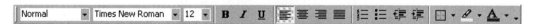

Figure 2.20.   The full Formatting toolbar on one row.

To apply any of the attributes available on the Formatting toolbar to text already typed into your document, you must select the text first.

OTHER TOOLBARS

Lots of people prefer to use toolbars, so Microsoft developed a broad variety of them to accommodate the "button clickers." There are toolbars for entering **AutoText** (recorded blocks of text you use frequently), for creating forms, and for adding special elements to your forms such as check boxes and labels. There's a toolbar to help you create a database, one for creating drawings, and another for adjusting pictures you import into your documents.

You can use a toolbar to work with tables and borders or to work with inserted WordArt. You can use the Web toolbar to access information you need. When you get really good at word processing, you might even use the Visual Basic toolbar, or create your own custom toolbar for special projects.

Turn a toolbar on or off:

1   Choose **View>Toolbars** to display a menu of available toolbars and the **Customize** command.

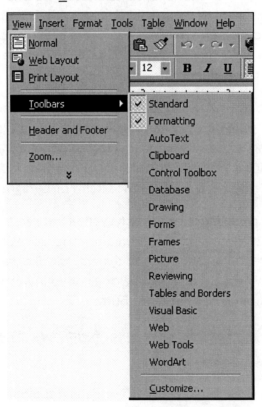

Figure 2.21.   The list of available toolbars on the **Toolbars** submenu.

2   Choose the toolbar you want to turn on or off. A check mark next to the name of the toolbar indicates the toolbar is displayed.

 TIP: To display a shortcut menu for toolbars, right-click anywhere in the toolbar area.

Float like a butterfly. Sting like a bee. Move your toolbars away from the perimeter of the window, and you have floating toolbars that look like palettes (see Figure 2.22).

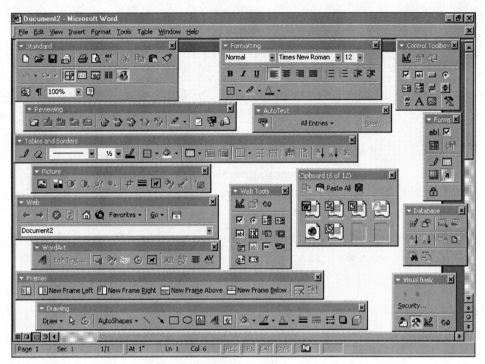

Figure 2.22.   All 16 Word toolbars displayed and floating.

To float a toolbar:

1   Position your pointer over the toolbar handle at the left end of the toolbar you want to float.

2   Hold down the mouse button, and drag the toolbar into the document area of the window.

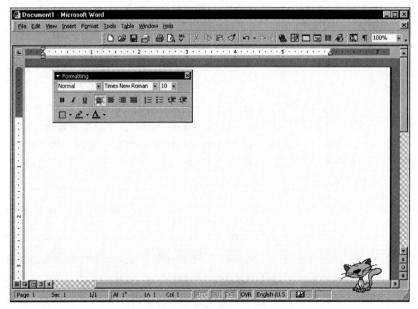

Figure 2.23.   Move the toolbar and position it where you choose.

3   Release the mouse button, and the toolbar floats in the
    document window.

If you want to move the floating toolbar to a different position, drag the title bar of the
floating toolbar elsewhere in the window.

To dock a floating toolbar:

*   Position your pointer over the title bar of a floating toolbar and
    drag the toolbar to the perimeter of the Word window; you can
    "dock" a toolbar on any side of the window (top, bottom, left,
    or right).

 TIP: You can also change the placement of the Standard and
Formatting toolbars at the top of the Word window using the
toolbar handles.

As you become more proficient in Word, you may find the toolbars a very effective
way to increase productivity.

Practice Exercise 2-2

Understanding Toolbars

1   Use 📂**02Ex2-1** still open from Practice Exercise 2-1, or open
    📂**02Ex2-2** from the **WORDCert\Word A** folder. Make sure that
    you are at the top of the document. The insertion point should
    be on the first line of the document.

2   View the Standard and Formatting toolbars (they should both be
    visible and sharing one row).

 NOTE: If the Standard and Formatting toolbars are not visible,
choose **View>Toolbars>Customize**, choose the **Toolbars** tab,
and choose the Standard and Formatting toolbars and the
Menu Bar as the only Toolbars displayed. Remove any check
marks from all other selected check boxes. Then choose **Close**.

 3   Point to the very last button on the Formatting toolbar. When
    you see its ScreenTip, click the button. View the buttons that
    are hidden when the toolbar is not fully extended.

4   Click anywhere in the document to close the **More Buttons**
    palette.

5   Choose **View>Toolbars>Customize** from the menu bar.

6   Complete the following steps in the **Customize** dialog box:

    *   On the **Options** tab, deselect the **Standard and Formatting
        toolbars share one row** check box.

    *   Choose **Close**.

7 View the toolbars now. Move back to the top of the document. The **Bold** and **Align Left** buttons should look like they are "pressed in," or selected.

8 Move the insertion point to various parts of the document and note any changes on the Formatting toolbar.

9 Choose <u>V</u>iew><u>T</u>oolbars from the menu bar. Choose **Tables and Borders** to turn on that toolbar. Then, complete the following steps:

- Point to various buttons on the Tables and Borders toolbar to view their ScreenTips.

- Drag the toolbar handle of the Tables and Borders toolbar so that the toolbar is floating in the document window.

 • Close the Tables and Borders toolbar by clicking its **Close** button. (If you can't see a **Close** button on the toolbar's title bar, right-click on the toolbar and choose **Tables and Borders** from the shortcut menu to turn it off.)

10 Close the document without saving any changes. Choose <u>F</u>ile><u>C</u>lose from the menu bar.

View the toolbars. Notice that most of the buttons are not available because you don't have a document window open.

11 Click the **New Blank Document** button on the Standard toolbar.

View the toolbars. Most of the buttons are now available.

12 Close the new document without saving any changes.

Use the Mouse

If you've ever played Solitaire on your computer, you've practiced your mouse skills. Moving the pointer, clicking on items, and dragging and dropping selected items are basic mouse skills. But there's more than games for mousing about.

Use the mouse to position the insertion point and then type your text. The mouse can also be used to select text and to move the insertion point to a different place within text for typing or editing. All of these tasks can be done with the mouse, customarily using its left button.

The mouse pointer changes its shape according to where it's located in the document. The following table explains some of the pointer shapes:

POINTER SHAPE	FUNCTION
↖	Click to make a window active. Choose menus and menu commands. Click scroll box, scroll bar, or scroll arrows to view a different part of the document. Click **Minimize**, **Maximize**, and **Close** buttons. Click and drag title bar to move a window. Select and choose options in dialog boxes, and select lines or paragraphs of text.
⌛	Tells you to wait until a job is done.
I	Click to position insertion point.
I⁼ I ⁼I	Double-click to position insertion point. Word automatically inserts line breaks, tabs, and paragraph formatting.
↔ ↕ ↘ ↗	Click and drag to resize windows and floating toolbars.
✥	Click and drag to move toolbars and drawing objects. In Outline view, selects heading level and all sub-levels.
✥	Click and drag to move headings in Outline view.

CLICK AND TYPE

Click and Type is a new feature in Word 2000. This feature is both wonderful and possibly confusing. Earlier versions of Word only allowed you to enter text at the top of the page in a new document; you had to press the **Enter** key repeatedly to begin lower down on the page. Now, you can double-click in any blank area of a page and begin typing—at the top, near the top, in the center, or even at the bottom of the page.

To use Click and Type:

1   Point in the workspace where you want to position the insertion point.

2   Double-click to place the insertion point.

3   Type your text.

SHORTCUT MENUS

Shortcut menus are available all over the place in Word. (See some examples in Figure 2.24.) To access a shortcut menu, click the right mouse button or press the **Application** key on some of the newer keyboards. Based upon the location of the pointer when you right-click or use the **Application** key, a shortcut menu appears with specific options. The options are the most frequently used commands that apply to the thing you clicked on. For instance, as you saw in the previous exercise, a right-click while your pointer is over one of the toolbars displays the list of available toolbars. No need to move your tired arm all the way up to the **View** menu.

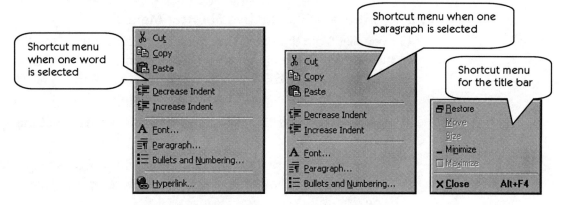

Figure 2.24. Shortcut menus.

If you right-click on a word in your document, the shortcut menu displays frequently used commands related to text, such as **Cut, Copy, Paste**, and access to the **Font or Paragraph** dialog box.

  TIP: For the lefties in the world, it's possible to switch the mouse button's actions. Use the taskbar to choose **Start>Settings>Control Panel** to open the **Control Panel** dialog box. Double-click on the Mouse icon to open the **Mouse Properties** dialog box. Choose **Left-handed**, and adjust the **Double-click speed**, if you like. (Your dialog box may be different, so you may need to search for an option that allows you to change the mouse button.) When your changes are all made, close the **Mouse Properties** dialog box by clicking **OK**, and then close the **Control Panel** dialog box using the **Close** button.

Mouse

You can right-click some of the things in the status bar and even in the title bar. For instance, when you right-click the **Spelling and Grammar Status** indicator in the status bar, you see a shortcut menu of choices to **Hide Spelling Errors, Hide Grammatical Errors,** and other **Options**. A right-click in the title bar opens a shortcut menu to **Restore, Move, Size, Minimize, Maximize,** or **Close** the Word window.

 NOTE: If you don't see all three choices on the shortcut menu for the **Spelling and Grammar Status** idicator, you may need to turn some options on. Choose **Tools>Options** and then the **Spelling & Grammar** tab. In the Spelling section, select the **Check spelling as you type** check box; in the Grammar section, select the **Check grammar as you type** check box. Then, choose **OK** to close the dialog box.

Use the shortcut menus:

1 Point to the word, paragraph, or window element you want to see commands for.

2 Right-click or press the **Application** key to display the shortcut menu.

3 Choose a command from the menu or close the menu by clicking anywhere off the shortcut menu or pressing **Esc**.

Practice Exercise 2-3

Practice Mouse Skills and Use Shortcut Menus

1 Choose **File** from the menu bar. Select 🗁 **02Ex2-1** from the file list at the bottom of the menu. If you did not do the previous two exercises, open 🗁 **02Ex2-3** from the **WORDCert\Word A** folder.

2 Practice mousing about by doing the following:

- Move the pointer to a word and double-click to select the word.

- Move the pointer to the selection area of the workspace and point to a short line of text. Click once to select the entire line.

- Point to a multiple-line paragraph and double-click to select the paragraph. Do not deselect this paragraph.

- Point to the horizontal ruler and view the changes in the pointer.

- Point to the toolbar handle to the left of one of the toolbars and view the pointer.

3 Practice using shortcut menus by doing the following:

- Point to the selected paragraph of text. Right-click to display the shortcut menu.

- Point anywhere else in the document, and right-click to display the shortcut menu. Click anywhere in the document to close the shortcut menu without invoking a command.

- Press the **Application** key to display the shortcut menu. Press **Esc** to close the shortcut menu.

- Point to the dimmed **Track Changes** indicator (**TRK**) on the status bar. Right-click to display its shortcut menu. Press the **Esc** key to close the shortcut menu without invoking a command.

- Point to either toolbar and right-click to display the shortcut menu. Choose **WordArt** to turn on the toolbar.

4   Point to the title bar of the floating WordArt toolbar. Click-and-drag it to the left of the workspace. When it docks on the left side of the window, release the mouse button.

5   Right-click anywhere on the WordArt toolbar and choose **WordArt** again to turn it off.

6   Click the **New Blank Document** button on the Standard toolbar.

7   Move the pointer to the middle of the workspace and double-click (Click and Type) to position the insertion point.

8   Type your name.

9   Close both documents without saving any changes.

Use the Keyboard

Those who don't have any passion for the mouse may prefer to keep their hands on the keyboard. You'll quickly discover many ways to execute certain commands with the keyboard. For instance, pressing the **Enter** key is generally the same as clicking **OK** in dialog boxes. The **Esc** key cancels any choices you've made and closes a dialog box.

Figure 2.25.   The Microsoft Word menu bar.

Take a look at the words in the menu bar shown in Figure 2.25. Each word has one letter underlined. For instance, **File** has the **F** underlined. Technically, these are called **access keys**. Using a key combination of **Alt+F** (the underlined letter) opens the **File** menu. Once a menu is open, you can select any command shown by pressing just the underlined letter shown in the command you want.

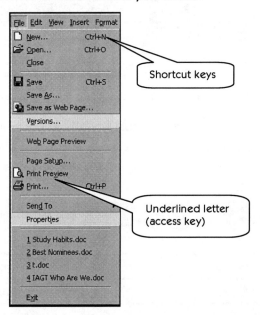

Figure 2.26.   Notice the underlined letters (access keys) in the File menu.

With a sharp eye, you'll see underlined letters all over the place in Word. In some cases you need a companion key, such as **Alt** or **Alt+Shift**, and some require nothing more than the underlined letter. When accessing a menu you can press and release the **Alt** key and then press the underlined letter of the menu you want to display. Shortcut keys are different in that they require the combination of keys be held down simultaneously to execute the command.

Access menu bar commands using the keyboard:

1   Hold down the **Alt** key and press and release the underlined letter for the menu you want to display.

2   Press and release the underlined letter of the command you want to use.

 TIP: Once you start getting used to keyboard shortcuts, you will probably prefer them instead of the access keys. For instance, to start a new document, use **Ctrl+N** instead of **Alt+F** then **N**.

Listing all the keyboard shortcuts would require a lot of room, so experiment. Try different keys alone or in combination with **Ctrl** or **Alt**. Scout out those underlined letters in menus and dialog boxes. For a list of some shortcut keys, see Appendix D on the CD-ROM that came with book.

MOVE WITHIN A DOCUMENT

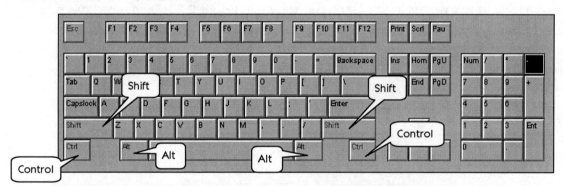

Figure 2.27.   **Control, Shift** and **Alt** used in combination with other keys provide fast shortcuts.

While you're typing text, your hands are obviously on the keyboard. So it is often quicker to use the keyboard than the mouse to move around in the document. No matter where in the document your cursor is located, use these keystrokes to reposition the insertion point:

PRESS	TO MOVE
Home	Beginning of a line
Ctrl+Home	Beginning of a document
Ctrl+End	End of the document
Left Arrow	Left one character

PRESS	TO MOVE
Right Arrow	Right one character
Ctrl+Left Arrow	Left one word
Ctrl+Right Arrow	Right one word
Ctrl+G or F5	Display the **Go To** dialog box.

Practice Exercise 2-4

Use the Keyboard

1   Use the keyboard to select the **File** menu (**Alt+F**): press and hold the **Alt** key, and then press the **F** key. Using the keyboard, choose the **Open** command: press the **O** key.

The insertion point is in the **File name** box.

2   Begin typing O2Ex2-4 in the **File name** box. Word completes the file name for you. Choose **Open** by pressing the **Enter** key.

3   Use the keyboard to select the **Edit** menu (**Alt+E**). Press and hold the **Alt** key, and then press the **E** key.

4   Use the **up** and **down** arrow keys to move through the commands on the **Edit** menu. When you get to the expand arrows, the **Edit** menu expands.

5   Press the **Esc** key to close the **Edit** menu. Notice that the menu bar is still active; **Edit** is raised, not dimmed. Use the **Left** and **Right Arrow** keys to move to different menus on the menu bar.

The full menus are displayed immediately.

6   Move to the **View** menu and press **Enter**.

7   Press **Esc** twice to close the **View** menu and move off the menu bar. (Your insertion point should now be blinking in the document.)

8   Use the access keys to display the other menus: **Alt+I**, **Alt+O**, **Alt+T**, **Alt+A**, **Alt+W**, and **Alt+H**. Press the **Esc** key twice.

9   Use the keyboard to move in the document:

- Press **Ctrl+Home** (to move to the beginning of the document).
- Press the **Right Arrow** five times (to move one character at a time to the right).
- Press **Ctrl+Right Arrow** five times (to move one word at a time to the right).

- Press the **Left Arrow** five times (to move one character at a time to the left).

- Press **Ctrl+Left Arrow** five times (to move one word at a time to the left).

- Press **Ctrl+End** (to move to the end of the document).

10 Use the keyboard shortcut to start a new blank document.

 NOTE: Look at the <u>F</u>ile menu if you don't remember what the shortcut is.

11 Type your name. Use the keyboard shortcut to save the document with the name 🖫**02Name**.

12 Use the access keys to close all open documents (**Alt+F** then **C**). Do not save any changes.

LESSON 3: CREATE, OPEN, AND SAVE DOCUMENTS

One of the reasons to use a word-processing application such as Word is to produce documents. After these letters, memos, reports, and other papers are created and saved, you will need to locate, open, and work with them. Working with existing and multiple documents requires some new skills.

In this lesson, you will learn to:

> Create a document using a template

> Locate and open an existing document

> Begin a new document during a work session

> Work with multiple documents

> Work with multiple windows displaying the same document

> Save a copy of a document

> Save multiple documents simultaneously

> Close documents

> Close multiple documents simultaneously

Figure 3.1.   A letter and an agenda each generated with the help of templates.

Your productivity will soar when you've mastered these skills, as will your confidence.

 Caution: The exercises in this lesson build off one another and need to be done sequentially to avoid confusion.

Create a New Document Using Templates and Wizards

 By now you surely have noticed that there is a **New Blank Document** button on the Standard toolbar for starting a new document. Using this button opens a default blank page. Though it looks as if nothing has been done to the page, it actually is a new document based on Word's Blank Document template (NORMAL.DOT). The purpose of templates is to use predetermined attributes, such as margins, paragraphs style, and fonts. All you need to do is start entering text. For this lesson, you'll use the Word template designed for sending a fax.

 NOTE: To start a document based on another of the many templates provided with Word, you *must* use the menu **File>New**. The menu command opens a dialog box showing several tabs, each of which displays some of the available templates.

FILE>NEW

As a novice Word user, you'll love the advantages of templates. Each template is specially designed and formatted for various generic kinds of business and personal documents as well as Web-page and e-mail documents. You need only add the text specified within placeholders in the template, or type over existing text, and then save it to create a polished document.

Create a fax based on a template:

1   Choose **File>New** from the menu bar to open the **New** dialog box.

 TIP: You can also use the access keys, **Alt+F** then **N**, to open the **New** dialog box.

2   Choose the **Letters & Faxes** tab. (See Figure 3.2.)

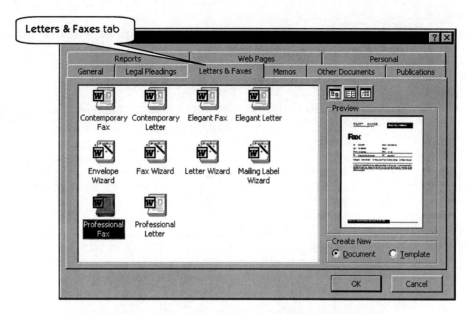

Figure 3.2.   The **New** dialog box with the **Letters & Faxes** tab selected.

3   Double-click the fax template that suits your purposes: **Contemporary Fax**, **Elegant Fax**, or **Professional Fax**.

4   Highlight the placeholder text shown within brackets and begin typing the requested information.

5   Choose **File>Save** from the menu bar and give your fax a file name that you will recognize later if you need to reopen it.

6   Determine where you want to store the saved fax in the **Save in** box of the **Save As** dialog box, and choose **OK**.

Quickly, and without your needing to know about formatting or how to apply it, your fax is ready to send. You can use any of the Word templates over and over, because the template remains unchanged when you save the document based on a template. The document is a duplicate of the template with your text in it and is, by default, saved in **Word Document (*.doc)** format. (You'll learn more about saving documents in various file formats later in this chapter.)

Practice Exercise 3-1

Create a Fax with the Elegant Fax Template

1   Start Word, if necessary.

2   In the blank document, type the name of your favorite vacation spot.

3   Choose **File>New** from the menu bar to open the **New** dialog box.

4   Choose the **Letters & Faxes** tab.

Elegant Fax

5   Select **Elegant Fax**. Look at the **Preview** box to see the
    fax layout.

6   Choose **OK** to open the **Elegant Fax** template.

7   Following the onscreen instructions, type the following text:

Company Name:	PRW Computer Training & Services
To:	Laura Morris
From:	Patty Winter
Company:	Denver Design Center
Date:	Today's Date (should be filled in for you)
Fax Number:	(303) 555-3426
Total No. of Pages:	2
Phone Number:	(303) 555-0099
Re:	The Information you Requested
Notes/ Comments:	Call me if you have any questions.
Return Address:	720 Skyline Drive, Idaho Springs, Colorado 80452

NOTES: For areas where you don't have text to type, delete the
placeholder. (Click the placeholder and then press the **Delete**
key.) Otherwise, the placeholders themselves appear in the
document.

Make sure you scroll down to see the bottom of the page with
the return address placeholder.

8   Save the document with the name 🖫**03Fax**.

9   Choose **File>Close** from the menu bar to close **03Fax**.

NOTE: Document 1, the Word default document with your
vacation spot on it, should still be open.

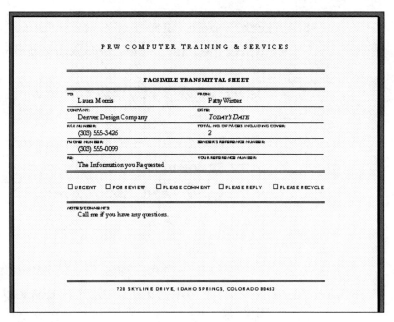

Figure 3.3. A sample of the Elegant Fax document.

10 Continue on to Practice Exercise 3-2.

Practice Exercise 3-2

Create a Letter with the Letter Wizard

1 Choose **File**>**New** from the menu bar to open the **New** dialog box.

2 Choose the **Letters & Faxes** tab.

3 Double-click **Letter Wizard**.

The Office Assistant opens with two choices.

4 Choose the **Send one letter** option from the Office Assistant.

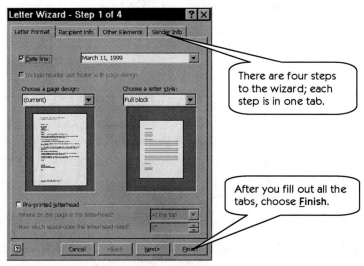

There are four steps to the wizard; each step is in one tab.

After you fill out all the tabs, choose **Finish**.

Figure 3.4. When using the Letter Wizard you can choose the tabs or click the **Next>** button to move among the tabs.

5   In Letter Wizard - Step 1 of 4, **Letter Format**, do the following:

  • Select the **Date line** check box and choose today's date, if necessary.

  • Select **Contemporary Letter** in the **Choose a page design** list.

  • Choose **Next>**.

6   In Letter Wizard - Step 2 of 4, **Recipient Info**, do the following:

  • In the **Recipient's name** box, type: Sahra Moalegi .

  • In the **Delivery address** box, type: 720 Chiefton Drive .

  • Press **Enter** and type: Ogallala, NE 71789 .

  • Choose **Next>**.

7   In Letter Wizard - Step 3 of 4, **Other Elements**, do the following:

  • Select the **Reference Line** check box and choose **RE:** from the list.

  • Choose **Next>**.

8   In Letter Wizard - Step 4 of 4, **Sender Info**, do the following:

  • In the **Sender's name** box, type: Roxana Squyres-Price .

  • In the **Return address** box, type: 6427 W. Canal Drive .

  • Press **Enter** and type: Baltimore, MD 21210 .

  • In the **Complementary closing** box, type: Sincerely yours, .

  • Choose **Finish**.

  The document opens with the text you added in the wizard. If you missed one of the steps or made a mistake, you can choose **Tools>Letter Wizard** from the menu bar and correct any omission. The dialog box opens again without the **Next>** and **Finish** buttons, but you can choose each of the tabs to make changes.

9   Dismiss the Office Assistant:

  • Notice the question from the Office Assistant.

  • Choose **Cancel** to hide the Office Assistant and continue to work on your letter.

10 In the letter, drag the I-beam over the following text placeholder: **Type your letter here.** To add, remove, or change letter elements, choose **Letter Wizard** from the **Tools** menu. Once the placeholder is selected, replace it with the following text:

  Thank you for being such a great customer. Please come back.

 11 Save the document with the name 03Letter.

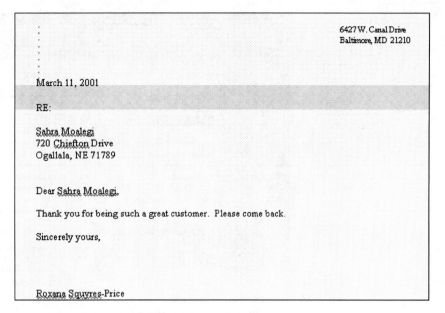

6427 W. Canal Drive
Baltimore, MD 21210

March 11, 2001

RE:

Sahra Moalegi
720 Chiefton Drive
Ogallala, NE 71789

Dear Sahra Moalegi,

Thank you for being such a great customer. Please come back.

Sincerely yours,

Roxana Squyres-Price

Figure 3.5. The finished letter.

12 Keep the documents open as you continue with this lesson.

Open Existing Documents

After a document is created and saved to the hard drive, a floppy disk, or other external storage media, you need to be able to find that document. Perhaps you'll need to edit some of the text or add to the document's content.

There are several ways to locate and open existing documents. The method you choose may differ according to the situation. If you know where the document is located, you'll use one method. If you're not sure where it is, but know the name of the document, you'll use a different method of opening it. If you've recently worked on a document and closed it, you'll discover there is yet another, speedy way to reopen it.

FILE>OPEN

The **Open** dialog box provides many additional ways of locating and opening existing files. Which method you use depends solely upon how much information you already have about the document. If you know the name of the document, your task is simplified. If you also know where the document is stored, the task is even simpler.

Simple ways to open a document:

1   Choose **File>Open** from the menu bar. The **Open** dialog box appears, as shown on the following page.

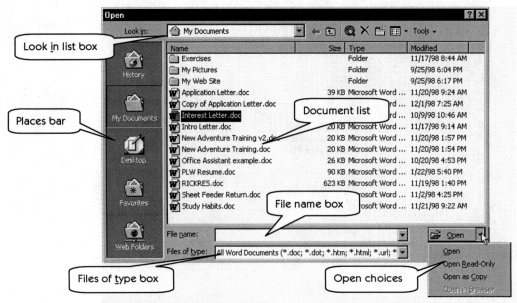

Figure 3.6.   The **Open** dialog box.

2   Look at the **Files of type** box to be sure the **Open** dialog box displays files saved in the format of you are seeking (e.g., **All Word Documents**).

 TIP: If you can't find your file, choose **All Files (*.*)** from the **Files of type** list. It might provide a daunting list of files, but somewhere in the list of file names your file will appear.

3   Locate and select the folder where the document is stored. (The name of the current folder is shown in the **Look in** box.)

•   Click one of the following icons on the **Places** bar.

History	History shows a list of the last 20 to 50 documents and folders you've worked with.
My Documents	My Documents shows the list of files stored in this folder.
Favorites	Favorites shows the list of files stored in this folder.
Desktop	Desktop shows a list of files and folders placed directly on the desktop.
Web Folders	Web Folders shows the folder shortcuts for Web servers to find files on the Web.

• Click the arrow on the **Look in** box and select a location from the list that is displayed.

 • Double-click a folder in the contents part of the dialog box.

 • Click the **Back** button to go back to the last location you used.

 • Click the **Up One Level** button to move up in the list one level at a time.

4 Click to highlight the name of the document you want to open.

5 Choose **Open** on the bottom of the **Open** dialog box.

 NOTE: If you want to open the document in read-only mode (you can't save any changes with the same document name) or open the document as a copy (you can make changes and when you save, **Copy of** is added to the document name), click the arrow on the **Open** button and choose the command you need.

As you continue to use Word, you'll come across situations in which you have limited information about documents you want to open. Word provides several ways to search for and locate documents.

Other tools on the Open dialog box for locating documents include:

 • The **Views** button changes the way files are displayed. You can see the file type icon and the document's name in all views, but in **Details** you will also see file size, type, and modified date/time. In **Properties** view you will see document statistics; in **Preview** view a "snapshot" of the document is displayed in the **Open** dialog box.

 • The **Tools** menu allows you to use the **Find** command to be more specific about your search criteria. You can also choose to **Delete** or **Print** selected files from this menu.

    • **Column heading** buttons in **Details** view allow you to sort the displayed list in ascending or descending order. Simply click the heading you want to sort by. The list of files will then be sorted in order. If, for example, you created a document a month ago, you could sort the files by modified date. The first click on the Modified heading button sorts the files in ascending order; click again to sort the files in descending order so the most recent files are listed first.

- **Files of type** list choices seek files saved in specific formats, such as: Rich Text Format (*.rtf), which allows other platforms and other word-processing programs to open the file and see it exactly the same as you created it, with formatting intact; Word Documents (*.doc) with both text and formatting readable by others who use Word to open the document; and a host of other format options. (For more about saving and file formats, please refer to **Save Documents** later in this lesson.)

When you become familiar with the simple search capabilities, you may want to use the more sophisticated Search features to locate documents.

More advanced ways to locate and open a document:

Figure 3.7.   The **Tools** menu on the **Open** dialog box.

- The **Find** command on the **Tools** menu opens a dialog box (see Figure 3.8) with powerful options for searching for words in documents; document **Property**, **Condition**, and **Value**; and the location in which the file may be stored. You can also save the search parameters for reuse at a later time.

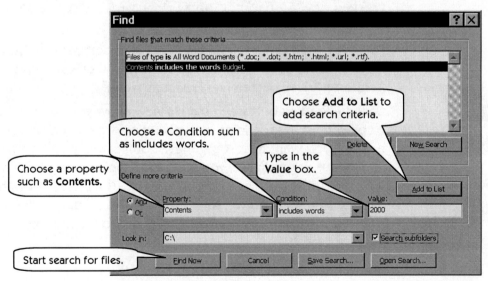

Figure 3.8.   In the **Open** dialog box, choose the **Tools** menu and choose **Find** to open the **Find** dialog box.

- After you fill out the **Find** dialog box and choose **Find Now**, the **Open** dialog box reappears with the results of your search. Select the file you want, if necessary, and choose **Open**.

START>DOCUMENTS

The Start menu on the Windows desktop has a feature that lists the names of recently used documents. The **Start** menu **Documents** list includes the most recently opened documents shown in alphabetical order (see Figure 3.9).

The list is not limited to any particular application; it shows the last documents opened, no matter which application created them. You might see documents created in a mixture of applications, such as Notepad, Microsoft Excel, Paint, and Microsoft Word. If you recently opened and worked on a Word document and then closed it, the name of the document appears in the **Documents** list in the **Start** menu.

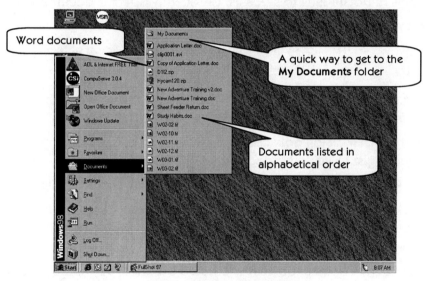

Figure 3.9.   The 15 most recently used documents are listed.

Open a recently used document from the Start menu:

1   Click **Start** on the taskbar.

 TIP: The keyboard shortcut for the **Start** menu is **Ctrl+Esc**. On some newer keyboards you even have an easier keyboard shortcut—you have the Windows Key. Generally, it is located on the bottom row of the keyboard between the **Ctrl** and **Alt** keys.

2   Choose **Documents** on the **Start** menu. A list of recently opened documents appears.

3   Choose the name of the document you want to open.

 TIP: Choose the **My Documents** folder at the top of the list to open any document stored in the default location.

The **Start** menu list of documents changes as you continue to work, opening and closing documents.

Practice Exercise 3-3

Open Documents in Many Ways

1   With Word open, choose **File>Open** from the menu bar to display the **Open** dialog box.

2   Begin typing the file name 📁**03Ex3-3** (in the **WORDCert\Word A\Samples** folder). When you see the full name displayed in the **File name** box, stop typing. Choose **Open** or press the **Enter** key.

3   Click **Start** on the taskbar to open a recently used document.

4   Point to **Documents** to see a list of recently opened documents.

5   Move to the list of documents and select 📁**03Fax**.

 NOTE: Choose the **My Documents** folder at the top of the list if 02Ex2-1 is not in the list of documents.

6   Use the **Open** command again. This time use the keyboard shortcut **Ctrl+O**.

7   In the **Open** dialog box, click the arrow on the **Views** button. Choose **List** to view the documents in a list.

8   Click the arrow on the **Views** button again and select **Details**.

9   Click the **Modified** column heading button to sort the list in ascending order. Click the **Modified** column heading button again to sort the list in descending order.

10 Select any document that was created before today and choose **Open**.

11 Open another document created before today using any of the three methods used above.

12 Keep all documents open as you continue with this lesson.

Start>Find>Files or Folders

Using the **Start** menu on the Windows taskbar allows you to do two things at once, if necessary. Presuming it is not already open, you can open the application and the document created by the application simultaneously from the **Start** menu.

If the application is already open and running, only the document opens and is displayed.

Find an existing document to open from the Start menu:

1   Click **Start** on the taskbar.

2   Point to **Find** to access the menu of options.

3   Choose **Files or Folders** to open the **Find: All Files** dialog box.

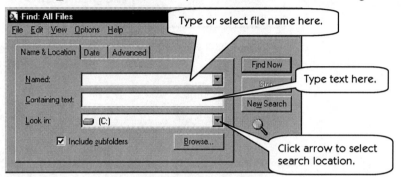

Figure 3.10.   Define your search criteria using the options on different tabs.

4   Make your search choices on the tab(s) at the top of the **Find: All Files** dialog box: **Name & Location**, **Date**, or **Advanced**.

TAB	DESCRIPTION
Name & Location	In the **Named** box, type all or part of a file name. Or if you don't know the file name, in the **Containing** text box, type a distinctive word or phrase in the document. In the **Look in** box, select a location to search (see Figure 3.10 above).
Date	To limit your search, use the **Find all files** choices: **Modified**, **Created**, or **Last accessed**. Further limit the list by using the **between** [date] and [date] boxes or **during the previous** [number] **month(s)/day(s)** options (see Figure 3.11).

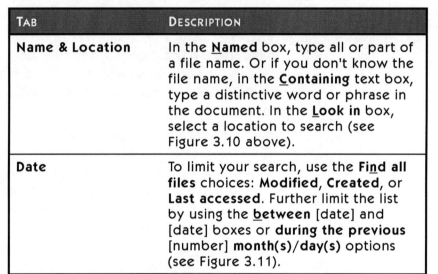
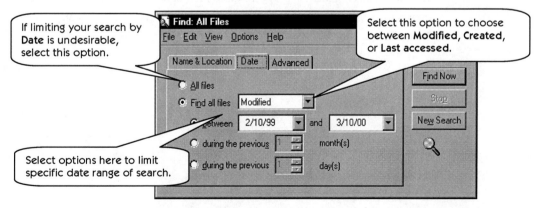

Figure 3.11.   Use the **Date** tab alone or in conjunction with the other tabs.

Tab	Description
Advanced	Use the **Of type** list to specify the type of document you are looking for (e.g., Microsoft Word Document). Use the **Size is** options to search by file size. (See Figure 3.12.)

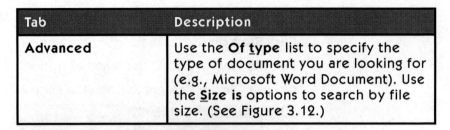
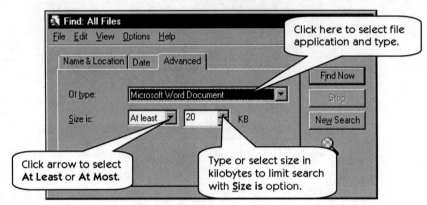

Figure 3.12. Look for specific types of files and/or limit the size of files you are trying to locate.

5   On the **Name & Location** tab, enter the document search criteria, including the **Look in** list, and the **Include subfolders** check box to instruct where the search is conducted (see Figure 3.10 above).

> NOTE: If you are unsure of the location of a file, choose the highest level you want to begin the search in the **Look in** box and make sure you select the **Include subfolders** check box. For instance, choose the **C:** drive (your computer's hard drive) and select the **Include subfolders** check box, to search the entire drive.

6   Choose **Find Now**.

The **Find: Files named ...** dialog box expands to show a list of all files that match the criteria, and the text you entered in the **Named** box is appended to the title of the dialog box window as Figure 3.13 shows.

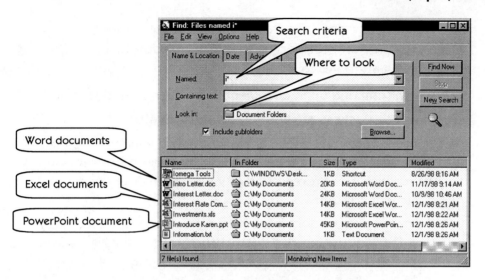

Figure 3.13.   Files that begin with the letter I.

To open a document in the list, double-click the appropriate name. Whether or not the application associated with the document is open, both the application and document are displayed. The **Find: Files named ...** dialog box remains available as a button on the taskbar so that you can return to the dialog box if needed.

Practice Exercise 3-4

Find Files from the Start Menu

1   Click **Start** on the taskbar.

2   Point to **Find** and choose **Files or Folders** from the submenu.

    The **Find: All Files** dialog box appears; the **Name & Location** tab is selected.

3   In the **Named** box, type: 03 .

4   Verify that **Document Folders** is displayed in the **Look in** box.

5   Select the **Include subfolders** check box, if necessary.

6   Choose **Find Now** to start the search.

7   Several file names should appear in the **Find: All Files** dialog box. Find the document **03Poem** and double-click it to open it.

    Make sure the CD-ROM that came with this book is inserted in your CD-ROM drive, or 03Poem may not appear.

8   Leave all documents open and continue on with the lesson.

Switch to Another Open Document

It's not at all uncommon to have more than one document open at a time. The reasons for simultaneously opening multiple Word documents vary, but one instance might be when you want to copy text from an existing document into, say, a letter you are composing.

The document window in the foreground is called the active document window. It is the document in which you can work; cut, copy or paste information via the clipboard; enter text; or apply formatting attributes to existing text.

It's a simple matter to switch from one open document to another open document.

Two ways to access different open documents:

- If you see only one document in your Word window, use the **W**indow menu to select the name of the open document you want active in the foreground of your screen. Every open document is listed.

- If a portion of the document window is visible, but not active, click the window to bring it to the foreground (see Figure 3.14).

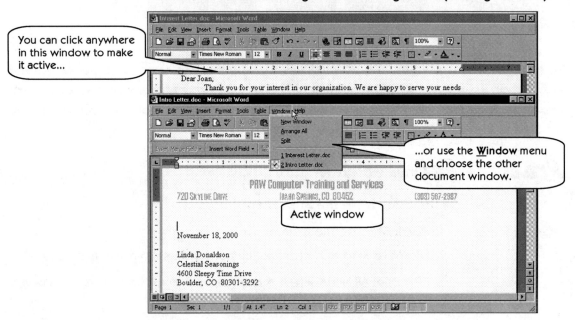

Figure 3.14.   Switching to a different open document.

You can have as many documents as you want opened simultaneously. The only limitations are the amount of RAM in your computer and common sense. If you no longer need to use an open document, close it. You can always reopen it. If you think you might want to use or work on a document even though you are working on another Word document, keep it open. You can begin new documents and open additional existing documents during any work session.

TASKBAR

You can also use the taskbar to switch to another Word document (see Figure 3.15). With Office 2000, all document windows have an associated taskbar button. When you open a document window in any application, the button on the Windows taskbar is connected to the document. This makes switching among document windows easier.

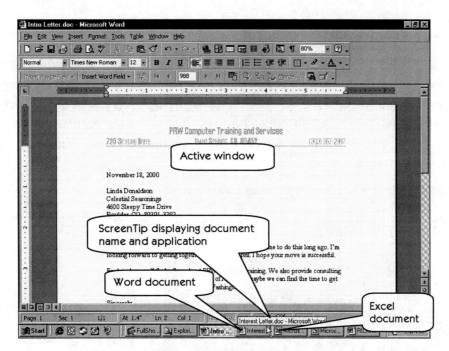

Figure 3.15.   Use taskbar buttons to switch to another document.

Simply point and click the button on the taskbar (let your pointer hover if you can't read the button) for the document you want to use.

 NOTE: Word 97 and earlier versions of Word use the taskbar in a slightly different way. The taskbar only displays minimized applications. Minimized applications hold all open document windows. If you minimize an open document, it becomes an icon in the lower portion of the Word application window, which typically means it is difficult to see and use.

WINDOW MENU

Every business hopes to accomplish lots of work in the most efficient manner. Often you're expected to do two things at once, and using the **Window** menu, you almost can! Work with multiple windows displaying the same document, or access another open document via Word's **Window** menu. In either of these cases, you probably need to arrange the windows so you see and have access to multiple windows.

You can also divide a single document window into two sections that scroll independently by using the **Split** command on the **Window** menu. Each section is called a **windowpane**. Finally, as discussed earlier, you can activate any open document from the **Windows** menu.

New Window

You may wonder why on earth you'd ever want two or more windows displaying the same document. Say you are working with a very long document, one that exceeds the size of your monitor and requires lengthy scrolling to see all of its parts. Say also that you want to work at the beginning of your document but need to refer to information entered at the end of your document. Simply open a second window displaying the same document (see Figure 3.16).

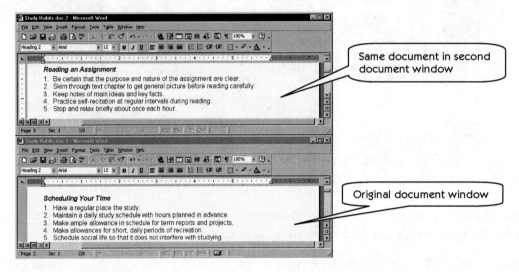

Figure 3.16.   Two windows tiled horizontally for the same document.

Because each window operates independently, you can leave one window displaying the beginning of the document while you scroll the second window to display the end of the document. It's exactly the same document. Information or text you enter in one document window automatically appears in the other document window(s).

You can also apply different views to each window. For example, one window might show the complete text in Normal view while another window of the same document displays the Outline view.

Open an additional window displaying the same document:

- With a document open, choose **W**indow>**N**ew **Window** from the menu bar.

The second view of the same window opens on top of the original view of the document. Both windows are fully functional, that is, you can scroll each independently, enter or edit text in either window, apply formatting–in short, do anything to the document in either window.

To display additional new windows, or other open documents, for that matter, use the **Window** menu again. Select the name of the document to bring it to the foreground of your Word application window. A sequential number following the name of the original document identifies each window of a document. For instance, the document, **My Fax**, displays **My Fax:1** for the original window displaying **My Fax**. The second window displays the name **My Fax:2**. The document name with the sequential number appears in the title bar of the document window and on the list of open windows shown at the bottom of the **Window** menu (see Figure 3.17).

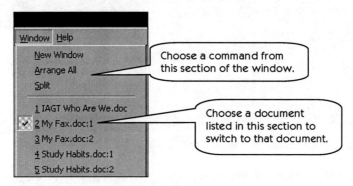

Figure 3.17. The **Window** menu with two documents in two windows.

Access any open window:

- Choose **Window** from the menu bar.
- In the list of open documents, choose the name of the window you want to view or work with.

Arrange All

Activating other open documents from the **Window** menu is simple. Simply choose the name of the document you want in the foreground. You might, however, prefer to have two or more windows showing onscreen at the same time. That way you can scroll to see different portions of the same document, cut and paste easily between open documents, compare data, and perform any number of other tasks. When you have multiple open windows displaying documents, you can create a grid-like effect, shrinking open windows so that all are visible onscreen at the same time, (as shown in Figure 3.18).

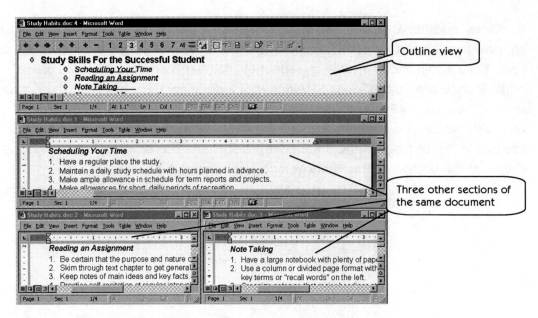

Figure 3.18.   One document displayed in four windows.

According to the number of windows you have open, the arrangement of the windows differs. Two or three windows appear horizontally. Beyond that number, windows are arranged both horizontally and vertically and sized to fit all the open document windows within the Word window.

To see all open windows on screen simultaneously, choose **Window>Arrange All** from the menu bar.

 CAUTION: If you have more than two open document windows and both default toolbars displayed, using **Arrange All** may make it impractical to perform any work in the windows because each workspace is so small.

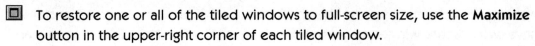 To restore one or all of the tiled windows to full-screen size, use the **Maximize** button in the upper-right corner of each tiled window.

Split

Another way to view different portions of the same document is by splitting the active window. This gives you two horizontal panes, as shown in Figure 3.19. The effect is similar if you chose **New Window**, and then **Arrange All** with only one window open. So why have a **Split** command?

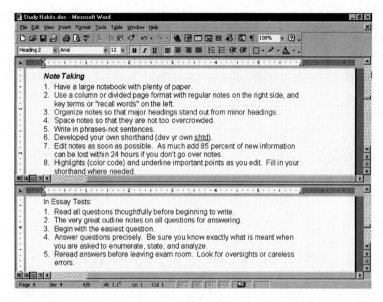

Figure 3.19.   One document split into two sections.

The reasoning behind the **Split** command is that you may have multiple windows displaying documents, but you want to maximize only one window and split that maximized window into panes rather than open yet another new window. Also, the split window doesn't include the window controls that a new window does and therefore allows you to see more of your document. It makes no difference how many documents or windows displaying documents you have open, you can still apply the **Split** command to any active document window.

The **Split** command on the **Window** menu toggles between **Split** and **Remove Split**. When you no longer need two separate panes, simply return to the **Window** menu and choose **Remove Split**.

Practice Exercise 3-5

Switch Between Open Documents

1 Choose the **Window** menu.

2 Choose **03Poem** from the list of documents at the bottom of the menu.

3 Look at the taskbar at the bottom of the screen. Point to the **Word** buttons on the taskbar and wait for the ScreenTip to see the full name of the document associated with each button.

4 Find the button for the **03Fax** document you created in Practice Exercise 3-1. Click that button to switch to that document. Notice **03Poem** still has a button on the taskbar.

5   Choose **Window>Arrange All** to see all the Word windows you
    currently have open. This will look very messy, but don't worry;
    you are going to fix it.

6   Find the active window (blue title bar, and usually at the top of
    the screen). Maximize this window; click the **Maximize** button on
    the top-right corner of the window.

7   Using the taskbar, click the other open Word windows and
    maximize each one.

 TIP: Right-click the taskbar button and choose **Maximize**.

8   Switch to **03Poem**. (Click the taskbar button.)

9   Choose **Window>Split** to split the window into two sections.
    Move the border for the split to where you want it, and click
    once. Scroll each section of the document to see how the
    sections move independently.

10 Choose **Window>Remove Split** to return the document to one
    section.

11 Leave the documents open and continue with this lesson.

Save Documents

If you've used a computer at all before entering the world of Microsoft Word 2000,
you know about saving a document. The principle is simple but essential. If you don't
save your work, it's lost when you close the document or when a disaster strikes such
as a power outage.

If you look at the **File** menu, you'll see there's more than one way to save a document.
The differences in saving are subtle. They allow you to create backup versions of a
document and to quickly save all open documents.

FILE>SAVE

We've said it before, but we'll say it again: save, save, save! That's the most useful
advice anyone can learn when working with computers. When you choose **File>Save**,
you are said to be **writing to disk** (which is a rather stuffy bit of computer jargon that
really means you are creating a file to hold your document with all the text and
formatting you've entered). Unless you save your work to disk, you run the risk of losing
all your work.

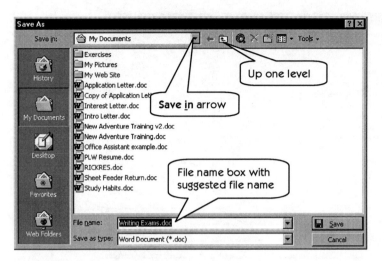

Figure 3.20.   The **Save As** dialog box.

When you save, the file must have a name that differs from all other files in the same folder and should be named using words that will help you recognize the document's contents. For instance, a name such as **My First** is not very helpful to you or anyone else who might need to locate, open, and use the file. It gives no indication of what's in the file. **1st Letter to Jon** is better, and **Jon Jones Letter 1** would be even more identifiable.

By default, Word displays the first words entered in the document in the **File name** box (see Figure 3.20). Most people prefer to give documents a different name. Simply replace the words in the **File name** box with a name that suits the document better.

 TIP: Windows allows you to use real words and spaces between words to name your documents. You can use up to 255 characters (letters, numbers, and spaces all count as characters). Word automatically appends the proper extension (a dot plus three letters following the file name) to identify the format in which a file is saved.

Understand the Save Process

The first time you save a document by choosing **File>Save**, the **Save As** dialog box opens because Word doesn't know the name of your document yet. As you work with the document after you've named it, the **Save** command updates the original saved version of the document file by again writing the file to disk. For example, assume you have begun a fax. You entered the recipient's name and address and saved the document, giving it a name. Then you add text in the body of the fax and save again. The first saved version without body text is replaced by the updated version of the document with body text.

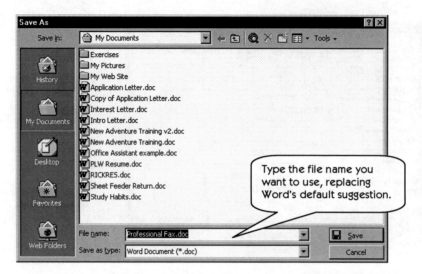

Figure 3.21.   The **Save As** dialog box for a fax the first time around.

Save and name a file:

 1   Choose **File>Save** to open the **Save As** dialog box.

   TIP: The keyboard shortcut for the **Save** command is **Ctrl+S**.

2   In the **File name** box, enter the name for your document.

   CAUTION: There are certain characters that are unacceptable in file names, such as: / \ < > ? : ; [ ] * | " If you inadvertently enter a forbidden character, a **Warning** dialog box appears when you choose the **Save** button. The Warning gives you a message that essentially means your file name includes unacceptable characters. Simply choose the **OK** button in the dialog box, delete the unacceptable character(s), and use something else that Word will accept.

3   Look at the **Save as type** box. Most likely it says, **Word Document (*.doc)**. If not, click the arrow to display the **Save as type** list and choose **Word Document (*.doc)**.

4   In the **Save in** box, indicate where you want to store the file.

   NOTE: You can use the buttons on the Places bar in the **Save As** dialog box to quickly change the location you want to use.

To be sure you are saving the document file in the folder where you want it stored, look at the folder name shown in the **Save in** box at the top of the dialog box. If the folder shown is incorrect, use the arrow beside the **Save in** box or the buttons to the right of that box, to navigate, locate, and select the correct folder for storing your document file.

> **5** Choose **Save** at the lower right of the **Save As** dialog box to write your file to disk.

Saving and naming your document assures that you have a permanent copy of the document on your hard disk (or external media) and that you can reopen it at any time.

File>Save All

By this lesson, you're far enough along in learning Word to pick up a trick or two. As you work with multiple open documents, you may want to save changes made in several of the open documents. Naturally, you could bring each document to the foreground of the Word window and save, but that's rather cumbersome.

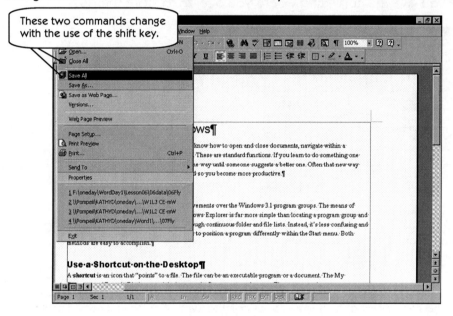

Figure 3.22. Save all the open documents at one time.

Amaze your colleagues by pressing the **Shift** key as you choose the **File** menu with multiple documents open. Surprise! The **File** menu has additional commands, one of which allows you to save all open documents with one menu choice, **Save All** (see Figure 3.22).

- Press the **Shift** key, and choose **File>Save All**.

  This procedure works best when every open document has already been saved at least once and has a name and storage location. If any of the open documents has never been saved, the **Save As** dialog box opens, and you have the opportunity to enter all the first-time Save options discussed earlier in the lesson.

FILE>SAVE AS

Though the **Save As** dialog box opens for each initial saving of a document, you can also use the **Save As** command to open the same dialog box and make a duplicate of the file. There are several reasons to make duplicate files. Perhaps you want to have a backup copy stored in a different location on your network, or on external media, such as a floppy disk. Possibly you'd like to continue working on the document but are unsure if your edits will work, so you can make a duplicate, and revise the copy while retaining the original document in its current state of development.

The steps involved in making a copy are essentially the same as the steps used to originally save a document. The primary differences lie in the **File** menu command you choose, the name you give the copy, and where you decide to store the duplicate.

Figure 3.23.   Use **File>Save As** to save a document with a new name.

 CAUTION: If you are storing a duplicate copy of a document in the same folder with the original file, be sure to revise the name of your copy to avoid overwriting the original file.

If you are creating a backup copy of your document stored in a different folder from the original or on external media, you can use exactly the same name the original document file has without overwriting the original.

Duplicate (copy) a document using Save As:

1   Choose **File>Save As** to open the **Save As** dialog box.

2   Use the **Save in** box to determine where the copy will be stored.

   • If you want to store the duplicate in the same folder with the original, change the name of the duplicate file.

   • If you want to store the duplicate elsewhere, you can leave the name of the duplicate unchanged.

3   If necessary, use the **Save as type** box to change the format for saving the duplicate file. (For more information, see **Appendix B** in the **WORDCert** folder on the CD-ROM with this book.)

4   Choose **Save** to close the **Save As** dialog box.

Be aware that when you create a duplicate file using the **Save As** command, the original file automatically *closes* when you choose the **Save** button in the **Save As** dialog box, and the *duplicated* document is in the foreground of the Word window.

CREATE A NEW FOLDER

Oops, no place to put your file? Not to worry. While you are in the **Save As** (or the **Open**) dialog box, you can create a new folder to store documents.

Store document in new folder:

1   Choose **File>Save As** from the menu bar to open the **Save As** dialog box.

2   Use the **Save in** box to navigate to where you want to place the new folder.

3   Click **Create New Folder** or press **Alt+5**. A **New Folder** dialog box will open (see Figure 3.24).

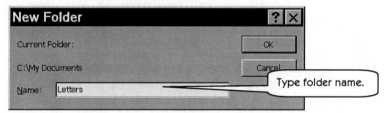

Figure 3.24. Verify the name of the folder where the new folder will go. In this example *Letters* will be a subfolder of **My Documents** on the **C:** drive. If this is incorrect, press the **Esc** key.

4   In the **Name** box, type the new folder name and choose **OK**.

The new folder now appears in the **Save in** box.

5   To save the file, type its name in the **Save As** dialog box's **File name** box and choose **Save**.

Practice Exercise 3-6

Saving Documents

1   Start a new blank document using the **New Blank Document** button on the Standard toolbar.

2   Type your name and address on three separate lines.

3   Choose **File>Save** from the menu bar to save the document.

4   Notice the suggested file name is *Your Name*. Choose the **Save** button in the dialog box to accept this name and save the document.

5   Save all eight open documents. Hold down the **Shift** key then click the **File** menu. Notice that the **Save** command has changed to **Save All**. Choose **Save All**.

   - If it looks like nothing happened, the **Save All** command worked and you are finished with this exercise.

   - If the **Save As** dialog box is displayed, this means you have a document you have not saved at least once. Continue with this exercise.

6   Choose **Cancel** in the **Save As** dialog box. Use the **Window** menu to find the document you have not yet saved. Look for the default document name, **Document1**; choose the name from the **Window** menu to switch to that document. Save the document with the name ⊟**03Spot**.

7   Try saving all the documents again.

8   Create a new folder and save the active document in the folder using the following steps:

   - Choose **File>Save As** to open the **Save As** dialog box. Navigate to the **My Documents** folder or to the folder your instructor indicates.

   - Click the **Create New Folder** button.

   - Type Examples in the **Name** box and choose **OK**.

   - Type 03Spot, if necessary, in the **File name** box to save this document in the **Examples** folder. Choose **Save**.

9   Leave the documents open and continue the lesson.

Close Documents

Whether your work session is ended, interrupted, or a document is completed, at some time you'll want to close documents. You can close a single document or all open documents using the **File** menu.

It's a good idea to execute the **Save** command before closing a document. However, if you attempt to close a document and have unsaved changes, the Office Assistant displays a message or Word displays a dialog box asking if you want to save the changes (see Figure 3.25). You can choose **Yes**, **No**, or **Cancel** in either message dialog box. **Yes** saves the changes and then closes the document. **No** closes the document and discards unsaved changes. **Cancel** stops the process of closing the document, and you can review, edit, or continue using the document.

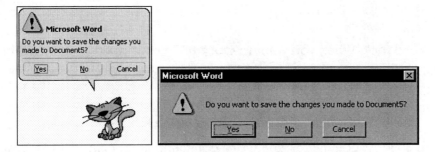

Figure 3.25. The message from the Office Assistant and Microsoft Word.

If you attempt to close a document that has never been saved, you see the same message dialog box, so there's no chance of losing either the document you're closing or the changes made to a document.

FILE>CLOSE

The **File** menu always displays the **Close** command (see Figure 3.26). Use it when you want to close only the active document in the foreground of your Word window.

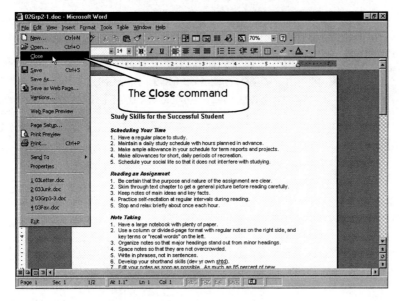

Figure 3.26. Use the **Close** command to close each document individually.

Close a single document:

 • With the document in the foreground of your Word window, choose **File>Close**.

 TIP: You can also use **Ctrl+W** or **Ctrl+F4** to close a document.

File>Close All

Here's another Word trick. When you want to close all of your open documents in one stroke, press the **Shift** key as you choose the **File** menu, just as you did when saving all open documents with one command.

- Press the **Shift** key and choose **File>Close All**.

Like the **Save** and **Save All** commands, the **Close** command is replaced by **Close All** when you press the **Shift** key as you choose the **File** menu. Choose **Close All**, and every open document automatically closes, leaving only the Word application itself open.

Practice Exercise 3-7

Close Document Files

1 On the document window that is currently active, choose **File>Close** from the menu bar to close this document.

2 Look at the taskbar to see how many document windows you currently have open.

3 Hold down the **Shift** key while you choose the **File** menu. Notice the **Close** command changed to **Close All**. Choose **Close All** to close all the Word document windows that are currently open.

LESSON 4: EDIT DOCUMENTS

When creating documents, you almost always need to make some changes. Perhaps you need to change a word, or restructure a sentence, or move a paragraph to a different position in the body of text. Editing documents is a necessary task, so learning how to edit in Word will further your mastery of the program.

In this lesson, you will learn to:

> Select text using the mouse and the keyboard

> Insert and delete text

> Copy and move text

> Use the Undo and Redo features

> Use AutoCorrect, AutoComplete, and AutoText

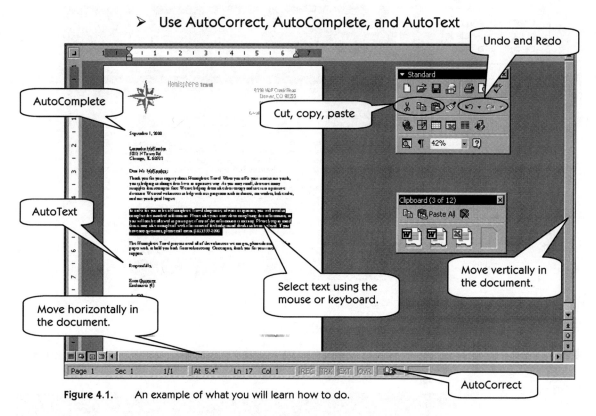

Figure 4.1.   An example of what you will learn how to do.

Once you master the skills in this lesson, you will be able to productively edit not only your documents but co-workers' documents as well.

Select Text

In order to edit text, you must select text you want to replace and then type the new text. As soon as you begin typing, the selected text is replaced with the new text. Selecting text is also the first step in copying text to the clipboard so you can paste it somewhere else. When you want to change formatting, you also need to know how to select text. You can use the mouse or the keyboard to select text. Once you have tried both methods of selecting text, you can determine which one works better for you.

USE THE MOUSE

Editing text often means that you need to retype letters or words. To replace text, it must be selected. With text selected, you simply begin typing, and the selected text is replaced by the letters or words you type. There are several ways to select text with the mouse in Word.

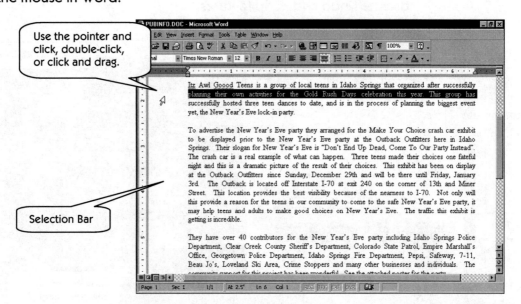

Figure 4.2.   Using the mouse to select text.

Mouse selection methods:

 NOTE: Remember, the selection bar is the white area to the left of the left margin. You learned about this in Lesson 2.

	MOUSE ACTION	SELECTS
I	Drag **I-beam pointer** across selection.	One character at a time, or word by word
I	Double-click **I-beam pointer** on the word.	One word
↗	With the pointer in the **selection bar**, click.	One line

MOUSE ACTION		SELECTS
	With the pointer in the **selection bar** (white arrow), click and drag.	Multiple lines
	With the pointer in the **selection bar**, double-click.	One paragraph

NOTE: See **Appendix B** in the **WORDCert** folder on the CD-ROM that came with this book for more selection techniques while using the mouse.

USE THE KEYBOARD

If you're a keyboard maven, Word provides ways to select text you want to replace. The effect is identical to selecting text with the mouse, but sometimes it is faster and more precise.

Keyboard selection methods:

1   Move the insertion point to the beginning or end of the selection you want to make.

2   In all but one case below (**Select All, Ctrl+A**), you will hold down the **Shift** key to "modify" the basic navigation keys you learned earlier. In some cases, the **Ctrl** key is also used as a modifier key.

• Use one of the following key combinations:

PRESS	SELECT TO
Shift+Home	To the beginning of line
Shift+End	To the end of line
Ctrl+Shift+Home	To the beginning of document
Ctrl+Shift+End	To the end of document
Shift+Left Arrow	Left one character
Shift+Right Arrow	Right one character
Ctrl+Shift+Left Arrow	Left one word
Ctrl+Shift+Right Arrow	Right one word
Ctrl+A	All document text (Select All)

- Use the **Extend Selection** command:
  - Press **F8** to turn on Extend Selection.
  - Use any of the following keyboard movement keys to select the text:

KEY	TO MOVE AND SELECT
Home	To the beginning of line
End	To the end of line
Ctrl+Home	To the beginning of document
Ctrl+End	To the end of document
Left Arrow	Left one character
Right Arrow	Right one character
Ctrl+Left Arrow	Left one word
Ctrl+Right Arrow	Right one word

USE THE MOUSE AND KEYBOARD TOGETHER

You can also use a combination of the mouse and keyboard to select text. This works best when you are trying to select a large portion of text that extends across multiple pages.

Select text using the mouse and keyboard concurrently:

1 Select a portion of the text using the mouse or keyboard.

2 Move the pointer to the end of what you want to select. Use the scroll bars if necessary.

3 Hold down the **Shift** key, or press **F8** (**Extend Selection**), then click the mouse at the end of the selection.

This is where moving the document using the scroll bars is extremely valuable. When you move the document using the scroll bars, the insertion point *does not* move. This allows you to bring into view the area of the document you need to see to use the Shift-and-click method of selecting text.

Practice Exercise 4-1

Select Text

1 Open 📁04Ex4-1 from the **WORDCert\Word A** folder.

2 Select text in the document using the mouse and the Shift-and-click method:

- Point to the left of the word **Office** in the first line and click and drag across the word (to select it).

- Point to the word **Microsoft** and double-click it (to select the word quickly).

- Point to the first line of text after the bulleted list that begins with **"The One-Day series currently..."** from the selection bar and click (to select that line).

- While still pointing at the selected line of text, double-click (to select the entire paragraph).

- Use the scroll bar to move to the end of the document. Point to the end of the last line in the document, hold down the **Shift** key, and click (to select from the location of the insertion point to the end of the document).

3 Select text in the document using the keyboard. Hold down the **Shift** key while pressing the following keyboard movement keys:

- Press **Ctrl+Home** (to select from the insertion point to the beginning of the document).

     NOTE: To deselect text between steps, click away from the selected text or press an arrow key.

- Press the **Right Arrow** five times (to select text one character at a time to the right).

- Press **Ctrl+Right Arrow** five times (to select one word at a time to the right).

- Press the **Left Arrow** five times (to select text one character at a time to the left).

- Press **Ctrl+Left Arrow** five times (to select one word at a time to the left).

- Press **Ctrl+End** (to select text from the insertion point to the end of the document).

4 Close the document without saving any changes.

Insert and Delete Text

As you edit a document, you may need to insert and delete text. You can replace text by selecting the text and then typing the new text. Or, if you prefer, you can type over existing text.

INSERT, DELETE, AND REPLACE TEXT

Highlight the text you want to delete and begin typing in the new text. Immediately the old text is gone, and your new text replaces it. (You already saw an example of replacing selected text when you worked with placeholders in Lesson 1.)

 TIP: Use **Ctrl+Backspace** to delete one word at a time to the left of the insertion point. **Ctrl+Delete** deletes one word at a time to the right of the insertion point.

If you simply need to add text—perhaps inserting a word or a sentence—position the insertion point where you want the new text to appear and begin typing.

As you type in Insert mode (default), anything to the right of the insertion point is pushed to the right and down the page with the help of word wrap.

To insert text:

1 Move the insertion point to the position in which you want to insert text.

2 Begin typing the new text.

To delete text one character at a time:

1 Position the insertion point.

2 Use the **Backspace** or **Delete** key:

   • Press **Backspace** to delete text to the left of the insertion point.

   • Press **Delete** to delete text to the right of the insertion point.

To delete or replace selected text:

1 Select the text you want to delete.

2 Press the **Backspace** key or the **Delete** key, or type replacement text.

TYPE OVER TEXT (OVERTYPE MODE)

If you want to type over existing text:

1 Press the **Insert** key to switch from **Insert** mode (default) to **Overtype** mode.

   On the **status bar**, you will see the **Overtype** indicator (**OVR**) in bold when you are in **Overtype** mode.

    NOTE: Double-clicking the **OVR** indicator on the status bar will also switch modes.

2 Type the new text.

   Each character is replaced by what you type.

3 Press the **Insert** key again to return to **Insert** mode.

    NOTE: If you do not get the same results as explained in the above steps, some of the options for editing may have been changed. Choose **Tools**>**Options** and then choose the **Edit** tab to review the options that are set on your computer. To see a definition of an option, right-click the option and choose **W**hat's This?.

Practice Exercise 4-2

Insert and Delete Text

1 Open 📂**04Ex4-2** from the **WORDCert\Word A** folder. Save the document as 💾**04AppL**.

2 Insert text by completing the following steps:

- Move to the beginning of the salutation line, **Mr. Stone**.
- Type Dear at the beginning of the line.
- Move to the beginning of the second sentence in the second paragraph, **When completing this information ...**
- Type Please take your time

3 Delete and insert text by completing the following steps:

- Press the **Delete** key to delete the **W** in the word **When**.
- Type a lowercase **w**.
- Move to the left of the period in the first sentence in the first paragraph, **Thank you for your interest ...**
- Press the **Backspace** key to delete the space after **TEENS** and before the period.
- Notice that the wavy, green line disappeared.

4 Select and replace text:

- Select the word **is** in the second line of the first paragraph.
- Type are to correct the grammar of the sentence.
- In the second paragraph's first line, select the word **a** in front of **ITZ AWL GOOOD TEENS.**
- Type an to correct the grammar.

5 Type over text using **Overtype** mode:

- Move to the beginning of the document, before the recipient's name, **Earl Stone.**
- Press **Insert** to turn on **Overtype** mode.
- Type Jose Vigil.
- Move down to the beginning of the next line.
- Type 1634 Humbolt Avenue.
- Move down to the end of the next line.
- Press **Ctrl+Backspace** to delete the zip code.
- Type 80111.
- Move to the salutation line in front of **Stone**.
- Type Vigil.
- Press **Insert** again to return to Insert mode.

6 Save and close the document.

Itz Awl Goood Teens

July 23, 2001

Jose Vigil
1634 Humbolt Avenue
Denver, CO 80111

Dear Mr. Vigil,

Thank you for your interest in ITZ AWL GOOOD TEENS. When you offer your time to our youth, you are helping to change their lives in a positive way. As you may recall, there are many struggles that teenagers face. We are helping them take their energy and use it in a positive direction. We need volunteers to help with our programs such as dances, car washes, bake sales, and our youth pool league.

In order for you to be an ITZ AWL GOOOD TEENS chaperone, advisor or sponsor, you will need to complete the attached information. Please take your time when completing this information, as you will not be allowed to participate if any of the information is missing. Please keep in mind that it may take a couple of weeks for some of the background checks to be completed. If you have any questions, please call me at (303) 567-2987.

When you return your packet, it should contain the following:

➤ Application (2 pages including Skill sheet & Sexual Misconduct/Child Abuse Statement) *
➤ CBI Background check *
➤ Central Registry check *
➤ DMV License check *
➤ Two (2) written references
➤ Proof of Auto Insurance
➤ Copies of any Training Certificates (First Aide, CPR, WFR, Life Guard, etc.)
  * Form is provided

The ITZ AWL GOOOD TEENS projects need all of the volunteers we can get, please do not allow this paper work to hold you back from volunteering. Once again, thank you for your interest and support.

Respectfully,

Patty Winter
Enclosures (4)
cc: Joan Vieweg

Figure 4.3.   Your edited document should look like this.

Move or Duplicate (Cut or Copy)

When you want to move or duplicate text or graphics, first select the text or graphics, then cut or copy the selection. The selection is held in a temporary storage area called the **Clipboard**. Move to the desired location on the document and then paste the selection from the Clipboard (see Figure 4.4).

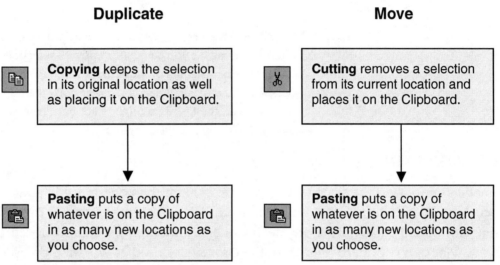

Duplicate   **Move**

Copying keeps the selection in its original location as well as placing it on the Clipboard.

Cutting removes a selection from its current location and places it on the Clipboard.

Pasting puts a copy of whatever is on the Clipboard in as many new locations as you choose.

Pasting puts a copy of whatever is on the Clipboard in as many new locations as you choose.

Figure 4.4.   A visual representation of duplicating and moving text.

MOVE TEXT (CUT AND PASTE)

Using **Cut** (found on the **Edit** menu) removes the selected items from the document to the Clipboard. You can then paste the text from the Clipboard. Move to the position in which you want the Clipboard contents to appear, and choose **Edit>Paste**.

Move text with cut-and-paste:

1   Open or switch to the document that contains the items you want to move.

2   Select the text you want to move.

   3   Choose **Edit>Cut** from the menu bar.

   TIP: The keyboard shortcut for the **Cut** command is **Ctrl+X**.

Word removes (cuts) your selection from the document and stores it in the Clipboard.

4   Move the insertion point to the location where you want to paste the item.

5   Choose **Edit>Paste** from the menu bar.

TIP: The keyboard shortcut for the **Paste** command is **Ctrl+V**.

Word inserts the cut selection at the location of the insertion point. The text has been moved.

NOTE: A new feature, the Office Clipboard now stores up to 12 items. This means you can cut or copy 12 selections to the Clipboard and paste any of those items wherever and whenever you choose. When you cut or copy the thirteenth item, however, the first item on the Clipboard is removed. See **Multiple Cut/Copy and Paste** ahead.

COPY AND PASTE

Sometimes you need the same text or graphic in more than one place in your document. There's no need to recreate the wheel. Just copy and paste. Things copied from your document leave the original intact and temporarily stores a duplicate copy on the Windows Clipboard (and now, the Office Clipboard as well—see below). You can repeatedly paste the Clipboard contents into other places in your document, or into other documents, without copying or cutting them again.

NOTE: Deleting selected text using the **Delete** or **Backspace** key has no effect on the selection in the Clipboard.

Copy and paste:

1   Select the text or graphics you want to copy.

2   Choose **Edit>Copy** from the menu bar.

TIP: The keyboard shortcut for the **Copy** command is **Ctrl+C**.

Word copies the selection to the Clipboard.

3   Move the insertion point to the position you want to paste the selection.

4   Choose **Edit>Paste** from the menu bar.

The contents of the Clipboard are inserted at the location of the insertion point.

MULTIPLE CUT/COPY AND PASTE

 To cut/copy and paste multiple selections, Word has a new feature; it uses the Windows Clipboard, working in much the same way as it does for single selections when you use cut/copy and paste. The major difference is your ability to make multiple selections available throughout your document pages. As you add selections using **Copy** or **Cut**, the original contents of the Office Clipboard are *not* replaced. You can compile as many as 12 different selections on the Office Clipboard using the new Clipboard toolbar.

The first selection you place on the Clipboard is no different from any other cut or copy action. It's the second selection that activates the new feature, the Clipboard toolbar. Word copies and adds each successive selection to the Clipboard toolbar and identifies where the selection came from with an application icon (see Figure 4.5).

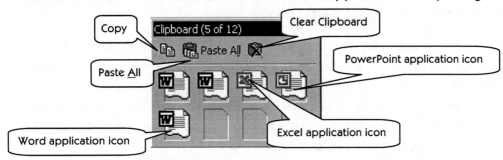

Figure 4.5.   The Clipboard toolbar.

 TIP: If the Clipboard toolbar fails to appear, right-click any toolbar and choose **Clipboard**.

Buttons on the Clipboard toolbar:

- Move the mouse pointer over one of the icons, and hover to see a ScreenTip of the item in the Clipboard.

- Click the desired icon to paste the item.

- Click the **Paste All** button to paste all the items on the Clipboard into your document.

- Click the **Clear All** button to remove all the items from the Clipboard.

- Click the **Close** button to hide the Clipboard toolbar.

- You can also use the **Paste** button on the Standard toolbar, or press **Ctrl+V**, to paste into your document the last item that was cut or copied.

Use the Clipboard toolbar for multiple cut/copy selections:

1   Select the text or graphic you want to cut or copy.

2   Choose **Edit** from the menu bar, then choose **Cut** or **Copy**.

3   Repeat steps 1 and 2 (up to 11 times) for other items to cut or copy.

4   Move the insertion point to the position to paste the text.

5   Click one of the items on the Clipboard toolbar to paste the selection.

6   Repeat steps 4 and 5 for each selection you want to paste.

MOVE AND COPY TEXT (DRAG AND DROP)

Yet another quick and easy way to move or copy a selection is the drag-and-drop method. This method produces essentially the same result as cut or copy and paste, and it can be a more convenient way to move or copy text if the selection needs to be moved within text that is already visible onscreen. This method is not suggested for those times when you need to move or copy text to another page. Highlight the selection, then *drag* it to the new position, and *drop* it.

Move text or graphics using drag-and-drop:

1   Select the text you want to move.

2   Move the mouse pointer onto the selection. When the pointer becomes an arrow, click and hold the left mouse button down.

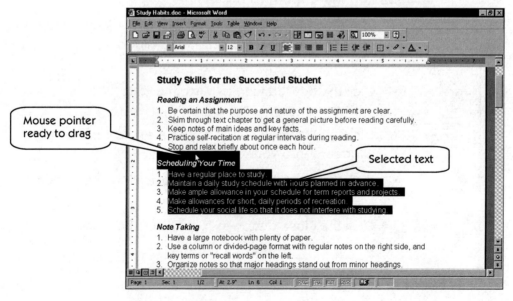

Figure 4.6.   Point to the text you want to move and click and drag it.

3 Drag the highlighted selection to the new position.

As you drag the selection, a hatched insertion point is displayed where the selection will be inserted.

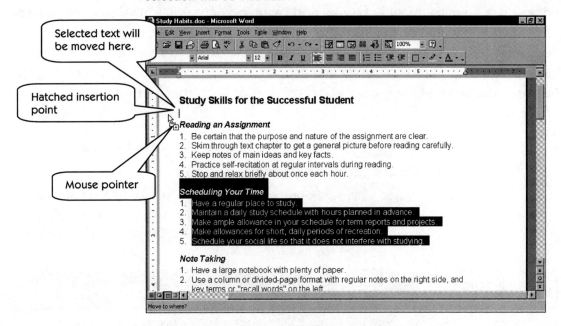

Figure 4.7.   Drop the selected text where you want it to appear.

4 When you reach the new position for the selection, release the mouse button.

The entire selection has been moved from its original location.

Copy text or graphics using drag-and-drop:

1 Select the text or graphics you want to copy.

2 Move the mouse pointer onto the selection. When the pointer becomes an arrow:

- Hold down the **Ctrl** key on the keyboard.

- Click and drag the highlighted selection to the new position.

 As you drag the selection, a hatched insertion point is displayed where the selection will be inserted. The plus sign beside the pointer indicates that you are copying.

GO TO

The **Go To** command (found on the **Edit** menu) allows you to reposition the insertion point at a particular page in your document. There are many reasons to use **Go To**, but since you're learning about **Cut/Copy** and **Paste**, perhaps you'll have an occasion when you've cut or copied text but you want to paste it on a different page in your document. Rather than scroll through all those pages after you have the Clipboard loaded, you can instead efficiently and accurately move to the correct page using **Go To**. After you arrive at the proper page, you can position the insertion point anywhere on the page.

Move the insertion point to the top of a specific page:

1 Choose **Edit>Go To** from the menu bar.

 TIP: As shown earlier in this lesson, the **Go To** command has two keyboard shortcuts, **Ctrl+G** and **F5**. Also, as you saw in Lesson 2, you can double-click the left side of the status bar to display the same tab.

Page is just one of the items you can **Go To**.

Some **Go To** elements allow you to move backward as well as forward in a document.

Figure 4.8. The **Find and Replace** dialog box with the **Go To** tab selected. **Go To** has many elements you can choose from to move the insertion point.

2 Select **Page** in the **Go to what** list, if necessary. (It should be selected by default.)

3 Type the page number to go to in the **Enter page number** box.

4 Choose **Go To** or press **Enter**.

The insertion point moves to the top of the page you entered.

5 Choose **Close** or press **Esc** to close the **Find and Replace** dialog box.

Practice Exercise 4-3

Cut/Copy and Paste Text

1   Open 📁**04Ex4-3** from the **WORDCert\Word A** folder. Save the document as 💾**04Quest**.

2   Near the beginning of the document, select the two lines beginning with **Please supply copies of your tax returns ...** and include the two blank lines after them. (You may see paragraph marks [¶] on the blank lines.)

> Please supply copies of your tax returns from the last 5 years.
> This questionnaire must be witnessed by 2 individuals, and signed
> and dated by you below.

3   Choose **Edit>Cut** from the menu bar to remove the selection and place it on the Clipboard.

> **TIP:** The keyboard shortcut for the **Cut** command is **Ctrl+X**. You can also use the right mouse button to display the shortcut menu and then choose **Cut**.

4   Move to the bottom of the document, directly above the signature line, and choose **Edit>Paste** to paste the Clipboard contents.

> **TIP:** The keyboard shortcut for the **Paste** command is **Ctrl+V**. You can also use the right mouse button to display the shortcut menu and then choose **Paste**.

> Please supply copies of your tax returns from the last 5 years.
> This questionnaire must be witnessed by 2 individuals, and signed
> and dated by you below.
>
>
> Signature:
> Witness 1:
> Witness 2:
> Date:

5   Select the first line at the beginning of the document, **New Account Questionnaire**, and the blank line below it.

6   Choose **Edit>Copy** from the menu bar to copy the selection to the Clipboard.

> **TIP:** The keyboard shortcut for the **Copy** command is **Ctrl+C**. You can also use the right mouse button to display the shortcut menu and then choose **Copy**.

7   Move to the top of page 2.

> **TIP:** Use the **Go To** feature.

8   Choose **Edit>Paste** to paste a copy of the selection at the top of page 2.

9   Select the name and address of the company at the beginning of the document. (Do not select any blank lines.)

> Superior Securities & Investments
> 1 Superior Way
> Superior, Wisconsin 10903

10 Choose **Edit>Copy** from the menu bar to copy the selection to the Clipboard.

11 Display the Clipboard toolbar, if necessary. (Right-click any toolbar and choose **Clipboard** from the list.)

12 Move to the end of the document.

> **TIP:** Remember the keyboard shortcut, **Ctrl+End**.

13 Move to the beginning of the line with the 800 number.

14 Choose **Edit>Paste** to paste the name and address of the company.

> Mail to:
> Superior Securities & Investments
> 1 Superior Way
> Superior, Wisconsin 10903
> 1-800-GET RICH (438-7424)

15 Select all four lines of question 3 and the following blank line.

16 Click the selection and drag it to move it, placing it so that the questions are in numerical order, as shown in Figure 4.9.

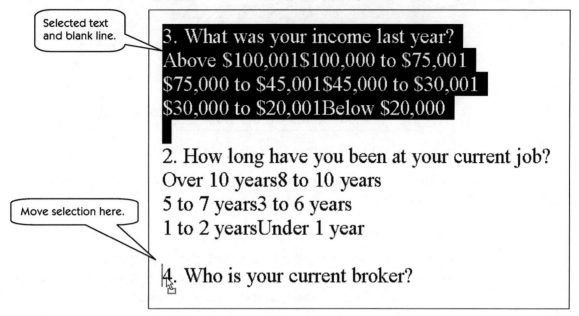

Figure 4.9.   Drag and drop.

17 Save and close the document.

A completed example of **04Quest** is available in the **WORDCert\Word A\Samples** folder on the DDC CD-ROM.

Undo and Redo

If you make a mistake—and who doesn't?—use the **Undo** button on the Standard toolbar to repair the damage. Some folks like to call this the "Ungoof" button. Word records up to 100 actions in the Undo list, so you can undo previous mistakes by repeatedly clicking the **Undo** button.

 CAUTION: Undo does not work with all commands, especially many of those on the **File** menu such as **New**, **Close**, **Save**, and **Send To**.

Each **Undo** is sequential. Each click moves back sequentially through your actions, starting by undoing the most recent action; each click removes the next, and the next, and the next action, and so on.

If you click too far, you can "undo your Undo" with the **Redo** button, also on the Standard toolbar. Just as the **Undo** clicks are sequential, so are the **Redo** clicks, adding back one action with each click.

The **Undo** and **Redo** buttons also have attached arrows that show a list of tasks that you can undo or redo at one time. When you choose an item on the list, you undo or redo that action and all items leading up to it.

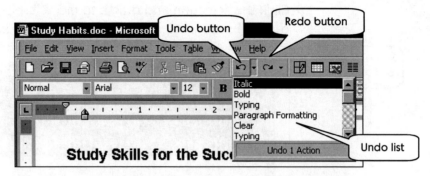

Figure 4.10.   Click the **Undo** arrow and choose the action(s) to undo.

If you have multiple documents open, each document has its own set of **Undo** and **Redo** actions listed in the drop-down list of each button.

Undo a mistake:

1   To undo the last thing you did, click the **Undo** button on the Standard toolbar. If necessary, continue to click the **Undo** button to return the document to the state you want.

 TIP: The keyboard shortcut for the **Undo** command is **Ctrl+Z**; for **Redo** it is **Ctrl+Y**.

2   To reverse the last **Undo** action, click the **Redo** button.

When you can no longer undo/redo an action, the button is dimmed.

Practice Exercise 4-4

Undo and Redo Typing

1   Start a new blank document. Save the document as ⊞**04UndoN**.

2   Type your name.

3   Start another new blank document and save it as ⊞**04Undo**.

4   Type To: , press **Tab**, and type Chief Operating Officer .

5   Click the **Undo** button on the Standard toolbar enough times to remove **Chief Operating Officer** and type: Information Officer .

 TIP: The keyboard shortcut for the **Undo** command is **Ctrl+Z**.

 NOTE: The **Undo** button can be a fickle beast that behaves differently depending on your typing speed and accuracy. Watch the screen as you use the **Undo** button so you only undo what you want to undo. You may need to retype **To:** in the step above.

6 Choose **Window>04UndoN** to return to the first document.

> **TIP:** Remember that you can also use the document's taskbar button.

7 Click the **Undo** button to remove your name.

8 Click the **Redo** button to reinsert your name.

9 Select the entire document (**Ctrl+A**) and press **Delete**.

10 Click the **Undo** button to undo the deletion.

11 Close both of the documents without saving the changes.

Automatic Entries

 Word has three great productivity boosters: **AutoCorrect**, **AutoComplete**, and **AutoText**. These features function differently, but each is a method of entering text automatically. **AutoCorrect** recognizes commonly misspelled or mistyped words and replaces them with the correct word or spelling. **AutoComplete** attempts to identify words as you type and finishes typing the word for you. (You already saw an example of **AutoComplete** earlier, when typing letters; today's date was given in a ScreenTip and you approved the automatic entry.) **AutoText** is a method of recording and inserting frequently used blocks of text, such as your company name, address, and phone numbers.

AUTOCORRECT

AutoCorrect corrects common mistakes without your doing anything (except not turning it off). When you're using Word 2000, if you've noticed that your spelling has improved on words you "always" misspell, you can thank Microsoft for that—it's probably the **AutoCorrect** feature!

AutoCorrect uses two entries to make corrections: one that is recognized as incorrect, and one that replaces the incorrect entry. Word is pre-programmed to fix things like missed capitalization at the beginning of a sentence, and it replaces a solo i with I in all sentences. Commonly misspelled words are also corrected; for instance, **AutoCorrect** replaces **teh** with **the** and **cheif** with **chief**.

AutoCorrect is also a clever way to enter common symbols such as the registered mark ®, trademark ™, and copyright ©.

Enter symbols in your document using AutoCorrect:

- The following table shows you what to type to enter the symbol:

You Type	To Enter AutoCorrect Character
(c)	©
(r)	®
(tm)	™
...	...
:)	☺
-->	→

You can also add your own **AutoCorrect** entries, symbols or text.

Define AutoCorrect entries and options:

1   Choose **Tools>AutoCorrect** from the menu bar. The **AutoCorrect** dialog box is displayed, as shown in Figure 4.11.

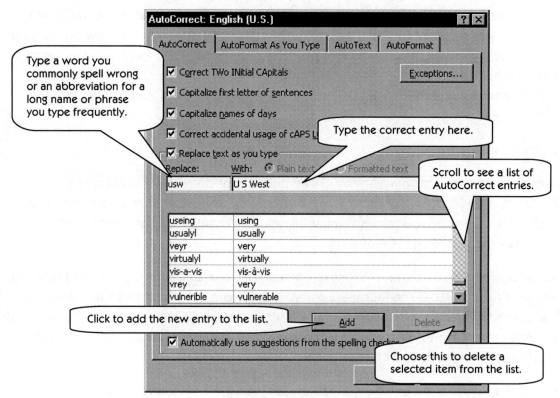

Figure 4.11.   The **AutoCorrect** dialog box with the **AutoCorrect** tab selected.

2 Select/deselect any of the options on the dialog box to turn the option on or off:

OPTION	DESCRIPTION
Correct TWo INitial CApitals	When you accidentally type two capital letters at the beginning of a word, the program corrects the word to one capital letter when you press the spacebar or type punctuation.
Capitalize first letter of sentences	When you type a period (.) and then a space (or two spaces), Word capitalizes the next word you type.
Capitalize names of days	When you type weekdays (Monday, Tuesday, Wednesday, etc.), Word capitalizes the day for you if you don't.
Correct accidental usage of cAPS LOCK key	If you accidentally type with Caps Lock on and use the **Shift** key to capitalize words, Word will correct the mistyped words and turn Caps Lock off.
Replace text as you type	As you are typing, Word substitutes the word in the **Replace** list with the word that is in the **With** list. (See notes below for more information.)
Automatically use suggestions from the spelling checker	When you type an incorrect word, this option replaces words using the Spelling dictionary.
Exceptions button	This allows you to define abbreviations, words, or terms with mixed capitalization that you don't want Word to automatically correct.

 CAUTION: When creating an **AutoCorrect** entry in the **Replace text as you type** box, don't type a word that you might use in the future, because that word will *always* be replaced!

 TIP: If you want to add a symbol to the **AutoCorrect** list, first place the symbol in your document (**Insert>Symbol**). Then place the symbol in the clipboard (**Ctrl+X**). Finally, paste the symbol in the **With** text box of the **AutoCorrect** dialog box (**Ctrl+V**).

3   After making all your selections, choose **OK** to close the
AutoCorrect dialog box.

NOTE: You can also add words you incorrectly type while you
are running the **Spelling** feature. While in the **Spelling and
Grammar** dialog box, choose the correct spelling of the
identified word and choose the **AutoCorrect** button.

Define AutoCorrect Exceptions

Fortunately, AutoCorrect is not an all-or-nothing feature. If you have specific situations
in which you don't want AutoCorrect to override your typing, you can designate those
deviations in the **AutoCorrect Exceptions** dialog box. For example, while you may like
the **Correct TWo INitial Capitals** feature in the **AutoCorrect** dialog box (this feature is
selected by default), you don't want the two caps that represent part of a company
name to be changed. You should specify this exception in the **INitial CAps** tab of the
AutoCorrect Exceptions dialog box.

On the **First Letter** tab, there are common abbreviation entries. When you type the
abbreviation with its ending period, the next word will not be capitalized
automatically.

Figure 4.12.   The first tab in the **AutoCorrect Exceptions**
dialog box is only one option.

Other abbreviations that you type can be added in the dialog box. Another option is
to select the **Automatically add words to list** check box. When you do so and type an
abbreviation, Word automatically capitalizes the next word. Press **Backspace** to delete
the word and then retype it. The abbreviation is then automatically added to this list of
exceptions.

NOTE: AutoCorrect exceptions aren't added automatically if you use **Undo** to reverse the
AutoCorrect change; you must use **Backspace**.

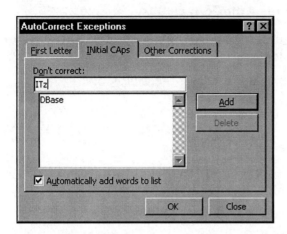

Figure 4.13.   The second tab in the **AutoCorrect Exceptions**
dialog box is for two INitial capital letters.

The **AutoCorrect Exceptions** tab is for the correction of proper names or for acronyms with two initial embedded capital letters, such as **AService** for the company name **AService Company** or **RScA** for **right scapuloanterior**. Again, you can add words to the list in the dialog box or have Word automatically add words for you. As mentioned in Lesson 7, **Spell Check Options**, words in *all* caps are automatically ignored by default.

Figure 4.14.   The third tab in the **AutoCorrect Exceptions** dialog box.

The third tab, **Other Corrections**, is for Word to not change what are normal spelling corrections. You can use this feature instead of adding the words to the custom dictionary. This option allows you to ignore incorrect spellings temporarily; you can later go back to this dialog box and choose **Delete** to remove the entry. For example, **Itz Awl Goood Teens** is the name of a group. While you are working on documents for this group, you could add **goood** to the exception list and then later remove it so you don't accidentally miss what would be a typo in other documents.

Define exceptions for AutoCorrect:

1   Choose **Tools>AutoCorrect** from the menu bar to display the **AutoCorrect** dialog box.

2   Choose **Exceptions** at the top of the dialog box.

3   Choose desired tab(s):

   • **First Letter** — Defines an abbreviation, including its period, so the next letter is not capitalized.

   • **INitial CAps** — Defines words that are supposed to begin with two initial capital letters.

   • **Other Corrections** — Defines all other exceptions.

4   In the **Don't capitalize after** or **Don't correct** box, type the word/abbreviation you want to define.

 NOTE: The entries you type cannot include any spaces. If you type a space, the **Add** button is dimmed (unavailable).

5   Choose **Add** to add the word to the exceptions list.

6   Choose **OK** when you are finished defining AutoCorrect exceptions.

   You return to the **AutoCorrect** dialog box. If you need to make any changes to these options, you can do so at this point.

7   Choose **OK** to return to your document.

AUTOCOMPLETE

As you have seen in previous lessons, **AutoComplete** is a pre-programmed feature that automatically provides a ScreenTip that permits you to insert text quickly—text such as months, today's date, days of the week, your name, and other **AutoText** entries. This feature is active by default; Word tries to help you as you type. As soon as Word recognizes a series of letters or numbers you type as the beginning of an **AutoComplete** entry, it provides a ScreenTip. By pressing **Enter** you can have Word complete the entry for you. If Word guesses incorrectly, simply continue typing to remove the incorrect text as you enter the correct text.

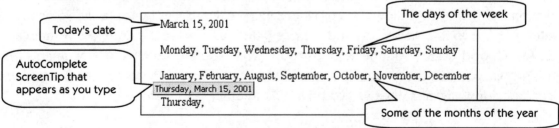

Figure 4.15.   Some examples of **AutoComplete**.

If **AutoComplete** annoys you, you can turn it off. Choose <u>I</u>nsert>**<u>A</u>utoText>AutoTe<u>x</u>t** from the menu bar and then deselect the **<u>S</u>how AutoComplete tip for AutoText and dates** check box.

AUTOTEXT

AutoText entries are blocks of text or graphics that you want to use over and over. AutoText differs slightly from AutoCorrect. **AutoCorrect** automatically fixes an entry. AutoText lets you enter a shortcut name used to identify an AutoText entry that will expand to insert the text or graphics that you have stored.

Generally, you'll find **AutoCorrect** most useful for correcting misspelled words and inserting symbols, while **AutoText** is more appropriate for phrases and blocks of formatted text. A good use for an AutoText entry, for example, would be company names and/or addresses you use repeatedly.

Create an AutoText entry:

1 Type the entry and format the text as desired.

2 Select the text.

3 Choose <u>I</u>nsert>**<u>A</u>utoText><u>N</u>ew** from the menu bar.

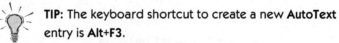 **TIP:** The keyboard shortcut to create a new **AutoText** entry is **Alt+F3**.

4 Type a name for the **AutoText** entry (see Figure 4.16).

Figure 4.16.   Keep AutoText entry names easy to remember.

5 Choose **OK** or press **Enter**.

Use an AutoText entry:

1 Begin typing the **AutoText** name you just created.

2 When the ScreenTip displays the entry, press **Enter** or **F3** to insert it.

Delete an AutoCorrect or AutoText entry:

1 Choose **<u>T</u>ools><u>A</u>utoCorrect** from the menu bar.

2 Choose the **AutoCorrect** or **AutoText** tab.

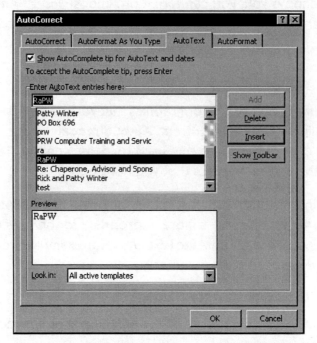

Figure 4.17. The **AutoCorrect** dialog box with the **AutoText** tab selected. Delete **AutoCorrect** and **AutoText** entries you no longer use to keep your lists manageable.

3   Select the entry to delete.

4   Choose the **Delete** button.

5   Repeat steps 2-4 as necessary.

6   Choose **OK** when you are done updating the automatic entry list(s).

Practice Exercise 4-5

Working with AutoComplete and AutoText

1   Start a new blank document. Save the document as ⊟04Motor.

2   Start typing the name of the current month. If you get a ScreenTip showing the month, press **Enter**.

   •   Press **spacebar**, and today's date will appear as a ScreenTip. Press **Enter**.

3   Press **Enter** two more times to add a blank line.

4   Type the following name and address:

   Janice French
   Motor Sports, Inc.
   3453 Detroit Street
   Denver, CO 80222

5 Create an **AutoText** entry by completing the following steps:

- Select the name and address you just typed.

- Choose <u>I</u>nsert>**<u>A</u>utoText**><u>N</u>ew to display the **Create AutoText** dialog box.

   TIP: The keyboard shortcut to create a new **AutoText** entry is **Alt+F3**.

- Type myclient in the **Create AutoText** dialog box and choose **OK**.

6 Delete the client's name and address in the document and begin typing the new AutoText name: myclient . When you see the ScreenTip, press **Enter**.

7 Press **Enter** twice to skip a line and type Dear Ms. French: .

- If the Office Assistant appears, choose **Cancel** to hide the assistant and continue your letter.

8 Press **Enter** twice to skip a line.

9 Type the following text, exactly as shown:

> I will be sending you teh invoice as soon as i count how many CErelli ElephantBots(r) yuo purchased.

Notice that when you pressed the spacebar after each incorrect word, the word corrected itself: words are capitalized and spelled correctly, and the **r** in parentheses turns into a registered symbol.

10 Add and test an AutoCorrect Exception:

- The word CErelli should be spelled with the two initial caps. Choose **<u>T</u>ools**>**<u>A</u>utoCorrect** and choose **<u>E</u>xceptions**.

- If necessary, select the **INitial CAps** tab.

- In the **<u>D</u>on't correct** box type: CErelli then choose **<u>A</u>dd**. Choose **OK** twice to close the dialog boxes and return to your document.

- Select the word **Cerelli** in the document and retype it with the two initial caps and press the spacebar.

Notice it is still marked as an unrecognized word (with the red underline) but Word did not change the capitalization.

11 Move to the end of the paragraph and press **Enter** twice to skip a line. Begin typing your name. If a ScreenTip appears showing your name, press **Enter**.

   NOTE: Your name will not appear as a ScreenTip in the step above unless it is stored in options (**<u>T</u>ools**>**<u>O</u>ptions**). In the **User Information** tab, type your name in the **<u>N</u>ame** box.

12 Choose **Insert>AutoText>AutoText**.

13 In the **AutoText** tab, select **myclient** from the list and choose **Delete**.

14 Choose **OK** to close the **AutoCorrect** dialog box.

15 Save and close the document.

A completed example of **04Motor** is available in the **WORDCert\Word A\Samples** folder on the DDC CD-ROM.

LESSON 5: CHANGE DOCUMENT APPEARANCE

Whether you begin a new document using the Blank Document template (NORMAL.DOT) or one of the other templates available in Word, certain decisions are already in place. The page margins are set with space allotted for the body of the document and the header and footer areas. The fonts and paragraph shapes are pre-determined. You may wonder if you can change any of these settings. The answer is a definitive *Yes*.

In this lesson, you will learn to:

> Apply font attributes

> Insert special characters

> Use AutoFormat

> Create drop caps

> Change paragraph margins

> Apply borders and shading

> Set page margins

> Establish printing instructions for pages

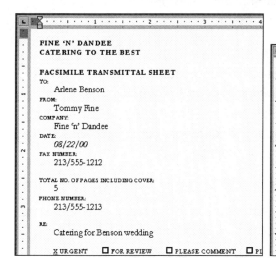
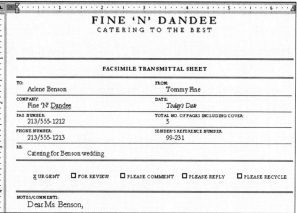

Figure 5.1.   By comparing a simple, text-only document and the same document with formatting applied, you can easily see that formatting creates a more visually appealing document, one that makes a stronger impression.

Character Formatting

Probably the easiest place to begin learning about formatting attributes is with letters and words. As you have seen, each letter is considered a "character," which is why it's called **character formatting**. When working with character formatting, Word provides you with several ways to apply the same effect. You can use a dialog box, the Formatting toolbar, or shortcut keys to apply most formatting attributes.

When you want to change the attributes applied to a single character, a word, or a group of words, you must highlight the text you want changed. (**Highlight** and **select** are synonymous and are often used interchangeably.) Remember the old word-processors' adage:

Select it to affect it!

FORMATTING TOOLBAR

The Formatting toolbar (see Figure 5.2) has an array of buttons for applying attributes to characters. You can change the font, font size, font style (e.g., bold, italic, underline), and even the font color of characters using the Formatting toolbar.

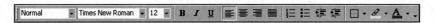

Figure 5.2.   In most cases, simply select the text and click the button you want to use.

(In addition to character attributes, the Formatting toolbar has buttons for working with paragraphs. These are discussed later in this lesson.)

Character formatting adds "spice" to your words, allowing you to emphasize single words or phrases. You might also need, for example, to indicate the titles of books, magazines, and online magazines. (You may want to refer to *The Chicago Manual of Style* (14th edition), the *MLA Handbook for Writers of Research Papers* (4th edition), or *The Associated Press Style Book and Libel Manual* (1998 edition) for suggestions concerning the standard formatting of bibliographical information.)

Apply character attributes:

1   Highlight the character(s) you want to format (e.g., a single letter, word, or group of words).

2   Click any desired Formatting toolbar buttons to apply character attributes:

B   • Bold

I   • Italic

U   • Underline

• Highlight (selected color) The default is *Yellow*.

 • Font Color (selected color) The default is *Red*.

 TIP: The keyboard shortcut for Bold is **Ctrl+B**; for Italic, **Ctrl+I**; for Underline, **Ctrl+U**. See **Appendix D** in the **WORDCert** folder on the CD-ROM that came with this book for a list of shortcut keys.

You can apply a single attribute or any combination of attributes to a selection. It's a little like getting dressed in the morning. You try on one set of "attributes," and if they don't suit you, it's possible to change any or all of them. If you apply an attribute that doesn't quite work for you, remove it exactly as you applied it—by clicking a toolbar button or via the keyboard shortcuts.

Again: *Select it to affect it!*

Remove character attributes:

1 Highlight the character(s) to change.

2 Click the button(s) that applied the attribute you no longer want.

To apply a different attribute while the character(s) are still selected, simply click another character attribute button.

Change the font or font size:

1 Highlight the character(s) you want to format (e.g., a single letter, word, or group of words).

2 Click the arrow of one of the following Formatting toolbar buttons to select the desired font and/or font size:

 • Font

 • Font Size

FONT DIALOG BOX

While the Formatting toolbar offers quick and frequently used character attributes, it is far from a complete selection of the font attributes available in Word. As you develop more and more skill with Word, you'll discover that you can apply multiple attributes to a selection using the many choices found in one place, the **Font** dialog box. As always, the characters you want to format must be highlighted before you display the **Font** dialog box. Figure 5.3 displays the **Font** dialog box.

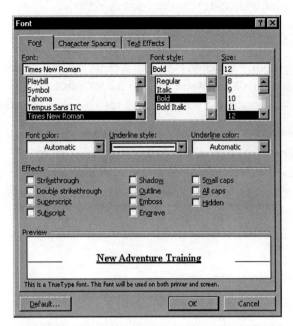

Figure 5.3.   Apply multiple character attributes in the
                   Font tab of the **Font** dialog box.

 NOTE: Fonts shown in the **Font** list reflect all of the fonts installed and activated in your Windows system. To add fonts to (or remove them from) the scrolling list, please refer to your Windows documentation.

By selecting or deselecting the various **Effects** check boxes, and by choosing from the available options in the lists, you create a preview at the bottom of the dialog box that gives you a close approximation of how your choices will look with your formatting options applied. The **Preview** box helps you determine if your choices please you. If not, simply change your choices before closing the **Font** dialog box.

Apply multiple character attributes:

1   Highlight the character(s) you want to format.

2   Choose **Format>Font** from the menu bar.

 TIP: The keyboard shortcut to display the **Font** dialog box is **Ctrl+D**.

3   Select all the formatting options you want to apply to the highlighted text in the **Font** dialog box.

4   When the Preview looks good to you choose **OK** to close the dialog box.

Your character formatting is applied, and you're ready to proceed to other tasks.

REPEAT

The **Repeat** feature (found in Word's **Edit** menu) changes its name and function based upon the last action you performed. If you've applied character formatting to a selection of text, for example, the menu may display **Repeat Font Formatting** or **Repeat Bold**. To apply the same formatting you just applied to other text in your document, highlight the text you want to format, and choose **Edit>Repeat Formatting** from the menu bar.

 TIP: There are two keyboard shortcuts for the **Repeat** command, **Ctrl+Y** and **F4**.

The Repeat feature remembers *the last action you performed* in a document; so you can continue making text selections and apply the same set of formatting attributes as many times as you like—until you perform another task.

FORMAT PAINTER

 Different from **Repeat**, the **Format Painter** functions exactly like a brush dipped in a bucket of paint. You load the **Format Painter** with character or paragraph formatting by selecting the formatted text and clicking the **Format Painter** button to activate the brush. Next, drag the **Format Painter I-beam** over the text to apply the copied format(s).

Format Painter allows you to copy formatting you like to other sections of your document after the fact. The **Repeat** command is useful if you know immediately that you want to use the formatting you just applied.

Use Format Painter:

1   Select the text whose formatting you want to copy.

 NOTE: To copy paragraph formatting, you must also select the paragraph mark at the end of the paragraph.

 2   Click the **Format Painter** button on the Standard toolbar.

The pointer changes to an I-beam with a paintbrush.

3   Select the text you want to copy the formatting to.

 You can also copy formatting to multiple locations using **Format Painter**. Select the formatted text, and then double-click the **Format Painter** button. Select the text in each location you want to copy the formatting to. When you are finished, click the **Format Painter** button again to deselect it, or press **Esc** on the keyboard.

Practice Exercise 5-1

Add Character Formatting

1 Open 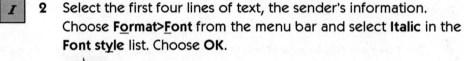**05Ex5-1** from the **WORDCert\Word A** folder. Save it as **05Format**.

 2 Select the first four lines of text, the sender's information. Choose **Format>Font** from the menu bar and select **Italic** in the **Font style** list. Choose **OK**.

> TIP: The keyboard shortcut for Italic is **Ctrl+I**.

 3 Select the first line of text, **New Adventure Training**. Choose **Format>Font** and select **Bold** in the **Font style** list. Choose **OK**.

> TIP: The keyboard shortcut for Bold is **Ctrl+B**.

 4 Select the line **Word for Windows – Beginning**. Choose **Format>Font** and choose **Bold** in the **Font style** list, then select the single line in the **Underline style** list. Choose **OK**.

> TIP: The keyboard shortcut for Underline is **Ctrl+U**.

> NOTE: If the underline starts at the beginning of the line (where there is no text), select that area of the underline. Click the **Underline** button on the Formatting toolbar to deselect it.

 5 Use **Format Painter** to copy character formatting by doing the following:

- Select only the word **Beginning** in Word for Windows – Beginning.

 - Click the **Format Painter** button on the Standard toolbar.

- Select the phone number in the final paragraph with the Format Painter I-beam to copy the formatting to it.

Your document should resemble that shown in Figure 5.4.

6 Save and close the document.

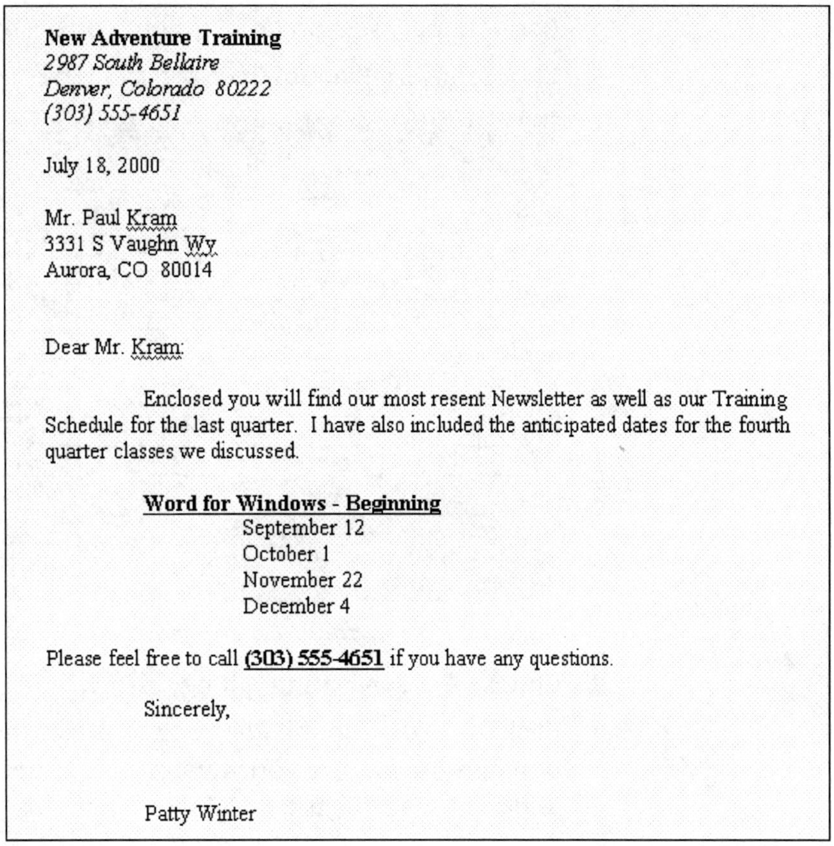

> **New Adventure Training**
> *2987 South Bellaire*
> *Denver, Colorado 80222*
> *(303) 555-4651*
>
> July 18, 2000
>
> Mr. Paul Kram
> 3331 S Vaughn Wy
> Aurora, CO 80014
>
>
> Dear Mr. Kram:
>
>   Enclosed you will find our most resent Newsletter as well as our Training
> Schedule for the last quarter. I have also included the anticipated dates for the fourth
> quarter classes we discussed.
>
>   <u>**Word for Windows - Beginning**</u>
>   September 12
>   October 1
>   November 22
>   December 4
>
> Please feel free to call **(303) 555-4651** if you have any questions.
>
>   Sincerely,
>
>
>
>   Patty Winter

Figure 5.4.   Your letter with formatting.

Special Formatting

As you know, many symbols and special characters (@, #, $, &, %) are accessible
directly from the keyboard by pressing the **Shift** key as you type a number key at the
top of the keyboard. Others, as you saw in Lesson 4, can be inserted using
AutoCorrect. Others still must be inserted using the **Symbol** dialog box.

SYMBOLS AND SPECIAL CHARACTERS

The **Symbols** tab on the **Symbols** dialog box contains characters such as bullets, small
pictures, and foreign language symbols. The **Special Characters** tab contains characters
such as dashes, quotes, and ellipses.

Insert symbols:

1   Position the insertion point where you wish to insert a symbol.

2   Choose **Insert>Symbol** from the menu bar.

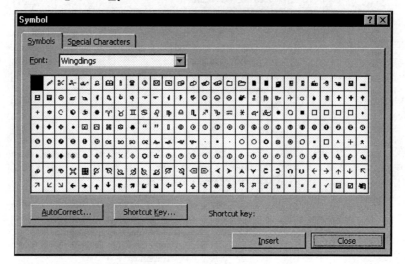

Figure 5.5.   Use symbols to add spice to your documents.

3   Choose the **Symbols** tab, if necessary.

4   Click the arrow on the **Font** box to select the font set that contains the symbol you want to use. For example, select **Wingdings** (see Figure 5.5)

5   To view a symbol displayed in the table, click the symbol to make it larger and easier to view.

6   When you find the symbol you want to place in your document, click it and choose **Insert**.

> **TIP:** You may need to move the **Symbol** dialog box so you can see different parts of your document. If you want to insert a symbol in another location in your document, move the dialog box if necessary, reposition the insertion point, select the desired symbol, and choose **Insert** to place another symbol.

7   When you are finished inserting symbols choose **Close** to return to your document.

Insert special characters:

1   Position the insertion point where you want to insert a special character.

2   Choose **Insert>Symbol** from the menu bar.

3 Choose the **Special Characters** tab to insert a special character (see Figure 5.6).

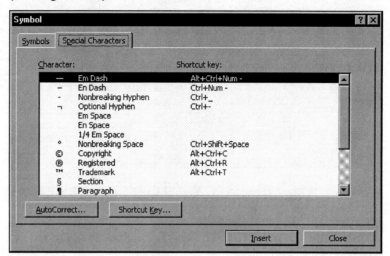

Figure 5.6.   Use the **Special Characters** tab to find Copyright and Trademark characters and nonbreaking spaces and hyphens, as well as many others.

4 Choose the **Character** you want to insert.

5 Choose **Insert**.

6 When you are finished inserting special characters choose **Close** to return to your document.

DROP CAPS

Drop caps, used with discretion, can change a rather ordinary newsletter or flier into an interesting, attention-getting, and more effective document. You've seen them ever since you were a child.

> Once upon a time, in the Land of Nonce, there lived a prince who loved horses. Each morning, when the prince awoke, he stretched and went straight to the window of his sleeping chamber to look toward the meadow where his beloved horses gamboled in the tall grass. It thrilled him to see the graceful creatures in their element.

You can drop one or more letters at the beginning of a paragraph, and you can even change the font of the dropped letters from the **Drop Cap** dialog box (see Figure 5.7).

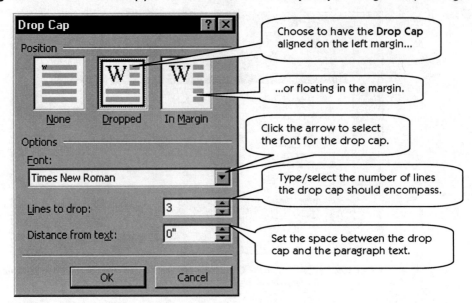

Choose to have the **Drop Cap** aligned on the left margin...

...or floating in the margin.

Click the arrow to select the font for the drop cap.

Type/select the number of lines the drop cap should encompass.

Set the space between the drop cap and the paragraph text.

Figure 5.7.   Drop caps can add interesting effects to your documents.

There are no set rules for applying drop caps. It's a design element, and your own good taste determines how many letters you drop, whether the drop cap is placed in the margin or inside the boundaries of the paragraph, the font to use, and how far down to drop the cap. Experiment with different settings until you achieve the effect you think most suitable to your document.

Apply a drop cap:

1   Position your cursor in the paragraph you want to begin with a drop cap, or select the letters to drop if you want to drop more than one letter.

2   Choose **Format>Drop Cap** from the menu bar.

    The **Drop Cap** dialog box displays.

3   Choose the drop cap **Position** by selecting either **Dropped** or **In Margin**.

     NOTE: If desired, click the **Font** arrow and select a font for the drop cap letter.

4   Type/select a number from the **Lines to drop** box. The default is **3**. This setting determines the size of the drop cap and how far down in the text your cap drops.

5   If necessary, type/select the amount of space between the letter and the text in the **Distance from text** box. The default is 0", which is acceptable in most instances.

6   Choose **OK** when you are finished.

AUTOFORMAT

There are those who prefer never to learn anything about word processing beyond typing in the content. Save the day. Send for a bird, a plane? No. Try **AutoFormat**.

After all the text is entered in a document, say a business letter, you can use the **AutoFormat** feature. Choose **Format>AutoFormat** from the menu bar. A dialog box, shown in Figure 5.8, opens to offer you options for automatically formatting the text.

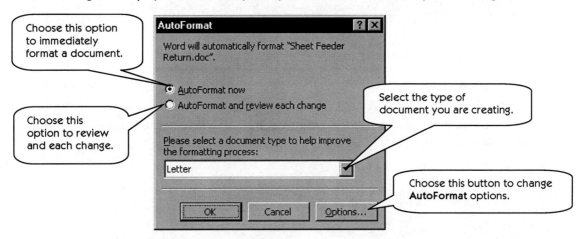

Choose this option to immediately format a document.

Choose this option to review and each change.

Select the type of document you are creating.

Choose this button to change **AutoFormat** options.

Figure 5.8. Use **AutoFormat** to make your document look professional quickly.

You can format a letter, an e-mail message, or a general document such as a report. It's usually best to create all the document content first and then apply **AutoFormat**. After it is applied, you can make revisions to any of the text or formatting.

Use AutoFormat:

1   Start a new blank document and insert all the document text as desired.

2   Save the document.

3   Choose **Format>AutoFormat** from the menu bar.

4   Choose **AutoFormat now** in the **AutoFormat** dialog box.

 NOTE: If you prefer to have more control over the document layout, you may wish to choose **AutoFormat and review each change** instead.

5   Click the arrow on the **Please select a document type...** box and select the kind of formatting you want to apply: **General document**, **Letter**, or **Email**.

6   Choose **OK**.

  • If you chose **AutoFormat and review each change** in step 4, a dialog box opens allowing you to accept, reject, or review changes, or to choose a template from the Style Gallery (see Figure 5.9).

Figure 5.9.   Choose to accept or reject all the changes, review the changes
               individually, or select a template from the Style Gallery.

If you choose the **Review Changes** button in the **AutoFormat** dialog box, you are able
to peruse the formatting changes that Word wants to apply, and accept or reject them.
If you elect to use this option, you'll probably still need to do some formatting in the
document before printing it and sending it out, but that's an improvement over
applying all the formatting yourself.

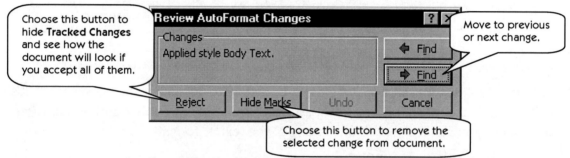

Figure 5.10.   The change is highlighted with an explanation in the dialog box.

Practice Exercise 5-2

Use Special Formatting in a Document

1   Open 📁**05Ex5-2** from the **WORDCert\Word A** folder. Save it as
    💾**05Symbol**.

2   Format the document using **AutoFormat** by doing the following:

    •   Choose **Format>AutoFormat** from the menu bar.

    •   Choose **AutoFormat now** in the **AutoFormat** dialog box.

    •   Select **General document** as the document type.

    •   Choose **OK** to have Word automatically format the document
        for you.

3 Apply a drop cap to the second paragraph by doing the following:

- Move the insertion point into the second paragraph, **ITZ AWL GOOOD TEENS....**

- Choose **Format>Drop Cap** from the menu bar.

- In the **Position** area, select **Dropped.**

- Choose **OK** to close the dialog box.

- Click anywhere in the document to deselect the drop cap box and see the paragraph with the change.

4 Insert a trademark symbol (™) by doing the following:

- Move the insertion point to the second line of the third paragraph directly after **Outback Outfitters.**

- Choose **Insert>Symbol** from the menu bar.

- Choose the **Special Characters** tab in the **Symbol** dialog box.

- Select **Trademark** from the **Character** list.

- Choose **Insert** and then choose **Close.**

5 Insert symbols in the document by doing the following:

- Move to the last paragraph of text, **If you are interested in covering....**

- Move the insertion point in front of the first phone number.

- Choose **Insert>Symbol** from the menu bar.

- Choose the **Symbols** tab in the **Symbol** dialog box.

- Click the arrow on the **Font** box and select **Wingdings.**

- Select the telephone symbol in the first row (eighth from the left).

- Choose **Insert** to insert the symbol. If necessary, move the dialog box so you can see where the symbol was inserted.

- Click in the document in front of the cellular phone number and choose the **Insert** button to insert the symbol again.

 TIP: You could also copy and paste this symbol.

Your document should resemble that shown in Figure 5.11.

- Choose **Close.**

6 Save and close the document.

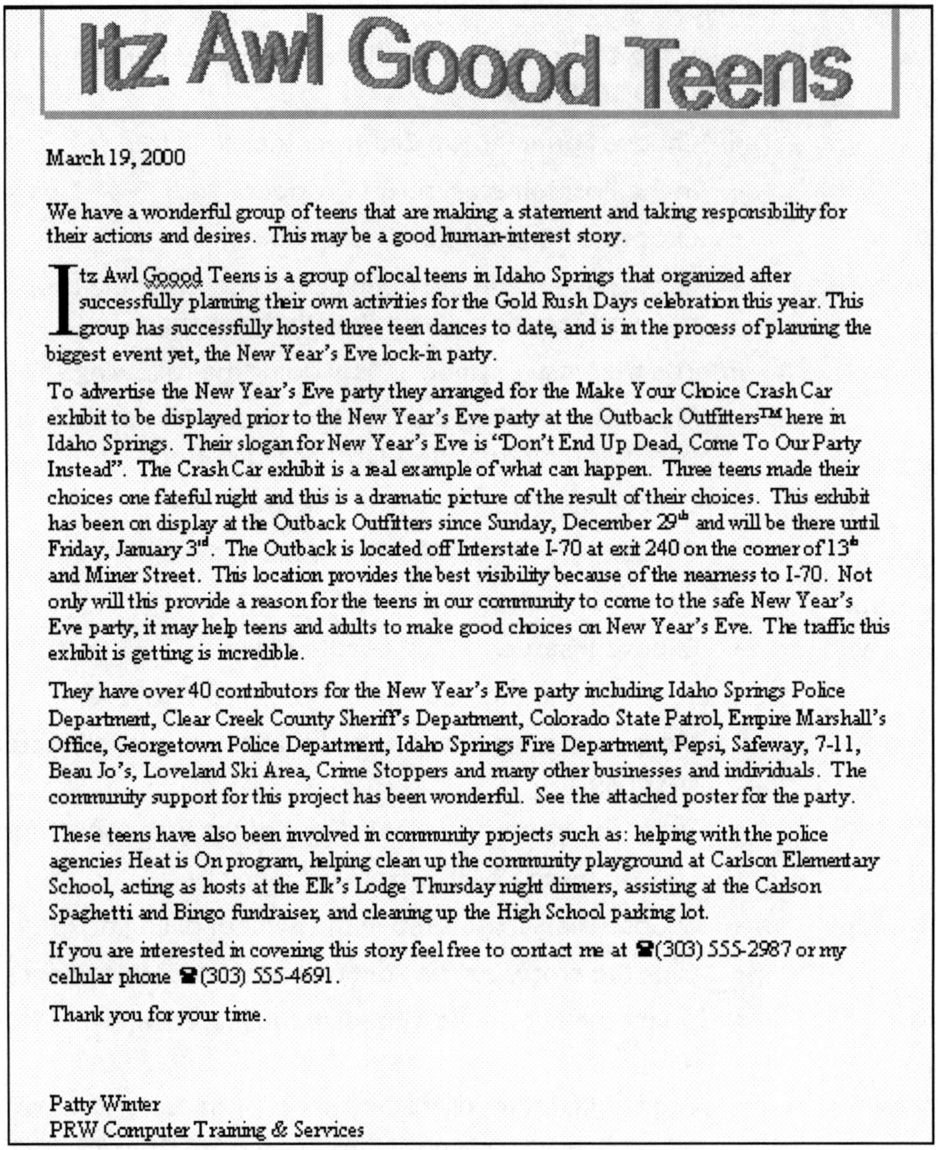

Itz Awl Goood Teens

March 19, 2000

We have a wonderful group of teens that are making a statement and taking responsibility for their actions and desires. This may be a good human-interest story.

Itz Awl Goood Teens is a group of local teens in Idaho Springs that organized after successfully planning their own activities for the Gold Rush Days celebration this year. This group has successfully hosted three teen dances to date, and is in the process of planning the biggest event yet, the New Year's Eve lock-in party.

To advertise the New Year's Eve party they arranged for the Make Your Choice Crash Car exhibit to be displayed prior to the New Year's Eve party at the Outback Outfitters™ here in Idaho Springs. Their slogan for New Year's Eve is "Don't End Up Dead, Come To Our Party Instead". The Crash Car exhibit is a real example of what can happen. Three teens made their choices one fateful night and this is a dramatic picture of the result of their choices. This exhibit has been on display at the Outback Outfitters since Sunday, December 29th and will be there until Friday, January 3rd. The Outback is located off Interstate I-70 at exit 240 on the corner of 13th and Miner Street. This location provides the best visibility because of the nearness to I-70. Not only will this provide a reason for the teens in our community to come to the safe New Year's Eve party, it may help teens and adults to make good choices on New Year's Eve. The traffic this exhibit is getting is incredible.

They have over 40 contributors for the New Year's Eve party including Idaho Springs Police Department, Clear Creek County Sheriff's Department, Colorado State Patrol, Empire Marshall's Office, Georgetown Police Department, Idaho Springs Fire Department, Pepsi, Safeway, 7-11, Beau Jo's, Loveland Ski Area, Crime Stoppers and many other businesses and individuals. The community support for this project has been wonderful. See the attached poster for the party.

These teens have also been involved in community projects such as: helping with the police agencies Heat is On program, helping clean up the community playground at Carlson Elementary School, acting as hosts at the Elk's Lodge Thursday night dinners, assisting at the Carlson Spaghetti and Bingo fundraiser, and cleaning up the High School parking lot.

If you are interested in covering this story feel free to contact me at ☎(303) 555-2987 or my cellular phone ☎(303) 555-4691.

Thank you for your time.

Patty Winter
PRW Computer Training & Services

Figure 5.11. Your document with special formatting.

Paragraph Formatting

The shapes of paragraphs and their relationships to one another help you effectively convey information in a document. For instance, the address block of a business letter has paragraphs shaped differently from the paragraphs in the body of the letter. Typically, the name and address paragraphs are closer together and are all on the same margin, creating a unified effect for the address block. Paragraphs in the body of the letter are separated farther to make reading easier and may have different margins to set off specific information.

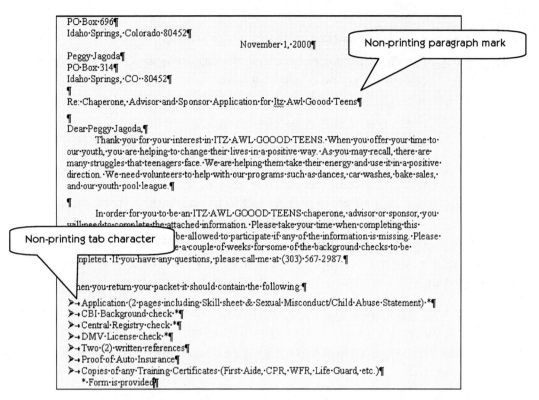

Figure 5.12.   The paragraph formatting is contained within the nonprinting paragraph marks.

¶ As you type, each time you press the **Enter** key, you create a new paragraph. It may help you to know that, as with table layouts, the instructions determining the shapes of paragraphs are actually contained in the nonprinting paragraph marks (¶) at the end of each paragraph (see Figure 5.12). The paragraph mark travels to the right of the cursor as you type. When you press the **Enter** key, a new paragraph mark is created that *duplicates the formatting of the preceding paragraph*. You can display these paragraph marks by selecting the **Show/Hide ¶** button on the Standard toolbar. Deselect the button to hide nonprinting characters.

RULER

Set different indents for a paragraph using the indent markers on the horizontal ruler. You can click and drag the markers (illustrated below) along the ruler to position them as desired.

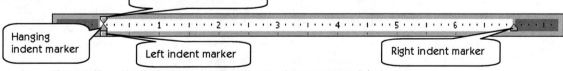

Figure 5.13.   The horizontal ruler allows you to change paragraph indents.

The indent markers on the left function independently or in unison.

- • The **First Line Indent** marker (the upside-down triangle) moves only the first line of a paragraph.

- • The **Hanging Indent** marker (the triangle) controls the remaining lines in a paragraph. A hanging indent is when the top line of the paragraph is farther to the left than the rest of the paragraph, as in a bibliography, for example.

- • The **Left Indent** marker (the square beneath the Hanging Indent marker) moves all text in the paragraph from the page margin. Both the First Line Indent and Hanging Indent markers move in unison when you drag the square.

 The **Right Indent** marker (the triangle on the right side of the ruler) establishes the right paragraph indent.

It isn't necessary to highlight the entire paragraph when you want to change indents in a single paragraph, but your cursor must be in the paragraph you want to change. If you want to change indents in more than one paragraph, however, you must select the paragraphs you want to change.

Change paragraph indents:

1   Place cursor in paragraph to indent, or select paragraphs to indent.

2   Point to the indent marker you want to move:

- • First Line Indent

- • Hanging Indent

- • Left Indent

 TIP: In Word 2000, if you hover the pointer on the marker, a ScreenTip appears. This helps you be more confident that you are moving the correct marker

3   Click and drag the marker into position using the tick marks on the ruler as a guide for setting the left indent (see Figure 5.14).

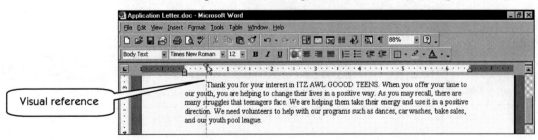

Figure 5.14.   Drag the indent markers to change the paragraph.

As you drag an indent marker, a vertical, dotted line appears in the document area of your Word window, giving you a visual guide for positioning the marker. When you release the mouse button, the dotted line disappears, and text in the paragraph reflows to accommodate the new setting.

    4   Click and drag the **Right Indent** marker into position, if desired.

PARAGRAPH DIALOG BOX

An alternative way to set paragraph indents appears on the **Indents and Spacing** tab of the **Paragraph** dialog box (see Figure 5.15). This dialog box is used when your document has to conform to very detailed specifications, the kind of thing you can't do with accuracy when using the mouse methods shown above. This method lets you establish text alignment settings (left, centered, right, or justified), the kind of indentation you want, the space allotted before and/or after the paragraph, as well as the line spacing within the paragraph (leading). The **Paragraph** dialog box also has a Preview box to give you an idea of how the selected paragraph will look in relation to the other paragraphs in your document.

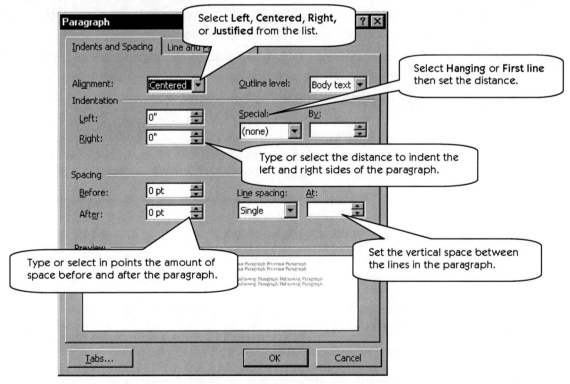

Figure 5.15.   Each setting you make in the **Indents and Spacing** tab of the **Paragraph** dialog box determines how the shape of your paragraph appears onscreen and when printed.

If you are in the habit of separating paragraphs by hitting the **Enter** key twice or more times to create space between paragraphs, you're about to learn how to step beyond that rudimentary level of word processing. Though **Enter-Enter** works, it is not the most elegant way to separate paragraphs. Ideally, you want paragraphs separated automatically with one **Enter**, and, because you're using a word processor on a computer, not a mechanical typewriter, you can specify exactly how far apart those paragraphs should be. It's far more versatile and visually appealing than the **Enter-Enter** method.

Design a paragraph:

1   Click the paragraph you want to revise, or select desired paragraph(s).

2   Choose **Format>Paragraph** from the menu bar.

3   Choose the **Indents and Spacing** tab in the **Paragraph** dialog box, if necessary (see Figure 5.15).

4   Select desired **Alignment**: Left, Centered, Right, or Justified.

5   Set the **Indentation** you want for the selected paragraph(s) in the **Special** box: (none), First line, or Hanging. Then type or select the distance for your indentation in the **By** box.

6   Type or select the amount of **Spacing** to precede or follow the paragraph in the **Before** and **After** boxes.

 NOTE: As a novice word processor, you may find it easiest for now to set spacing for only **Before or After** your paragraph. These settings are cumulative; that is, 4 points of space before a paragraph and 4 points of space after the paragraph add up to a total of 8 points of space between paragraphs when you press the **Enter** key.

7   Select desired **Line spacing** option: Single, 1.5 lines, Double, At least, Exactly, or Multiple.

 NOTE: If you choose At least, Exactly, or Multiple, you can then type or select the vertical space in the **At** box.

8   Look at the **Preview** of your paragraph. Revise any of your settings as necessary.

9   Choose **OK** to close the **Paragraph** dialog box.

 TIP: To apply the same paragraph formatting after the fact to other paragraphs throughout your document, choose **Edit>Repeat Paragraph Formatting** from the menu bar. Remember, the keyboard shortcuts are **Ctrl+Y** or **F4**.

Practice Exercise 5-3

Change Paragraph Formatting

1 Open ⊟05Ex5-3 from the **WORDCert\Word A** folder. Save it as ⊟**05Para**.

2 Place the insertion point in the first section of the document. Move the pointer into the first multiline paragraph and click (the two columns for **Who We Are**).

3 Justify paragraph text by doing the following:
   • Choose **Format>Paragraph** from the menu bar.
   • Choose the **Indents and Spacing** tab in the **Paragraph** dialog box, if necessary.
   • Choose **Justified** from the **Alignment** box.
   • Choose **OK** to accept your change.

4 Place the insertion point in the second section of the document, **Meetings**.

5 Center the paragraph text as follows:
   • Choose **Format>Paragraph**.
   • Choose **Centered** from the **Alignment** box.
   • Enter/select **6** in the **Before** and **After** boxes.
   • Choose **OK** to accept your changes.

6 Place the insertion point in the **Eye-of-the-Tiger Contest** paragraph.

7 Change the paragraph's left and right indents using the horizontal ruler:
   • Point to the **Left Indent** marker and drag it to 1" on the ruler.
   • Point to the **Right Indent** marker and drag it to 6" on the ruler.

8 Save and close the document.

   A completed example of **05Para** is available in the **WORDCert\Word A\Samples** folder.

Add Borders and Shading

In situations where you want to emphasize a paragraph or create a graphic effect for a page, borders and shading can be very useful. If you have a color printer, you can use any color available in the palette. If you have a black and white printer, try the shades of gray for the borders and shading.

Borders surround paragraphs and pages of text. Shading is applied behind paragraph or page text. For this reason, you need to set both text color and shading color with some awareness of the printed result. If you choose a mid-tone gray for the shading, and only a slightly darker mid-tone gray for the text, legibility will definitely be an issue when you print. Black and white printers convert all colors to shades of gray, so choosing shading and text colors for a document you'll print on both color and black and white printers is a real challenge. Your best bet is to run a test print on any printer you're likely to use before considering the document completed.

FORMATTING TOOLBAR

The quickest way to apply a border to one or more paragraphs is to click the **Border** button on the Formatting toolbar. This button's name and appearance changes according to the border style currently selected in the button palette. Click the **Border** arrow to open the palette and select another border style.

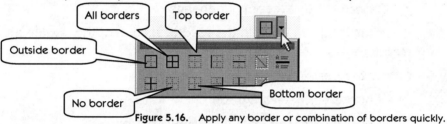

Figure 5.16. Apply any border or combination of borders quickly.

As with all formatting, you must either place the insertion point in the paragraph to frame or select multiple paragraph(s) to frame or shade.

Borders and shading aren't limited to paragraphs and pages only, however. You can also apply a border or shading to a single word or group of words. It all depends on the objects you select before applying borders or shading.

Apply borders:

1   Select the text (character, word, sentence, or paragraph[s]) you want to frame.

2   Click the **Border** button on the Formatting toolbar to apply the selected border style.

OR

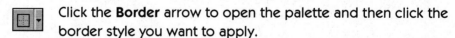 Click the **Border** arrow to open the palette and then click the border style you want to apply.

 CAUTION: You may discover that the border applied to a paragraph conforms to the margins set for the paragraph. If you've surrounded multiple paragraphs with varied margins, Word may break the border, independently surrounding each paragraph with differing borders.

Borders and Shading Dialog Box

Apply border and shading options to selected text when you choose **Format>Borders and Shading** from the menu bar to display the **Borders and Shading** dialog box, as shown in Figure 5.17. This dialog box has three named tabs: **Borders**, **Page Border**, and **Shading**.

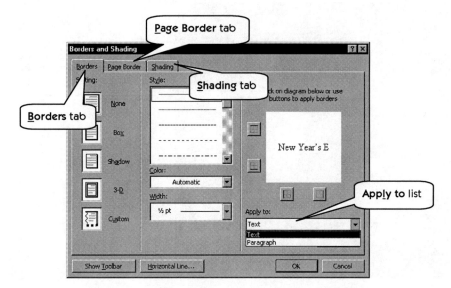

Figure 5.17.   Choose **Format>Borders and Shading** from the menu bar to display the **Borders and Shading** dialog box.

Borders Tab

On the **Borders** tab (shown above), the **Setting** area gives you a choice of outline styles (**None**, **Box**, **Shadow**, **3D**, or **Custom**) around the text or paragraph. You can also change the line **Style**, **Color**, and **Width**. Finally, you can choose to remove any number of the four sides of the border by clicking on a button in the Preview area. (Doing so changes the Setting option to **Custom**.) If you have text selected, you can choose **Apply to: Text** or **Paragraph**. If you choose **Text**, the border surrounds the selected entry *only*; if you choose **Paragraph**, it surrounds *each* paragraph within the selection. The **Options** button allows you to set the distance between the text and each individual side of the border.

Page Border Tab

The **Page Border** tab places a border around each page of your document. Most of the options on this tab are similar to those on the **Borders** tab. Additionally, you have an **Art** drop-down list that allows you to add a repeated graphic (champagne bottles, seasonal symbols) or a stylized border (Greek key, Art Deco, etc.)

around the page. By default, every page displays the selected page border (Whole document). The **Apply to** box allows you to specify another setting: **Whole document, This section, This section – First page only, This section – All except first page**. See Figure 5.18.

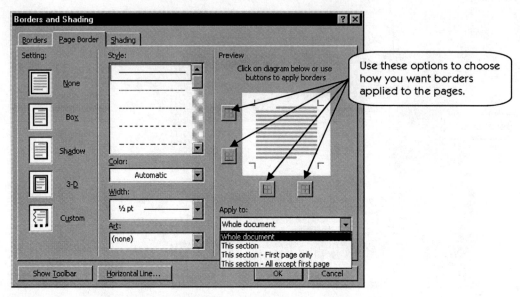

Figure 5.18.   Choose the **Page Border** tab to apply borders to the pages.

Shading Tab

The **Shading** tab, shown in Figure 5.19, will add color or a pattern around text or paragraphs. When you select a color in the **Fill** palette, the color name or the percentage of gray on the white-to-black continuum appears to the right of the palette. If you want additional color options, choose the **More Colors** button. ScreenTips appear with the name of each color. It is important to remember that shading style is applied "over" the fill color. If you want to vary the blackness, select from **5%** to **Solid** in the Patterns **Style** list. If you choose **Solid**, the color is black. You can also choose a Grid, Trellis (crosshatched), or lined (vertical, horizontal or diagonal) pattern. If you have a pattern percentage, you can choose a second color in the Patterns **Color** list. If you have text selected, select **Text** in the **Apply to** box to apply shading to the selected text only; select **Paragraph** to apply the shading to all selected paragraph(s).

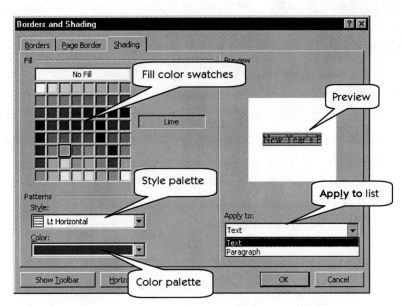

Figure 5.19. Choose the <u>S</u>hading tab to apply shading to the selected **Text** or **Paragraph**.

Apply borders and/or shading:

1 Select the text (character, word, sentence, or paragraph[s]) you want to frame or shade.

 NOTE: If you want your choices applied to pages, you don't need to make a selection above. Choose the **Page Border** tab in step 3, below.

2 Choose **For<u>m</u>at>Borders and Shading** from the menu bar.

3 In the **Borders and Shading** dialog box, choose the appropriate named tab for your changes: **<u>B</u>orders**, **<u>P</u>age Border**, or **<u>S</u>hading**.

4 Select from the available options.

 TIP: You can use any or all of them, including applying borders to characters, words, paragraphs, and pages. Do be cautious, though; too much of a good thing spoils the effect.

5 Choose any other tabs, as necessary.

6 Choose **OK** when you are finished making your selections on all tabs in the **Borders and Shading** dialog box.

Practice Exercise 5-4

Apply Borders and Shading to Document Elements

1   Open 📁**05Ex5-4** from the **WORDCert\Word A** folder. Save it as 💾**05Border**.

2   Apply an outside border to a paragraph by doing the following:

   • Select the centered **Meetings** paragraph and the heading itself.

   • Click the **Borders** arrow on the Formatting toolbar to open the palette.

   • Click the **Outside Border** button on the palette.

3   Apply a top border by doing the following:

   • Select the heading, **Gold Rush Days - Mini Star Search**.

   • Click the **Borders** arrow on the Formatting toolbar

   • Click the **Top Border** button on the palette.

4   Apply a bottom border by doing the following:

   • Select both columns of text underneath the heading **Gold Rush Days**.

   • Click the **Borders** arrow on the Formatting toolbar.

   • Click the **Bottom Border** button on the palette.

5   Add shading to text by doing the following:

   • Select the indented paragraph explaining the Eye-of-the-Tiger Contest.

   • Choose **Format>Borders and Shading** from the menu bar.

   • Choose the **Shading** tab in the **Borders and Shading** dialog box, if necessary.

   • Select **20%** from the **Style** box in the **Patterns** section.

   • Select **Gold** from the **Color** box.

   • Choose **OK**.

6   Save and close the document.

   A completed example of **05Border** is available in the **WORDCert\Word A\Samples** folder.

Page Formatting

Though you learned how to format characters and paragraphs before now, in actual practice, you'll probably set the page formatting first of all. **Page Setup** formatting determines the overall margins, the size of paper you'll print on, the printer used, and the page layout of your document.

PAGE SETUP DIALOG BOX

The function of the **Page Setup** dialog box goes beyond making an attractive page. Every document you create needs set margins and other basic instructions that will ensure that the document will print correctly. In the **Page Setup** dialog box, you see named tabs for setting instructions about page **Margins**, **Paper Size**, **Paper Source** (default printer), and page **Layout** (see Figure 5.20).

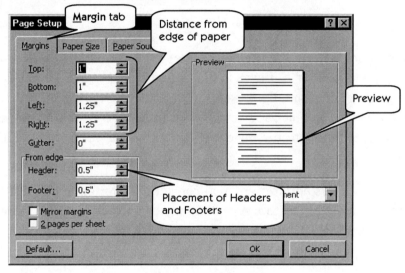

Figure 5.20.   Choose **File>Page Setup** from the menu bar to display the
              Page Setup dialog box.

 TIP: A shortcut to diplay the **Page Setup** dialog box is to double-click in the dark gray area on the horizontal or vertical ruler.

Typically, when you start a new blank document that will need some specific design specifications, first open a new document, and then choose **File>Page Setup** from the menu bar.

Adjust document's page setup:

1   Choose **File>Page Setup** from the menu bar.

2   In the **Page Setup** dialog box, choose any or all of the tabs: **Margins, Paper Size, Paper Source, Layout**. See tab descriptions below.

3   Select the options appropriate for the printing and design of your document.

 TIP: Be sure to glance at the **Preview** box located at the lower right of each tab to determine if your choices please you. If not, simply revise your choices while the **Page Layout** dialog box is still displayed.

4   Choose **OK** when all the page attributes are set to close the **Page Setup** dialog box.

Margins Tab

The **Margins** tab (see Figure 5.20 on the previous page) allows you to establish the **Top, Bottom, Left,** and **Right** margins for all pages in the document. Margins are to be considered more a guide than a limitation, except that you must allow a minimum amount of space for a printer to pull paper through its rollers. You can still, however, set paragraph indents to extend into the page margins, provided your printer can print what is in the margin.

If you intend to include headers and footers, you can set the allotted space for these in the **From edge** area of the **Margins** tab. As with many other dialog boxes, there is a Preview to help you determine which settings will work best for your document.

Paper Size Tab

On the **Paper Size** tab of the **Page Setup** dialog box (see Figure 5.21 on the following page), you can set the paper dimensions (**Width** and **Height**) as well as the direction that your document will print on the paper. The direction text will print is known as the page's *orientation*. Text prints either vertically (**Portrait**), which is the default setting, or horizontally (**Landscape**).

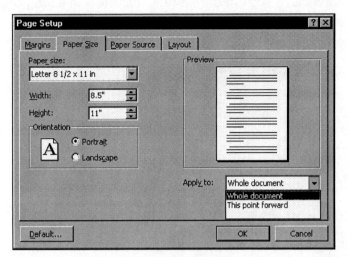

Figure 5.21.   Choose the **Paper Size** tab to choose the size of the paper
(Letter [8½ x 11 in] , Legal [8½ x 14 in], etc.) and the way
you want the writing oriented on the page.

Paper Source Tab

The **Paper Source** tab has options that apply to multiple page documents and
envelopes. See Figure 5.22.

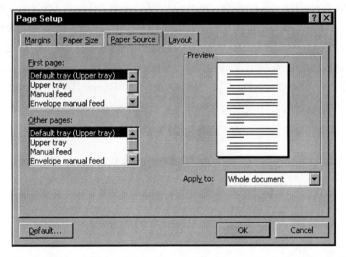

Figure 5.22.   Choose different paper trays if your letterhead is in one tray
and subsequent pages need to be printed, for example, on blank paper.

Layout Tab

During your word-processing career, most of your documents will follow a standard
page design—such as business letters, memos, reports, and the like. As you develop
more confidence in Word, however, you may want to let your creative juices flow. The
Layout tab of the **Page Setup** dialog box lets you determine the characteristics of long

documents, such as the appearance of section breaks (e.g., chapters in a long book document). You can also specify different headers and footers for left- and right-facing pages in a two-sided (duplexed) document.

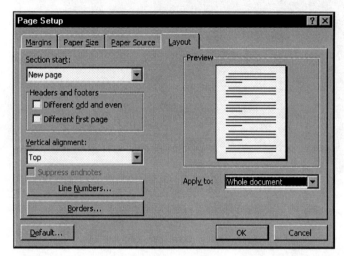

Figure 5.23.   Click the **Layout** tab to choose header and footer options and how the text is vertically aligned on the page.

For those creative touches, try using an often overlooked, but very interesting document attribute found in the **Layout** tab of the **Page Setup** dialog box: **vertical alignment**. This feature is a handy way to create interesting visual effects for one-page fliers, attention-getting brochures, unusual covers for reports, or anything you can think up. Change the vertical alignment setting from the standard **Top** to **Center**; this causes text you enter to flow both upward and downward, positioning the total amount of text entered on the page exactly in the center of the page, between the top and the bottom margins. **Justified** vertical alignment stretches the total amount of text on the page equally between the top and bottom margins of the page.

Although, on the other hand, it's common to adjust the page setup for a document at the start of creating it, you certainly can change it after the document is well under way—or completed, for that matter.

Practice Exercise 5-5

Change Page Formatting

1   Open 📁**05Ex5-5** from the **WORDCert\Word A** folder. Save it as 💾**05Fine**.

2   Change the document margins by doing the following:

•   Choose **File>Page Setup** from the menu bar.

•   Choose the **Margins** tab in the **Page Setup** dialog box, if necessary.

3   Change the following margins:

MARGIN	SETTING
Top	2"
Bottom	2"
Le**f**t	1"
Ri**g**ht	1"

4   Choose **OK** to change the margins.

Observe that by changing the page setup, text has flowed to a new page, creating a two-page document. The total number of pages must now be changed on the fax cover sheet.

5   Change the number in the **Total number of pages including cover** box to **5**.

6   Save and close the document.

Headers and Footers

Headers and footers help you identify documents quickly. While there are few rules concerning the content of headers and footers, convention dictates that for business letters longer than two pages you include the name and return address of the company and/or sender and the date the letter is created or mailed. You can also include graphics, such as a company logo and decorative lines to separate the header from the body of your document.

The footer often carries page numbering for long documents and can include any other identifying data relating to the document, such as government identifying numbers or legal filing numbers.

When you want to enter text in either the header or the footer, you should be in Print Layout view. If you're in Normal view and choose **V**iew>**Header and Footer** from the menu bar, Word automatically switches to Print Layout view and opens the Header pane and a toolbar designed specifically for working with headers and footers.

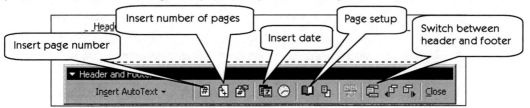

Figure 5.24.   The Header and Footer toolbar is accessible only by choosing **Header and Footer** from the **V**iew menu; you cannot display it using the toolbar shortcut menu.

Begin entering header and footer data:

1   Choose **View>Header and Footer** from the menu bar.

    The Header pane and the Header and Footer toolbar appear.

     NOTE: If you would prefer not to see the document text in this view, hide it by clicking the **Show/Hide Document Text** button (to select it) on the **Header and Footer** toolbar.

    On the other hand, if you later want a sense of how your header and footer appear in relation to the contents of the body of your document, click the **Show/Hide Document Text** button to deselect it.

2   Begin typing the header information, or position the insertion point in the **Header** pane using Click and Type and then type.

     TIP: Common header information is: company and/or personal name, address information, phone number(s), and an e-mail or web-page address.

3   Continue entering information as desired, using the Header and Footer toolbar buttons or the **Insert** menu to insert date, time, page numbers, or other data.

4   When you are satisfied with the header, you can, if necessary, switch to the footer. Click the **Switch Between Header and Footer** button on the Header and Footer toolbar.

5   Begin typing the footer information as desired, using the Header and Footer toolbar buttons or the **Insert** menu.

     TIP: If you decide to use automatic page numbering, you can also type some identifying word or abbreviation, such as **Page** or **pg.**, and a space before clicking one of the page numbering buttons in the Header and Footer toolbar to insert the numbering code.

6   Click the **Close Header and Footer** button on the Header and Footer toolbar to close the toolbar and the **Header/Footer** pane.

     NOTE: After you create a header or footer, by default, the same data appear in exactly the same place on every page in the document. It is possible, however, to create different headers and footers for facing pages and for different sections of long documents. However, in this lesson we'll keep it simple and discuss only one of the many available header and footer alternatives.

DIFFERENT FIRST PAGE

Often, in multiple-page documents, you will want a header or footer that differs on the first page from the remaining pages of the document. Using the Header and Footer toolbar, you can assign the first page to have a different header or footer.

Create a different first page:

1   Click the **Page Setup** button on the Header and Footer toolbar to display the **Page Setup** dialog box.

 NOTE: If you do not have the **Header** or **Footer** pane open, choose **File>Page Setup** from the menu bar to display the **Page Setup** dialog box.

2   Choose the **Layout** tab, if necessary.

3   Select the **Different first page** check box.

4   Choose **OK** to close the **Page Setup** dialog box.

When the **Page Setup** dialog box closes, notice that the header now reads, **First Page Header**; the footer is distinguished by the words **First Page Footer**. You can enter any data you want restricted to the first page header and/or footer of your document in these panes. Use the **Switch Between Header and Footer** button to move between them. The **Show Previous** and **Show Next** buttons on the Header and Footer toolbar allow you to toggle between the **First Page Header** and **Footer** panes, and the header and footer for remaining pages.

Practice Exercise 5-6

Add Headers and Footers to Document

1   Open 📂**05Ex5-6** from the **WORDCert\Word A** folder. Save it as 💾**05First**.

2   Set up a different first page header and footer:

   • Choose **File>Page Setup** from the menu bar.

   • Choose the **Layout** tab in the **Page Setup** dialog box, if necessary.

   • Select the **Different first page** check box.

   • Choose **OK** to close the **Page Setup** dialog box.

3   Create a header for the first page of the document:

   • Choose **View>Header and Footer** from the menu bar.

   The **Header** pane and the Header and Footer toolbar appear.

 NOTE: If necessary, click the **Show Previous** button on the Header and Footer toolbar to go back to the **First Page Header** pane.

- In the **First Page Header** pane, type The Learning Tree.

- Press the **Tab** key twice and click the **Insert Date** button.

4   Create the footer for the first page of the document:

- Click the **Switch Between Header and Footer** button to switch to the First Page Footer pane.

- Type Reply to Request for Information.

- Press the **Tab** key once to move the insertion point to the center of the **First Page Footer** pane.

- Type Page and include one space after the word.

- Click the **Insert Page Number** button.

- Type one space after the number, then type the word of and another space.

- Click the **Insert Number of Pages** button.

To see the header and footer, click the **Close Header and Footer** button on the Header and Footer toolbar.

When you close the **Header and Footer** pane, you should be viewing the bottom of page 1 and the top of page 2. Notice there is no header on page 2.

5   View the first page header and footer. Scroll to the top of page 1 to see the header. Scroll through page 2 to see that there is no header or footer.

6   Create a header for the remaining pages:

- Choose **View>Header and Footer**.

The **Header** pane and the Header and Footer toolbar appear.

- If necessary, click the **Show Next** button on the Header and Footer toolbar to exit the **First Page Header** pane and to go to the **Header** pane for the rest of the document.

- In the **Header** pane, type the following:

    Mr. Alexander Eleve
    Educational Information
    Today's Date

- Click the **Close Header and Footer** button on the Header and Footer toolbar.

7   View the headers and footers. Scroll to the top of page 1 to see the first page header. Scroll to the bottom of page 1 to see both the first page footer and the second page header. Scroll to the bottom of page 2 to see there is still no footer on page 2.

8   Save and close the document.

An example of **05First** is available in the **WORDCert\Word A\Samples** folder.

LESSON 6: INTRODUCTION TO TABS, TABLES, AND COLUMNS

Use tabs, a table, or columns to enhance long and short documents. Each of these Word features creates an orderly arrangement of text, numbers, and/or graphics. The method you choose for arranging content depends on the information itself and the visual effect you prefer.

In this lesson, you will learn to:

> ➤ Set tabs using the ruler
>
> ➤ Move or delete tabs
>
> ➤ Create a table from existing text
>
> ➤ Use the Insert Table button
>
> ➤ Edit table contents
>
> ➤ Insert and delete cells, columns, and rows
>
> ➤ Adjust column width and row height using the rulers
>
> ➤ Use the Tables and Borders toolbar
>
> ➤ AutoFormat tables
>
> ➤ Create newspaper-style columns

With these skills, your reputation for creating organized, effective documents will spread far and wide. Figure 6.1 shows how the use of columns, tables, and tabs can enhance a document.

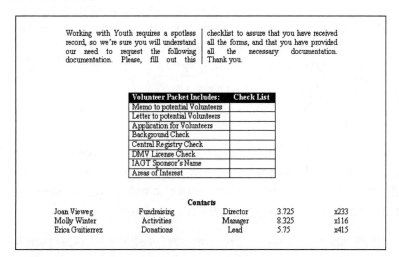

Figure 6.1.   An example of columns, tables, and tabs.

Use Tabs

Tabs (sometimes called **tab stops**) are paragraph instructions for positioning text or numerals in paragraphs. Each time you press the **Tab** key, a tab marker separates text or numbers in exactly the same location on each line of a paragraph. You can have as many tabs as you want in any paragraph, and you may use any combination of tab types: left; center; decimal; bar; and right (see Figure 6.2).

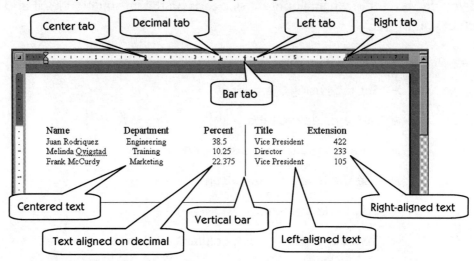

Figure 6.2.   Word provides five tab types: left; center; decimal; bar; right.

There's also a relationship between tabs and tables. Tabs are often used to separate numbers, words, or groups of words that will appear in a table since Word lets you convert tabbed text to a table or vice versa. That's not to say that tabbed data is the only method of creating a table, but it certainly is a common and easy way.

DEFAULT TABS

Default tabs are available automatically in every new document. If you look carefully at the ruler, you'll see faint tick marks along the lower edge of the horizontal ruler. These marks indicate the position of each default tab in each paragraph of the document. The default tabs are left tabs, which create left-aligned text and appear every half-inch.

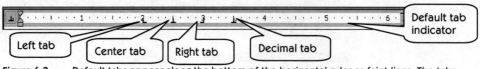

Figure 6.3.   Default tabs appear along the bottom of the horizontal ruler as faint lines. The tabs you set are indicated by black tab markers on the ruler itself.

If you view the header or footer (**View>Header and Footer**), you'll see that both the header and the footer have two default tabs: one center tab and one right tab. These tabs, however, are denoted by black tab markers—not the tick marks usually reserved for default tabs. The different kinds of tab markers are explained below.

It is important to note that, once you insert a tab manually, all the default tabs to the left of the new one are cleared.

TAB MARKERS ON THE RULER

If you find Word's default tabs don't meet your needs, set up your own tabs. When you do so, you can choose the alignment and position of each tab. Look to the left side of the horizontal ruler, and you'll see a button. Each click on that button displays one of the five kinds of tabs. Keep clicking until you get the tab type you want. Each tab type produces a different appearance for your text. The tab displayed on the button is the tab you will insert each time you click the ruler. The table below describes the five tab types and their effect on your text.

TAB TYPE	BUTTON	RESULT
Left Tab	⌊	Begins text at the exact position of the tab marker and streams text to the right of the marker. For example: ⌊ flow right
Center Tab	⊥	Begins entering text exactly at the tab marker, but streams text both left and right equally, so that the tab marker is always located dead center, no matter how much text is entered. For example: flow equally, left ⊥ and right of tab
Right Tab	⌋	Begins entering text exactly at the position of the tab marker but streams text to the left of the marker. This is often used on the right side of letterheads. For example: flow left ⌋
Decimal Tab	⊥	Begins entering text at the tab marker, but when a decimal point (period) is entered, the decimal point becomes the character that the tab aligns. For example: ⊥ 10.00 .10 1000.10
Bar Tab	┃	Inserts a vertical line at the tab marker. Note how this creates a vertical line whether or not the **Tab** key is pressed. You only need to press **Enter** for the line to appear. For example: ┃ align on vertical bar ┃ text after bar tab text before bar tab ┃ text after bar tab

NOTE: Notice also that Word 2000, has buttons for setting the First Line Indent, and a Hanging Indent. To return to the tab choices, continue to click the tab type button until the Left Tab is displayed. To change paragraph indents, refer to Lesson 5 for more information.

SET TABS USING THE RULER

The tab type button on the ruler cycles through all five tabs available in Word. Each time you want to change to a different kind of tab, you must click the tab type button repeatedly until it displays the tab type you desire.

Each time you use the ruler to place a tab in a paragraph, you must click the lower portion of the ruler.

Use the tab type button:

1   Position your cursor in the paragraph in which you want to insert one or more tabs.

2   Use the pointer to click the tab type button (located at the far left of the ruler) until the kind of tab you want appears on the button.

   TIP: If you don't remember what the symbols on the tab type button mean, hover the pointer over the button to see the ScreenTip.

3   Position your pointer over the lower portion of the ruler, and click at the place you want the tab marker to appear.

When you click the ruler, a black marker indicates where the tab is located. Clicking again on the ruler inserts the same kind of tab markers where your curser is located.

   TIP: If you want to change to a different kind of tab, return to the tab type button, select another tab type, and click the ruler where you want to insert a tab.

4   Type text and press the **Tab** key to advance to the tab position. Enter tab-aligned text or numbers.

   NOTE: Because the paragraph mark carries the paragraph instructions (including tabs), and travels in advance of the cursor as you type, when you press the **Enter** key to create a new paragraph, the new paragraph has the same tab markers as the preceding one.

MOVE/CLEAR TABS ON THE RULER

If you discover that the position of your tabs is just a little bit off, you can adjust them. Since tabs are associated with paragraph instructions, changes can be made on a paragraph-by-paragraph basis; revising tab markers in one selected paragraph does not change the tab stops in any other paragraph.

Move tabs using the ruler:

1   Position the insertion point in the paragraph where the tab is located, or select multiple paragraphs.

2   Point to the tab you want to move and click-and-drag it to the desired position on the ruler.

Clear tabs using the ruler:

1   Position the insertion point in the paragraph where the tab is located, or select multiple paragraphs.

2   Point to the tab you want to clear and click-and-drag it down into the document, pulling it off the ruler.

DEFINE TABS USING THE TABS DIALOG BOX

While the ruler provides access to all five-tab types, the **Tabs** dialog box offers an assortment of **tab leaders**, those dots and dashed lines that run between tabbed data. Tab leaders are often used, for example, in tables of contents, in indexes, and in theater programs that list the names of the actors across from the names of the characters. You can also clear tabs using the **Tabs** dialog box. Figure 6.4 illustrates the **Tabs** dialog box.

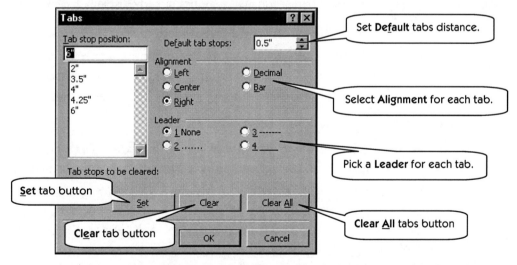

Figure 6.4.   As you set each tab, all the tabs are listed in the **Tab stop position** list of the **Tabs** dialog box.

Each tab is set individually, but you may set as many tabs as you like while the **Tabs** dialog box remains open. You can also reopen the **Tabs** dialog box to add, edit, or clear tabs.

Set tabs:

1   Position the insertion point in the paragraph you want to set tabs for, or select multiple paragraphs.

2   Choose **Format>Tabs** from the menu bar.

    The **Tabs** dialog box is displayed.

3   Enter a **Tab stop position** for a single tab (e.g., 1.25 inches).

4   Select desired **Alignment** and **Leader** options for new tab.

5   Choose **Set**.

    The new tab is displayed in the **Tab stop position** list.

6   Repeat steps 3-5 for each tab you want to set.

7   Choose **OK** to close the dialog box when done setting tabs.

Practice Exercise 6-1

Define, Move, and Delete Tabs

1   Open 📂**06Ex6-1** from the **WORDCert\Word A** folder. Save it as 💾**06Tabs**.

    Notice that this document already has tabbed text starting with the second "paragraph."

     NOTE: If paragraph marks are not already displayed, click the **Show/Hide ¶** button on the Standard toolbar. ¶

2   Position the insertion point next to the last paragraph mark in the document, across from **Background Check**, and press **Enter**.

3   Type Central Registry Check and press **Tab**, then press **Enter**.

4   Type DMV License Check and press **Tab**.

5   Select the tabbed text: **Volunteer Packet Includes…DMV License Check**. Include the paragraph mark at the end of the document.

6   Notice that the ruler shows one tab marker (a left-aligned tab at 3" on the horizontal ruler) that applies to all of the selected paragraphs. Notice also that all of the default tabs to the left of that marker have been removed.

7   Position your pointer over the tab marker at 3". Hold down the mouse button, and drag the tab marker to 2.5".

    Notice that the selected text and all of the paragraph marks are simultaneously moved to the left. The default tab marker at 3" reappears.

8   Drag this tab marker off the ruler to clear the tab.

Notice that the tab alignment has reverted to the default tabs indicated by faint tick marks on the lower edge of the horizontal ruler.

9   Save your work and close the document.

A completed example of **06Tabs** is available in the **WORDCert\Word A\Samples** folder.

Create Tables

Tables are one of Word's richest features—so rich, in fact, that there's an entire menu dedicated to table options (see Figure 6.5).

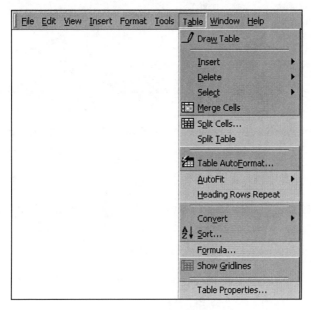

Figure 6.5.   The **Table** menu contains a variety of options for creating and formatting tables.

You can align text neatly in a document by creating tables without visible borders. However, a wide assortment of borders and shading is also available if you wish to emphasize data in a table. You can convert existing data to a table, or create a table and then fill in the data.

Plain or fancy, all tables are comprised of **rows and columns**. The intersection of a row and column is a **cell**. Tables can have numerous rows and columns. Each cell in a table contains a specific amount of data, text, or numbers and can "grow" vertically (height) while maintaining the horizontal size (width) of other cells in a column.

You can merge, split, or delete cells. You can sort data and enter a calculating formula in a cell—in fact, there's remarkably little you *can't* do in a table.

CONVERT TEXT TO TABLE

If you begin entering text and later realize you want to insert it in a table, tabs may be the best way to separate the text you want to convert. Each time you press the **Tab** key as you type, a nonprinting tab marker appears in the document (→). Each time you insert a tab, Word uses it to identify the end of the contents intended for one cell in a table. Pressing the **Enter** key signifies the end of a row. Look at the two documents displayed in Figure 6.6.

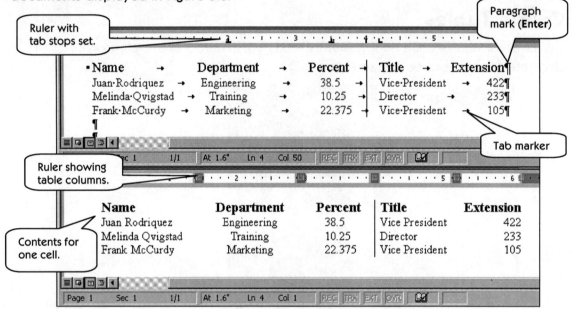

Figure 6.6.   The same document using tabs to convert data into a table.

It certainly is easy enough to create a table using conversion, and, with the aid of the Table **AutoFormat** feature, tables couldn't be faster.

 NOTE: Technically, this kind of information is said to be in **tab-delimited text** format, a useful term to know if you plan to learn about Access databases or Excel spreadsheets.

Convert typed data directly to a table:

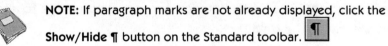 **NOTE:** If paragraph marks are not already displayed, click the **Show/Hide ¶** button on the Standard toolbar. ┃¶┃

1   Select all of the tabbed data you want to place in a table.

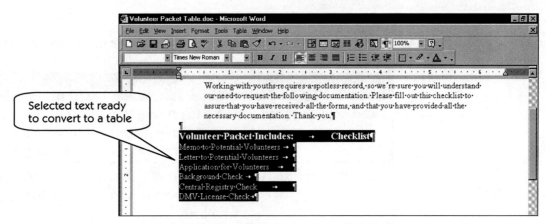

Figure 6.7. Tabbed text, indicated by the tab markers (arrows), is highlighted and will be converted into a table.

 2 Choose **Table>Insert>Table** from the menu bar.

Use the Convert Text to Table dialog box:

1 Select all of the tabbed data you want to place in a table.

2 Choose **Table>Convert>Text to Table** from the menu bar.

The **Convert Text to Table** dialog box opens (see Figure 6.8).

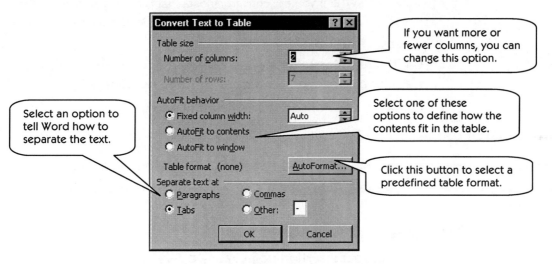

Figure 6.8. Use the **Convert Text to Table** dialog box for more options.

3 The **Number of columns** reflects the number of columns you have defined by the number of tabs in the selected text.

4   In the **AutoFit behavior** section, choose one of the following options:

Option	Description
Fixed column **w**idth	Use to choose the size in inches for the columns. **Auto** will insert columns of equal size between the margins.
Auto**F**it to contents	Automatically sizes the columns to fit the amount of text typed in the column.
AutoFit to win**d**ow	Automatically sizes the table to fit within the window of a web browser. When the window size of a web browser changes, the table automatically adjusts to fit the window.

5   In the **Separate text at** section, verify that **T**abs is selected.

     NOTE: If you are converting data that is not separated by tabs, you could choose one of the other options in the **Separate text at** section of the dialog box.

6   Use the **A**uto**F**ormat button to change the format of the table. (See the next section for details on Table AutoFormat.)

7   Choose **OK** to convert the selected text to a table.

TABLE AUTOFORMAT

Whether you begin creating a table from existing data or create the table and then fill in the data, you can use the **Table AutoFormat** dialog box to tweak your table design at any time.

Enhance or edit a table:

1   Position your insertion point in any cell in your table.

     2   Choose **T**able>Table Auto**F**ormat from the menu bar.

The **Table AutoFormat** dialog box is displayed (see Figure 6.9).

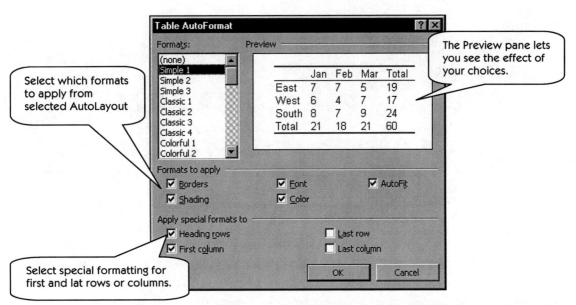

Figure 6.9. Let Word's **Table AutoFormat** command help polish the look of your tables.

3   Scroll through the **Formats** list and select the design you want to use. Look at the **Preview** section to get an idea of what your table would look like.

4   You can select and deselect options under **Formats to apply**, such as **Borders**, **Shading**, **Font**, **Color** and **AutoFit**, in the Table **AutoFormat** dialog box.

5   You can also include or eliminate predesigned special formatting for **Heading rows**, **First column**, **Last row**, and **Last column**.

6   Choose **OK** to apply your selections and close the dialog box.

 TIP: If you don't like the way the table looks, remember that you can always use the **Undo** feature (**Edit**>**Undo Text to Table**).

If you aren't satisfied with the design choices you've made, you can return again and again to the **Table AutoFormat** dialog box or apply your own formatting until your table is exactly as you want it to be.

INSERT OR DELETE COLUMNS, ROWS, OR CELLS

Again, in the **Table** menu, you find choices for inserting and deleting parts of a table. The **Insert** and **Delete** submenus list choices for columns, rows, and cells. On the **Table**>**Insert** menu you have the choice of inserting columns to the left or right, and rows above or below, the location of the insertion point. You can also choose **Cells** to display the **Insert Cells** dialog box. Also, on the **Table**>**Delete** menu you can choose to delete the entire table or selected columns, rows, or cells. Figure 6.10 illustrates these two submenus.

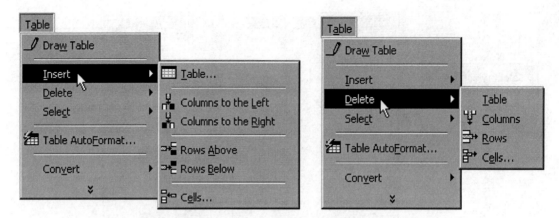

Figure 6.10.   Personalized versions of the **Table>Insert** and **Table>Delete** submenus.

This may all seem overwhelming to read about, but it will make perfect sense as you begin to use the **Table** menu. Make a selection, or position your cursor inside the table, and select the table element(s) to insert or delete using the **Table** menu.

Insert cells, columns, or rows:

1   Position the insertion point in the table where you want to make the insertion.

2   Choose **Table>Insert** from the menu bar.

TIP: There is also a shortcut menu and a toolbar button on the Standard toolbar available to you if you wish to insert a column to the *left* only. Select the column, point to the selection, and right-click. Choose **Insert Columns** from the shortcut menu. An **Insert Rows** button is also available if you wish to insert a row *above* the current one only.

3   Choose one of the following submenu commands:

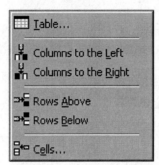

Figure 6.11.   The **Insert>Table** submenu

If you choose one of the column or row commands, the column or row is inserted.

If you choose **Cells**, the **Insert Cells** dialog box is displayed for you to further define how you want the cells inserted. Make the desired selection and then choose **OK** to complete the command.

CHANGE COLUMN WIDTH/ROW HEIGHT

Before getting down to the business of changing column width or row height, position your cursor inside a table, and look at the horizontal ruler. Markers indicating the width of each column in the table appear there; they can be moved to increase or decrease column width (see Figure 6.12).

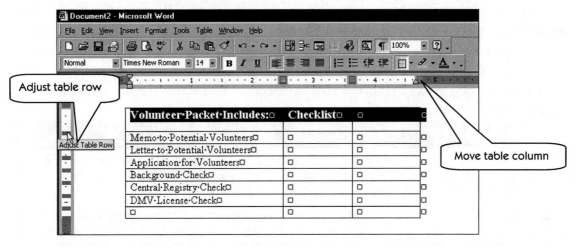

Figure 6.12.   As you move the arrow pointer over a column or row marker, it changes shape to a sizing arrow so you can click and drag to resize a column or row.

Look also at the vertical ruler. Guess what? You can also adjust the row height using the row markers on the vertical ruler.

Drag to change column width or row height:

1   Move the insertion point in the table.

2   Use the pointer to click and drag the column or row marker to increase or decrease the size of the column or row.

MOVE A TABLE

⊞   While you are in a table in Print Layout view, there is a square with four arrows above the first cell. This is called the **table move handle**. Drag this handle to move the entire table.

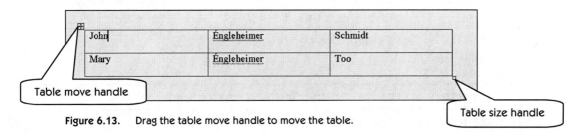

Figure 6.13.   Drag the table move handle to move the table.

RESIZE A TABLE

While the pointer is in a table in Print Layout view, there is a square at the bottom-right corner of the table. This is called the **table size handle**. Drag this handle to resize the entire table (see Figure 6.13 above).

ENTER TABLE DATA

If you decide to create a table first and then fill in the data, you must click inside a cell to begin entering data. When you want to move to another place in the table to enter more data, you can, of course, click inside the new location and begin entering data, but there are several other ways to move from cell to cell. You will also find that there are particular keystrokes that allow you to select cells, add rows, enter data, and create special formatting in cells.

KEYSTROKE	RESULT
Tab	Moves one cell to the right in a row. At the end of a row, pressing **Tab** moves the cursor down to the leftmost cell of the next row.
	If you press the **Tab** key in the last cell of the last row, a new row is added to the table automatically.
Shift+Tab	Moves to the preceding cell.
Ctrl+Tab	Enters a tab within the contents of the cell.
Arrow keys	Moves up or down one cell and left or right one character. If you are at the beginning or end of a cell, however, you will move to the previous or next cell when you press the left or right arrow key.
	If you press the down arrow key while your cursor is inside the last row of a table, the cursor moves outside the bounds of the table and to the next available paragraph mark or line of text. Similarly, if you are in the first row of a table and press the up arrow key, you will move to the next available paragraph mark or line of text.
Enter	Begins a new "paragraph" inside a cell.
Shift+Enter	Creates a new line for text inside a cell without creating a new paragraph.
Alt+5 (number pad, NumLock off)	Selects the entire table.
Alt+PageUp	Moves to the first cell in a column.
Alt+PageDown	Moves to the last cell in a column.
Alt+Home	Moves to the first cell in a row.
Alt+End	Moves to the last cell in a row.

Practice Exercise 6-2

Convert Text to Table and Revise the Table

1   Open 📁**06Ex6-2** from the **WORDCert\Word A** folder. Save it as 💾**06Packet**.

2   Convert tabbed text to an **AutoFormat** table:

- Select the tabbed text: **Volunteer Packet Includes ..DMV License Check**. Include the paragraph mark at the end of the line.

- Choose **Table>Convert>Text to Table** from the menu bar.

- Verify that the **Number of columns** setting is **2**.

- Verify that **Tabs** is selected under **Separate text at**.

- Choose **AutoFormat** to open the **Table AutoFormat** dialog box.

- In the **Formats** list, select **Colorful 1**.

- Choose **OK** twice.

- Click away from the **AutoFormat** table to deselect it.

3   Continue entering data in the table:

DOCUMENTATION	CHECKLIST	THEN, PRESS
Row 2, Memo	Sent 02/16/00	**Tab** twice
		Moves to the third row, second column.
Row 3, Letter	Sent 02/22/00	**Tab** twice
		Moves to the fourth row, second column.
Row 4, Application	Sent 02/22/00	**Tab** twice
		Moves to the fifth row, second column.
Row 5, Background Check	Pending as of March 1, 2000	**down arrow**
		Advances to the sixth row, second column.
Row 6, Central Registry Check	Pending as of March 1, 2000	**down arrow**
		Advances to the seventh row, second column.
Row 7, DMV	Received 02/27/00	———

4   Insert a column:

  • Position the insertion point in the **Checklist** column.

  • Choose **T<u>a</u>ble>I<u>n</u>sert>Columns to the <u>R</u>ight** from the menu bar.

5   Resize columns by dragging the column marker:

  • On the **Checklist** column, drag the right side of the column to approximately 3.5" on the horizontal ruler.

  • On the new column, drag the right side of the column to approximately 5.25" on the horizontal ruler.

6   Enter new table data:

  • The insertion point should be in the first row of the new column (the heading row); if not, move it there.

  • Type Filed in Drawer # .

  • Center the new heading.

Your table should look similar to the following:

Volunteer Packet Includes:	Checklist	Filed in Drawer #
Memo to Potential Volunteers	Sent 02/16/00	
Letter to Potential Volunteers	Sent 02/22/00	
Application for Volunteers	Sent 02/22/00	
Background Check	Pending as of March 1, 2000	
Central Registry Check	Pending as of March 1, 2000	
DMV License Check	Received 02/27/00	

7   Delete a column from the table:

  • The insertion point should be in the **Filed in Drawer #** column; if not, move it anywhere in the column.

  • Choose **T<u>a</u>ble>D<u>e</u>lete><u>C</u>olumns** from the menu bar to remove the column from the table.

8   Save your work and close the document.

Create Newspaper Columns

While tables offer a tidy way of organizing data in rows and columns made up of cells, newspaper columns organize text and graphics in a different kind of column. The text and graphics stream (or *snake*) from the top to the bottom of one column and then move to the top of the next column to the right to fill downward, and so on.

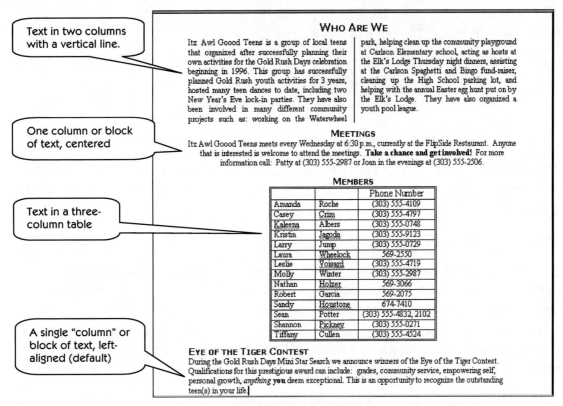

Figure 6.14. Combine blocks of single-column text with two-column newspaper columns and tables for more interesting documents.

Word allows you to enter text and then highlight the text and convert it to newspaper columns, or you can designate the number of columns for text before you start typing. In either case, mixing blocks of text with text in multiple columns creates separate sections within your document (see Figure 6.14). A new section need not break on to a new page, but each section does display a different section number at the left side of the status bar.

COLUMNS BUTTON

 Perhaps the simplest way to create newspaper columns is by using the **Columns** button on the Standard toolbar. You can begin by entering all or most of the text you want arranged in columns. The words flow in the default block paragraph format as you type. Type as many paragraphs as you need.

Next comes the conversion from a single "column," block-paragraph style to text arranged in multiple columns.

Create columns using the Columns button:

1 Click anywhere within document text to position the insertion point, or select specific text to place in columns.

 2 Click the **Columns** button on the Standard toolbar to display the menu of column number options (see Figure 6.15).

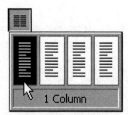

Figure 6.15. The **Columns** button drop-down palette. Drag the pointer to the right to insert as many newspaper columns as you like.

3 Point to the number of columns you want, then click.

This method of creating columns is fast, direct, and sure. You see exactly the number of columns you'll get. For more elaborate column controls, try the next method, using the **Format** menu.

FORMAT MENU COLUMNS

When you use the **Columns** button on the Standard toolbar, each column is pre-designed by Word, and all columns are created equally. For example, if you apply three columns using the **Columns** button, all three are of equal width. While defining the columns, you have no control over the distance between columns or the width of each column—nor can you apply a vertical line between columns, something used frequently in desktop publishing.

Using **Format>Columns** from the menu bar allows you to define the number of columns you need, add a dividing line (vertical rule), and dictate the width of each column and the distance that separates each column from the next. Your options can apply to the entire document or to selected text. The **Columns** dialog box is shown in Figure 6.16.

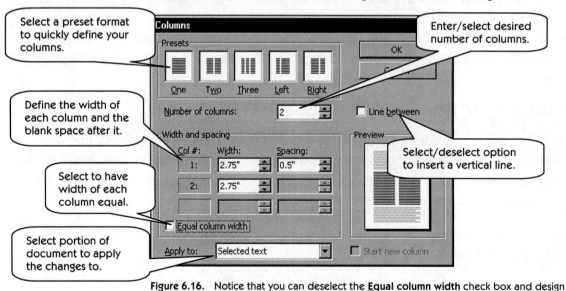

Figure 6.16. Notice that you can deselect the **Equal column width** check box and design columns of any width to suit your needs.

Clearly, using the **Columns** dialog box is the best choice for documents requiring a small dose of visual variety in page layout design and for documents that don't require text to flow in columns.

Create columns using the Format menu:

1   Click anywhere within document text to position the insertion point, or select specific text to place in columns.

 NOTE: It is not necessary have all your column text entered now.

2   Choose **F**o**rmat**>**C**olumns from the menu bar.

The **Columns** dialog box is displayed. (See Figure 6.16.)

3   Choose one of the **Presets**, if desired.

OR

Enter/select the **N**umber **of columns** you want.

4   Select the **Line b**e**tween** check box to insert vertical rules between all your columns, if desired. (Applies to all columns or none.)

5   Enter/select column **W**i**dth** and **S**pacing in the boxes to the right of each **C**ol #, if desired. Check how your settings will look in the **Preview** pane. If necessary, revise settings.

 TIP: If you want multiple columns to be exactly the same width, select the **Equal column width** check box. This overrides any setting you made in the **Width and spacing** section of the **Columns** dialog box.

6   In the **Apply to** box, select whether you want to apply the column settings to Selected text, Selected sections, This section, This point forward, or Whole document.

7   Choose **OK**, when all is set, to close the **Columns** dialog box.

You've spent a lot of time in this dialog box, but even so, you may discover that the column widths you chose aren't as suitable as you'd hoped. There is a solution to this problem, as the next section explains.

CHANGE COLUMN WIDTH WITH THE RULER

Similar in many respects to the appearance of the ruler when you have a table in your document, newspaper columns also have column markers in the horizontal ruler. These markers also allow you to adjust column width.

You can drag a column marker to expand or reduce the width of any column. If you set your columns to **Equal column width** in the **Columns** dialog box, changing the column width in the ruler affects all of your columns.

 TIP: You can also increase or decrease the distance between columns in the ruler. Simply drag a Left Margin or Right Margin marker to expand/reduce the amount of space between columns.

Change column width using the ruler:

1 Move the insertion point into the columns so you can see the column definitions on the horizontal ruler.

Figure 6.17.   Use the column markers to adjust column width.

2 Click and drag the marker for the element you want to resize:

- The Left Margin marker resizes the column's left margin and the space between the columns.

- The Right Margin marker resizes the column's right margin and the space between the columns.

- The column marker resizes the right side of the left column and the left side of the right column, keeping the distance between the two columns the same.

- If the columns are set to **Equal column width** in the **Columns** dialog box, column markers are not available. You can, however, change column margins.

ENTER AND EDIT TEXT IN COLUMNS

After you apply columns to text, adding to or editing existing text follows the same rules and takes advantage of the same shortcuts as typing or editing any other text. Position the insertion point where you want additional words and begin typing, or highlight and delete words you don't want. Each addition or deletion of text changes the flow of text in the columns you set up.

Move to	Press
Top of previous column	**Alt+Up arrow**
Top of next column	**Alt+Down arrow**

 As available in a single "column" document, the selection bar is available in every column and is directly to the left of the left margin. When the pointer is in the selection bar, it becomes a right-pointing arrow so you can select text using the mouse.

If you prefer to have your columns break at a specific place in the text, try this:

Create a column break:

1   Position the insertion point at the end of the line, where you want to insert a column break.

2   Choose **Insert>Break** from the menu bar.

The **Break** dialog box opens (see Figure 6.18).

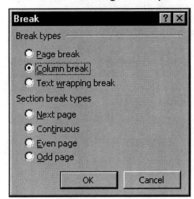

Figure 6.18.   Don't use the lower portion of the **Break** dialog box if you choose to create a **C**olumn break.

3   Select **Column break**, if necessary.

4   Choose **OK**.

   NOTE: If you discover that your new column break doesn't suit you, remember the **Undo** feature.

Practice Exercise 6-3

Create and Format Columns:

1   Open 06Ex6-3 from the **WORDCert\Word A** folder. Save it as 06Cols.

2   Select the paragraph that begins with **Working with youths...**

3   Choose **Format>Columns** from the menu bar.

The **Columns** dialog box is displayed.

4   Complete the following steps:

• Click **Two** in the **Presets** section.

• In the **Width and spacing** section of the dialog box, enter/select **0.2"** in the **Spacing** box for **Col #1**.

• Select the **Line between** check box.

- Check how your settings will look by glancing to the right at the **Preview** pane.

- Choose **OK** when the Preview suits you to close the **Columns** dialog box.

5   The space between the columns is too tight. Drag margin marker to make the space between the columns approximately .5".

6   Save your work and close the file.

A completed example of **06Cols** is available in the **WORDCert\Word A\Samples** folder.

LESSON 7: FINISH YOUR WORK

Check Spelling and Grammar

Nothing can spoil a great-looking document quicker than a mispeled word. (See what we mean?) Spelling in English isn't easy or natural for many folks—including native speakers—so Microsoft has included a remarkably thorough spell checking capability in Word. You can also use Word's grammar checking feature to find common usage errors, or check the document's readability, that is, the reading level may be too complex or simple for your audience.

In this lesson, you will learn to:

> ➢ Check spelling and grammar in multiple languages
> ➢ Use automatic spelling and grammar check
> ➢ Add words to Word dictionaries and AutoCorrect
> ➢ Use auxiliary dictionaries
> ➢ Use Word's Thesaurus feature
> ➢ Find and replace text, numerals, and formatting
> ➢ Understand soft page breaks and hard page breaks
> ➢ Use Print Preview
> ➢ Set printing options
> ➢ Print a finished document

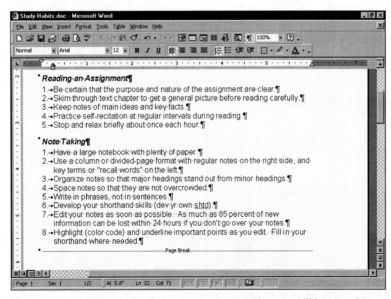

Figure 7.1. Use Word's spelling and grammar checking capabilities to polish your documents.

SPELL CHECK

Spell checking takes only a moment, but its rewards last a long, long time. You may have a beautifully designed document with finely tuned content, and it may be printed on elegant paper, but one tiny spelling error can destroy the whole thing. As you type, and certainly before running a final print, use the Spelling feature in Word.

 CAUTION: A spell checker can catch incorrectly spelled words, not words spelled correctly but used incorrectly... as in **to**, **too**, and **two**; **bear** and **bare**.

No spell checker can include every word you're likely to use, so it's nice to know that you can add words to the Word dictionary, or create custom dictionaries. For instance, jargon particular to your profession may not be included in Word's standard dictionary. You can even spell check documents written in languages other than English as well as documents containing multiple languages, such as French, Spanish, and English.

The two ways for checking spelling are as follows:

- While you enter document contents, use Word's automatic spell checking in conjunction with AutoCorrect.

 - After the document has been completed, choose **Tools>Spelling and Grammar** from the menu bar, click the **Spelling and Grammar** button on the Standard toolbar, or press **F7**.

Automatic Spell Check

If you leave the default spell checking option (**Check spelling as you type**) selected in the **Options** dialog box (this is the default setting), you'll discover a wonderfully easy way to add words to the dictionary or to AutoCorrect. Right-click a word that has a wavy red underline to access a shortcut menu. (Wavy green underlines indicate lapses in grammar, discussed later in this lesson.)

Figure 7.2.   Right-click a word with a wavy red underline to access Word's suggestions for replacement words.

MENU ITEM	DESCRIPTION
Suggested word(s)	Corrects this occurrence of the misspelled word.
Ignore All	This and every occurrence of this spelling will be overlooked in all documents until you quit this session of Word.
Add	The wavy red line disappears, and the word, exactly as typed, is added to the currently active dictionary.
AutoCorrect	Opens a menu displaying the same choices Word offers at the top of the shortcut menu. You can select the correct spelling from the list to add an AutoCorrect entry of the misspelled word and its correction.
Language	Allows you to set a new language for the spell check and other proofing tools. (See also **Custom Dictionaries** later in this lesson.)
Spelling	Opens the standard **Spelling and Grammar** dialog box.

To disable automatic spell check in the current document, select the **Hide spelling errors in this document** check box in the **Spelling & Grammar** tab of the **Options** dialog box (**Tools>Options**). To disable it in all documents, deselect the **Check spelling as you type** check box. For more details about what Word flags as possible errors (and ignores), see **Spell Check Options** later in this section.

You can use one method or the other—or both for a double measure of safety. The choice you make depends on your work style and the complexity of your document. No matter which choice you make, at some point you'll encounter the **Spelling** dialog box. The dialog box shown below is associated with the English (U.S.) dictionary.

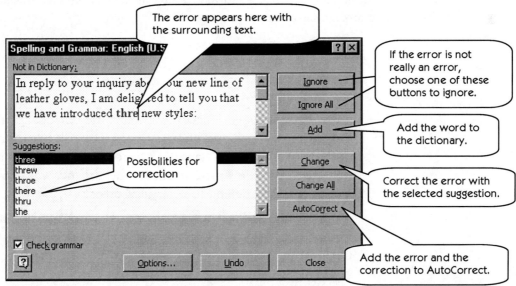

Figure 7.3.   The **Spelling and Grammar** dialog box displays the first misspelled word in red.

Misspelled words (or words not included in the dictionary) appear in red in the **Not in Dictionary** box of the **Spelling and Grammar** dialog box. A list of suggested alternatives appears in the **Suggestions** box. You have several options of what to do next. If the correct spelling appears under **Suggestions**, click the correct spelling and choose **Change** to insert the correction—or you can choose **Change All** to revise every occurrence of this misspelling throughout the document. If you find yourself consistently making the same typographical error, it may be a good idea to add that correction to your AutoCorrect list. Choose **AutoCorrect** in the **Spelling and Grammar** dialog box to make that entry automatically. (Review Lesson 4 if necessary.)

Alternatively, you can choose **Ignore** to bypass this instance of the word—or you can choose **Ignore All** to have Word bypass every instance of this word throughout the document.

 TIP: Remember, *nothing* takes the place of good proofreading. If you value your reputation, never rely upon yourself to proof your own writing or typing. Fresh eyes can find things you've looked at a dozen times and never noticed.

Spell-check a document:

1   When a wavy red line appears under a word in the document, right-click it and choose the correct spelling from the shortcut menu (see Figure 7.2).

OR

 • Choose **Tools>Spelling and Grammar** from the menu bar or press **F7**.

If there are errors, the **Spelling and Grammar** dialog box is displayed and the first spelling error is shown in a red font. (See Figure 7.3) Grammar errors are shown in a green font.

 NOTE: Repeated words, such as **he** in ...then **he he** went to... are considered spelling errors in Word.

2   Do one of the following:

• If the word is spelled incorrectly, click the correct spelling in the Suggestions list and choose **Change** to edit this instance of the word. Choose **Change All** to replace all misspellings of this word. Choose **AutoCorrect** to add the incorrect spelling and suggested spelling to the AutoCorrect list.

• If the word is spelled correctly, choose Ignore to skip this instance of the word. Choose **Ignore All** to skip the word throughout the document. Choose **Add** to include the word in the dictionary so you won't be prompted to correct the word again in any Word document.

- If there is a grammar error, click a correction in the Suggestions list and choose **Change** or, to skip this rule throughout the document, choose **Ignore Rule**. Choose **Next Sentence** to skip any grammar problems in this sentence and move to the next.

  The grammar checker is discussed in more detail later in this lesson.

3 Repeat step 2 as needed. If you didn't start **Spelling and Grammar** at the top of the document, Word may ask if you want to continue checking the remainder of the document. Choose **Yes** and repeat step 2.

  The Office Assistant notifies you when the spelling and grammar check is complete.

By now, you're probably getting the impression that there are plenty of ways to go about spell checking, and you're correct. Just remember that all ways lead to the same two outcomes: standard spelling, and a document you can be proud of.

Spell-Check Options

If you want to turn automatic spell check on or off, or if you wish to change or verify any other Spelling features, choose **Tools>Options** from the menu bar and choose the **Spelling & Grammar** tab for the following options:

OPTION/BUTTON	DESCRIPTION
Check spelling as you type	As you type, misspelled words are underlined with a wavy red line. In some instances the incorrectly typed word is automatically corrected, provided the incorrect word has a listing in AutoCorrect.
Hide spelling errors in this document	Deactivate automatic spell checking on a document-by-document basis.
Always suggest corrections	Word offers its best guess as to what you really meant to type. The guesses appear in the **Suggestions** list when you spell-check the document. Suggestions always appear on the shortcut menu when you right-click.
Suggest from main dictionary only	Typically, this is the option you want for most documents. If, however, the document relies on a different dictionary (e.g., a custom dictionary), deselect this option.
Ignore words in UPPERCASE	Words, such as acronyms and trade names, typed in all caps (not those assigned the small caps font attribute) will not be included in the spell check.

OPTION/BUTTON	DESCRIPTION
Ignore words with numbers	Words with numbers embedded, such as Y2K and 2Style, will not be included in the spell check.
Ignore Internet and file addresses	As Word 2000 is Internet savvy, it skips addresses during a spelling check.
Custom dictionary list	Lists CUSTOM.DIC by default, the custom dictionary provided by Word, but also displays any dictionaries you locate and select using the **Dictionaries** button.
Dictionaries...	Allows you to locate additional dictionaries stored on your hard drive and select and make those dictionaries available to Word during any spell check. (Word provides many auxiliary dictionaries in different languages, and you can create your own custom dictionaries.)

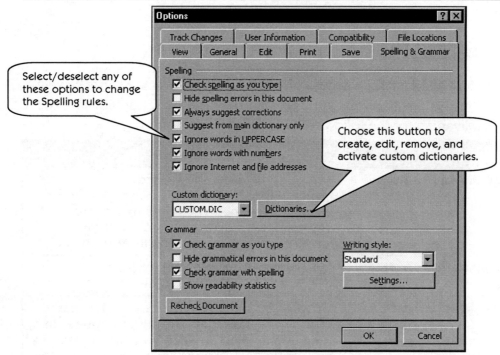

Figure 7.4.   The **Spelling & Grammar** tab of the **Options** dialog box.

Set spell checking options:

1   Choose **Tools>Options** from the menu bar to display the **Options** dialog box.

2   Choose the **Spelling & Grammar** tab, if necessary.

3   Select/deselect desired Spelling features.

4   Choose **OK**.

Custom Dictionaries

Different dictionaries may be used during spell checking. For instance, Microsoft has numerous dictionaries in languages other than standard U.S. English. You can also create your own dictionaries for particular projects, or purchase dictionaries for terminology in professions such as law and medicine.

Activate custom dictionaries: A three-part process

1 The dictionary must be available to your computer (possibly on a network server or installed on your hard drive).

2 The dictionary must be listed in the **Custom Dictionaries** dialog box.

3 The dictionary must be selected in the **Custom dictionary** list of the **Options** dialog box.

 To spell-check documents in languages other than English, select the foreign text, then choose **Tools>Language>Set Language** from the menu bar to display the **Language** dialog box. In the **Mark selected text as** list, select the language, then choose **OK**. A check mark appears to the left of the dictionaries you can access. The Spelling feature refers to the assigned dictionary during a spell check of selected text and then returns to using the English (U.S.) dictionary for all remaining text.

To have the spell check bypass words in a particular language for which you have no dictionary, select the **Do not check spelling or grammar** check box.

GRAMMAR CHECK

Language is a tool of communication, and as such it has certain standards upon which most speakers and writers of English agree. The common language in the United States, is known as **Standard American English** (or **General American**) usage and is the basis on which Word's Grammar feature determines correct versus incorrect usage. This feature is far from infallible, but it can often help you decide if the words you've chosen are saying what you intend to communicate.

It might be helpful to know the different kinds of errors Grammar looks for. Not only does it look for grammar errors, it looks into the overlapping area of punctuation—as well as mechanics and (to a lesser degree) diction and rhetoric.

Word has five sets of writing styles for checking English grammar: Casual, Standard, Formal, Technical, and Custom (see Figure 7.5). Ultimately, the standard you use will be determined by trial and error. Try working with one of the writing style standards, and if you find that it growls at you too often, try another one until you find the one that works most effectively for you.

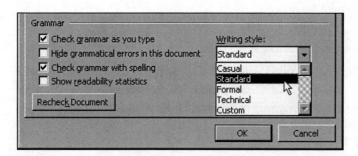

Figure 7.5.   Pick the **Writing style** that seems most appropriate for your document.

Microsoft understands that English grammar is not cast in stone, so you have a wide measure of control in determining what the grammar checker looks for—and what it overlooks.

Set Grammar options by choosing **Tools>Options** from the menu bar. Then, choose the **Spelling & Grammar** tab in the **Options** dialog box (see Figure 7.4).

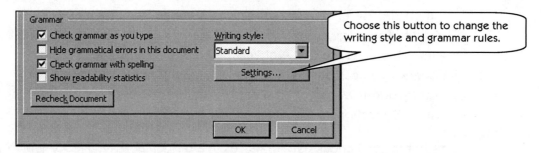

Figure 7.6.   If the wavy green underlines indicating grammar errors in documents bother you,
deselect the **Check grammar as you type** check box.

You set general behaviors for the Grammar feature in the **Options** dialog box. These options determine whether wavy green lines denote grammatical errors or if those lines are hidden in a particular document, whether Word will automatically check grammar as it checks spelling, and whether or not you are given readability statistics (see Figure 7.6).

Readability statistics are based on word choice and sentence structure. Ernest Hemingway would probably have received about an eighth-grade rating. William Faulkner would probably rate at post-graduate level if that were an available readability level in Word. Gertrude Stein would, no doubt, rate as simply incoherent.

 TIP: For more sophisticated control of the grammar checker, choose **Tools>Options** from the menu bar. Then choose the **Spelling & Grammar** tab. Choose **Settings** in the lower portion of the dialog box to activate or deactivate specific style and grammar elements.

Each time you change **Writing style** in the **Options** dialog box, the defaults for the chosen style appear in the **Grammar Settings** dialog box (accessed via the **Settings** button). Unfortunately, there is no way to save your settings when you change writing styles, so you must verify your preferred settings every time you change styles.

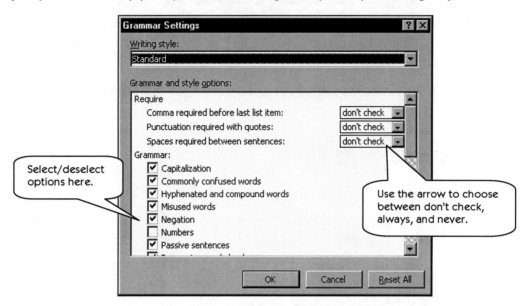

Figure 7.7. Change grammar settings here by choosing the **Settings** button on the **Spelling & Grammar** tab of the **Options** dialog box.

As you check grammar, it would be helpful if Word explained the reason for flagging words and sentences. This is one area where the Office Assistant can be very helpful. If you turn on the Office Assistant, you will get explanations as you move through the **Spelling and Grammar** dialog box.

 NOTE: If you would like to see more precise definitions of any of the Grammar terms, you can choose **Help>Microsoft Word Help** from the menu bar and type ⌈grammar⌉ in the Office Assistant Help bubble. Choose **Search**, then from the list under **What would you like to do?**, choose **Grammar and writing style options**.

No grammar checker is perfect. Therefore, depending on a grammar checker to cure all your writing ills can be a sure route to embarrassment. There will be instances when the grammar checker flags something that is perfectly acceptable. It is, after all, only a database of common deviations from language standards, and anything that doesn't agree with the database is suspect. If you're not a grammarian, use the grammar checker—but also have a friend or colleague who is sharp-eyed and language savvy proofread your final draft to catch any oversights.

Turn off automatic grammar checking:

1   Choose **Tools>Options** from the menu bar to display the **Options** dialog box.

2   Choose the **Spelling & Grammar** tab, if necessary.

3   Select the **Hide grammatical errors in this document** check box to disable automatic grammar check in the current document.

OR

Deselect the **Check grammar as you type** check box to disable it in all documents.

Practice Exercise 7-1

Check Spelling and Grammar

1   Open 📁**07Ex7-1** from the **WORDCert\Word A** folder. Save it as 💾**07Spell**.

2   Notice the word **skedule** is marked with a wavy red line, indicating that it is misspelled.

3   Change **Spelling** options:

•   Choose **Tools>Options** from the menu bar and choose the **Spelling & Grammar** tab, if necessary. Select the **Hide spelling errors in this document** check box, and then choose **OK** to see the effect in your document. (Existing spelling errors in the current document are no longer underlined.)

•   Return to the **Spelling & Grammar** tab of the **Options** dialog box. Deselect the **Hide spelling errors in this document** check box, then choose **OK**.

4   Spell-check your document:

•   Position your insertion point at the beginning of the document, if necessary, using the keyboard shortcut, **Ctrl+Home**.

•   Choose **Tools>Spelling and Grammar** from the menu bar to display the **Spelling and Grammar** dialog box.

TIP: The keyboard shortcut for the **Spelling and Grammar** command is **F7**.

•   Observe that the word **skedule** appears in red, indicating that it is either misspelled or not found in Word's dictionary.

•   Select **schedule** from the **Suggestions** list, if necessary, and then choose **Change**.

- Because you didn't choose **Change All** in the above step, **Skedule** is again indicated in red. This time, select **Schedule** in the **Suggestions** list and choose **AutoCorrect**, since this could be a regularly repeated typing error.

Now every time someone types **skedule** on your computer, the misspelling will automatically be replaced by **schedule**.

5 Continue to correct the document by fixing the grammar errors:

- The next error flagged is **don't**, a grammatical error. Observe the **Suggestions** and choose **Change**.

- The next error flagged is a typing mistake: two spaces. Again, observe the **Suggestions**, and choose **Change**.

6 Address additional spelling errors:

- The next flagged spelling error **shtd** is actually correct, so choose **Ignore**.

- You will see a message that the spelling and grammar check is complete. If the Office Assistant displays the message, click the document to activate it and close the message. If Word displays the message in a dialog box, choose **OK** to return to the document.

7 Add a shortcut in the **AutoCorrect** dialog box:

- Select the word, "SkoolDAZE," and choose **Tools>AutoCorrect** from the menu bar.

- In the **Replace** box, type: $\boxed{sk}$. Choose **Formatted text**, and then choose **Add**. Choose **OK** to close the dialog box.

8 Use your Spelling and AutoCorrect settings:

- Move to the end of your document.

- Press **Enter** and type the following paragraph *exactly* as it appears below (to demonstrate the effect of step 7):

> Sk is the foremost provider of educational materials for lerners in Industry. Imagine your progress after only one lesson.

- Right-click the word **lerners**, and select the correct spelling from the shortcut menu.

10 Save your work and close the document.

A completed example of **07Spell** is available in the **WORDCert\Word A\Samples** folder.

Thesaurus

A thesaurus is a collection of words grouped with other words that mean the same thing (synonyms) and with those that are opposite in meaning (antonyms). The Word thesaurus also includes related words.

USE THE THESAURUS

Professional writers use a thesaurus regularly for those times they're at a loss for just the right word to express their meaning. Fresh language conveys information more effectively. Perk up your documents with alternatives to words you use often (perhaps too often!). To use the Thesaurus in Word, select the word for which you want to find an alternative, and then choose **Tools>Language>Thesaurus** or press **Shift+F7** (see Figure 7.8).

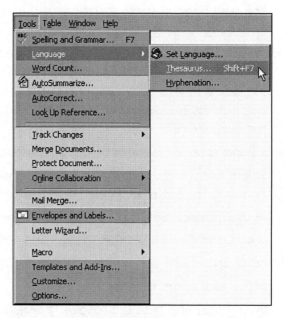

Figure 7.8.   When the perfect word eludes you, use Word's thesaurus to locate it.

 NOTE: By default the thesaurus is automatically installed during a full installation of Office 2000. If **Thesaurus** does not appear after you choose **Tools>Language** from the menu bar, you should install the thesaurus using the Microsoft Office 2000 CD-ROM.

In the **Thesaurus** dialog box (see figure 7.9 below), the word you selected is in the **Looked Up** box. Words will be added to the **Looked Up** list as you use the thesaurus. If you want to return to a word you looked up, you may select it from the box, or choose **Previous** to return to the last word you looked up.

The **Meanings** list contains some possible definitions of the word. Click any word listed to see suggestions of additional words in the **Replace with Synonym** list. If any word in the dialog box puzzles you, select that word and then choose **Look Up**. A whole new set of words appears in the dialog box. In some cases, you may see antonyms listed in the **Replace with Synonym** list. You can also choose to look up additional words that are similar to the antonym.

When you see the word you would like to use, simply select it, and then choose **Replace**.

Use the thesaurus:

1   Select the word or place the insertion point in the word in your document that you want to look up or replace.

2   Choose **Tools>Language>Thesaurus** from the menu bar to open Word's thesaurus. (See Figure 7.9).

 TIP: The keyboard shortcut for the Thesaurus feature is **Shift+F7**.

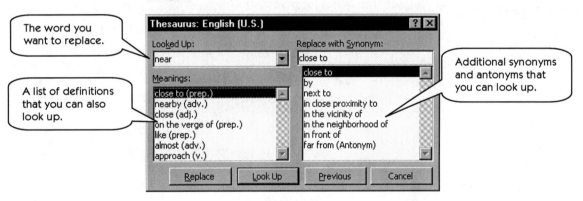

Figure 7.9.   In the **Thesaurus** dialog box, you can select a different word to use or look up antonyms.

3   In the **Meanings** list, select the word or phrase you want to explore. Repeat for each word or phrase that you want to investigate.

The **Replace with Synonym** list will change to display additional words and phrases related to your selection in the **Meanings** list.

• If you find a word or phrase for which you would like to look up additional meanings, select it from either list and choose **Look Up**.

• If you have looked up more than one item, you can return to the last item by choosing **Previous**.

- If you want to return to an earlier item that you looked up, click the **Loo_ked Up** arrow to display a list of where you have been. Select the item you would like to return to.

- If you don't want to use any of the alternatives, choose **Cancel** to close the dialog box and return to your document without making any changes.

4   After you have found the word or phrase you want to use, select it from the **Replace with _Synonym** list and choose **_Replace**. The dialog box closes and your alternative word or phrase replaces the original.

Practice Exercise 7-2

Use the Thesaurus

1   Open 📂**07Ex7-2** from the **WORDCert\Word A** folder. Save it as 💾**07Poem**.

2   Select the word **heartless** in line 2.

3   Choose **_Tools>_Language>_Thesaurus** from the menu bar.

    TIP: The keyboard shortcut for the Thesarus feature is **Shift+F7**.

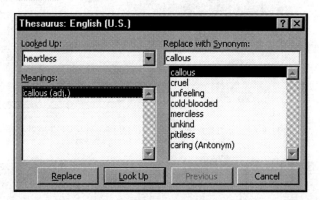

Figure 7.10.   There are several choices you can use to replace **heartles**.

4   Replace the selected word using the **Thesaurus** dialog box:

- Select the word **callous** in the list of synonyms.

- Choose **Look Up** to locate and read the **Meanings** for **callous**.

- Now select **cruel** from the bottom of the **Replace with _Synonym** list. Choose **Look Up** to see what the meanings are and then choose **_Replace**.

5   Save your work and close the document.

Find and Replace

Some users find that scrolling or navigating through text to locate specific words is just plain tedious. It's much easier to type in the text you are trying to find and let Word do the searching. The Find feature can locate parts of words, whole words, phrases, all forms of a word, and other words that sound like the typed one. Word 2000 searches the entire document, up or down from the insertion point. Headers and footers are also included in searches.

The gist of the Find and Replace feature is to establish exactly what you want to find by entering a text string, and further limiting the search with the search options available in the **Find and Replace** dialog box.

The **Find and Replace** dialog box has three tabs available for specifying search parameters: **Fin<u>d</u>**, **Re<u>p</u>lace**, and **<u>G</u>o To** (see Figure 7.11).

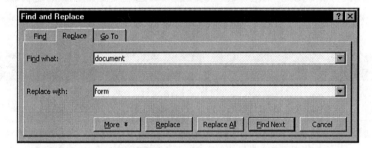

Figure 7.11.   For a more complex search, you can expand the size of the
                Find and Replace dialog box by choosing **<u>M</u>ore**. (See also Figure 7.12.)

Fin<u>d</u> is the tab on which you enter a text string (letters, words, numbers, symbols, or special characters) that tells Word what you are looking for. The **Re<u>p</u>lace** tab has exactly the same options as the **Fin<u>d</u>** tab plus an additional text box to use for a text string to replace the found text string (**Replace w<u>i</u>th**). Enter the text to find and the text to insert in place of the found text string.

<u>G</u>o To, on the other hand, is a simple search device that allows you quickly to jump to a particular place in your document. In this way, the **<u>G</u>o To** feature has similar search capabilities as Find and Replace—the reason the **<u>G</u>o To** tab appears in the **Find and Replace** dialog box.

 TIP: The following shortcut keys display different tabs in the **Find and Replace** dialog box: **Ctrl+F** displays the **Fin<u>d</u>** tab, **Ctrl+H** displays the **Re<u>p</u>lace** tab; and **Ctrl+G** displays the **<u>G</u>o To** tab.

As mentioned above, when conducting Find and Replace searches, you can narrow the search by selecting or excluding options and using the Search Options available after choosing **<u>M</u>ore** (see Figure 7.12).

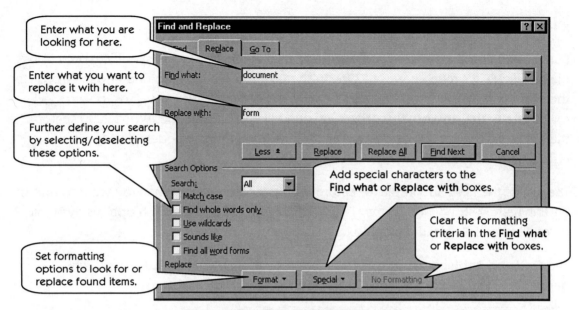

Figure 7.12.   The **Find and Replace** dialog box expands to reveal these additional search
options if you choose **More**.

OPTION	DESCRIPTION
Match case	Finds only words that match the text and letter case(s) of the words typed in the **Find what** box.
Find whole words only	Locates only those words that match the spelling of the word typed in the **Find what** box: nothing more, nothing less will do. For instance, without this option selected, a search to locate **love** will find **love**, but also **clove, foxglove, glove, lovely, lovesick**, and so forth.
Use wildcards	Allows you to use wildcards in place of specific text. A wildcard tells Word to search for any letter, number, or special character found in the position where the wildcard is placed. The most common are the asterisk (*) for any number of characters, and the question mark (?) for any single character. For example, *edding locates **bedding, bobsledding, shredding, wedding**; wed* locates not only **wedding** but **Weddell Sea, wedge, Wedgwood**, and **Wednesday**. However, if you enter **w?d**, Word finds only **wad** and **wed**, the only two words that start with a **w** and end with a **d**.
Sounds like	Locates different spellings of words that sound the same as the text string you typed in the **Find what** box. For example, **for** in the **Find what** box locates **for, fore**, and **four**.
Find all word forms	Results locate any variation of the word typed in the **Find what** box. For example, **house** results in **housed, houses**, and **housing**.

You can further limit the search by selecting from the list of options available through the **Format** button. You can also apply these formatting options to replacement text by selecting among the **Format** button options with the cursor inside the **Replace with** box.

The **Find** tab and the **Replace** tab both have a **Special** button. This button displays a list of non-printing characters, wildcards, and punctuation marks, that can be searched for and replaced.

Find and replace text strings:

1   Position the insertion point anywhere in the document. It's always a good idea to start at the top.

2   Complete one of the following steps to display the **Find and Replace** dialog box:

   •   Choose **Edit>Find** from the menu bar to set up search parameters that will locate text strings.

   •   Choose **Edit>Replace** to access options for locating *and* replacing text strings.

3   In the **Find what** box, type in the text you want to find. To replace found text, type replacement text in the **Replace with** box.

4   Choose **More**, if necessary, to select any additional **Search Options**. To further limit the search, choose **Format** and/or **Special**.

5   Choose **Find Next** to begin your search.

6   When the text string is found, complete one of the following steps:

   •   Choose **Find Next** to skip to the next occurrence of the **Find what** text string.

   •   Choose **Replace** to replace the found text with the **Replace with** text string.

   •   If you're positive you want all occurrences of the text string replaced with the **Replace with** text string, you can save time by choosing **Replace All**.

As you continue working with Find and Replace and your skills develop, you'll find that you can search for and replace things you hardly imagined—such as replacing a paragraph marker with a space, or converting some instances of a particular font to a different one. The more you use Find and Replace, the more uses you'll find for it.

Practice Exercise 7-3

Find and Replace

1   Open 📁**07Ex7-3** from the **WORDCert\Word A** folder. Save it as 💾**07Glove**.

2   Choose **Edit>Replace** from the menu bar to display the **Find and Replace** dialog box.

   NOTE: The keyboard shortcut for the **Replace** command is **Ctrl+H**.

3   In the **Find what** box, type: | love |.

4   Choose **Find Next**, and observe that the word, **gloves**, in the first line is partially selected. Continue choosing **Find Next**, and observe all the words found in the search.

The Office Assistant displays a message when you reach the end of the document.

5   With the **Find and Replace** dialog box still open, conduct another search with more specific search criteria:

- Choose **More**.

- Select the **Find whole words only** check box.

- In the Replace with box, type: | like |.

- Choose **Find Next**.

- Choose **Replace All** to replace all occurrences of **love** with **like**.

The Office Assistant displays a message telling you that Word found two places to replace **love** with **like**.

- Choose **Cancel** on the **Find and Replace** dialog box to return to the document.

- Review your document:

- Observe the name of the first glove model—**Like Handles**?!?

- Choose **Edit>Undo Replace All** from the menu bar to return your document to the state it was in before step 5.

6   Conduct another search with additional search criteria:

- Move to the top of the document.

- Choose **Edit>Replace** to redisplay the **Find and Replace** dialog box.

- Select the **Match case** check box. Verify that the **Find whole words only** check box is still selected.
- Choose **Replace All**.

Word made only one replacement.

- Choose **Cancel** on the **Find and Replace** dialog box to return to the document.

7 Save your work and close the document.

A completed example of **07Glove** is available in the **WORDCert\Word A\Samples** folder.

Page Breaks

You've already learned that, as you type, text wraps from line to line until you press the **Enter** key to create a paragraph break. If you continue typing, though, sooner or later you're going to fill up a page with text—and what happens then? Just as text automatically wraps, pages automatically "break."

We refer to automatic page breaks as **soft page breaks**. This term helps distinguish between an automatic page break and one you intentionally insert, called a **hard page break**.

The placement of a soft page break is always affected by any change in font style and size, and by the page and paragraph margins. Hard page breaks, on the other hand, always remain at the same point in the text (but not necessarily on the page), no matter what formatting revisions you make.

INSERT A HARD PAGE BREAK

The logic of hard page breaks is evident. If you feel you must have certain information on a particular page, you'll probably insert a hard page break to ensure that no other data appears on the page. A hard page break is actually a non-printing code that tells Word where to start a new page.

Insert a hard page break:

1 Position the insertion point at the end of the line, where you want to insert the page break.

2 Choose **Insert>Break** from the menu bar.

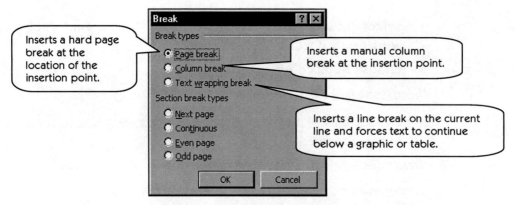

Figure 7.13. There are four kinds of breaks available in this
dialog box: page, column, text wrapping, and section.

3   Select **Page break**, if necessary (see Figure 7.13).

4   Choose **OK**.

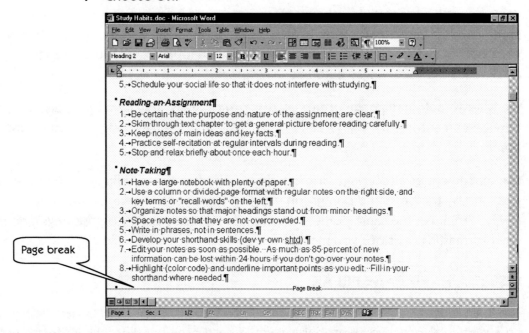

Figure 7.14. The type of break you insert is indicated on-screen in your document.

With non-printing characters displayed, your page break is a dotted line spanning the
screen whether you are looking at the document in Normal, Web Layout, or Outline
view, as you can see in Figure 7.14). In Print Layout View you actually see the pages.

DELETE A HARD PAGE BREAK

Removing a hard page break is as simple as deleting a word. Select the page break
marker by clicking in the selection bar and then pressing the **Delete** key. If the page
break is not visible, first click the **Show/Hide ¶** button on the Standard toolbar to
select it.

Practice Exercise 7-4

Work with Page Breaks

1 Open 📂**07Ex7-4** from the **WORDCert\Word A** folder. Save it as 💾**07Break**.

2 Insert a page break:

- Scroll down in the document until you locate the heading, **Memory and Concentration**. Position the insertion point before the word **Memory**.

- Choose **Insert>Break** from the menu bar to display the **Break** dialog box.

- Select **Page break**, if necessary, choose **OK**.

3 Delete a page break:

- Continue to scroll down in the document; notice how little information is on page 2.

- Position the insertion point at the beginning of the page break on page 2.

- Press **Delete** to remove the page break.

4 Save your work and close the document.

A completed example of **07Break** is available in the **WORDCert\Word A\Samples** folder.

Print a Document

Although some documents you create will be directed toward on-screen viewing (e.g., Internet, intranet), you will want to print most of the documents you develop in Word.

Whether you send your document out to a professional printing house or a service bureau or use your desktop printer, you'll definitely want to see how the document looks before you spend ink and paper on the final output.

 NOTE: Each kind of printer affects the appearance of your document, so it's important to have the correct printer selected as the default printer when you preview your document.

PRINT PREVIEW

After you've completed your document (and run Spelling and Grammar), you are ready to print the document. You'll probably find that it's necessary to make several prints of most documents: at least one for proofreading, and others to verify corrections you've made to each set of proofs.

TIP: To save trees and cut the cost of paper, you may wish to run your first test print on the back of a piece of paper you've already printed on—unless, of course, this would damage your printer.

Before expending any resources, however, you can get a pretty good idea of how your document will print just by looking at it in Print Preview. The Print Preview window differs from the document window in many respects. The most noticeable feature of Print Preview is its ability to give an overview of a full page or of multiple pages (up to six) of the document. This feature is useful for checking page breaks and the general layout and design elements of the document. Print Preview has a unique toolbar (see Figure 7.15) and, as you view your document in it, all other toolbars are hidden.

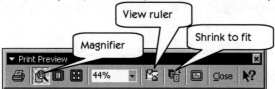

Figure 7.15.   The Print Preview toolbar offers selections appropriate to tasks you may need to perform before printing a document

TOOLBAR BUTTON	NAME	DESCRIPTION
	Print (default printer)	Prints the document immediately. The name of the default printer appears in the button's ScreenTip. To select a different printer, see the next section.
	Magnifier	Increases the size of the page you are viewing and lets you edit text in Print Preview. Move the pointer onto the document (the pointer should look like a magnifying glass) and click the area you want to enlarge; click again to return the view to its original settings. Deselect the **Magnifier** button to enter Edit mode, where you can adjust margins and edit text.
	One Page	Displays one full page of your document onscreen. This is the default view in Print Preview.
	Multiple Pages	Specify the number of pages you want to view onscreen using the drop-down palette.
19%	**Zoom**	As with the **Zoom** button on the Standard toolbar (see Lesson 2), this button allows you to increase/decrease the percentage of the document visible on the screen.
	View Ruler	Displays/hides the horizontal and vertical rulers—similar to Print Layout view. You may adjust page margins when this button is selected (see Lesson 2).
	Shrink to Fit	Adjusts font sizes and other document elements to make all your text fit neatly on the pages with no stragglers (known as widows) left on the last page.

TOOLBAR BUTTON	NAME	DESCRIPTION
	Full Screen	Hides most screen elements so you have room to view your document. To return to the Print Preview window, click **Close Full Screen** or press **Esc**.
Close	**Close Preview**	Allows you to exit Print Preview. If you are in Full Screen mode, clicking this button hides the taskbar and the Print Preview toolbar.
▲?	**Context Sensitive Help**	Accesses the What's This? Help feature. See **Appendix A**: **Finding Help** for more information.

Use Print Preview before printing:

1   Choose **File>Print Preview** from the menu bar to switch to Print Preview.

2   Use the Print Preview toolbar buttons to view and/or edit your document.

3   Click **Close** on the Print Preview toolbar to exit Print Preview.

PRINT OPTIONS

Although some of your documents may be intended for on-screen viewing, it's reasonable to expect that the majority of them will be printed. Once you know how to spell check, grammar check, and use Print Preview, you will be ready for this final step.

There are two basic ways to print. First, you can send the document directly to the printer using the **Print** button on the Standard toolbar—or on the Print Preview toolbar, if you prefer. The second way is to print via the **Print** dialog box, where you can set print options each time you initiate the **Print** command. It is helpful to know how much of the document you want to print (**Page range**) and the **Number of copies** you need.

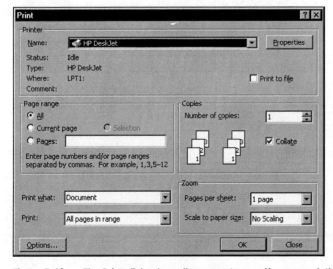

Figure 7.16.   The **Print** dialog box allows you to specify many printing parameters.

OPTION	DESCRIPTION
PRINTER	
<u>N</u>ame	Displays the default printer. Click the arrow to display a list of available printers.
Properties	Allows you to change the attributes associated with the selected printer, including paper and print quality. A Restore Defaults button allows you to reset the printer defaults quickly.
Print to fi<u>l</u>e check box	Prints the document to a file on disk so you can move the file to another computer or send it to a service bureau.
PAGE RANGE	
<u>A</u>ll	Prints all the pages of the document. (This is the default setting.)
Curr<u>e</u>nt page	Prints only the page on which the insertion point is located.
Pa<u>g</u>es	Prints only the pages you enter in the box. You can enter multiple individual pages or page ranges.
<u>S</u>election	Select text in the document, and then choose this option to print the selected text only.
COPIES	
Number of <u>c</u>opies	Type or select the number of copies you want to print.
Colla<u>t</u>e check box	Prints copies in order. For example, if you want two copies of a six-page document, the first copy of pages 1 to 6 will print and then the second copy will follow. (This is the default setting.)
ZOOM	
Pages per s<u>h</u>eet	Shrinks the text to fit more than one page on a sheet of paper, to make booklets, for example.
Scale to paper si<u>z</u>e	Select this option to reduce or enlarge the document to fit on a specific paper size, similar to what you can do with a photocopy machine.
OTHER OPTIONS	
Print <u>w</u>hat	Print just the part of the document you specify.
P<u>r</u>int	Click the arrow to print only Odd pages or Even pages. (All pages in range is the default setting.)
Options...	Customizes printing options.

Define printing options and print a document:

1 Choose **File>Print** from the menu bar to display the **Print** dialog box.

> **TIP:** The keyboard shortcut for the **Print** command is **Ctrl+P**. To display the **Print** dialog box, do not use the **Print** button on the Standard toolbar. Doing so will print the document immediately; it does not display the dialog box.

2 Make desired changes to the settings in the **Print** dialog box.

3 Choose **OK** to print the document or **Cancel** to return to your document without printing.

Practice Exercise 7-5

Preview and Print a Document

1 Use the file **07Break** you created in the previous exercise or open 📂**07Ex7-5** from the **WORDCert\Word A** folder. Save it as 💾**07Print**.

2 Choose **File>Print Preview** from the menu bar to see how the document will look when printed.

3 Click the **Multiple Pages** button on the Print Preview toolbar. Select **2 x 2 Pages** from the drop-down palette.

There are three pages; the last page has only a small amount of text on it.

4 Click the **Shrink to Fit** button.

5 Choose **File>Print** to display the **Print** dialog box.

> **TIP:** The keyboard shortcut for the **Print** command is **Ctrl+P**.

6 Verify that the correct printer appears in the **Name** box. (Select the printer you want to use, if necessary.)

7 In the **Pages per sheet** box, select **2 pages**.

8 Choose **OK**.

9 Save your work and close the document.

LESSON 1: WORK WITH TABLES

You may already be familiar with the basics of tables in Word from what you learned in **Section A**, but there is so much more to know! In this lesson, you'll become a table master, learning the following skills:

> ➤ Creating a new table

> ➤ Formatting a table, either manually or automatically

> ➤ Adding borders and shading to a table

> ➤ Merging and splitting table cells

> ➤ Changing the way that text flows in a cell

> ➤ Sorting table contents

> ➤ Using math formulas and functions in tables

> ➤ Setting number formatting

> ➤ Inserting an Excel worksheet into a document

You'll have the chance to practice creating, editing, and formatting tables in the exercises in this chapter.

Item	Color	Number	Price	Quantity in Stock
Wool Sweater	Green	234985G	$39.99	1
	Blue	234985B	$39.99	0
	Red	234985R	$39.99	10
Wool gloves	Black	23940932	$12.50	2
			Item Count	4
			Quantity Total	11

Shaded cells — *Information centered in column* — *Merged cells* — *Formulas that calculate values*

Figure 1.1. This table showcases some of the table formatting and setup skills you will learn in this lesson.

Create Tables: A Review

A table is a great tool for precisely aligning several columns of information. (Figure 1.1 shows an example.) There are several ways you can create a table in Word. You can place a new, blank table in your document, you can draw a table, or you can convert existing text (in tabbed columns) into a table.

CREATE A NEW TABLE

 The most basic way to create a table is with the **Insert Table** button on the Standard toolbar. Click it to open a drop-down grid; move the mouse across it to choose the number of rows and columns you want; and then click, as shown in Figure 1.2.

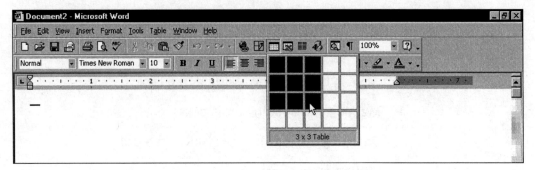

Figure 1.2.   The **Insert Table** button provides an easy way to create a standard table.

If you want a table with special options, such as a specific column width, either create a table as shown above and then format it, or create it using the **T**a**ble>I**nsert>**T**able command instead. The following steps show how.

Create a table:

1   Choose **T**a**ble>I**nsert>**T**able. The **Insert Table** dialog box opens. (See Figure 1.3.)

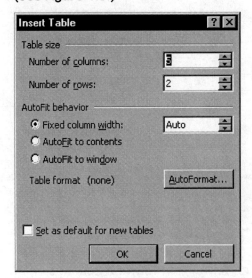

Figure 1.3.   Specify the type of table you want in the **Insert Table** dialog box.

2   Enter the number of columns and rows you want.

3 Select an **AutoFit** option:

   Fixed column width: Lets you specify a precise width for each column, or choose **Auto** to space the columns evenly over the entire available page width.

   AutoFit to contents: Automatically widens or narrows each column to fit the contents you enter.

   AutoFit to window: Sizes the table so that it fits the window size exactly.

4 (Optional) If you want to AutoFormat the table, choose the **AutoFormat** button. Choose an AutoFormat, and then choose **OK**.

5 Choose **OK**. The table appears in your document.

 NOTE: You learned about AutoFormatting in **Section A**.

After creating a table, you can enter text into it, change its column widths or its overall width, add rows, format it, and do more. You will learn how to do all of these things later in this lesson.

 NOTE: You can also create a table by drawing one or by converting text into a table. You learned how to do both of these things in **Section A**. You'll review these skills in the following topics.

Practice Exercise 1-1

Create Tables

1 Start a new document and save it as 🖫**01Tabl1**.

2 Choose the **Insert Table** button on the Standard toolbar. A grid opens.

3 Move the mouse across the grid to select three across and three down, and then click the mouse button.

4 Click below the table, and press **Enter** a few times.

5 Choose **Table>Insert>Table**. The **Insert Table** dialog box opens.

6 Enter **5** in the **Number of columns** box.

7 Enter **4** in the **Number of rows** box.

8 Choose **AutoFit to contents**.

9 Choose **OK**.

10 Save your work; leave the document open for the next exercise.

A completed example of **01Tabl1** is available in the
WORDCert\Word B\Samples folder on the DDC CD-ROM.

Draw a Table

If you need a table with columns of various sizes or with a different number of columns from one row to another, you might find it easier to draw the table rather than creating a generic one and modifying it. In **Section A**, you learned how to draw a table; let's quickly review that now.

Draw a table:

1   Choose **Table>Draw Table,** or choose the **Tables and Borders** button on the Standard toolbar. The Tables and Borders toolbar appears, and the mouse pointer turns into a pencil.

2   Drag on the workspace to draw a box that will form the outside of the table.

3   Drag lines in the box to create the table rows and columns. (See Figure 1.4.)

Figure 1.4.   Draw a table line by line.

TIP: When you draw a table, you don't have to have the same number of rows in each column, or vice versa.

4   If you want to delete a drawn line on the table, click the **Eraser** button on the Tables and Borders toolbar and then click on the line you want to remove.

5   Choose the **Draw Table** button on the Tables and Borders toolbar, turning off table-drawing mode.

Practice Exercise 1-2

Draw a Table

1   Start in **01Tabl1** from the preceding exercise, or open ⌷**01Ex1-2** from the **WORDCert\Word B** folder.

2   Save the file as ⌷**01Tabl2**.

3   Add a few blank lines at the bottom of the document.

4 Choose **Table>Draw Table**.

5 Draw a box to form the outside of your table.

6 Draw three vertical lines and two horizontal ones, creating three rows and four columns. Figure 1.5 shows a sample; yours may look somewhat different, depending on the row heights and column widths you drew.

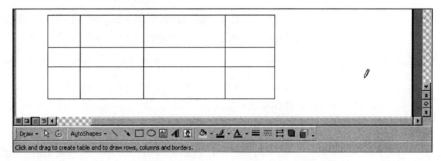

Figure 1.5.   Cells in a drawn table do not have to be a uniform size.

  7 Choose the **Eraser** button on the Tables and Borders toolbar.

8 Click on several of the lines in the table, removing them. Figure 1.6 shows an example.

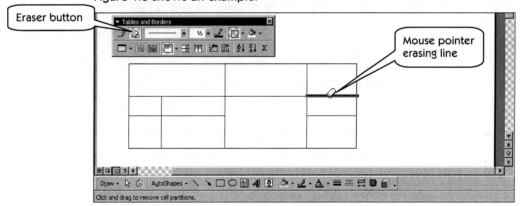

Figure 1.6.   You can erase individual lines with the **Eraser** tool.

  9 Choose the **Eraser** button again, or press **Esc**, to turn off the eraser.

10 Save your work; leave the document open for the next exercise.

Enter and Edit Data in a Table

To enter data in a table, use the following procedure.

Enter text in a table:

1   Click in the cell in which you want the text to appear, to move
    the insertion point into that cell.

2   Type the text you want, just as you would type any ordinary text.

3   Move to the next cell in which to type by doing any of the
    following:

    • Click in the desired cell.

    • Press the **Tab** key to move to the next cell (that is, the cell to
      the right, or to the next row if you are in the rightmost
      column).

    • Press **Shift+Tab** to move to the previous cell.

4   To start a new row in the table, place the insertion point in the
    last cell of the last row and press **Tab**.

 NOTE: If your table is created with the **AutoFit to contents** option,
each column expands as you add text in it.

Edit text in a table:

1   Click in the cell where you want to edit.

2   Press the **Backspace** or **Delete** key to delete characters to the left
    or right of the insertion point, respectively.

    OR

    Double-click to select entire words, and then type over them to
    replace the text.

    OR

    Triple-click to select the cell's entire contents, and then
    type over it.

3   Type new text as needed.

Practice Exercise 1-3

Entering and Editing Data

1   Start in the **01Tabl2** document from the previous exercise, or
    open 🗁**01Ex1-3** from the **WORDCert\Word B** folder.

2   Save the document as 🖫**01Tabl3**.

3 Click in the first cell (top left) of the first table, and type Chemistry . Then press **Tab**. Type Math , and press **Tab** again.

4 Continue typing the names shown in Figure 1.7, pressing **Tab** to move from cell to cell in the table.

Chemistry	Math	Biology
Sociology	English	Physics
Computer Science	Physical Education	Music

Figure 1.7.   Enter these words into the cells of the first table.

5 Click in the first cell of the second table, and type **First Name**. Notice that the column expands to hold your typing.

6 Type the text shown in Figure 1.8 into the second table, pressing **Tab** to move from one cell to another.

7 When you reach the last cell of the last row, press **Tab** to create an extra row.

First Name	Last Name	Grade 1	Grade 2	Grade 3
Tom	Smith	A	B	B
Nancy	Phillips	B	B	A-
Cindy	Kelly	C	C	C
Loren	Colvin	C	A	B

Figure 1.8.   Type this text into the cells of the second table.

8 Click in the last cell of the second table (Figure 1.8), and press **Shift+Tab** three times, moving the insertion point to the cell that contains **Colvin**.

9 Press **Backspace** and delete **Colvin**. Then type Coleman .

10 Type the text shown in Figure 1.9 into the third table:

 NOTE: If you are using the table you created in Practice Exercise 1-2, it may look slightly different than the one below.

Inspiration		Joy	Happiness
Kindness	Compassion	Euphoria	
Excitement	Peace		Comfort

Figure 1.9.   Type this text into the third table.

11 Double-click on **Excitement**; type **Bliss**, replacing **Excitement**.

NOTE: Notice that the cells of the third table resize themselves automatically as the longest value in the column changes. For example, in step 11, when you replace **Excitement** with **Bliss**, the column may narrow.

12 Save your work; leave the document open for the next exercise.

A completed example of **01Tabl3** is available in the **WORDCert\Word B\Samples** folder on the DDC CD-ROM.

Change Column Widths and Row Heights

You can resize columns and rows manually or automatically based on either a fixed width or the contents.

RESIZE ROWS AND COLUMNS MANUALLY

To resize one row or column, use this procedure.

Resize a row or column:

1 Position the mouse pointer on the border below the row, or to the right of the column, to be resized. The mouse pointer becomes a double-headed arrow.

2 Drag the border to a new position. (See Figure 1.10.)

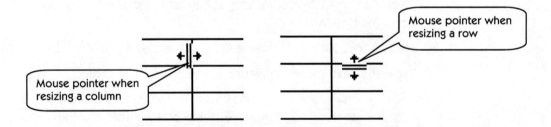

Figure 1.10. Resize a row or column by dragging its border.

CAUTION: When you resize a column manually, you turn off its ability to AutoFit to the contents. You must turn **AutoFit to contents** back on for the table, as described in the following section, if you want to return to using AutoFit.

TIP: You can double-click a column divider to AutoFit the column to the text.

CHANGE A TABLE'S AUTOFIT SETTING

As you have seen, when you create a table with the AutoFit option, each column expands and contracts based on the longest line of text in one of its cells.

You can change a table's AutoFit setting at any time, as shown in the following steps.

Change a table's AutoFit setting:

1   Select the table.

 NOTE: To select the table, click its selection button, as shown in Figure 1.11.

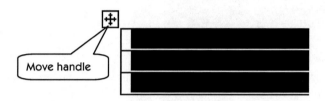

Move handle

Figure 1.11.   Select the entire table by clicking its move handle, which is located in its the upper-left corner.

2   Choose **Table>AutoFit**. A list of AutoFit settings appears.

3   Choose one of the following settings:

- **AutoFit to contents:** Resizes each column depending on the data entered in it.

- **AutoFit to window:** Resizes the table so you can see the whole table on-screen, regardless of the size of the Word window.

- **Fixed column width:** Turns off AutoFit so that the column widths do not vary with either the contents or the window area.

 NOTE: You will learn about the last two commands on the submenu, both of which deal with distribution, in the following topic.

 TIP: The bottom left button on the Tables and Borders toolbar can be any of a variety of buttons. Open its drop-down list to choose the button that you want it to show. All three of the **AutoFit** commands are available from there, for example. (See Figure 1.12.)

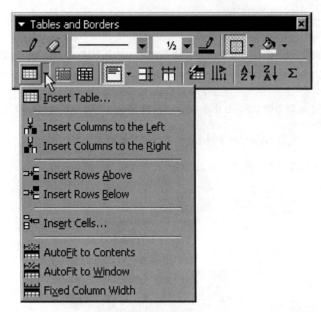

Figure 1.12. Select which command will be the button in the bottom left position of the Tables and Borders toolbar.

DISTRIBUTE TABLE CELLS EVENLY

When you first create a table, all the rows and columns are the same size (unless you have drawn the table), so you usually do not need to use the **Distribute** commands on a blank table. But as you work with a table, you might make manual or automatic adjustments to the rows and columns, making them different sizes. If you later decide you want to reset them so that they are all the same height and width again, use the following procedures.

Distribute column widths evenly:

1   Choose **Table>AutoFit>Distribute Columns Evenly**.

Distribute row heights evenly:

1   Choose **Table>AutoFit>Distribute Rows Evenly**.

 TIP: There are buttons on the Tables and Borders toolbar that provide shortcuts to these **Distribute** commands.

Practice Exercise 1-4

Resize Rows and Columns

1   Start in the **01Tabl3** document from the last exercise, or open 📁**01Ex1-4** from the **WORDCert\Word B** folder.

2   Save the file as 💾**01Tabl4**.

3 Select the first table, and choose **Table>AutoFit>AutoFit to contents**.

 NOTE: You will be working exclusively with the first table in the file for this exercise.

4 Choose **Table>AutoFit>Fixed column width**, setting it back to **non-AutoFit** usage.

 NOTE: Notice that the column widths do not change back to the original size; the AutoFit feature is merely turned off.

5 Drag the border between the second and third columns to the left, so that **Education** does not fit on the first line.

 NOTE: Notice that the bottom row grows in height to accommodate a second line.

 6 Choose **Table>AutoFit>Distribute Rows Evenly**, so that all of the rows in the table are the same height as the bottom (the largest) one.

7 Drag the right border of the table to the 6" mark on the ruler.

 8 Choose **Table>AutoFit>Distribute Columns Evenly**, so that all the columns are the same width again.

9 Save your work; leave the document open for the next exercise.

A completed example of **01Tabl4** is available in the **WORDCert\Word B\Samples** folder on the DDC CD-ROM.

Add and Remove Rows, Columns, and Cells

In this section, you will learn how to alter a table radically by changing the number of rows and columns it contains. You can do so by inserting and deleting, or by merging or splitting, existing cells.

INSERT AND DELETE ROWS AND COLUMNS

You have already seen how to add another row to the bottom of a table: Just position the insertion point in the bottom right cell and press **Tab**.

You can also add a new row anywhere you want with the following procedure.

Add a table row:

1   Select a row (or more than one; see the tip below step 2) above
    or below which the new row(s) should appear.

    OR

    Move the insertion point into a row.

2   Choose **Table>Insert>Rows Above** to insert new rows above the
    selected row(s).

    OR

    Choose **Table>Insert>Rows Below** to insert new rows below the
    selected row(s). (See Figure 1.13.)

TIPs: To insert more than one row at once, select more than one first.

The Standard toolbar has an **Insert Rows** button that is a shortcut for
Table>Insert>Rows Above.

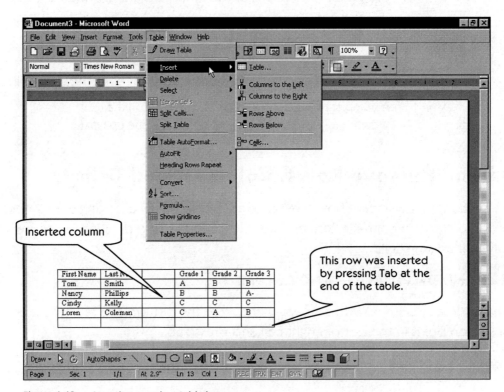

Figure 1.13.   Inserting rows in a table is easy.

Columns work the same way. To add a column, use the following procedure.

Add a table column:

1 Select one or more columns, or move the insertion point into a column.

2 Choose **T<u>a</u>ble>I<u>n</u>sert>Columns to the <u>L</u>eft** to insert columns to the left of the selected column(s).

OR

Choose **T<u>a</u>ble>I<u>n</u>sert>Columns to the <u>R</u>ight** to insert columns to the right of the selected column(s).

 TIP: The **Insert Columns** button on the Standard toolbar is a shortcut for inserting columns to the right.

To delete one or more rows or columns, use the following procedure.

Delete a row or column:

1 Select the row(s) or column(s) you want to delete.

2 Choose **T<u>a</u>ble><u>D</u>elete>Rows** to delete the selected row(s).

OR

Choose **T<u>a</u>ble><u>D</u>elete>Columns** to delete the selected column(s).

 TIP: You can also use the **Cut** button on the Standard toolbar to remove rows; if you don't paste them later with the **Paste** button, it's the same as deleting them. However, you cannot use the keyboard **Delete** key to delete rows or columns; pressing this key merely clears their contents, because it is a shortcut for the **<u>E</u>dit><u>C</u>lear** command.

INSERT AND DELETE CELLS

You can insert or delete individual cells anywhere in your table. For example, you may want to make room for individual values that you forgot to include in a tabular list.

Insert cells:

1 Select the cell(s) where you want to insert.

 TIP: If you select more than one cell in step 1, the procedure will insert the same number of new cells.

2 Choose **T<u>a</u>ble>I<u>n</u>sert>C<u>e</u>lls**. The **Insert Cells** dialog box appears. (See Figure 1.14.)

3 Select the way you want the old cells to move to make room: **Shift Cells <u>R</u>ight** or **Shift cells <u>d</u>own**.

4 Choose **OK**.

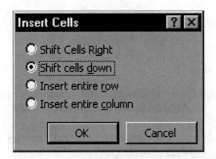

Figure 1.14.   Choose how you want the remaining
cells to behave when the chosen cell is removed.

If you shift cells down when inserting new cells, Word inserts an entire new row.
However, if you shift cells right, Word adds only a single cell and pushes all other cells
in that row to the right. In both cases the data shifts to make room for only the
individual cell you are adding; the remainder of the blank row or column appears at
the bottom or right, respectively, of the table. Figure 1.15 shows a table with a cell
added in the middle and existing data shifted down.

First Name	Last Name	Grade 1	Grade 2	Grade 3
Tom	Smith	A	B	B
Nancy	Phillips		B	A-
Cindy	Kelly	B	C	C
Loren	Coleman	C	A	B
	New cell	C		

> This row was added so
> the last cell in the
> column would not be in
> a row by itself.

Figure 1.15.   A new cell has forced the values in the third column to shift down.

MERGE AND SPLIT CELLS

Merging cells refers to combining two or more cells by removing the divider line(s)
between them so they form one big cell. This can be especially useful when you are
trying to center a heading over several cells; if you merge all the cells in the row into
one big cell and then set the text in it for Center alignment, the heading will be
perfectly centered. Similarly, *splitting cells* refers to inserting a divider line in a cell,
creating two separate cells.

There are several ways to merge and split cells in a Word table.
One way is to draw or erase divider lines using the **Draw Table** and
Eraser buttons on the Tables and Borders toolbar. This method is
extremely flexible; you can place or remove dividers anywhere you
like.

NOTE: When you use the Eraser tool to erase a line between
two cells containing data, the content merges unless the cells are
unequal in height or width. If you merge cells with different
heights or widths, they continue to be separate cells, but the
divider between them no longer shows.

Merge and split with the Table drawing tools:

1 Display the Tables and Borders toolbar if it doesn't already appear.

 TIP: You can choose the **Tables and Borders** button on the Standard toolbar to show or hide this toolbar.

2 To merge two cells, choose the **Eraser** button and then click on the line to erase.

3 To split a cell, choose the **Draw Table** button and then draw where you want to place a divider.

4 When you are finished, press **Esc** to exit table-drawing mode.

 Another way is to select the cell(s) to affect and then choose **Table>Merge Cells** or **Table>Split Cells**. When you are merging cells, the action takes place immediately. When you opt to split a cell, a **Split Cells** dialog box opens (see Figure 1.16) to help you specify whether you want a vertical or horizontal split and the number of pieces you want it split into. There are shortcut buttons for both the merging and splitting commands on the Tables and Borders toolbar.

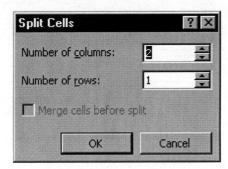

Figure 1.16. Specify how you want the cell(s) to be split.

Merge cells with the Table menu:

1 Select two or more cells to merge.

2 Choose **Table>Merge Cells**.

Split cells with the Table menu:

1 Select the cell(s) to split.

2 Choose **Table>Split Cells**.

3 Enter the number of columns and/or rows into which you want to split.

4 Choose **OK**.

Practice Exercise 1-5

Change the Number of Rows, Columns, and Cells in a Table

1   Start in the file **01Tabl4** from the last exercise, or open
    📁**01Ex1-5** from the **WORDCert\Word B** folder.

2   Save the file as 💾**01Tabl5**.

3   Add a row and a column to the second table by doing the
    following:

*   Select the last cell in the second table, and press **Tab**, adding
    a new row.

*   Add a new student in that row: **Tim Bradley**,
    with grades of **D**, **B**, and **C**.

*   Select the third column.

*   Choose **Table>Insert>Columns to the Left**, adding a column.

*   Add the heading **Level** to the new column, and enter **1** in
    each row, so that each student is in level 1.

The results appear in Figure 1.17.

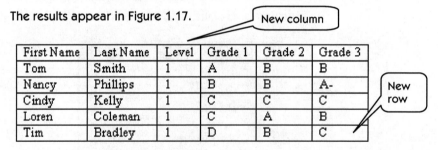

First Name	Last Name	Level	Grade 1	Grade 2	Grade 3
Tom	Smith	1	A	B	B
Nancy	Phillips	1	B	B	A-
Cindy	Kelly	1	C	C	C
Loren	Coleman	1	C	A	B
Tim	Bradley	1	D	B	C

Figure 1.17.   The second table in **01Tabl5**, with a new row and a new column added.

4   Display the Tables and Borders toolbar if it does not appear.

5   Make sure the **Draw Table** button is selected (so that it looks
    "pressed"). If it is not, click it. Then draw a vertical line splitting
    the **Joy** cell in half in the third table. (See Figure 1.18.)

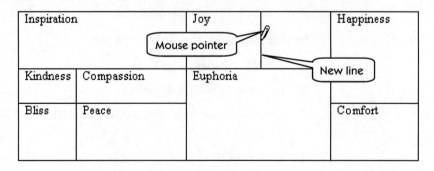

Figure 1.18.   Split the **Joy** cell by drawing a line in it.

6 Choose the **Eraser** button on the Tables and Borders toolbar, and click the divider between **Joy** and **Euphoria**, erasing it.

> **NOTE:** Notice that because the cells were unequal widths in step 5, they maintain their separateness. The divider line merely disappears between them.

7 Click the **Eraser** button again, turning off the Eraser feature.

8 Select the same two cells (**Joy** and **Euphoria**) as well as the new, empty cell.

9 Choose **Table>Merge Cells**. The selected cells are combined into a single cell, with the two words separated by a paragraph break. (See Figure 1.19.)

Inspiration		Joy Euphoria	Happiness
Kindness	Compassion		
Bliss	Peace		Comfort

Figure 1.19.   The **Joy** and **Euphoria** cells have been merged.

10 Save your work; leave the document open for the next exercise.

A completed example of **01Tabl5** is available in the **WORDCert\Word B\Samples** folder on the DDC CD-ROM.

Format a Table

You can format the text in a table in much the same way you format any other text. For example, you can apply all kinds of character formatting, such as changing the font, size, and attributes. You can also apply paragraph formatting, such as adjusting text alignment and revising spacing settings, to each cell. (Each cell is considered an individual "paragraph." If you have more than one paragraph in a cell, each paragraph in it can be formatted separately too.)

FORMAT A TABLE AUTOMATICALLY WITH AUTOFORMAT

In **Section A**, you learned about table autoformatting. It provides an easy way to apply borders, shading, fonts, and other formatting to a table based on any of several preset schemes. Beginners find it very helpful, but advanced users often find that their own manual formatting pleases them more. You will learn about adding your own borders, shading, and gridline settings later in this lesson.

Apply table AutoFormatting:

1   Select the table.

2   Choose **Table>Table AutoFormat**, or choose the **Table AutoFormat** button on the Tables and Borders toolbar.

3   Select the AutoFormat that you want to use. (See Figure 1.20.)

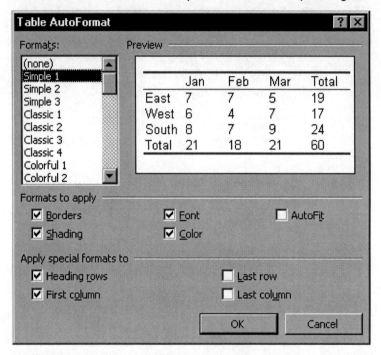

Figure 1.20.   Choose an AutoFormat for your table.

NOTE: If you want to exclude any properties of the chosen scheme, deselect the appropriate checkboxes in the **Formats to apply** section of the dialog box shown in Figure 1.20.

4   If your table has labels or headings in the first or last row or column, make sure that the appropriate checkbox is marked in the **Apply special formats to** section.

NOTE: For example, in step 4, if your first row contained column labels and your last row contained totals of each column of numbers, you would mark the **Heading rows** and the **Last row** checkboxes.

5   Choose **OK**. The AutoFormat is applied.

If later you want to remove the AutoFormat, repeat this procedure but choose **(none)** from the list of AutoFormats.

CAUTION: AutoFormatting often does not work very well for tables with unusual layouts, such as the third table in the **01Tabl05** example you have been working with. That's because Word cannot figure out which is the first or last row or column that should be treated in a different way.

REPEAT TABLE HEADINGS ON EACH PAGE

If you have a large table that prints on more than one page, you may want to repeat your headings on each page of the printout. That way, people reading later pages will not be confused about what each column represents.

Set heading row(s) to repeat:

1 Select the row(s) that contain(s) the headings.

2 Choose **Table>Heading Rows Repeat.**

To turn the feature off, repeat the steps to toggle the command off again.

ADD BORDERS

By default, each table that you create has a plain, black, 1/2-point border around each cell. As a result, you can easily see the table's borders on-screen. These borders also prints on your printouts.

 NOTE: A "point" is a typesetting measurement. One point equals 1/72 of an inch.

You can change the border for any side of an individual cell or change the table (or a group of selected cells) as a whole. You can make the border thicker, give it a different color or line style, or even remove it altogether.

The Tables and Borders toolbar provides a series of buttons that can help you change the borders for a cell (or group of cells). Table 1.1 contains these buttons and the procedures for using them.

Table 1.1: Tables and Borders Toolbar Controls for Borders

Button	Description
	Select a line style (dotted, dashed, double, etc.) from this drop-down list.
½	Select a line thickness, from 1/4 point to 6 points, from this drop-down list.
	Choose a color for the border from the pop-up palette of colors.
	Select which side(s) of the selected cell(s) will be affected. Or, to remove the border, choose the No Border button.

Change a cell's border with the toolbar:

1 Select the cell(s) to be affected.

2 Use the controls shown in Table 1.1 to select a border style, thickness, and color.

3 Open the **Border** palette; choose which side(s) of the selected cell(s) should be affected. (See Figure 1.21.)

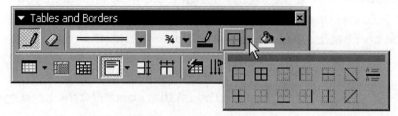

Figure 1.21.   You can choose a single side of the selected area to affect, or you can choose an outside border or all borders.

4 If you chose a single side in step 3, repeat step 3 to choose other sides if needed.

NOTE: After you choose a specific border style, weight, and color, Word uses those same selections to other borders you apply from the **Borders** button on the toolbar.

You can also change the borders for a cell or group of cells with the **Borders and Shading** dialog box, as outlined in the following steps. This method gives you more precise control but takes a little longer to accomplish than the toolbar method.

Change borders with a dialog box:

1 Select the cell(s) to be affected.

2 Choose **Format>Borders and Shading**.

3 Choose the **Borders** tab if it is not already on top. (See Figure 1.22.)

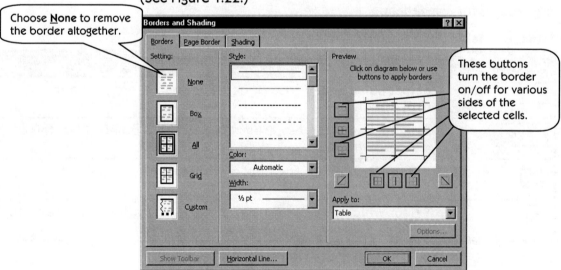

Figure 1.22.   Set borders for the selected cell(s) using these controls.

4 Select a setting from the **Setting** area. If you want to remove the border, choose **None**.

NOTE: Choose **None** and then **Custom** if you want to select lines individually in the **Preview** area. Choosing **None** erases the existing borders, and choosing **Custom** prepares the dialog box to receive custom settings.

5   Choose a line style from the **Style** list.

6   Choose a color from the **Color** drop-down list.

7   Choose a line width from the **Width** drop-down list.

8   If you chose **Custom** in step 4, click the buttons surrounding the Preview to turn the borders on or off for each side of the cell(s).

9   Choose **OK**.

SET CELL SHADING

Shading refers to the color or pattern in the background of a cell. You can set the shading for each cell individually; thus, it's easy to make certain cells stand out with special colors, patterns, or shades of gray. For example, many people like to shade their heading rows so that it's apparent those rows are not part of the data. Figure 1.23 shows an example.

First Name	Last Name	Level	Grade 1	Grade 2	Grade 3
Tom	Smith	1	A	B	B
Nancy	Phillips	1	B	B	A-
Cindy	Kelly	1	C	C	C
Loren	Coleman	1	C	A	B
Tim	Bradley	1	D	B	C

Figure 1.23.   This table's headings stand out because they are shaded.

You can set shading with the **Shading Color** button on the Tables and Borders toolbar, or you can use the **Shading** tab in the **Borders and Shading** dialog box.

Set shading with the toolbar:

1   Select the cell(s) you want to shade (or remove shading from).

2   Open the **Shading Color** button's palette. Choose a color, or choose **No Fill** to remove shading.

NOTE: You can choose **More Fill Colors** to open a dialog box from which you can choose among a wider variety of colors.

CAUTION: The **Shading Color** button on the Tables and Borders toolbar looks just like the **Fill Color** button on the Drawing toolbar, but it's not the same control. When you are working in a table cell, the **Fill Color** button's commands are unavailable.

Using the **Shading** controls in the **Borders and Shading** dialog box is more work, but it also offers more options. For example, with this method, you can set a shading pattern that combines two colors. (See Figure 1.24.)

First Name	Last Name	Level	Grade 1	Grade 2	Grade 3
Tom	Smith	1	A	B	B
Nancy	Phillips	1	B	B	A-
Cindy	Kelly	1	C	C	C
Loren	Coleman	1	C	A	B
Tim	Bradley	1	D	B	C

Figure 1.24.   The heading cells have a two-color pattern applied to their shading.

Set shading with the dialog box:

1   Select the cell(s) you want to shade (or remove shading from).

2   Choose F**o**rmat>**Borders and Shading**.

3   Choose the **Shading** tab.

4   Select a fill color from the **Fill** area. (See Figure 1.25.) Or, choose **No Fill** to remove shading.

5   If you want to shade using a pattern, choose the pattern from the **Style** drop-down list, and then choose the pattern color from the **Color** drop-down list below it.

   NOTE: The **Color** drop-down list becomes available when you choose a pattern other than **Clear**. It is not available in Figure 1.25.

6   Choose **OK**.

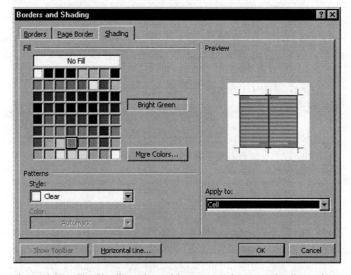

Figure 1.25.   The **Shading** tab enables you to choose a shading color and, optionally, a pattern.

CHANGE TEXT DIRECTION

 Text in a cell runs horizontally, left –to –right, by default. (That's no surprise; that's the way almost all text in the English language runs.) You can change its direction to vertical for some of your cells if it fits the needs of your project. To do so, simply select the cell and choose the **Change Text Direction** button.

Choosing the **Change Text Direction** button cycles through the available text directions each time you click on it. The directions are

- Horizontal, left to right (the default)
- Vertical, top to bottom
- Vertical, bottom to top

Practice Exercise 1-6

Format a Table

1   Start in the file **01Tabl5** from the preceding exercise, or open 📂**01Ex1-6** from the **WORDCert\Word B** folder. Then save the file as 🖫**01Tabl6**.

2   Remove the border from the first table by doing the following:

- Select the entire first table.

- Open the Border button's palette on either the Borders and Shading or the Formatting toolbar, and choose **No Border**. This removes the border from the table.

3   Select the entire first table, and choose the **Change Text Direction** button on the Tables and Borders toolbar, changing its direction. The result appears in Figure 1.26.

Chemistry		Math		Biology
Sociology		English		Physics
Computer Science		Physical Education		Music

Figure 1.26.   Here's how the first table will look after you've removed the borders and altered the text direction.

4 In the second table, apply a blue double border on the bottom of the first row, removing all other borders in that row:

- Select the first row of the second table.

- Choose **F**ormat>**B**orders and Shading. The Borders and Shading dialog box opens.

- Choose the **Borders** tab.

- Choose a double line from the **St**y**le** list.

- Choose a dark blue from the **C**olor drop-down list.

- Choose **N**one to remove existing borders.

- Choose the **Bottom Border** button from the **Preview** area.

5 On the **Shading** tab, set a green and yellow, striped background for the cells:

- Choose a medium green as the **Fill** color.

- Choose **Dk Vertical** from the **St**y**le** drop-down list.

- Choose a pale yellow from the **C**olor drop-down list.

- Choose **OK**.

6 In the remainder of the table (all rows except the first one), turn off all borders, and then add dotted vertical borders only:

- Select the cells.

- Choose **F**ormat>**B**orders and Shading, and choose the **Borders** tab.

- Choose **N**one.

- Choose **C**ustom.

- Choose a dotted line from the **St**y**le** list.

- Choose **Automatic** from the **C**olor list.

- Choose all three of the vertical line buttons at the bottom of the **Preview** area. (See Figure 1.27.)

- Choose **OK**.

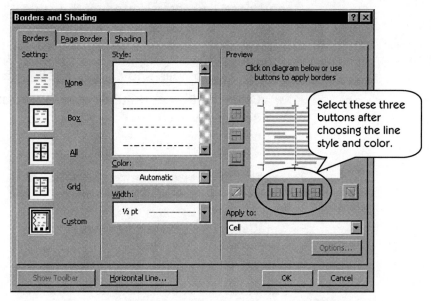

Figure 1.27. Set up dotted vertical borders, with no horizontal borders.

7 Center the entire table in the document, and then center the contents of each cell within the cell:

- Select the entire table.

- Choose the **Center** button on the Formatting toolbar, centering the table in the document.

- Select all the columns except one. (You'll select that column in a moment.)

 NOTE: Don't select the entire table, because Word will think that the centering should apply to the table as a whole.

- Choose the **Center** button, centering the contents of each cell in those columns.

- Select the other column, and click **Center** again, centering its contents.

 8 Select the first row, and choose the **Bold** button on the Formatting toolbar, making all the text bold.

9   Using the Tables and Borders toolbar, place a solid black horizontal line at the bottom of the table:

- Select the last row.

- Open the **Line Style** drop-down list on the Tables and Borders toolbar, and choose a solid line.

- Open the **Border** button's palette, and choose the **Bottom Border** button.

Figure 1.28 shows the finished table.

First Name	Last Name	Level	Grade 1	Grade 2	Grade 3
Tom	Smith	1	A	B	B
Nancy	Phillips	1	B	B	A-
Cindy	Kelly	1	C	C	C
Loren	Coleman	1	C	A	B
Tim	Bradley	1	D	B	C

Figure 1.28.   The table should look like this after the formatting has been applied.

10   Save your work; leave the document open for the next exercise.

A completed example of **01Tabl6** is available in the **WORDCert\Word B\Samples** folder on the DDC CD-ROM.

Sort Table Contents

You can sort the contents of a table alphabetically, either in ascending order (A to Z, 0 to 9) or in descending order (9 to 0, Z to A). You can sort by any column. This can be useful, for example, if you need to sort a table of addresses by last name or by ZIP code.

 NOTE: You can also sort regular paragraphs in Word using this feature. For example, you could use it to alphabetize the paragraphs in a list of definitions or in an index.

There are two ways to sort. One way is to use the **Sort Ascending** or **Sort Descending** button on the Tables and Borders toolbar to perform a sort by a single column:

Sort with the toolbar buttons:

1   Select the column by which you want to sort.

 2   Choose the **Sort Ascending** or **Sort Descending** button.

This kind of sort is very easy, as you can see, but limited. You cannot sort by more than one column at a time. Suppose, for example, that you wanted a list sorted first by ZIP code and then by last name. You would need to use the **Sort** dialog box for such an operation, as shown in the following steps.

Sort with the Sort dialog box:

1   Click anywhere within the table. (You do not have to select a particular column.)

2   Choose **T**a**ble>S**ort. The **Sort** dialog box opens. (See Figure 1.29.)

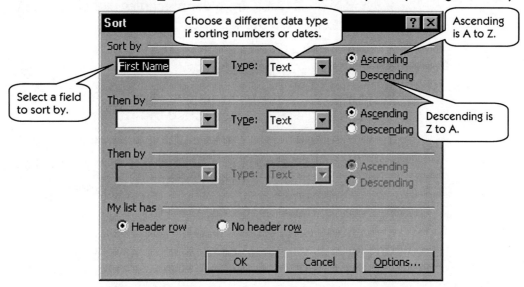

Figure 1.29.   Choose how you want the table data to be sorted.

3   At the bottom of the dialog box, choose **Header** **r**ow or **No header ro**w, depending on whether or not your first row contains column headings.

 NOTE: You perform step 3 before step 4 below, because if you have a header row, and you indicate this, the column names will appear on the list in step 4, making it easier to find the one you want.

4   Open the **Sort by** drop-down list; choose the column by which you want to sort first.

5   Choose a sort type from the **Type** drop-down list.

 NOTE: Setting a type is useful if you are sorting numbers or dates, because in those cases the first character in the cell is not necessarily what you want to sort by. For example, **Text** sorts by the first letter. If you choose **Number**, it sorts by number (for example, 2 comes before 10). If you choose **Date**, it sorts by date (for example, 12/31/98 comes before 1/1/99).

6   Choose **A**scending or **D**escending.

7   (Optional) If you want to sort by another field, choose it from the **Then by** drop-down list. Then set its **Type** and choose **Ascending** or **Descending**, just as you did in steps 5 and 6.

8   Choose **OK**. The table is sorted.

Practice Exercise 1-7

Sort a Table's Data

1   Start in the **01Tabl6** from the preceding exercise, or open 📂**01Ex1-7** from the **WORDCert\Word B** folder.

2   Save it as 💾**01Tabl7**.

3   Select the **First Name** column.

4   Choose the **Sort Ascending** button on the Tables and Borders toolbar. The table is now sorted by first name.

5   Choose **T**a**ble>**_S_**ort**. The **Sort** dialog box opens.

6   Open the **Sort by** drop-down list, and choose **Last Name**.

7   Choose **OK**. The table is now sorted by last name.

8   Save your work, and close the file.

A completed example of **01Tabl7** is available in the **WORDCert\Word B\Samples** folder on the DDC CD-ROM.

Use Math in Tables

Occasionally you might need to perform mathematical calculations on numbers in your table cells. For example, you might total or average the numbers in a column. Word enables you to use formulas and functions in cells, much as you use them in Excel.

NOTE: When referring to the various cells in your table, use Excel-type notation. Each row has a number, beginning with 1; each column has a letter, beginning with A. So, for example, the cell at the intersection of row 2 and column B is known as B2. The range of cells from A1 through C3 is known as A1:C3.

What's the difference between a formula and a function? A *formula* is an equation that can involve any combination of cell references, math operators, functions, and numbers. For example, =**C1+2** is a formula that takes the value in cell C1 and adds 2 to it. A *function* is a built-in, named math operation, such as =**AVERAGE**, that can be used in a formula. For example, the formula =**AVERAGE(C1:F1)** finds the average of the numbers in C1, D1, E1, and F1; **AVERAGE** is the function used in the formula.

CALCULATE WITH MATH OPERATORS

The simplest kind of formula involves one or more numbers or cell references plus a math operator, such as + (plus), - (subtract), * (multiply), / (divide), or ^ (raise to the power of). All formulas begin with an equals sign, to differentiate them from ordinary text. Here are some sample formulas:

=C1+C2	=C1+3/12
=C1*5	=C1^3

Formulas like these can calculate all kinds of useful values. For example, if C2 contains a yearly interest rate (an APR), you could use C2/12 to divide the annual rate by 12, producing a monthly interest rate.

Create a formula with math operators:

1 Select the cell in which you want to enter the formula.

2 Choose **Table>Formula**. The **Formula** dialog box opens. (See Figure 1.30.)

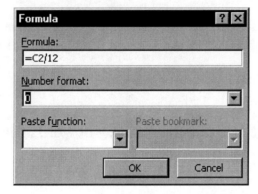

Figure 1.30. Enter your formula in the **Formula** text box.

3 Select whatever is in the **Formula** box and delete it.

4 In the **Formula** box, type the formula. Make sure you begin it with an equals sign.

5 (Optional) Choose a number format for the output if desired. Table 1.2 shows the number formats.

6 Choose **OK**.

NOTE: Formulas that contain more than one operator are calculated using an order of precedence. Exponentiation is done first, then multiplication, division, and finally addition and then subtraction. To change the order of formula calculation, place the parts to be done first in parentheses. For example, 1+9/2 would be 5.5, because Word would calculate 9/2 and then add 1. However, (1+9)/2 would be 5, because Word would calculate 1+9 and then divide the answer by 2.

Table 1.2: Number Formats in Word

Format	Use
#,##0	Simple ordinal numbers separated by commas for thousands, etc., always rounded to the closest whole number
#,##0.00	Simple ordinal numbers separated by commas for thousands, etc., and including two places after the decimal point
$#,##0.00;($#,##0.00)	American dollar amounts with negative dollar amounts shown inside parentheses
0	Simple ordinal whole numbers
0%	Numbers are converted to a percentage of 100.
0.00	Ordinal numbers displayed using two places after the decimal point
0.00%	Percentages displayed using two places after the decimal point

USE FUNCTIONS

It's true that almost all calculations can be performed with basic math operators, but not always easily. For example, you could average the contents of cells C1:C4 with the following formula:

   (C1+C2+C3+C4)/4

However, it is much easier in many cases to use one of Word's built-in functions. For example,

   =AVERAGE(C1:C4)

performs the same calculation as the formula above it.

Each function has one or more *arguments* in parentheses after it. The arguments are the cells or numbers to include in the calculation. Two or more arguments in a function are separated with commas, like this:

   =AVERAGE(C1, C2, C5)

Table 1.3 lists the available functions in Word and describes what each of them returns (that is, what result it displays).

 NOTE: Not all functions can accept table cell references as arguments. The ones that can are **AVERAGE, COUNT, MAX, MIN, PRODUCT,** and **SUM.** The others must have numeric arguments.

Table 1.3: Functions Available in Word

Function	What it returns
ABS	The absolute value of a number
AND	The value 1 if the logical expressions in its arguments are all true, or the value 0 if any of its arguments are false (This is the opposite of NOT.)
AVERAGE	The average of a list of values
COUNT	The number of items in a list
DEFINED	The value 1 if the expression in the argument is valid, or 0 if the expression cannot be computed
FALSE	0 (zero)
INT	The numbers to the left of the decimal place in the value or formula in its argument
MAX	The largest value in a list
MIN	The smallest value in a list
MOD	The remainder that results from dividing one value by another a whole number of times
NOT	The value 0 if the logical expression in the argument is true, or the value 1 if the expression is false (This is the opposite of AND.)
OR	The value 1 if any of the logical expressions in the arguments are true, or 0 if all of them are false
PRODUCT	The result of multiplying a list of values given as arguments
ROUND	The value of the first argument rounded to the number of decimal places specified by the second
SIGN	The value 1 if the argument is a positive value, or the value -1 if the value is negative
SUM	The sum of a list of values or formulas
TRUE	1

Create a formula that includes a function:

1   Click in the cell where you want the result of your calculation to appear.

2   Choose **Table>Formula** to open the **Formula** dialog box. (See Figure 1.30.)

NOTE: By default, the formula =**SUM(ABOVE)** appears in the **Formula** dialog box. The =**SUM** function calculates the sum of the cells you specify. **ABOVE** refers to all the cells above the selected one in the table.

3   If you want to accept **=SUM(ABOVE)** as the formula to use, choose **OK**, and you're done. You can skip the rest of these steps.

If **=SUM(ABOVE)** is not what you want, delete that formula from the **Formula** box and continue on to step 4.

> **NOTE:** If **=SUM** is the function you want, but you want to total other cells than those above the selected one, leave **=SUM** in place but change the value in the parentheses. For example, to add cells C1 through C3, change the formula to **=SUM(C1:C3)**.

4   Open the **Paste** function drop-down list, and choose the function you want to use. It appears in the **Formula** text box, with parentheses after it. Table 1.3 lists the functions you can use.

5   In the parentheses, type the range of cells to affect.

6   (Optional) Choose a number format for the results from the **Number** format drop-down list. Table 1.2 lists the available formats.

7   Choose **OK**. The dialog box closes, and the formula is inserted into the cell. The result of the formula's calculation appears in the cell.

To edit a formula, you can turn on the display of field codes and then make your changes directly in the cell. Right-click the cell and choose **Toggle Field Codes**; when you are done, do it again to turn them off.

> **NOTE:** Word is not specifically designed for calculations and functions the way a spreadsheet program like Excel is. If you want to delve more deeply into formulas and functions, you may be interested in one of DDC Publishing's Excel books.

Practice Exercise 1-8

Insert Calculations

1   Open the file 01Ex1-8 from the **WORDCert\Word B** folder, and save it as 01Math.

2   Insert a formula in cell B5 that calculates the numbers above it:

• Click in the bottom cell in the second column (column B).

• Choose **Table>Formula**. The **Formula** dialog box opens.

• Leave the formula as is in the **Formula** box.

• Open the **Number** format drop-down list, and choose **$#,##0.00;($#,##0.00)**.

• Choose **OK**. The total appears in the cell.

• Repeat the procedure in cells C5, D5, and E5.

3 Place a formula in cell F2 that calculates the sum of B2:E2:

- Click in the last cell in row 2.
- Choose **Table>Formula**. The formula in the **Formula** box now reads **=SUM(LEFT)** because Word assumes you want to sum the numbers to the left.
- Change the Number format to $#,##0.00;($#,##0.00).
- Choose **OK**.

4 Repeat step 3 for cells F3, F4, and F5.

> **CAUTION:** As you calculate the numbers, make sure the **Formula** box continues to read **=SUM(LEFT)**. If the formula switches to something else, correct it.

5 Add another row at the bottom of the table (by pressing **Tab** in the last cell), and type **Average** in the first column. The new row is row 6.

6 Insert a formula in cell B6 that averages the values in column B:

- Click in cell B6, and then choose **Table>Formula**.
- Delete all text from the **Formula** box except the equals sign.
- Open the **Paste function** drop-down list, and choose **AVERAGE**.
- Between the parentheses in the **Formula** box, type **B2:B5**.

> **NOTE:** Yes, it's an error to include B5 in the average, since B5 contains a total. But making this error will give you something to correct in the next step, when you learn to correct formulas.

- Change the Number format to $#,##0.00;($#,##0.00).
- Choose **OK**. The average appears.

7 Edit the formula in B6 so that it refers to B2:B4:

- Right-click B6; choose **Toggle Field Codes**. Change B5 to B4.
- Right-click and choose **Toggle Field Codes** again.
- Right-click and choose **Update Field**.

8 The finished table appears in Figure 1.31. Save your work, and close the file.

	Q1	Q2	Q3	Q4	Total
Tom	$25,600	$23,450	$23,048	$38,509	$110,607.00
Dick	$30,492	$38,409	$8,503	$20,394	$97,798.00
Harry	$23,940	$30,292	$12,093	$58,093	$124,418.00
Total	$80,032.00	$92,151.00	$43,644.00	$116,996.00	$332,823.00
Average	$26,677.33				

Figure 1.31. The table after all row and columns have been totaled and the first quarter has been averaged.

A completed example of **01Math** is available in the **WORDCert\Word B\Samples** folder on the DDC CD-ROM.

Insert an Excel Worksheet in a Document

Excel is a full-featured spreadsheet program. If you have Excel installed on your PC, you can insert a mini-worksheet into a Word document and take advantage of Excel's expanded list of functions and other sophisticated controls right within Word.

When you insert an Excel worksheet, Word's toolbars and menu bar change to those of Excel, and the inserted worksheet sits in a framed box that looks very different from an ordinary Word table. However, when you click away from it, the Excel controls disappear and the resulting sheet closely resembles a regular Word table, both on-screen and in print.

Insert an Excel worksheet:

1   Position the insertion point in the document where you want the spreadsheet to appear.

2   Choose the **Insert Microsoft Excel Worksheet** button on the Standard toolbar.

3   Drag across the number of rows and columns you want to create the worksheet window. (See Figure 1.32.)

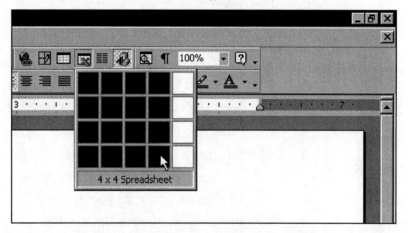

Figure 1.32.   Choose the initial size of the worksheet, just as you do when creating a table.

NOTE: When you release the mouse button, the worksheet appears in your document, as shown in Figure 1.33. Excel's toolbar and menus appear, replacing those of Word.

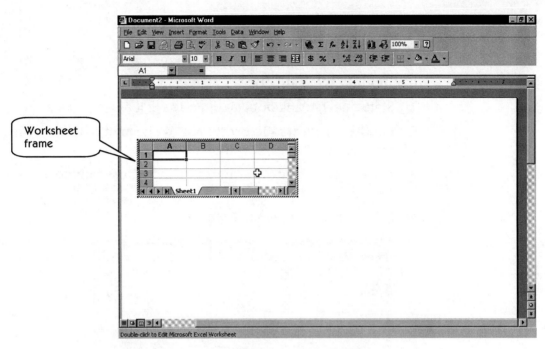

Figure 1.33. An Excel worksheet embedded in Word.

4   Enter data into the Excel worksheet, using any of Excel's features.

 NOTE: You can enter numbers, text, and formulas into the Excel worksheet, just as you would do in Excel.

5   Click outside of the worksheet frame to close Excel and return to Word.

6   To edit the worksheet more, double-click on it.

The inserted worksheet is actually much larger than can fit in the frame. You can scroll to different parts of it using the frame's scroll bars. It can be useful to have cells that are not in view; for example, you might scroll to the left and enter your raw data, and then scroll back to the right and enter formulas that calculate that data. Only the cells containing the calculations would appear in the frame (and thus, in your Word document).

If you want to make more or fewer cells visible in Word, simply resize the worksheet frame by dragging its selection handles.

To delete an embedded worksheet from your Word document, first click away from it to exit Excel's tools. Then click once on the worksheet box to select it, and press the **Delete** key.

Practice Exercise 1-9

Insert an Excel Worksheet

1   Start a new, blank document and save it as 🖫01Wksht.

2   Choose the **Insert Microsoft Excel Worksheet** button on the Standard toolbar.

3   Move the mouse down four rows and across four columns, and then click.

4   Enter the data shown in Figure 1.34.

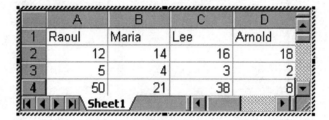

	A	B	C	D
1	Raoul	Maria	Lee	Arnold
2	12	14	16	18
3	5	4	3	2
4	50	21	38	8

Figure 1.34.   Enter this data into your embedded Excel sheet.

5   Click outside the Excel frame to deselect it.

6   Save your work, and close the file.

A completed example of **01Wksht** is available in the **WORDCert\Word B\Samples** folder on the DDC CD-ROM.

LESSON 2: WORK WITH COLUMNS

In the last lesson, you saw how to organize data in multiple columns using a table. In this lesson, you'll learn about a different kind of column: the snaking, newspaper-style columns that are frequently found in newsletters, magazines, and other publications.

In this lesson, you will learn to:

- ➤ Change the number of columns your document uses

- ➤ Convert a section of the document to a different column layout

- ➤ Change a column's width and spacing

- ➤ Balance the text across columns

- ➤ Insert manual column breaks

You will have a chance to practice these skills in the exercises in this lesson as well as in the Walk, Run, and Fly exercises at the end of the lesson.

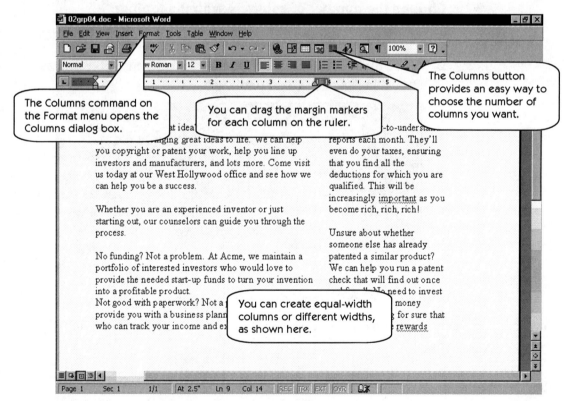

Figure 2.1. A multi-column layout.

Create a Multi-Column Layout

By default, every Word document starts out with its number of columns set to 1. A standard letter, for example, is a one-column document, where the width of the column equals the width of the page. You can change the default setting in either of two ways: with the **Columns** button on the Standard toolbar, or with the **Format>Columns** command.

 NOTE: Multiple columns do not appear side by side in Normal view. To see how the columns will look when printed, switch to Print Layout view (**View>Print Layout**).

USE THE COLUMNS BUTTON ON THE TOOLBAR

The **Columns** button provides a quick and easy way to change the number of columns in your document. However, it's not very flexible; it creates from one to four evenly spaced columns, with no special options or widths. (For more flexibility, try the **Format** menu method, described in the next section.)

Change the number of columns with the toolbar:

1   Choose the **Columns** button on the toolbar. A grid drops down.

2   Move the mouse across the number of columns you want, as shown in Figure 2.2, and then click.

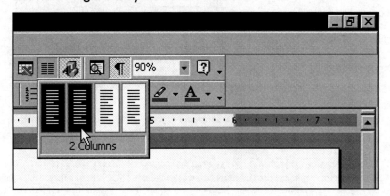

Figure 2.2.   Select the number of columns you want.

To go back to a single-column layout, repeat these steps but drag across a single column on the grid.

USE THE FORMAT MENU

The **Format>Columns** command opens a dialog box filled with many options for setting up your new columns. For instance, you can adjust the widths, change the space between columns, and place a vertical line between columns.

Set up columns with the Columns dialog box:

1 Choose **Format>Columns**. The **Columns** dialog box opens.
(See Figure 2.3.)

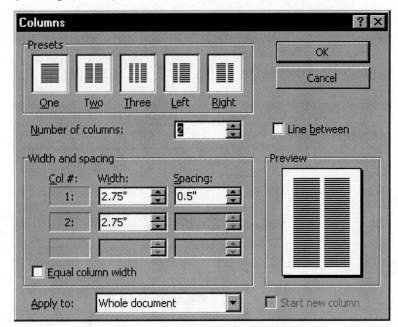

Figure 2.3. This dialog box lets you set up the columns you want.

2 Do one or more of the following:

- Choose one of the **Presets** buttons to select one, two, or three columns or to select a layout of two different-sized columns, with the smaller one either to the left or to the right.

- Set the number of columns in the **Number of columns** box.

- Set the **Width** (in inches) for each column.

- Set the **Spacing** (in inches) between columns.

- Choose the **Equal column width** checkbox to force all column widths to be the same.

- Choose the **Line between** checkbox to draw vertical lines between columns (like some newspapers have).

3 Choose **OK**.

Practice Exercise 2-1

Create a Multi-Column Layout

1 Open the file 🗁**02Ex2-1**, and save it as 🖫**02Col1**.

2 Choose the **Columns** button, and move the mouse across the grid to create three columns. Then click to select a three-column layout.

3   Choose **Format>Columns**. The **Columns** dialog box opens.

4   Choose the **Line between** checkbox.

5   Choose the **Equal column width** checkbox.

6   Change the value in the **Spacing** box to 0.2".

 TIP: If you are going to use a vertical line between columns, you might want to set the **Spacing** to less than the default (which is 0.5"), because the lines will prevent the readers' eyes from wandering to the wrong column.

7   Choose **OK**. The result appears in Figure 2.4.

8   Save your work; leave the document open for the next exercise.

A completed example of **02Col1** is available in the **WORDCert\Word B\Samples** folder on the DDC CD-ROM.

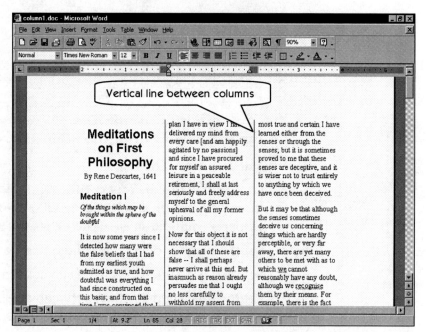

Figure 2.4.   The document after formatting it in three columns.

USE DIFFERENT COLUMNS IN THE SAME DOCUMENT

As you just saw, it's simple to change a document's overall Columns setting. The only thing that's tricky is setting up one part of a document to have a different number of columns than the rest. To do that, you must employ section breaks.

Each section of a document has its own Columns setting that specifies the number of columns to be used. By default, each document has one section. Figure 2.4 shows a single-section document set for a three-column layout. By adding a *section break*, you split the document into two sections, and each section can have its own Columns setting. Figure 2.5 shows the same document with a section break.

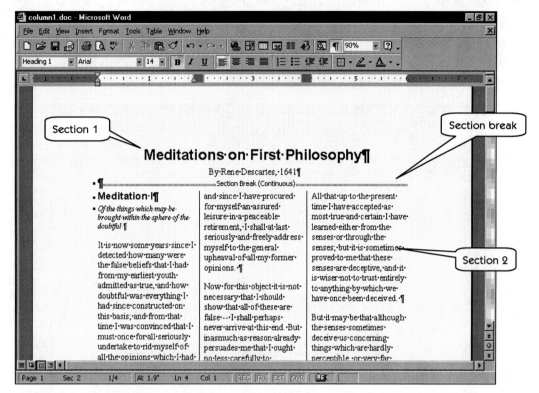

Figure 2.5. This document's title is in a one-column section, and the remainder of the document is in a three-column section.

 TIP: In Figure 2.5, hidden characters have been turned on so you can see the section break. To do this on your own screen, choose the **Show/Hide ¶** button on the Standard toolbar.

Insert a section break:

1   Position the insertion point where you want the break to occur.

 NOTE: It should be at the point where the number of columns should change in the document.

2   Choose **Insert>Break**.

3   Choose **Continuous**.

4   Choose **OK**.

5   Position the insertion point in the section you want to work with.

6   Change the **Columns** setting, as you learned in the preceding sections.

The makers of Word understand that sometimes you want to set up a few paragraphs of a document with a different number of columns than the rest and that you don't want to bother with inserting section breaks. So if you select some text before you change the number of columns, Word automatically inserts section breaks before and after the selected text. (See Figure 2.6.)

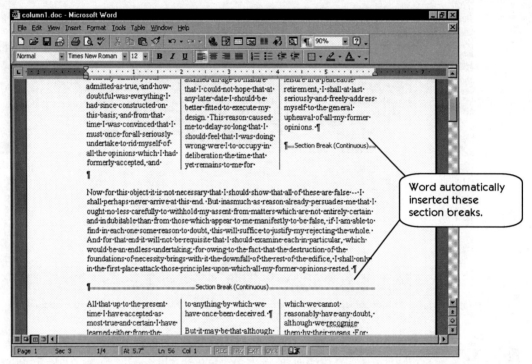

Figure 2.6.   When you select some text before changing the Columns setting, Word automatically inserts section breaks around it.

Apply a different Columns setting to selected text:

1   Select the text that should be formatted with a different Columns setting than the rest of the document.

2   Change the Columns setting, as you learned in the preceding sections.

The section breaks hold the settings for all the text above them. Therefore, if you delete a section break, the number of columns (as well as other settings) defaults to that of the next section break down or to that of the end-of-document marker (which serves the same purpose as a section break marker, holding section-wide settings). You will see this in Practice Exercise 2-2.

CHOOSE A DOCUMENT VIEW FOR WORKING WITH COLUMNS

When working with multi-column text, you can use either Normal view or Print Layout view. Figure 2.6 shows Print Layout view, which is great for seeing how your document will look when printed.

If you are focused on editing your text, you may prefer Normal view so you don't have to scroll up and down to move from one column to another. In Normal view, you see only one column, so you don't get the full picture of your document's layout. Figure 2.7 shows the document from Figure 2.6 in Normal view.

 NOTE: In Normal view, you can also see the section breaks without turning on all the other hidden characters with the **Show/Hide ¶** button, so it's easy to delete section breaks from Normal view by selecting them and pressing the **Delete** key.

You are probably already familiar with changing views: Use the **View** menu commands, or use the **View** buttons in the bottom left corner of the screen.

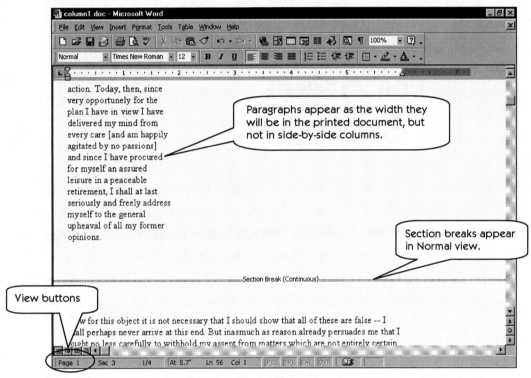

Figure 2.7.   In Normal view, the document appears as one long column—great for text editing, but not the best choice for page layout.

Practice Exercise 2-2

Use Different Column Settings

1   Start in the file **02Col1** from the preceding exercise, or open
    📂**02Ex2-2** from the **WORDCert\Word B** folder.
    Save the file as 💾**02Col2**.

2   Position the insertion point before **Meditation I**, and choose
    Insert>Break. Choose **Continuous**, and choose **OK**.

 3   Position the insertion point at the top of the document, and
    choose the **Columns** button. Drag across a single column,
    changing the first section to a single-column layout.

4 Select the paragraph that begins "All that up to the present time...."

5 Choose **Format>Columns**. Then choose the **Two** button, and choose **OK**. That paragraph now appears in two columns.

6 Choose **View>Normal** to switch to **Normal** view, and scroll down to locate the section breaks around the chosen paragraph. (See Figure 2.8.)

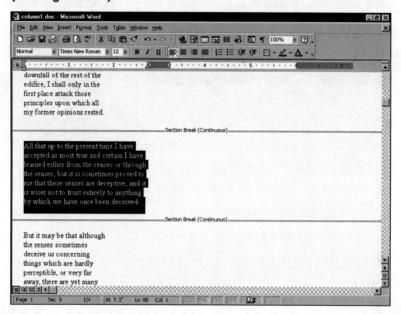

Figure 2.8.   The paragraph you selected is in its own section.

> **NOTE:** The section break above the paragraph tells Word to use three columns for all the text above it. The section break *below* the paragraph tells Word to use two columns for the text above it.

7 Click on the Section Break line above the paragraph and press **Delete**, deleting the break. The paragraph becomes part of the previous section, which now has two columns.

> **NOTE:** Why does the previous section now have two columns? Because the section break at the end of it specifies it.

8 Switch back to Print Layout view, and notice the number of columns in various points. Notice that

- The title is still in a single-column section by itself.

- The first part of the body has taken on the two-column layout. That's because you deleted the three-column section break.

- The last part of the body has a three-column layout. That's because the end-of-document marker specifies three sections.

9 Click at the end of the last paragraph in the two-column section and press **Delete**, removing the section break. The document body goes back to three columns.

10 Save your work, and close the file.

A completed example of **02Col2** is available in the **WORDCert\Word B\Samples** folder on the DDC CD-ROM.

Work with Text in Columns

After placing your text in multiple columns, you may want to edit it. Editing text in multiple columns is the same as editing text normally, except you may need to scroll up or down to bring the text you want into view.

 TIP: Many people find it easier to edit text in **Normal** view.

The main difference when editing text in multiple columns is that you may want to control where each column ends. The following sections explain ways to do that.

CREATE COLUMN BREAKS

Text flows automatically to the next column when it reaches the bottom of the current one, but you can also add manual column breaks.

Insert a column break:

1 Position the insertion point where you want the break to occur.

2 Choose **Insert>Break**.

3 Choose **Column break**.

4 Choose **OK**.

 TIP: Most people prefer using the shortcut keys instead of the above method: **Ctrl+Shift+Enter**.

You can remove a manual column break the same way you remove any character: Click on it and press the **Delete** key, or position the insertion point immediately after it and press **Backspace**.

BALANCE COLUMN LENGTHS

By default, text flows all the way to the bottom of the first column before it starts filling the next one. This is fine if you have enough text to fill all of the columns on the page, but if you have only a half-page full of text, for example, you might want the text spread out evenly over all the available columns. Otherwise, your text may fill the two leftmost sections of the page only, leaving the right side of the page blank.

If the document has more than one section, the text within a section is automatically balanced between all available columns. Therefore, you can balance text by inserting a section break at the end of the text to be balanced.

Practice Exercise 2-3

Break and Balance Columns

1   Open the file 📁**02Ex2-3** and save it as 💾**02Col3**.

2   Choose the **Columns** button, and drag across four columns, creating a four-column layout.

3   Position the insertion point after **Forrest** and press **Ctrl+Shift+Enter**, inserting a column break. Then press the **Delete** key once to remove the extra line. The result should resemble Figure 2.9.

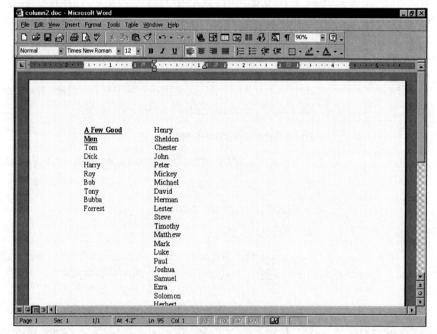

Figure 2.9.   Inserting a column break forces the rest of the list into the second column.

4   Press **Backspace**, removing the column break.

5   Position the insertion point after **Abraham** (at the end of the list).

6   Choose **Insert>Break**, choose **Continuous**, and choose **OK**. The names balance evenly in the four columns, as shown in Figure 2.10.

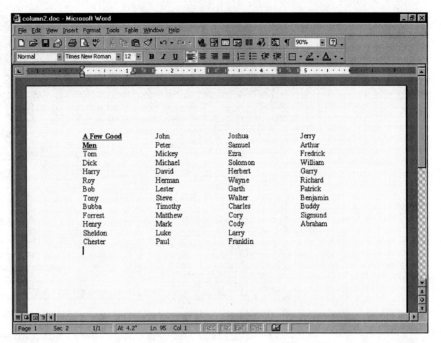

Figure 2.10. By inserting a section break at the end, you force all the columns to be used evenly.

7   Save your work, and close the document.

Change Column Width

You have already seen that you can create evenly spaced columns as you set up your columns with the **Columns** dialog box. You can revisit the **Columns** dialog box at any time to change the width precisely. Use the following procedure.

Change the column width:

1   Choose **Format>Columns**. The **Columns** dialog box opens, as shown in Figure 2.11.

2   Change the number in the **Width** column for each column in the document.

NOTE: When you make changes to a column's width or to the spacing between columns, the other columns' measurements change to compensate, so that the entire space between the right and left margins is accounted for. For example, if you change the width of Column 1 in Figure 2.11 to 1.3, the other columns change to 1.07" apiece, taking an equal amount of the needed space from each.

3   Type a different number in the **Spacing** column to adjust the spacing between columns in the document.

4   Click **OK**.

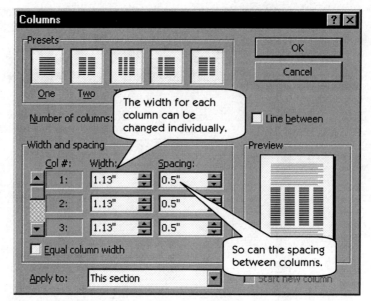

Figure 2.11.   Set precise column widths for each column here.

 TIP: If you want to change all the columns back to the same width again, just choose the **Equal column width** checkbox. Then clear it and make your width selections again.

You can also change the column width by dragging the column markers on the Ruler. As shown in Figure 2.12, each column has its own margins (the white areas). The gray areas represent the space between columns.

Change column width with the Ruler:

1   Position the mouse pointer over a column marker on the Ruler.

2   Drag it to adjust the column to its left. (See Figure 2.13.)

 TIP: When the insertion point is in a column, indent markers appear on the Ruler too. (See Figure 2.12.) It is hard to drag the margin markers when the indent markers are in the way, so click in some other column before you try to drag margin markers on the Ruler.

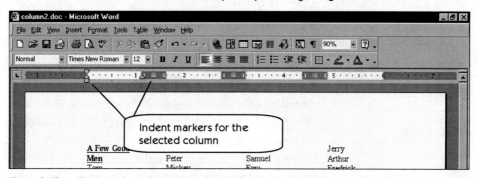

Figure 2.12.   The Ruler for a four-column layout. Each column has its own margins.

Figure 2.13.   To adjust a column's width, drag its margin marker on the right end.

Practice Exercise 2-4

Change Column Width

1 Open 📁 **02Ex2-4** from the **WORDCert\Word B** folder, and save it as 💾 **02Col4**.

2 Choose **Format>Columns**.

3 Choose the **Left** button. The column widths change.

4 Choose the **Equal column width** checkbox. The widths return to being identical.

5 Change the **Spacing** setting to 0.3". The number in the **Width** box increases to 2.85".

 NOTE: Why does the Width increase by only .1" when you decrease the Spacing twice that much? Because there are two columns, but only one space between them. Each column will receive .1", for a total of .2".

6 Remove the checkmark from the **Equal column width** checkbox.

7 Choose **OK**. The dialog box closes.

8 Drag the left margin of the second column to the 4" mark on the Ruler, increasing the space between columns.

9 Drag the right margin of the first column to the 3.75" mark on the Ruler, expanding the first column. The results appear in Figure 2.14.

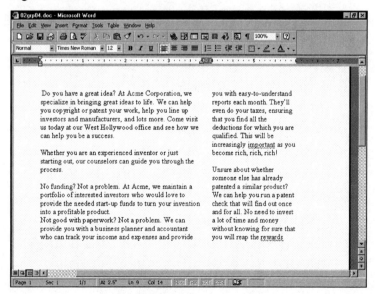

Figure 2.14. The document with altered column widths.

10 Save your work. Then close the file.

A completed example of **02Col4** is available in the **WORDCert\Word B\Samples** folder on the DDC CD-ROM.

LESSON 3: MAIL MERGE

Mail merge combines a form letter with a list of names to produce personalized letters suitable for a mass mailing. That's its most common function, but the Mail Merge feature in Word can also be used with other document types and other lists to produce items such as labels, envelopes, and catalogs.

In this lesson, you will learn to:

> ➤ Create a form letter or other main document
>
> ➤ Organize a list of names or other data to be used
>
> ➤ Use data from other sources, such as Access
>
> ➤ Insert mail merge fields in the main document
>
> ➤ Merge the list with a form letter
>
> ➤ Use the Mail Merge feature to create envelopes and mailing labels
>
> ➤ Use the Mail Merge feature to create catalogs

You will have an opportunity to practice these skills in the Practice Exercises in this lesson and the exercises at the end.

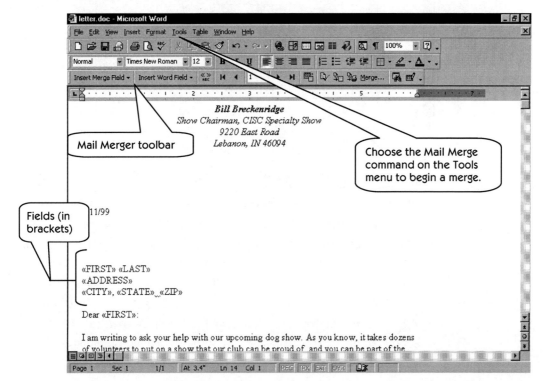

Figure 3.1.   You can create a letter or envelopes or labels that contain merge fields to pull in information from a data source such as a table.

Understand Mail Merge

Mail merge can save a lot of time because it can quickly generate many personalized copies of a letter, a report, an envelope, a label, or other kind of document.

Mail merge is a multi-step process:

1   Create the data source first. This can be a table in Word that contains the names and addresses of the people to send the mailing to, for example, as shown in Figure 3.2. Each person's name and address information is called a *record*. Column headings are called *field names*.

NOTES: Lesson 1 explained tables thoroughly, so you should have no trouble creating a table like the one in Figure 3.2.

If your data source is not created yet, you can create it on-the-fly using a form in Word, as you'll learn later in this lesson. You can also use data from another program, such as Access.

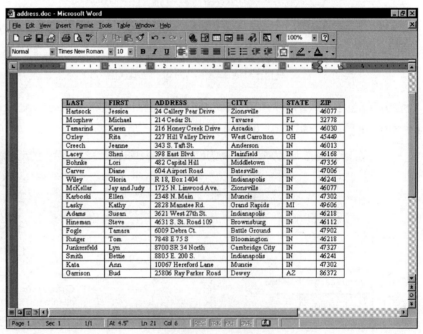

Figure 3.2.   This table holds information (the records) that will appear in the letters.

2   Create a document (usually a letter) that includes Word commands called *merge codes* in the places to be personalized. For example, there will be a **<<FIRST>>** field in the spot where the person's first name should go, as shown in Figure 3.3. Mail merge field names appear with double angle brackets around them.

NOTE: In this lesson, the term "field" will be used to refer to mail merge fields. Be aware that Word has other kinds of fields, too, that are not covered in this lesson.

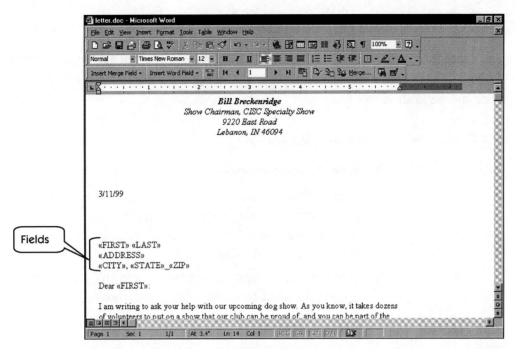

Figure 3.3.   This letter contains generic text that will appear in all letters plus the codes for the personalized data.

3   Tell Word to merge the table with the letter, creating personalized letters for each person in the table, as shown in Figure 3.4. Notice that the actual information replaces the mail merge fields.

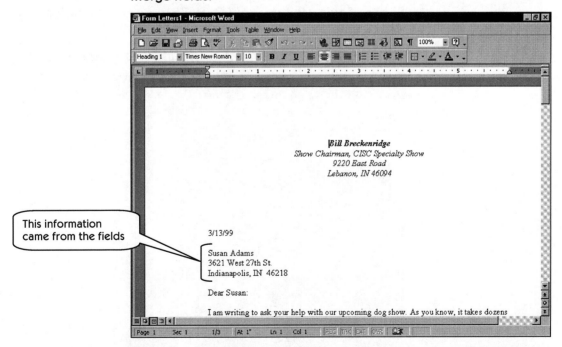

Figure 3.4.   Here's a letter created by merging the table in Figure 3.2 with the letter in Figure 3.3.

4   Check your work, and print the letters.

Perform a Basic Mail Merge

Let's start by performing a very simple mail merge with a list of names and a letter. This will give you an idea of how it all works. Then you'll learn how to do fancier things with mail merge later in this lesson.

PREPARE THE MERGE DOCUMENTS

To prepare for a merge:

1   Create a list of names and addresses in a Word table, and save your work with a name you will remember. Make sure you include table headings such as First, Last, ZIP, etc. (Use the table in Figure 3.2 as an example.)

2   Write the letter you want to send, leaving blank spaces for the areas you want to customize in each letter.

SET UP THE MAIL MERGE

After you have done the above steps, use the following procedure to begin the mail merge.

Start a mail merge:

1   Make sure the letter you have written is open and on-screen.

2   Choose **Tools>Mail Merge**. The **Mail Merge Helper** dialog box opens.

3   Choose the **Create** button. A menu appears. (See Figure 3.5.)

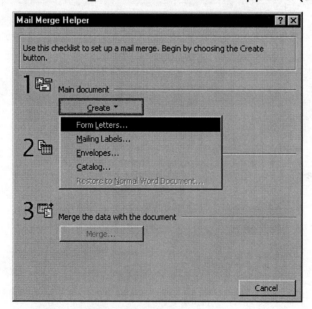

Figure 3.5.   Start a mail merge here.

4　Select **Form Letters**. A dialog box appears asking whether you want to use the **Active Window** or a **New Main Document**.

5　Choose **Active Window**.

6　Choose the **Get Data** button. A menu appears.

7　Choose **Open Data Source**. The **Open Data Source** dialog box appears.

8　Select the table of names and addresses you created when preparing for the mail merge. Then choose **Open**.

9　A message appears that Word found no merge fields in your main document. Choose **Edit Main Document**.

At this point, the **Mail Merge Helper** dialog box goes away, to allow you to insert merge fields in your document. An additional toolbar now appears at the top of your screen, the Mail Merge toolbar, as shown in Figure 3.6.

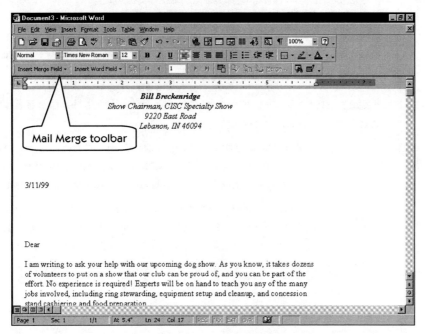

Figure 3.6.　The Mail Merge toolbar will help you place fields in the main document.

INSERT MERGE FIELDS IN THE MAIN DOCUMENT

Now you are ready to insert the merge fields. The merge fields are the field names (i.e., the column headings) from the table.

Insert merge fields:

1　Position the insertion point where you want the first field to appear.

2　Choose the **Insert Merge Field** button on the Mail Merge toolbar. A list of the fields appears.

3 Choose the field you want to insert. A code for it appears in the document, as shown in Figure 3.7.

List of available fields

Merge field inserted in the document

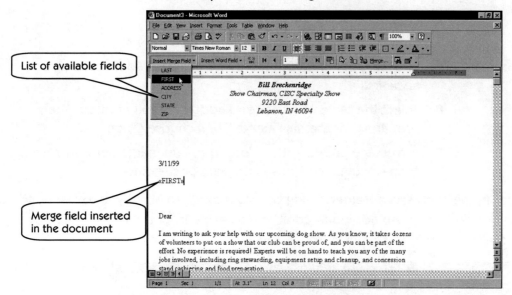

Figure 3.7. Select a field from the menu; it appears at the documents's insertion point.

4 Type spaces or text needed, or reposition the insertion point.

5 Repeat steps 2 through 4 to insert other fields. Figure 3.8 shows a letter with fields inserted.

 TIP: You can use the fields in more than just the address block. For example, in Figure 3.8, notice that the **FIRST** field is used after *Dear,* and the **LAST** field is used in the second paragraph.

 CAUTION: Don't forget to add a space between fields (like a space between **FIRST** and **LAST** names), or punctuation, such as a comma and a space between **CITY** and **STATE**.

These fields will print a recipient's name and address.

You can greet each recipient by name.

The LAST field is used here to personalize the message.

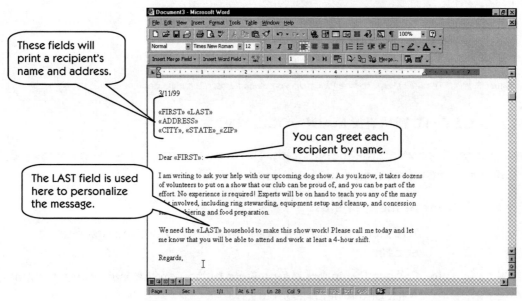

Figure 3.8. Insert merge fields just as if you were typing a name and address block.

PERFORM THE MERGE

When you have finished inserting fields, you are ready to merge. There are many ways to start the merging process, but the easiest is the following.

Merge to a new document:

Choose the **Merge to New Document** button on the Mail Merge toolbar.

When you do so, a new document is created containing all of the merged letters, with New Page section breaks separating them for easy printing.

You can scroll through the letters to check them, and then when you are ready, print them as you would print any other document.

As mentioned, there are other ways to perform the merge. Here are a few of them, along with an explanation of when each might be useful.

- **Merge to Printer**: Choose this to merge directly to the printer rather than to a new document. This saves time if you are very sure that there are no errors in your merge document; but it can waste a lot of paper if you print many copies that you later realize contain errors.

- **Mail Merge Helper**: Choose this button to return to the **Mail Merge Helper** dialog box if you need to set any special options before you merge, such as filtering (more on this later). Then from there you can choose **Merge** to open the **Merge** dialog box, and then choose **Merge** again to perform the merge.

- **Merge**: Choose this to open the **Merge** dialog box (the same as clicking the **Merge** button in the **Mail Merge Helper** dialog box). The **Merge** dialog box provides options for controlling which records should be included (by number) or setting up queries that filter the records.

That's it! That's all there is to a basic mail merge. Now that you know the basics, practice what you've learned in Practice Exercise 3-1, and then move on to more advanced merging options in the remainder of the lesson.

Practice Exercise 3-1

Perform a Simple Mail Merge

1   Open the file 📂**03Ex3-1a** from the **WORDCert\Word B** folder, and save it as 💾**03Letter**. Open 📂**03Ex3-1b**, and save it as 💾**03Data**.

2 Open the **Mail Merge Helper,** and set the active window as the main document:

- Switch to **03Letter** by choosing it from the **Window** menu.

- Choose **Tools>Mail Merge.**

- Choose the **Create** button, and choose **Form Letters.**

- Choose **Active Window.**

3 Choose **03Data** as the data source:

- Choose the **Get Data** button, and choose **Open Data Source.**

- Choose **03Data,** and choose **Open.**

4 Choose **Edit Main** Document. The dialog box closes.

5 Insert the fields to form the recipient's name and address, as you saw in Figure 3.8.

- Position the insertion point two lines above *Dear:*.

- Choose **Insert Merge Field** from the Mail Merge toolbar, and choose **FIRST** from the list.

- Press the **Spacebar** once. Then choose **Insert Merge Field** again, and choose **LAST** from the list.

- Press **Enter.** Then choose **Insert Merge Field** again, and choose **ADDRESS** from the list.

- Press **Enter.** Then choose **Insert Merge Field,** and choose **CITY** from the list.

- Type a comma and press the **Spacebar** once. Then choose **Insert Merge Field,** and choose **STATE** from the list.

- Press the **Spacebar** twice. Then choose **Insert Merge Field,** and choose **ZIP** from the list.

6 Position the insertion point between *Dear* and *:,* and press the **Spacebar** once. Then insert the **FIRST** field there.

7 Scroll down to the second paragraph, and insert the **LAST** field between *the* and *household.*

8 Choose the **Merge to New Document** button. A new document appears containing the letters. Scroll through it and examine them.

9 (Optional) If you have access to a printer, print the first page of the document so you can see how the letters will print.

10 Save the file as ▦**03Merged,** and close it. Then save your work in **03Letter** and **03Data,** and close them, too.

A completed example of **03Merged** is available in the **WORDCert\Word B\Samples** folder on the DDC CD-ROM.

Work with Data Sources

Depending on the situation, your name and address data may be in any of several formats. Fortunately, you can use several kinds of data sources for a Word mail merge, so you will probably not have to retype your data. This topic outlines the types of data sources Word's Mail Merge will accept and explains how to incorporate them.

To choose a data source, choose what you want from the **Get Data** button's menu in the **Mail Merge Helper** dialog box. This applies to all of the data source types you will learn about in the following topics.

USE A WORD TABLE

In the preceding topic, you saw how to use a Word table as your data source for a mail merge. Since you learned all about creating tables in Lesson 1 of this section, tables are probably fresh in your mind, so you won't need to review them here. The important thing to remember when using a Word table as a data source is to place the field names in the first row, as you saw in the example file **03Data** in the preceding practice exercise. You may also want to format the row containing the field names in some special way (such as making them bold) to set them off from the rest of the list.

USE NAMES FROM AN ADDRESS BOOK

Some people store names and addresses in contact management programs such as Microsoft Outlook or Schedule+. You can use such address books as a data source for your mail merge if you like.

 TIP: You will seldom want to create a mail merge that uses every single name in an address book; you will want to employ a query, explained later in this lesson in "Filter Records with a Query," to select just the names you want.

Use Address Book names for mail merge:

1   Start in the **Mail Merge Helper** dialog box. To reopen it, choose the **Mail Merge Helper** button on the Mail Merge toolbar.

2   Choose the **Get Data** button. A menu appears.

3   Choose **Use Address Book**. A list of available address books appears. (See Figure 3.9.)

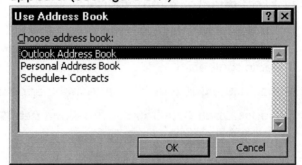

Figure 3.9.   Select the program whose address book you want to use.

4   Select the program you want, and choose **OK**.

5   If the **Choose Profile** dialog box appears, choose the profile to use from the **Profile Name** drop-down list; then choose **OK**.

 NOTE: If you do not know which profile to use, just click **OK** to choose the default one.

6   Complete the mail merge normally.

 TIP: When you perform a mail merge based on an address book, you will probably want to set up a query so that only the names you want are merged. To do so, refer to **Sort and Filter Merge Data** later in this lesson.

USE EXCEL DATA

If you are a Microsoft Office user, you probably have Excel installed on your computer, and possibly Access too. You can use data from either of these programs for your mail merge.

If you already have data in Excel that you want to use in your mail merge, first open it in Excel and check the following:

*   If you don't want to use the entire worksheet in the merge, create a named range in Excel for the range of cells to use. (See Excel's Help system if needed.)

*   Make sure there are no blank rows at the top of the worksheet if you are not using a named range.

*   Make sure that the first row in the worksheet or range contains the column headings to use as field names.

When you are satisfied with the setup of your data in Excel, save your work and close Excel. Then perform the following steps.

 CAUTION: Excel allows you to split and merge cells, just like Word does in tables, so that not every row has the same number of columns in it. This is very helpful for creating printed forms in Excel, but it can really mess things up in a mail merge. Don't use a worksheet with split or merged cells for mail merge data; if you must, unsplit or unmerge the offending cells first.

Use Excel data for a mail merge:

 1   Start in the **Mail Merge Helper** dialog box. If you need to reopen it, do so by choosing the **Mail Merge Helper** button on the Mail Merge toolbar.

2   Choose the <u>G</u>et Data button. A menu appears.

3   Choose **Open Data Source**. The **Open Data Source** dialog box appears.

4 Change the **Files of Type** setting to MS Excel Worksheets (*.xls).

5 Locate and select the Excel workbook containing the data, then choose **Open**. A **Microsoft Excel** dialog box appears, as shown in Figure 3.10.

Figure 3.10. Choose the range to use, or choose **Entire Spreadsheet** if there are no named ranges that you want.

6 Choose the named range if you created one, or choose **Entire Spreadsheet** to use the whole sheet. Then choose **OK**.

7 Complete the merge normally.

Microsoft has carefully designed all Office programs to work seamlessly together; this is why it's almost as easy to use Excel data as it is to work with data in Word itself. It's easy with Access too, as you'll see in the following topic.

USE ACCESS DATA

Access is a database program ideally designed for keeping track of things like addresses and other contact information. Therefore, it's a good bet that if you use Access, you've got some names and addresses stored in it.

To prepare to use Access data, open Access and remind yourself of the name of the database file and the table or query within it that holds the data you want. Then exit Access.

 NOTE: A query in Access is a set of criteria that plucks certain records from one or more tables and assembles them in a particular order. For example, you might have a query that picks out only people with ZIP codes greater than 55555. You can create simple queries as you merge in Word, as you'll see later in this lesson.

Use Access data for mail merge:

 1 Start in the **Mail Merge Helper** dialog box. If you need to reopen it, do so by choosing the **Mail Merge Helper** button on the Mail Merge toolbar.

2 Choose the **Get Data** button. A menu appears.

3 Choose **Open Data Source**. The **Open Data Source** dialog box appears.

4 Change the **Files of Type** setting to MS Access Databases (*.mdb; *.mde).

5 Locate and select the Access database containing the data, then choose **Open**. A **Microsoft Access** dialog box appears, listing the tables and queries.

6 Select the table or query you want, and choose **OK**.

7 Complete the mail merge normally.

USE A DELIMITED TEXT FILE

Text files can be the trickiest of data sources, not only because they're inherently difficult, but also because they tend to have errors in them more often than other types of sources do. These errors might have been introduced by sloppy data entry (for example, pressing **Tab** too many times between entries) or by a poorly designed or incorrectly used export utility in some other program.

For example, notice Figure 3.11. It is an ordinary text file (**.txt**) opened in Word. As you can see, the fields are separated into columns by tabs, but on some lines there is more than one tab between certain columns. Whoever created this table added the extra tabs to make the data line up neatly on-screen, but the extra tabs mess up a mail merge. Why? Because when importing data from text files, Word relies on delimiter characters to tell it when one column ends and the next one begins on each line. When Word encounters two tabs in a row, it thinks that the second tab represents another field and that there is simply no data in the space between them. Rows with extra tab stops end up with more columns than other rows, and Word becomes very confused.

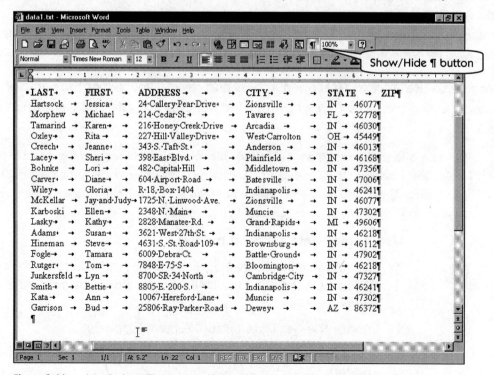

Figure 3.11. A typical text file separated into columns with tab stops.

To clean up a text file before using it as a data file, you must remove the extra tabs. There's no automatic way to do this; you must do it manually, moving the insertion point to each extra one and deleting it. It does help to turn on the display of hidden characters (such as tabs) with the **Show/Hide ¶** button.

 TIP: Word can search for and replace two tab stops in a row with a single tab stop. Use **Edit>Replace** and search for ^t^t. Replace it with ^t. Rerun the Replace until it finds no more. This will not take care of extra single tabs at the ends of lines, but it will save you some work searching for double tabs within lines.

After you remove all the extra tabs, check your work by converting the text to a table.

Convert text to a table:

1   Select all the data.

2   Choose **Table>Convert>Text to Table**. The **Convert Text to Table** dialog box opens.

3   Check the **Number of columns** setting. If it is not what you expected, choose **Cancel** and continue looking for errors in the tabs. If it is correct, choose **OK**.

4   Check for errors again, making sure that each cell has exactly one entry in it—no more, no less.

5   If needed, add a row at the top of the table for the headings, and type the headings above each column.

6   Save the data as a Word file, and use it to perform your mail merge.

You can also use the text file directly, without converting it to a Word table, if you are confident that there are no errors in it. To do so, follow these steps:

Use a text file as a merge source:

 1   Start in the **Mail Merge Helper** dialog box. If you need to reopen it, do so by choosing the **Mail Merge Helper** button on the Mail Merge toolbar.

2   Choose the **Get Data** button. A menu appears.

3   Choose **Open Data Source**. The **Open Data Source** dialog box appears.

4   Change the **Files of Type** setting to Text Files (*.txt).

5   Locate and select the text file containing the data, then choose **Open**.

6   Complete the merge normally.

NOTE: If you see the **Header Record Delimiters** box, shown in Figure 3.12, it means that there were errors that prevented Word from dividing the data neatly into fields. You can continue through the process by selecting the **Field** delimiter (for example, **Tab**) and the **Record** delimiter (for example, **Enter**) and choosing **OK**, but you will then need to open the text file and find the errors. It is better to choose **Cancel** if you see this, and then close all other dialog boxes and edit the text file.

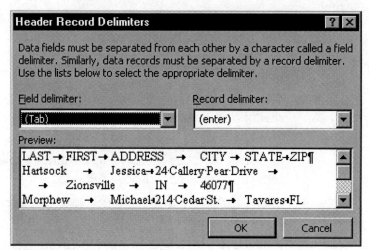

Figure 3.12. If this dialog box is displayed, Word is uncertain about the delimiter character because of errors in your text file.

Practice Exercise 3-2

Use Data from Other Sources

1   Open 📂**03Ex3-2a** from the **WORDCert\Word B** folder, and save it as 🖫**03Lettr2**.

 NOTE: If during this exercise the **Confirm Data Source** dialog box appears, choose **OK**, selecting the default choice.

2   Start the mail merge normally, by doing the following:

- Choose **Tools>Mail Merge**.
- Choose **Create**, and then choose **Form Letters**.
- Choose **Active Window**.

3 Select the Excel file **03Ex3-2b** for the data source by doing the following:

- Choose **Get Data**, and then choose **Open Data Source**.
- Change the **Files of type** to MS Excel Worksheets (*.xls).
- Choose **03Ex3-2b**, and choose **Open**.
- In the **Microsoft Excel** dialog box, choose **Entire Spreadsheet**, and choose **OK**.
- Choose **Edit Main Document**.

4 Change the data source to the Access database **03Ex3-2c** by doing the following:

- Choose **Tools>Mail Merge** to reenter the **Mail Merge Helper** dialog box.
- Choose **Get Data**, and then choose **Open Data Source**.
- Change the **Files of type** to MS Access Databases (*.mdb; *.mde).
- Choose **03Ex3-2c**, and choose **Open**.
- In the **Microsoft Access** dialog box, select the **Addresses** table, and choose **OK**.
- Choose **Edit Main Document**.

5 Change the data source to the text file **03Ex3-2d** by doing the following:

- Choose **Tools>Mail Merge** to reenter the **Mail Merge Helper** dialog box.
- Choose **Get Data**, and then choose **Open Data Source**.
- Change the **Files of type** to Text Files (*.txt).

    CAUTION: If the **Select Method** check box is deselected, click the box to select it.

- Choose **03Ex3-2d**, and choose **Open**.
- If the **Confirm Data Source** dialog box appears, make sure Text Files (*.txt) (the default choice) is selected and choose **OK**.
- If a box appears asking for header delimiters, accept the default (**None**) and click **OK**.
- Choose **Edit Main Document**.

6 Save your work; leave the document open for the next exercise.

A completed example of **03Lettr2** is available in the **WORDCert\Word B\Samples** folder on the DDC CD-ROM.

ENTER DATA IN A FORM

As you were using the Mail Merge Helper, you may have noticed that you could choose to create a data source file rather than open one. This method works well if you do not have the names and addresses already typed into the file ahead of time. Word prompts you to save your work when you're done, so you end up with a separate data file containing a Word table. It's simply a different way of getting to the same result.

Create a data file for a mail merge:

1   Start in the **Mail Merge Helper** dialog box. If you need to reopen it, do so by choosing the **Mail Merge Helper** button on the Mail Merge toolbar.

2   Choose the **Get Data** button. A menu appears.

3   Choose **Create Data Source**. The **Create Data Source** dialog box appears, as shown in Figure 3.13.

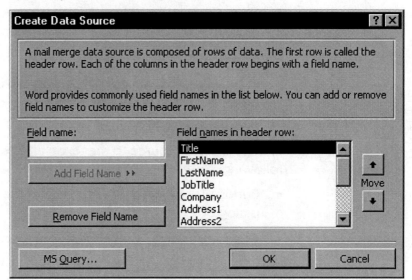

Figure 3.13.   Here's where you set up the fields (the column headings) you'll use in the data source.

4   Do any of the following as needed:

- Accept the ready-made list of fields that appear on the **Field names in header row** list.

- Remove a field that you don't want by choosing it and clicking the **Remove Field Name** button.

- Add a new field by typing its name in the **Field name** text box and then choosing the **Add Field Name** button.

- Rearrange fields by choosing the field you want to reposition and choosing the **Up** or **Down** arrow button in the dialog box.

5   When you are satisfied with the fields and their order, choose **OK**. The **Save As** dialog box opens.

6   Enter a name for your data file, and choose **Save**.

7   A message appears that your data source contains no records. Choose **Edit Data Source**.

8   Enter information into the fields for the first record. (See Figure 3.14.)

9   If you need to enter another record, choose **Add New** and then enter the data. When you are finished entering records, choose **OK**.

10 Continue with the merge normally.

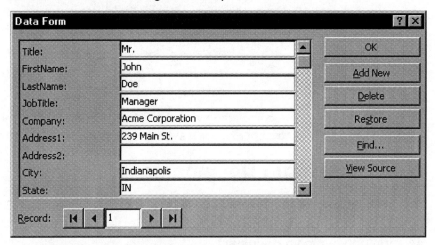

Figure 3.14.   Enter each person's name and address into the form, choosing **Add New** after each record.

Practice Exercise 3-3

Create a Data Source

1   Start in the file **03Lettr2** from the preceding exercise, or open 📂**03Ex3-3** from the **WORDCert\Word B** folder. Save the file as 💾**03Lettr3**.

2   Choose **Tools>Mail Merge** to reopen the **Mail Merge Helper** dialog box.

3   Choose the **Get Data** button, and then choose **Create Data Source**.

4   Choose the **HomePhone** field, and choose **Remove Field Name**. Do the same for **WorkPhone**.

5   Choose the **Company** field, and click the **Up** arrow button four times, moving **Company** to the top of the list. Then choose **OK**.

6   In the **Save As** dialog box, type ‾03Merge‾ for the file name and choose **Save**.

7   Choose **Edit** **D**ata **Source**.

8   Enter your own information in the **Data Form**, and then choose
    Add **New**.

9   Enter a friend's name and address in the **Data Form** (or make up
    a name and address), and choose **OK**. You now have two
    records in the data source.

> **NOTE:** If you have some extra time, you can try inserting the
> fields into the main document, as you learned to do earlier in
> the lesson.

10 Open the **Insert Merge Field** drop-down list to confirm that the
    field names appear there. Save your work, then close the file.

> **NOTE:** A dialog box appears asking if you want to save the
> data source, **03Merge**, that is attached to the **03Lettr3**
> document. Choose **Yes**.

A completed example of **03Merge** is available in the
WORDCert\Word B\Samples folder on the DDC CD-ROM.

Work with Main Documents

You have already seen how you can build a main document using a combination of
typed text and inserted fields. The following topics show some other tweaks you can
perform on your main document.

USE NON-BREAKING SPACES AND HYPHENS

As you are typing your main document (or any document, for that matter), you may
sometimes want to control how Word ends a line. By default, Word figures out the line
breaks for you. It breaks lines at spaces or at hyphens. However, this can sometimes be
awkward when you have a compound phrase or a hyphenated phrase that should stay
together. You can end up with breaks like these:

> *The last time I checked the outside temperature, the thermometer read -
> 3 degrees Fahrenheit.*

> *If you would like to congratulate Ben, write to him at this address: 909
> 1/2 Thomas Avenue, Springfield, IL 60394.*

In each case, the break has fallen at exactly the wrong spot, resulting in some potential
for confusion. The solution in both cases is to use a non-breaking space or hyphen.

Insert a non-breaking space:

• Press **Ctrl+Shift+Spacebar**.

Insert a non-breaking hyphen:

• Press **Ctrl+Shift+- (hyphen)**.

INSERT DATE AND TIME CODES

Besides the mail merge field codes, you can insert other codes in a document (any document, not just a mail merge one). For example, you can insert a code that will place the current date and/or time in the document, updating it automatically based on your computer's built-in clock/calendar.

Insert a date or time code:

1   Position the insertion point where you want the date or time to appear.

2   Choose **Insert>Date and Time**. The **Date and Time** dialog box opens. (See Figure 3.15.)

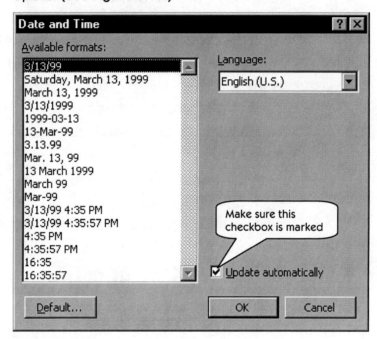

Figure 3.15.   Select the date or time format that you want.

3   Select the format you want.

4   Make sure the **Update automatically** checkbox is marked.

5   Choose **OK**. The code is inserted, and the current date or time appears.

   TIP: You can also insert the current date or time by pressing **Alt+Shift+D**. This inserts the date or time in the default format. To set the default format, choose a format in the **Date and Time** dialog box and then choose the **Default** button.

Practice Exercise 3-4

Add Non-Breaking Spaces and Date Codes

1   Open 📂**03Lettr3** from the preceding exercise, or open 📂**03Ex3-4** from the **WORDCert\Word B** folder and save it as 💾**03Lettr4**.

2   Position the insertion point at the end of the first body line (after *dozens*), then press **Delete**, removing the space between *dozens* and *of*. The resulting word, *dozensof*, appears on the next line.

3   Press **Ctrl+Shift+Spacebar**, inserting a non-breaking space between the two words. Now a space appears, but both words stay on the same line.

4   Select the current date in the document, and press **Delete**.

5   Choose **Insert>Date and Time**. The **Date and Time** dialog box opens.

6   Choose the second format on the list.

7   Make sure the **Update automatically** checkbox is marked.

8   Choose **OK**.

9   Save your work, and close the file.

A completed example of **03Lettr4** is available in the **WORDCert\Word B\Samples** folder on the DDC CD-ROM.

Preview Merged Letters One at a Time

To do a quick check before printing, many people find it useful to use Word's View Merged Data feature. This feature enables you to see one letter at a time on-screen exactly as it will print. You can scroll through the stack of letters with the controls Word provides.

TOGGLE MERGED DATA ON/OFF

 Choose the **View Merged Data** button on the Mail Merge toolbar. This toggles between displaying the merge fields (in arrow brackets) and displaying the actual names and addresses.

From there, you can scroll through the letters with the buttons immediately to the right of the **View Merged Data** button:

First Record button: Displays the first letter

Previous Record: Displays the letter before the currently displayed one

Go to Record: Displays the letter number that you specify

Next Record: Displays the next letter

Last Record: Displays the last letter

You can return to displaying the field names by clicking on the **View Merged Data** button again.

 NOTE: Many people prefer simply to merge to a new document and scroll through that document rather than previewing the letters like this.

Practice Exercise 3-5

Preview Merged Letters

1 Open the file 📁**03Ex3-5** from the **WORDCert\Word B** folder. Save it as 📁**03Lettr5**.

2 Choose the **View Merged Data** button. The first letter appears.

3 Choose the **Next Record** button. The next letter appears.

4 Choose the **Last Record** button. The last letter appears.

5 Choose the **View Merged Data** button. The field codes reappear.

6 Leave the document open for the next exercise.

Sort and Filter Merge Data

The default merge options may not be satisfactory in some situations. For example, if you are merging data from an address book, you may not want to create letters for every single person in your book. Or you may need the letters in a certain order (such as sorted by ZIP code for a mass mailing). In the following topics, you'll learn about sorting and filtering, two merge options you can set.

 NOTE: To set any of the **Merge** options, you must use the **Merge** dialog box. That means you can't go the shortcut route of choosing the **Merge to New Document** or **Merge to Printer** button on the Mail Merge toolbar when you are ready to perform the merge. Instead, you must choose the **Merge** button on the Mail Merge toolbar to open the **Merge** dialog box, and select the options you want to use.

SORT DATA

There are two ways to sort data in a particular order by one or more fields. One is simply to sort the Word table that contains it before you begin the merge process. Refer back to Lesson 1 of Section B to learn how to do that.

The other way is to do it while merging, as shown in the following steps.

Sort data to be merged:

1 Start a normal merge, and choose your merge type and data source.

2 In the **Mail Merge Helper** dialog box, choose the **Query Options** button. The **Query Options** dialog box opens.

3 Choose the **Sort Records** tab.

4 Open the **Sort by** drop-down list, then choose the field that you want to sort by. (See Figure 3.16.)

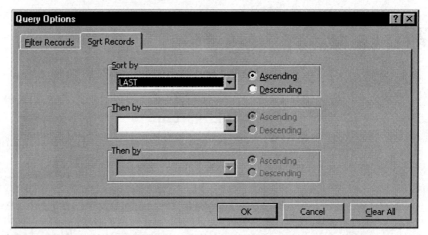

Figure 3.16.   Select up to three fields to sort by, in ascending or descending order.

5 Choose **Ascending** or **Descending**.

 NOTE: For a refresher on sorting, refer back to Lesson 1 of Section B.

6 If you want to sort by additional fields, select them in the **Then by** sections.

7 Choose **OK**.

8 Continue the merge normally.

FILTER RECORDS WITH A QUERY

A query is like a filter into which you pour your records. The ones you want are trapped by the filter and retained; the others fall through and are discarded. (Not permanently discarded; they're just not used in the particular mail merge you're doing.)

You can filter records either by field (based on criteria you choose) or by record number (based on their position in the data source file).

Filter records by field:

1   Start a normal merge; choose the merge type and data source.

2   In the **Mail Merge Helper** dialog box, choose the **Query Options** button. The **Query Options** dialog box opens.

3   Choose the **Filter Records** tab if it is not already on top.

4   Open the first **Field** drop-down list; choose the field containing the criterion by which to filter.

5   Open the first **Comparison** drop-down list, and choose the comparison operator you want.

6   In the first **Compare to** box, type the value to compare to. Figure 3.17 shows the settings for a filter that picks out everyone whose last name begins with the letters M through Z.

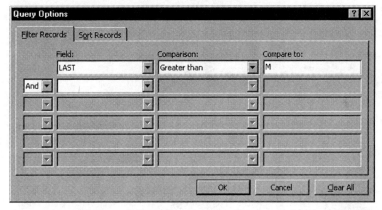

Figure 3.17.   This filter will select people with a last name beginning with M through Z.

 NOTE: How does the query shown in Figure 3.17 work? Names that begin with M are going to be "greater than" M by itself. They come after M in an alphabetical listing. By setting the value of **Greater than M**, you pull in those that begin with M plus those that come after them alphabetically (N through Z names).

7   To add other criteria, do so in the other rows. Then choose **OK**.

8   Continue the merge normally.

Another way to filter records is by their place in the data source file. Word considers the first record in the table (or other data source) to be record 1, the next one 2, and so on.

Filter records by record number:

1   Set up the merge normally, up to the point where you are ready
    to merge.

2   If the **Mail Merge Helper** box is open, choose the **Merge** button
    in it. If it isn't, choose the **Merge** button on the **Mail Merge**
    toolbar. The **Merge** dialog box appears. (See Figure 3.18.)

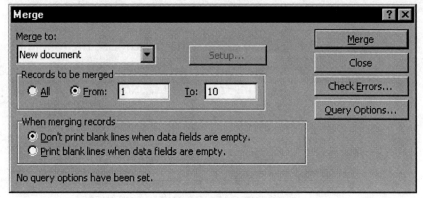

Figure 3.18.   Choose records by number in the **Merge** dialog box.

3   In the **Records to be merged** section, choose the option button
    next to **From** and enter the starting record number in the text
    box.

4   Enter the last record number in the **To** text box.

5   Choose **Merge** to complete the merge normally.

Practice Exercise 3-6

Sort and Filter Records

1   Start in the file **03Lettr5** from the preceding exercise, or open
    📂**03Ex3-6** from the **WORDCert\Word B** folder. Save the file as
    💾**03Lettr6**.

   2   Choose the **Merge** button on the Mail Merge toolbar.

3   Choose the **Query Options** button.

4   On the **Filter Records** tab, set up a filter that chooses only
    people in Indianapolis:

    •   Choose **City** from the **Field** drop-down list.

    •   Choose **Equal to** from the **Comparison** list.

    •   Type **Indianapolis** in the **Compare to** box.

5   Choose the **Sort Records** tab, and sort in descending order by
    ZIP code:

    •   Choose **ZIP** from the **Sort by** drop-down list.

    •   Choose the **Descending** button.

6 Choose **OK**. The **Merge** dialog box is in view again.

7 Choose **Merge**. The letters are merged to a new file.

8 Scroll through the file and confirm that only people with Indianapolis addresses are listed. Then close the document containing the letters without saving it.

9 **03Lettr6** is still open; save it and close it.

Create Merged Mailing Labels

Form letters are certainly not the only thing you can create with a mail merge. In fact, the most common thing that many people use mail merges for is creating sheets of mailing labels. Doing so is really no harder than creating a form letter.

Create mail-merged labels:

1 Start a new document, and choose **Tools>Mail Merge** to open the **Mail Merge Helper**.

2 Choose the **Create** button, and choose **Mailing Labels**.

3 A box appears asking whether you want to use the active window or start a new document. Choose **Active Window**.

4 Choose the **Get Data** button, and either open or create a data source, as you learned earlier in this lesson.

5 When you see a message that Word needs to set up your main document, choose **Set Up Main Document**.

6 A **Label Options** dialog box opens, as shown in Figure 3.19. At the top of the box, choose the type of printer you are using: **Dot matrix** or **Laser and ink jet**.

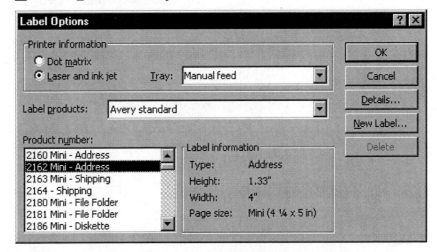

Figure 3.19. Word gives you the chance to set the label size and specifications.

7   In the **Tray** drop-down list, choose how you will feed the labels into the printer. Choose **Manual** if you will feed each sheet of labels in by hand, or choose a paper tray (such as **Upper** or **Lower**) if you are going to put the labels in the regular paper tray.

 TIP: Even though sheets of labels fit into a laser printer's tray, it is sometimes better to feed them in manually so they don't crumple or wrinkle as much.

8   Look on the box that your labels came in and find the Avery number. Even if the labels were not made by Avery, there should still be an Avery-equivalent number on them.

9   Select the Avery number from the **Product number** list.

 NOTE: If you don't have an Avery number, measure a single label on the sheet, and choose an Avery number that has the same measurements and number of labels per sheet. To find out how many labels there are per sheet, choose a label and then choose the **Details** button. However, because most label sheets designed for ink-jet or laser printers are normal paper size, if you match up with the right size label, the number of labels per sheet should automatically be correct.

10 Choose **OK**. The **Create Labels** dialog box appears. (See Figure 3.20.)

11 Choose the **Insert Merge Field** button, and choose the first field that you want on the label.

12 Add the rest of the fields you want, separating them with spaces and line breaks as needed to form an address block.

 TIP: You can change the label margins by clicking the **Details** button in the **Label Options** dialog box when you select the label in step 8.

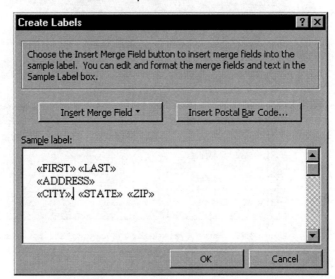

Figure 3.20.   Insert merge fields to form a normal address for a single label.

13 Choose **OK**. Word creates a sheet of label placeholders, which you can see on your screen behind the **Mail Merge Helper** dialog box.

14 Choose the **Merge** button (in the dialog box). Then in the **Merge** dialog box that appears, choose **Merge** again. Word creates a sheet of labels, ready to print, as shown in Figure 3.21.

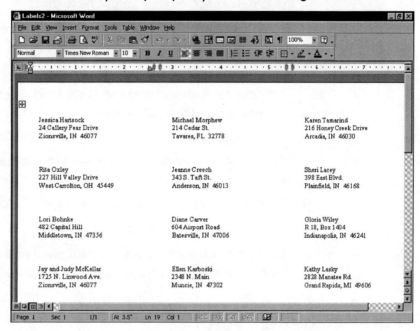

Figure 3.21. You can print this document on a sheet of label paper.

 CAUTION: Choose your labels carefully. There are label sheets designed for each type of printer: dot matrix, ink jet, and laser. If you use the wrong label type in your printer, it can damage the printer. In particular, labels designed for dot matrix or ink-jet use are apt to melt inside a laser printer, jamming up the printer mechanism and requiring costly repair.

Practice Exercise 3-7

Create Mailing Labels

1 Start a new document, and save it as 🖫03Labels.

2 Choose **Tools>Mail Merge**.

3 Choose **Create**, and then choose **Mailing Labels**. Then choose **Active Window**.

4 Choose **Get Data**, and then choose **Open Data Source**. Select **03data**, and choose **Open**. Then choose **Set Up Main Document**.

5 Make sure **Laser and ink jet** is selected as the printer information. In the **Product number** list, choose **5160 - Address**. Then choose **OK**.

6   In the **Create Labels** dialog box, insert fields to form the address:

- Press **Enter** once to create a blank space at the top of each label.

- Choose **In̲sert Merge Field**, and choose **First**. Then press the **Spacebar**, and insert the **Last name** field the same way.

- Press **Enter**, moving to the next line.

- Choose **In̲sert Merge Field**, and choose **Address**.

- Press **Enter**.

- Choose **In̲sert Merge Field**, and choose **City**. Follow it with a comma, a space, and the **State** field. Then add two more spaces and the **ZIP** field.

- Choose **OK**.

7   Choose **M̲erge**, and then choose **M̲erge** again. The labels appear, ready for printing.

8   Save the sheet of labels as 🖫**03Print**, and close the document.

9   Save **03Labels**, and close it.

Completed examples of **03Print** and **03Labels** are available in the **WORDCert\Word B\Samples** folder on the DDC CD-ROM.

Create Merged Envelopes

Creating envelopes is much the same as creating labels, except for a dialog box or two. Use this procedure when you want to print directly on a stack of envelopes rather than printing on labels and then sticking them onto envelopes.

 TIP: If you want to use a return address on the merged envelopes, set it up first. Choose **Tools>E̲nvelopes and Labels**, and enter a return address in the **R̲eturn address** box. When asked if you want it to be the default, choose **Y̲es**. Then choose **Change Document**.

Print mail merge envelopes:

1   Start a new, blank document, and choose **Tools>Mail Me̲rge** to open the **Mail Merge Helper**.

2   Choose the **C̲reate** button, and choose **Envelopes**. Then choose **A̲ctive Window**.

3   Choose **G̲et Data**, and either open or create a data source.

4   Choose **Set Up Main Document**.

5   An **Envelope Options** dialog box appears, as shown in Figure 3.22. Choose the envelope size you want from the **Envelope s̲ize** drop-down list.

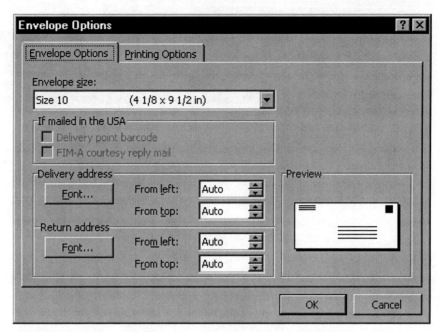

Figure 3.22. Set the envelope size and the position of the addresses on it.

 NOTE: The default envelope size is 10, which is a standard business envelope.

6 If you want to reposition the return address or the mailing address on the envelope, use the controls in the **Delivery address** and **Return address** sections.

7 Choose the **Printing Options** tab, and choose the correct orientation for your envelopes.

 TIP: If you are not sure of the correct envelope orientation, consult your printer manual, or experiment.

8 Choose **OK**. An **Envelope Address** dialog box appears. It's exactly the same as the box you worked with for mailing labels in Figure 3.20 except for its title.

9 Insert merge fields into the dialog box just as you did with mailing labels, and then choose **OK**.

10 Back in the **Mail Merge Helper**, choose **Merge**, and then choose the **Merge** button in the **Merge** dialog box that appears. Word creates the envelopes in a new document, as shown in Figure 3.23.

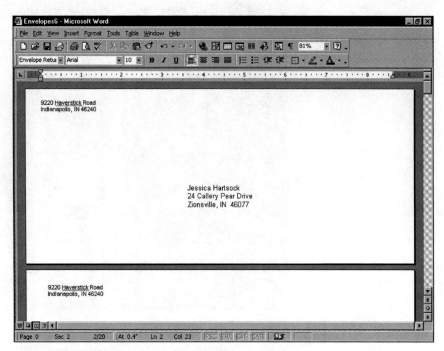

Figure 3.23. Each envelope is a separate section, ready to print.

11 Load your printer with envelopes, or feed them in manually, and print.

Practice Exercise 3-8

Print Envelopes with a Mail Merge

1 Start a new document, and save it as 🖫**03Env**.

2 Choose **Tools>Mail Merge**.

3 Choose **Create** and then **Envelopes**. Then choose **Active Window**.

4 Choose **Get Data** and then **Open Data Source**. Select **03Data**, and choose **Open**. Then choose **Set Up Main Document**.

5 In the **Envelope Options** dialog box, make sure that the **Envelope size** is set to **Size 10**.

6 Choose **OK**.

7 Insert fields in the **Sample envelope address** area to create the address block, the same as you did in earlier exercises. Then choose **OK**.

 TIP: Refer to step 6 of Practice Exercise 3-7 for detailed instructions.

8 Choose **Merge**, and then choose **Merge** again to create the envelopes.

NOTE: If you have a return address set up it will appear automatically on your envelopes.

9 Save the envelope file as 🖫**03Print2**, and close it.

10 Save 🖫**03Env**, and close it.

Completed examples of **03Print2** and **03Env** are available in the **WORDCert\Word B\Samples** folder on the DDC CD-ROM.

Create a Catalog

A catalog listing is just like any of the other merged documents except that more than one record appears per page. It's called a catalog because it creates a listing of the chosen fields from each record, one after the other, as shown in Figure 3.24. By now, the merge process should seem pretty familiar to you.

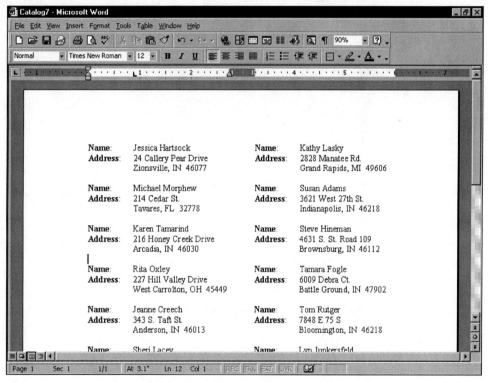

Figure 3.24. Here is a catalog of names and addresses.

Create a catalog:

1 Start a new document, and choose **Tools>Mail Merge**.

2 Choose the **Create** button, and choose **Catalog**.

3 Choose **Active Window**.

4 Choose the **Get Data** button, and either open or create a data source.

5 Choose **Edit Main** Document. The dialog box goes away, and you see your blank document.

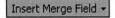 **6** Insert the fields for one record using the **Insert Merge Field** button on the Mail Merge toolbar.

> **NOTE:** Word will duplicate the fields for you to make the catalog.

7 Format any text around the fields, and format the fields themselves as desired.

> **NOTE:** For example, in Figure 3.25, field names have been added (**Name** and **Address**) and the fields have been aligned with tab stops. One extra line of space appears after the fields.

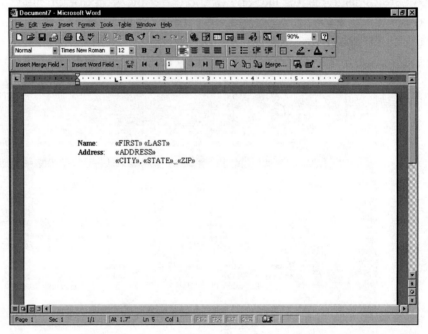

Figure 3.25. Set up a single record, just as you would set up the fields in a form letter.

 8 Choose the **Merge to New Document** button on the Mail Merge toolbar to perform the merge, as shown in Figure 3.26.

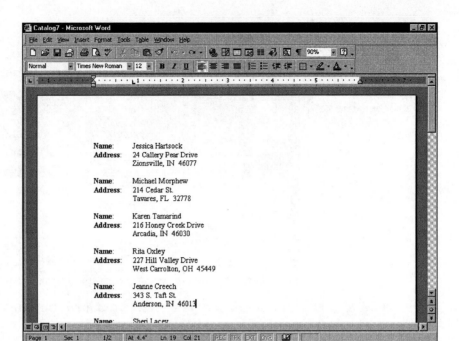

Figure 3.26. The results of merging the fields from Figure 3.25.

 TIP: Depending on the length of the data in each field, you might want to divide the list into two or more columns using the Columns feature you learned about earlier in this section, so that your catalog listing looks like the one back in Figure 3.24.

Practice Exercise 3-9

Create a Catalog

1 Start a new document; save it as 🖫**03Cat**.

2 Choose **Tools>Mail Merge**.

3 Choose **Create** and then **Catalog**. Then choose **Active Window**.

4 Select the Excel file **03Ex3-9** as your data source by doing the following:

- Choose **Get Data** and then **Open Data Source**.

- Choose **MS Excel Worksheets** from the **Files of type** list.

- Select **03Ex3-9**, and choose **Open**.

- If the **Confirm Data Source** dialog box appears, choose **OK**.

- In the **Microsoft Excel** dialog box, choose **OK**.

- Choose **Edit Main Document**.

5 Insert the **<<Product>>** merge field code. Then press **Enter**.

6 Type │Qty on hand:│ and format it as bold.

7 Insert the **<<Quantity>>** field after the text you just typed. Then press **Enter** twice. The screen should resemble Figure 3.27.

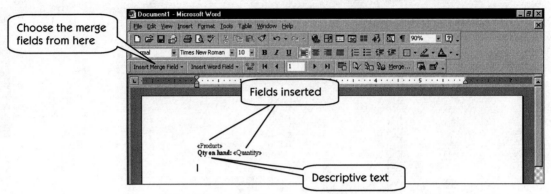

Choose the merge fields from here

Fields inserted

Descriptive text

Figure 3.27.   Set up your catalog to show the product and its quantity, like this.

8 Choose the **Merge to New Document** button on the Mail Merge toolbar. The catalog is created.

9 Format the document in four columns, as you learned in Lesson 2 of this section. Figure 3.28 shows the result.

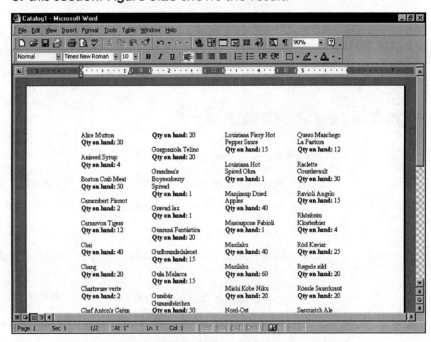

Figure 3.28.   The merged catalog file, formatted in four columns.

10 Save the merged file as 🖫**03Onhand**, and close it. Then save your changes to 🖫**03Cat** and close it. If the Excel worksheet used as a data source opened, close it as well.

LESSON 4: STYLES

Document formatting can become a real chore if the document is long. If you decide, for example, that you want all the headings to be 18-point instead of 16, you can waste a lot of precious time going through and manually reformatting each one. Fortunately, however, there is a solution. Word's **Styles** feature enables you to format characters and paragraphs according to a named style. Then, when you change the style's definition, all text using that style automatically changes, too.

In this lesson, you will learn to:

> ➤ Use styles to format documents
>
> ➤ Create your own styles
>
> ➤ Modify a style
>
> ➤ Copy styles between documents

You'll get hands-on practice with these features throughout the lesson, and then you'll review them in the exercises at the end of the lesson.

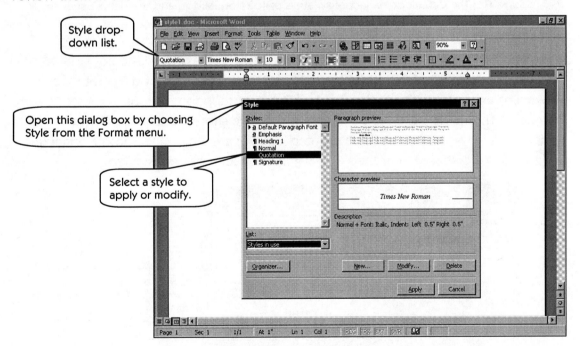

Figure 4.1.   You'll learn how to speed up your formatting in this lesson with styles.

What Are Styles?

Styles are named sets of formatting specifications. A style might specify a particular font, line spacing, indentation, tab stop, and so on. When you apply the style to some text, you apply all of its formatting in one action.

 NOTE: There are two types of styles: **Character** and **Paragraph**. Character styles apply only character formatting like font changes. Paragraph styles apply both character and paragraph formatting. Character styles are not often used; most styles that come with Word's templates are Paragraph styles.

Each template has a style called **Normal** on which all styles are directly or indirectly based. For example, Word's built-in Heading 1 style in the Normal (Blank Document) template is defined as the **Normal** style with these changes:

- Font: Arial 16-pt bold
- Kerning: at 16 pt
- Paragraph spacing: 12 points before, 3 points after
- Line and page breaks: Keep with Next
- Outline level: Level 1

 NOTE: The default document template is called **Normal.dot**, and the default style in a template is called **Normal**. Don't let the similar names confuse you.

When you assign the Heading 1 style to a paragraph, you assign all the above attributes automatically, plus all of the attributes of Normal style that are not different from the above. For example, notice that in Figure 4.2, the description for Heading 1 starts with "Normal+." This helps make the definition of the style shorter because only the deviations from Normal need to be pointed out. For example, since both Normal text and Heading 1 text are left-aligned, the alignment need not be specified.

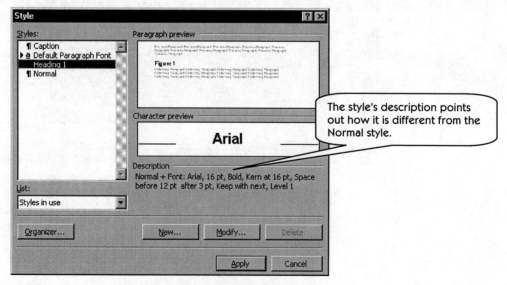

Figure 4.2.   Each style has a set of formatting attributes.

You can modify the Normal style just as you can modify any other style, so you can change the basis on which the other styles rely.

 NOTE: Style formatting can be overridden (for example, you could manually remove the Bold attribute from a heading).

 TIP: If characters within a paragraph have been manually formatted, you can return them to their default condition, as specified by the style assigned to the paragraph, by selecting the text and pressing **Ctrl+Spacebar**.

The styles available depend on which template the document was based on. Different templates have different styles. For example, the Elegant Letter template includes a style called Enclosure, while the Normal template does not.

Also, the same style might be defined differently from one template to another; for example, Heading 1 in the Normal template is 16-pt bold Arial, left-aligned, while Heading 1 in the Elegant Letter template is 10.5-pt, all-caps Garamond, centered.

OTHER USES FOR STYLES

Word uses styles in all kinds of ways that you might not expect. By learning about styles, you are plugging into a rich assortment of formatting features.

For example, when you generate a table of contents with the **Insert>Index** and **Tables** command (which will be covered in **Section C**), the table of contents is based on styles. Any paragraphs that have a heading style applied (Heading 1, Heading 2, and so on) are automatically included in the table of contents. The lines of the outline itself are also formatted with their own styles: TOC 1, TOC 2, etc. It's the same with tables of figures and tables of authorities. (See Figure 4.3.)

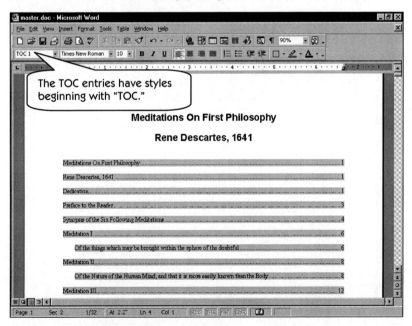

Figure 4.3.   This table of contents was created using the Heading styles in the document.

When you work in **Outline** view in Word, the various levels of the outline are also based on styles: Heading 1 for the first level in the outline; Heading 2 for the second level; and so on. You will learn about outlining in Lesson 5.

APPLY STYLES

Word offers several ways to apply a style:

- You can choose a style from the **Styles** drop-down list on the Formatting toolbar.

- You can choose **Format>Style** and select a style from the dialog box that appears.

- You can press the shortcut-key combination assigned to the style you want.

The shortcut-key method is the easiest, but you must remember the key combination for each style. This is not practical, especially for beginners. In addition, most styles do not have shortcut keys assigned by default, so you must set them up for the styles you use the most. (You'll learn to do this later in the lesson.)

The drop-down list method is faster and easier than the dialog box method, but you may not always be able to take advantage of it. The **Styles** drop-down list shows only the styles that are already in use in the document (with a few exceptions). If you want to use a style that has not already been used, and you don't see it on the **Styles** list, hold down the **Shift** key as you open the list, or open the dialog box.

Apply a style from the Styles list:

1   Select the text you want to apply a style to, or position the insertion point in a paragraph to apply it to the paragraph.

2   Open the **Styles** drop-down list on the Formatting toolbar; choose the style you want. (See Figure 4.4.)

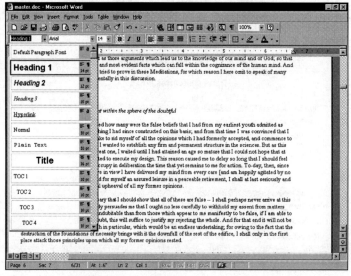

Figure 4.4.   A quick way to apply a style is to choose it from the **Styles** drop-down list.

CAUTION: If you select a portion of a paragraph before you apply the style, the style will apply only to the selected text. Therefore, if you want a style to apply to an entire paragraph, make sure you either select the entire paragraph first in step 1, or position the insertion point within the paragraph without selecting anything.

Apply a style with the Style dialog box:

1   Select the text you want to apply a style to, or position the insertion point anywhere in a paragraph to apply it to the whole paragraph.

2   Choose **F**ormat>**S**tyle. The **Style** dialog box opens. (See Figure 4.5.)

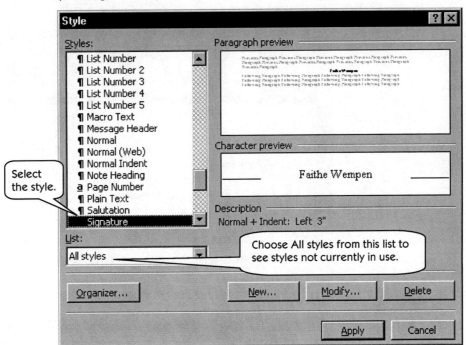

Figure 4.5.   Select the style you want from the **Styles** list.

3   Select the style from the **Styles** list.

 TIP: By default, the **Styles** list shows the styles that are currently in use in the document. If the style you want is not yet in use, open the **L**ist drop-down list and choose **All Styles**.

4   Choose **A**pply. The style is applied, and the dialog box closes.

Practice Exercise 4-1

Apply Styles

1   Start a new document; save it as ⊟**04Style1**.

2   Type your first and last names. Do *not* press **Enter** afterward.

3   Open the **Styles** drop-down list; choose Heading 1.

4   Select your last name (double-click it), and choose **Format>Style**.

5   Open the **List** drop-down list; choose **All styles**.

6   Choose **Signature** from the **Styles** list. Examine the **Description** for it: **Normal+Indent: Left 3"**.

7   Choose **Apply**. Then click away from it to deselect it. Figure 4.6 shows the result.

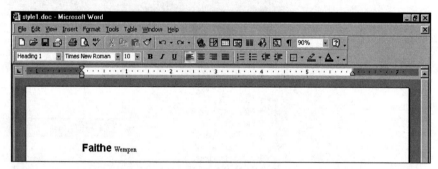

Figure 4.6.   The last name has the character portion of the Signature style applied.

 NOTE: Notice that the character part of the style was applied, but not the paragraph part. That's because you selected some (but not all) of the paragraph's text in step 4.

8   Select your entire name; press **Ctrl+Spacebar**. Figure 4.7 shows the result.

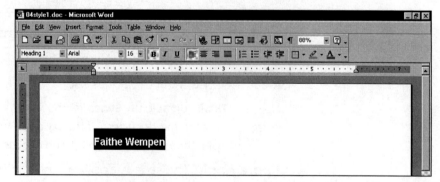

Figure 4.7.   Pressing **Ctrl+Spacebar** removes any character formatting that is not part of the paragraph style's definition.

NOTE: The character formatting is removed from your last name, leaving it with its paragraph style (Heading 1).

9   With the entire name still selected, open the **Styles** drop-down list; choose **Signature**. Figure 4.8 shows the result.

 NOTE: This time both the paragraph and the character formatting associated with the Signature style are applied. The Signature style now appears on the **Styles** drop-down list because it has been used in the document (in steps 6 and 7).

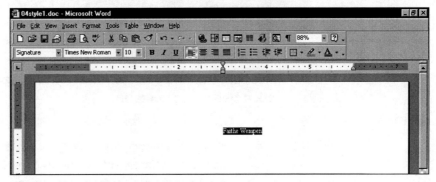

Figure 4.8.   When you select the entire paragraph and apply a style, all of the style's attributes affect the text (both character and paragraph).

10 Save your work; leave the document open for the next exercise.

Modify Styles

You can modify a style either through the **Styles** drop-down list on the Formatting toolbar or through the **Style** dialog box. As usual, the toolbar method is easier, but the dialog box method is more powerful.

 NOTE: The following procedure does not work when changing the Normal style. For that style, you must use the dialog box method, described later in this lesson.

Modify a style by example:

1   Apply the style to some text in your document.

2   Make changes to that text to match what you want the style to be in the future.

3   Click in the **Styles** drop-down list's text box. The name of the style will be highlighted.

4   Press **Enter**. A **Modify Style** dialog box opens, as shown in Figure 4.9.

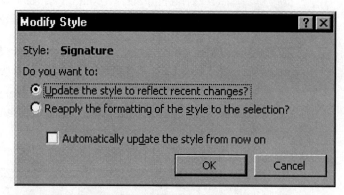

Figure 4.9.   Choose **Update the style to refect recent changes?** to change its definition to the new formatting.

5 Make sure that the **Update the style to reflect recent changes?** option button is selected.

6 Choose **OK**.

NOTE: If you select the **Automatically update the style from now on** checkbox, you will not see the dialog box in Figure 4.9 anymore; instead, pressing **Enter** in step 4 will automatically update the style without further intervention.

NOTE: The other option in Figure 4.9's dialog box, **Reapply the formatting of the style to the selection?**, removes all manual formatting from the text, restoring it to the settings specified by the style.

If you want to modify a style that is not in use in the document, or if you want to make changes to the style that you can't (or don't want to) make by example, you can use the **Style** dialog box to make the changes. The following steps show how.

Modify a style with the Style dialog box:

1 Choose **Format>Style**. The **Style** dialog box opens.

2 Select the style you want to modify from the **Styles** list.

TIP: Remember, if the style you want does not appear, open the **List** drop-down list and choose **All styles**.

3 Choose the **Modify** button. The **Modify Style** dialog box opens. (See Figure 4.10.)

Preparing for Microsoft Office Specialist Certification

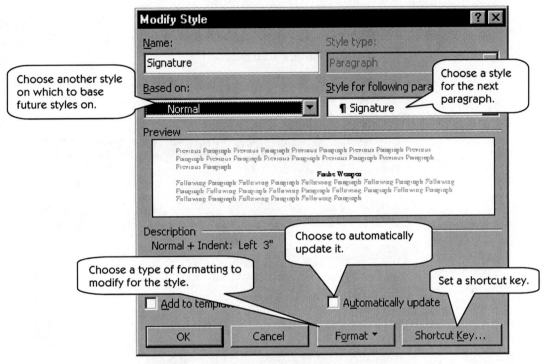

Figure 4.10. You can modify a style from here.

4 Change any of the following settings as needed:

- Rename the style in the **Name** text box. (You can do this only with styles you have created yourself, not with predefined styles that come with Word.)

- Change what other style it is based on.

- Change the **Style** for the following paragraph. (This is the style of the paragraph that will appear when you press **Enter** at the end of a paragraph of this type.)

     TIP: For non-heading styles, you will probably want the style of the following paragraph to be the same. For heading styles, you will probably want the style of the following paragraph to be different (body text usually follows a heading, for example).

- Choose the **Add to template** checkbox if you want the changes to be added to the template currently in use.

- Choose the **Shortcut Key** button to assign a keyboard shortcut. Then press the key combination you want to assign; choose **Assign**.

- Choose **Automatically update** so that you can more quickly modify the style from the toolbar, as you learned in the preceding steps.

NOTE: You can also delete a style that you have created by choosing the **Delete** button. You cannot delete Word's predefined styles.

5   Choose **Fo̲rmat**. A menu of formatting types opens. Then select the type of formatting you want to modify for the style. (See Figure 4.11.)

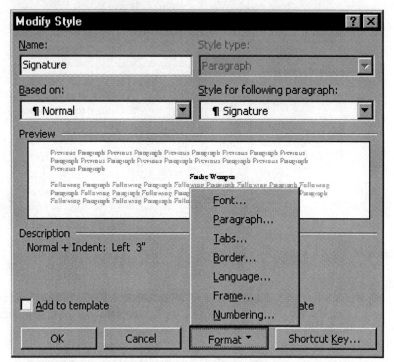

Figure 4.11.   Select the type of change you want to make to the style.

6   In the dialog box that appears (it varies depending on your choice in step 5), make formatting changes. Then choose **OK** to return to the **Modify Style** dialog box.

7   Choose **OK**. The style is changed.

 NOTE: All the other text in the document that uses the style should update automatically, but in some cases it doesn't. If a paragraph does not change automatically, reapply the style using the **Styles** drop-down list on the Formatting toolbar.

Practice Exercise 4-2

Modify a Style

1   Start in the file **04Style1** from the preceding exercise, or open 🗁**04Ex4-2** from the **WORDCert\Word B** folder. Save the file as 🗁**04Style2**.

2   Select the name; choose **Arial** from the **Font** drop-down list.

3   Click in the **Style** box on the Formatting toolbar, and press **Enter**. A **Modify Style** box appears.

4   Make sure **Update the style to reflect recent changes?** is selected.

5   Choose **OK**. The style is updated.

6   Choose **Format>Style**. The style **Signature** should already be selected on the **Styles** list. If not, select **Signature** from the list.

7   Choose **Modify**. The **Modify Style** dialog box opens.

8   Choose **Format** and then **Font**. The **Font** dialog box opens.

9   Change the **Font** to **Times New Roman**, as shown in Figure 4.12, and then choose **OK**. In the **Modify Style** box, choose **OK** again.

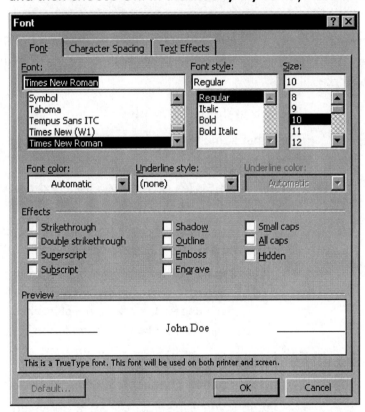

Figure 4.12.   The font is being changed for the style, not just for the selected text.

9   Choose **Apply**. The selected text changes to the new style definition.

10   Save your work; leave the document open for the next exercise.

Create Your Own Styles

You have seen already that Word provides many styles in each template, ready for your use. But you can also create your own styles if none of them suits you (or if you don't want to wade through them to check them out!).

 CAUTION: When you use the styles built into a Word template, the names are standardized; many templates use the same names. Therefore, if you attach a different template to the document later (with **Tools>Templates and Add-Ins**), the styles with the same names will automatically update. When you create your own style names, however, those names will probably NOT correspond to any of the styles in a different template that you might later attach. For this reason, some people prefer to modify the Word-provided styles, as you learned in the preceding section, rather than to create new ones.

You can create styles by example, or you can create them in the **Style** dialog box. The **Style** dialog box offers many more options but is more time-consuming than creating a style by example.

Create a style by example:

1   Format some text in the way you want the style to appear.

2   Select the text.

3   Click in the **Styles** drop-down list's text box on the Formatting toolbar.

4   Type a new name, replacing the name that is there, and press **Enter**. The new style is defined.

 NOTE: The new style will be saved with the document but not added to the template unless you enter the **Style** dialog box and choose the **Add to template** checkbox for it, which you learned about earlier in this lesson.

Create a style with the Style dialog box:

1   Choose **Format>Style**. The **Style** dialog box opens.

2   On the **Styles** list, select the style on which to base the new one.

3   Choose **New**. The **New Style** dialog box opens. (See Figure 4.13.)

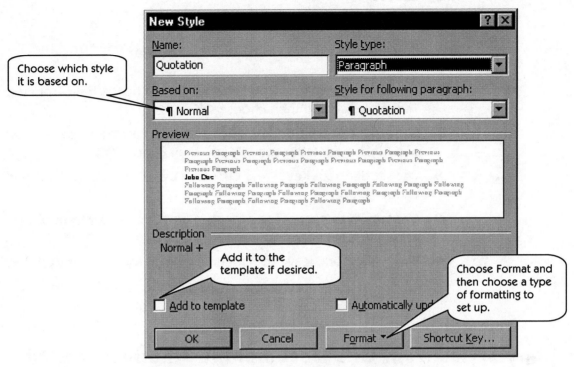

Figure 4.13. Create a new style by filling in the options here.

4 Type a name for the style in the **Name** box.

5 Check the **Based on** setting to make sure the new style is based on the one you want.

6 Choose the **Style for following paragraph.**

 TIP: To set a shortcut-key combination for the style, choose the **Shortcut Key** button and press the key combination you want to assign; then choose **Assign**.

7 Choose **Format**. A menu of formatting categories opens. Then select the type of formatting you want to set.

8 In the dialog box that appears (it varies depending on your choice in step 7), make formatting changes. Then choose **OK** to return to the **New Style** dialog box.

9 If you want to set any other attributes for the style, repeat steps 7 and 8. Otherwise, choose **OK**. The style is created.

Practice Exercise 4-3

Create a Style

1 Start in the file **04Style2** from the preceding exercise, or open ☐**04Ex4-3** from the **WORDCert\Word B** folder. Save the file as 🖫**04Style3**.

2 Choose **Format>Style**.

3   Choose **New**.

4   Type Quotation in the **Name** box.

5   If it does not already appear there, choose **Normal** from the **Based on** list.

6   Choose the **Format** button and then **Font**. Choose **Italic** from the **Font style** list, and then choose **OK**.

7   Choose the **Format** button again and then **Paragraph**. Set the **Left** and **Right** indentations to .5", and then choose **OK**.

8   Choose **Shortcut Key**. Press **Ctrl+Alt+Q**, and choose **Assign**. Then choose **Close**.

9   Choose **OK** to accept the new style and then **Apply** to apply it; close the dialog box.

10 Save your work; leave the document open for the next exercise.

A completed example of **04Style3** is available in the **WORDCert\Word B\Samples** folder on the DDC CD-ROM.

Copy Styles from One Document to Another

You can copy styles from one document to another. This can be useful, for example, if you have created several styles in a certain document and you want to use them in a new document.

 TIP: Another way to use the same styles in two different documents would be to add the styles to the template (with the **Add to Template** checkbox in the **Style** dialog box) and then use the same template for each. However, you may not always be free to add styles to the template; some organizations provide read-only templates on the network for employees to use.

 NOTE: The **Organizer** window, which you use to copy styles, can also be used to copy AutoText entries, toolbars, and macro project items. You may want to explore copying these items on your own.

Copying styles between documents:

1   Choose **Format>Style**, and then choose the **Organizer** button. The **Organizer** dialog box opens. (See Figure 4.14.)

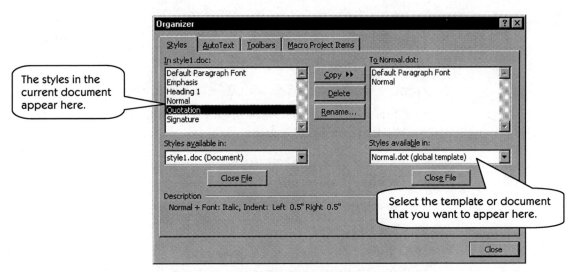

The styles in the current document appear here.

Select the template or document that you want to appear here.

Figure 4.14. You can copy, rename, and delete styles here.

2 Confirm that the document or template containing the style(s) appears in one of the panes.

3 Check to see if the document or template that you want to copy to appears in the other pane. If it does, skip to step 6. Otherwise, go on to step 4.

4 Choose the **Close File** button under the pane where you want the destination document or template to appear. The button changes to an **Open File** button.

5 Choose the **Open File** button. An **Open** dialog box appears. Choose the document or template that you want to copy to, and choose **Open**. Its styles appear in the **Organizer** dialog box.

> **NOTE:** By default, the file type in the **Open** dialog box is **Document Templates** (*.dot). If you want to copy the style(s) to a document instead, change the **Files of type** setting to **Word Documents** (*.doc).

6 Select the style that you want to copy, and then choose the **Copy** button.

7 Copy any other styles by repeating step 6; then choose **Close**.

8 A message appears asking whether you want to save the changes. Choose **Yes**.

You may have noticed in the **Organizer** dialog box two other buttons: **Delete** and **Rename**. You can use them to delete styles in either of the style lists, or to rename them. This might be useful, for example, if you are copying a style into another document but you realize that a style with the same name already exists there. You can delete it (with **Delete**), or you can rename it (with **Rename**) so that it no longer has the same name.

Practice Exercise 4-4

Copy Styles Between Templates

1   Prepare the files needed for this exercise by doing the following:

- Start in the file **04Style3**, or open 📂**04Ex4-4** from the **WORDCert\Word B** folder.

- Save that file as 💾**04Style4**.

- Open 📂**04Normal**.

- Save the file as 💾**04Copy**.

- Close **04Copy**.

2   In **04Style4**, choose **F**o**rmat>**S**tyle** and then choose the **Organizer** button. The **Organizer** dialog box opens. **04Style4**'s styles appear in the left pane.

3   Choose the **Close File** button under the right pane, and then choose the **Open File** button that appears.

4   Navigate to the folder that contains your sample files, and set the **Files of** t**ype** to **Word Documents (*.doc)**.

5   Select **04Copy**, and choose **O**p**en**.

6   Choose **Quotation** from the left list; choose the **C**o**py** button, copying it to the right list.

7   Choose **Close**. A message appears asking whether you want to save the changes. Choose **Y**e**s**.

8   Close **04Style4** (saving your changes), and open **04Copy**.

9   Open the **Styles** drop-down list; choose **Quotation**. (See Figure 4.15.)

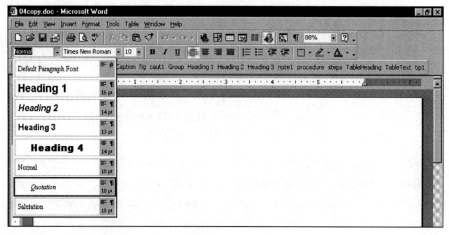

Figure 4.15.   The copied style appears in **04Copy**.

10 Save your changes; close **04Copy**.

LESSON 5: USE OUTLINES

Outlines can be a great help in organizing long documents (or even multi-document projects). You can create an outline as a standalone reference for yourself, or you can use an outline as a basis for your entire document. Then as your document's text takes shape, you can check your overall structure and organization by looking at your work in Outline view.

In this lesson, you will learn to:

> ➢ Type and edit an outline

> ➢ Expand and collapse an outline

> ➢ Reorganize an outline

> ➢ Automatically number outline headings

> ➢ Include or exclude certain paragraphs from an outline

> ➢ Apply styles to and customize outlines

You will have an opportunity to create and edit outlines in this lesson's exercises.

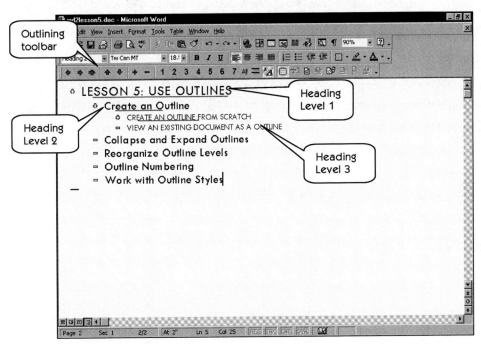

Figure 5.1. An outline in Word, shown in Outline view.

Create an Outline

The **Outline view** lets you look at a document where the document headings appear in a heirarchical, indented way. You can also hide the non-heading paragraphs so you can see the document's structure more clearly. Figure 5.1 shows an outline in Word.

You can view an existing document—and its outline—in Outline view, or you can create a new outline from scratch and add the text under the headings later.

CREATE AN OUTLINE FROM SCRATCH

To create an outline in a blank document, use the following procedure.

> **Start a new outline:**
>
> 1   Choose **View>Outline** to switch to Outline view.
>
> 2   Type the first line. Its style is Heading 1.
>
> 3   Press **Enter** to move to the next line.
>
> 4   To indent to a subordinate outline level, press **Tab**.
>
> 5   Continue typing your outline. To promote a line to a higher outline level, press **Shift+Tab**.
>
> NOTE: In Outline view, the **Tab** key doesn't work the same way it does normally; it demotes text to a lower outline level. You can't insert tabs in Outline view. Switch to another view, such as Normal or Print Layout, to do that.

When you switch to Outline view, the Outlining toolbar appears. It contains buttons that you can use as alternatives to many of the common commands for outlining. For example, the **Promote** and **Demote** buttons substitute for pressing **Shift+Tab** and **Tab**, respectively. (See Figure 5.2.)

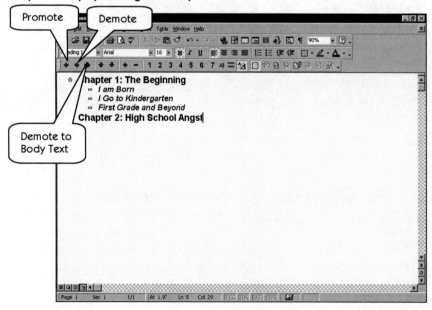

Figure 5.2.   You can use the Outlining toolbar to assist you in creating your outline.

TIP: Return to Normal or Print Layout view to type the text under your headings. Typing body text in Outline view is awkward because the line spacing (and sometimes the formatting) is not as you will see it on the printed page.

VIEW AN EXISTING DOCUMENT AS A OUTLINE

Any document that uses heading styles for its headings can be outlined. Heading styles include the styles provided in Word's templates (Heading 1, Heading 2, and so on) plus any styles that you set up to be headings.

View an existing document in Outline view:

1   Choose **View>Outline**.

The entire text of the document appears in Outline view, but not in an attractive way. The extra spacing between lines doesn't appear, and each paragraph appears indented according to its status in the outline. (See Figure 5.3.)

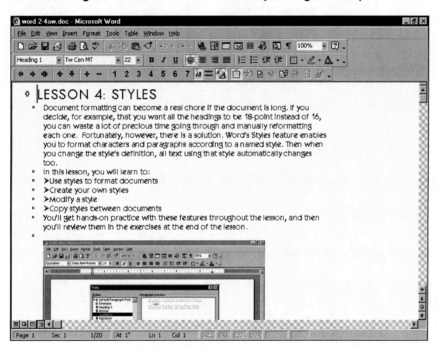

Figure 5.3.   A typical document displayed in Outline view.

From here, you can collapse the outline, as you'll learn in the following section, so that the body text doesn't show. You can then work with the outline as you would with one you created from scratch. You will practice this in Exercise 5-2 in the following topic.

Practice Exercise 5-1

Type a New Outline

1   Start a new document; save it as 05Out1.

2   Choose **View>Outline** to change to Outline view.

3   Type Chapter 1: The Beginning . Press **Enter**.

> NOTE: Refer to Figure 5.2 for a look at the outline you're creating in these steps.

 4   Press **Tab** to demote the next line to Heading 2 status, type I Am Born , and press **Enter**.

5   Type the following lines at this same outline level, pressing **Enter** after each:

> I Go to Kindergarten
> First Grade and Beyond

 6   On the line after the text you just typed, press **Shift+Tab** to promote the line to Heading 1 status.

7   Type Chapter 2: High School Angst .

8   Save your work, and close the file.

A completed example of **05Out1** is available in the **WORDCert\Word B\Samples** folder on the DDC CD-ROM.

Collapse and Expand Outline Levels

Most outlines have multiple levels of organization. In Figure 5.2, for example, are two levels, each designated by a heading style (1 and 2). Figure 5.3 contains an additional level: Body Text. Body text is anything formatted with a style other than a heading style.

You may not always want to see every level of the outline on-screen. For example, in Figure 5.3 you would probably want to hide the body text. There are several ways to choose which outline levels to display and which to hide; see the following list of Toolbar button and their actions.

 • Expands every hidden level under the currently selected line

 • Collapses every shown level under the currently selected line

 • Collapses everything except lines styled as Heading 1

• Collapses everything except lines styled as either Heading 1 or Heading 2 (There are also buttons 3 through 7 that work the same way with their respective levels.)

• Shows everything, including body text

 • Shows only the first line of each paragraph (toggle this on/off)

 • Shows or hides the character formatting for the outline text (font, font size, font attributes, and so on)

 NOTE: The buttons on the right end of the Outlining toolbar are used to manage master documents. You will learn all about them in **Section C**.

You can also expand and collapse by double-clicking the plus sign (+) next to headings. Double-clicking serves as a toggle: If it's expanded, it collapses; and vice versa.

Practice Exercise 5-2

Show/Hide Outline Levels

1   Open the file 📁**05Ex5-2** from the **WORDCert\Word B** folder; save it as 💾**05Out2**.

2   Choose **View>Outline** to see the document in Outline view. It resembles Figure 5.3.

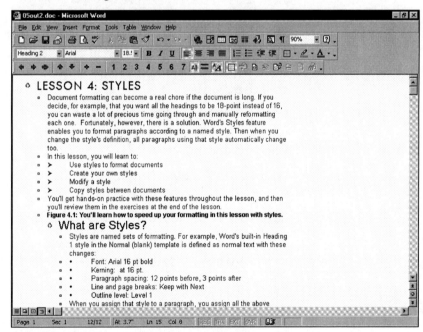

Figure 5.3.   The document in Outline view with all text showing.

3   Choose the **Show Heading 3** button on the Outlining toolbar. The body text disappears, and the first three levels of headings show. (See Figure 5.4.)

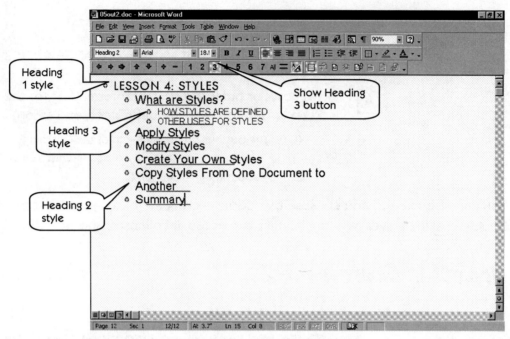

Figure 5.4.   The outline with three heading levels shown.

 NOTE: You can ignore the patterned underlines that sometimes appear in Outline view. They don't print. They merely tell you that there is text under that heading.

4   Double-click the plus sign next to *What Are Styles?*. The entire section of the document expands.

5   Double-click the same plus sign again. The entire section now collapses.

 6   Choose the **Expand** button on the Outlining toolbar. The outline for that section expands one level. Choose it a second time to open up another level.

7   Choose the **Collapse** button. The outline collapses one level. Choose it again; it collapses more.

8   Save your work; leave the document open for the next exercise.

A completed example of **05Out2** is available in the **WORDCert\Word B\Samples** folder on the DDC CD-ROM.

Reorganize an Outline

One of the nicest things about working with an outline in Word's Outline view is that you can easily rearrange entire sections of your document. With the text collapsed, it's easy to see the big picture and arrange the parts the best way.

When you rearrange the headings in an outline while the levels beneath are collapsed, the levels beneath move too. So if, for example, you move a heading with collapsed body text beneath it, the next time you expand the outline you will find that the body text has moved to stay with its heading.

You can move headings in any of several ways:

- Select a heading and choose the **Move Up** or **Move Down** button on the Outlining toolbar to move that heading one spot in either direction.

- Drag the heading (by its plus or minus sign) to the new position using drag-and-drop.

- Cut the heading (using **Edit>Cut**), reposition the insertion point, and paste it (using **Edit>Paste**).

TIP: Drag-and-drop is probably the easiest way, but it is also the most prone to mistakes. If you release the mouse button at the wrong time, you can end up with a section moved to the wrong spot. If this happens, use **Edit>Undo** Move to reverse the action, and then try again.

Practice Exercise 5-3

Rearrange an Outline

1   Start in the file **05Out2** from the preceding exercise, or open 📂**05Ex5-3** from the **WORDCert\Word B** folder and save it as 💾**05Out3**.

2   Collapse the outline to show only heading levels 1 and 2, unless the outline already appears that way.

3   Click on the plus sign next to **Apply Styles** to select that line. Then choose the **Move Up** button.

4   Choose the **Move Down** button, moving **Apply Styles** back where it started.

5   Drag **Apply Styles** directly above **Summary** and drop it there. (See Figure 5.5.)

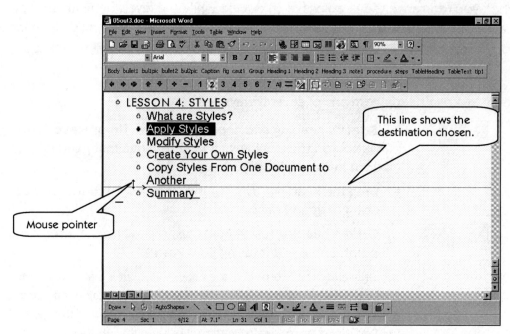

Figure 5.5. When dragging outline levels, a horizontal line shows where you are dragging.

6 Expand the outline to show all levels. Confirm that the **Apply Styles** text moved with its heading.

7 Collapse the outline back to just the first two heading levels.

8 Drag **Apply Styles** back to its original position (after *What Are Styles?*).

9 Save your work, and close the file.

Outline Numbering

When you are writing a multi-chapter document, you may want to number the chapters on the outline. If you type the numbers manually and then rearrange the chapters, you will need to renumber. If you let Word handle the numbering, however, it will renumber the chapters automatically each time you rearrange, add, or delete.

Outline numbering is also handy when you are writing extremely technical documents that need section numbers or even paragraph numbers. For example, you might have an organization like this:

> **Section A**
> > **Section A.1**
> > > **Section A.1.i**

Word can number each heading according to the scheme you specify, keeping every sequence accurate.

To set up the outline numbering, use the **Outline Numbered** tab in the **Bullets and Numbering** dialog box, as shown in the following steps.

Set up outline numbering:

1   View the document in Outline view.

2   Choose **Format>Bullets and Numbering**, and then choose the **Outline Numbered** tab.

3   Choose one of the numbering styles that include "Heading" codes in them. In Figure 5.6, the four styles on the bottom row all meet these criteria.

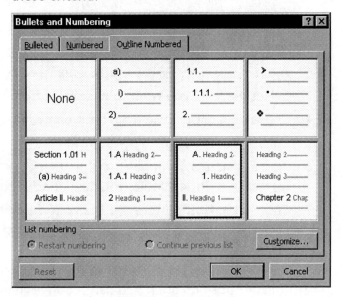

Figure 5.6.   Select an outline numbering scheme to be applied to your outline.

4   (Optional) Customize the numbering scheme, as explained in the text following step 5.

5   Choose **OK**. The numbering scheme is applied to your outline.

You can customize the numbering scheme if you like. Just choose the **Customize** button in the **Bullets and Numbering** dialog box (Figure 5.6). The following steps explain how customizing works.

 NOTE: If you customize a numbering scheme and then later want to return to the defaults for it, choose it in the **Bullets and Numbering** dialog box and then choose the **Reset** button.

Customize the outline numbering format:

1   If you are not already in the **Bullets and Numbering** dialog box, choose **Format>Bullets and Numbering**. Make sure the **Outline Numbered** tab is chosen.

2   Choose **Customize**. The **Customize Outline Numbered List** dialog box opens. (See Figure 5.7.)

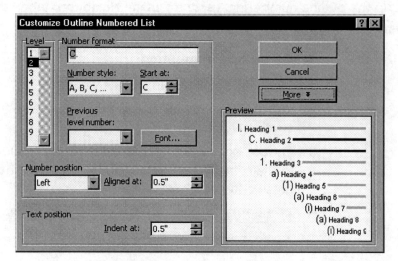

Figure 5.7. Customize how each outline level's numbering should be formatted.

3   Select the level you want to customize from the **Level** list.

4   Choose a number style from the **Number style** drop-down list.

5   Enter a starting value in the **Start at** box.

6   Add any special formatting to the number or letter in the **Number format** box. For example, you might add a period or dash after it.

7   Choose the **Font** button. Use the **Font** dialog box that appears to set text formatting for the number or letter characters. Then choose **OK**.

8   Set the position for the number (for Outline view only) in the **Number position** area. You can set an alignment (**Number position** drop-down list) and choose where on the ruler the number will appear (**Aligned at** text box).

9   Set an indentation for the text that follows the number in the **Indent at** text box.

10 (Optional) For more controls, choose the **More** button to open up the options shown in Figure 5.8. Then set any of them as needed:

•   **Link level to style**: Select the style that you want automatically applied to this level of the outline.

•   **Follow number with**: Select the character that will separate the number from the heading text. (**Tab** is the default.)

•   **ListNum field list name**: Type the label you want for lists that you generate by using the **LISTNUM** field. (This is for advanced users only.)

•   **Legal style numbering**: This changes the numbers in the current outline to their equivalent Arabic values. For example, it changes III or C to 3.

- **Restart numbering after:** Restart the numbering whenever this list level follows a higher list level.

- **Apply changes to:** This tells Word what part of the document you want to apply the outline number formatting to. (The default is the whole list.)

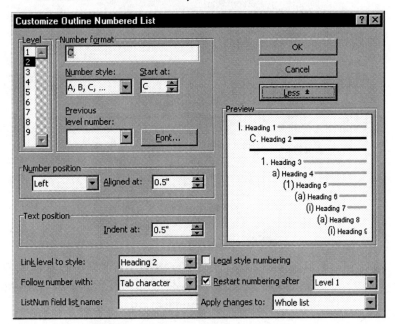

Figure 5.8.   Additional options are available when you choose **More** in the **Customize Outline Numbered List** dialog box.

11 Choose **OK**, accepting the customized list formatting.

Practice Exercise 5-4

Number an Outline

1   Open ☐05Ex5-4 from the **WORDCert\Word B** folder; save it as ☐05Out4. Change to Outline view (**View>Outline**) if not already there.

2   Set up outline numbering for the document by doing the following:

- Select the entire document (**Ctrl+A**).

- Choose **Format>Bullets and Numbering**, and choose the **Outline Numbered** tab.

- Choose the second outline scheme in the second row (1, 1.1, 1.1.1).

- Choose **OK**. The outline is numbered as shown in Figure 5.9.

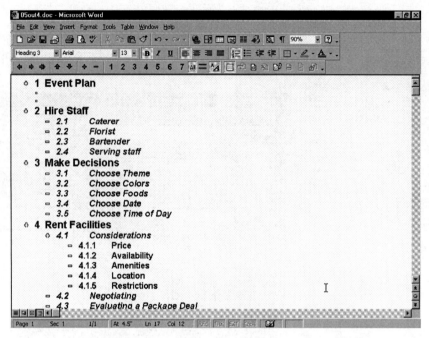

Figure 5.9.   The result of applying one of Word's outline numbering schemes.

3   Apply the **Title** style to the first line (**Event Plan**), excluding it from the automatic numbering.

4   Customize the numbering by doing the following:

- Position the insertion point in the **Hire Staff** line.

- Choose **Format>Bullets and Numbering** again.

- Choose the **Customize** button. The **Customize Outline Numbered List** dialog box opens.

- Choose **2** from the **Level** list.

- Open the **Number style** drop-down list; choose lowercase Roman numerals.

- In the **Number format** box, remove the **1.** code, leaving only **i**.

- Set the **Indent at** value to **0.2"**.

- If the **More** button appears, choose it. (The additional controls may already be displayed if you did the steps earlier in the lesson.)

- Make sure that the **Restart numbering after** checkbox is marked.

- Choose **OK**. The changed outline appears in Figure 5.10.

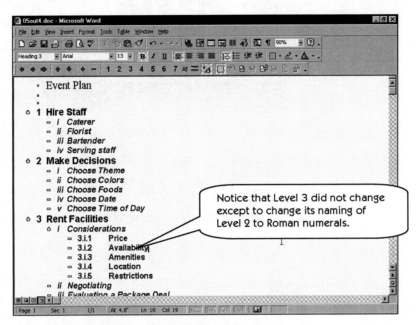

Figure 5.10. The outline with the changes just made.

5 Save your work; leave the document open for the next exercise.

Set the Outline Level for a Paragraph or a Style

You don't have to rely on Word's built-in styles to determine what paragraphs appear in Outline view. You can control them yourself, either at the individual paragraph level or at the style level.

SET THE OUTLINE LEVEL FOR INDIVIDUAL PARAGRAPHS

You can set up any of the styles you have created (see Lesson 4) to be included both at the various levels in Outline view and when Word generates items based on the document's outline (indexes, tables of contents, and so on). For example, perhaps you want your document's title, which is formatted in a custom style you created called **MyTitle**, to appear as Level 1 on all outlines. Set it up using the following steps.

 NOTE: You cannot change the outline level for Word's built-in heading styles (Headings 1 through 9).

Include or exclude certain paragraphs:

1 Select the paragraph(s) to be included or excluded. All of the paragraphs must be assigned a style you have created, not assigned a built-in one.

 NOTE: You do not have to be in Outline view; you can do this procedure in Normal or Print Layout view.

2 Choose **Format>Paragraph**; then choose the **Indents and Spacing** tab.

3   Open the **Outline level** drop-down list. Choose the outline level
     to assign to the paragraph: Body text or a level (Level 1, Level 2,
     and so on). See Figure 5.11.

4   Choose **OK**.

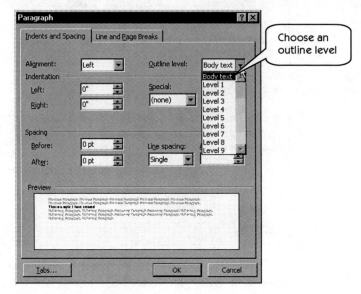

Figure 5.11.   Set the outline level for the paragraph(s).

After performing the above steps, if you are not already in Outline view, switch to it
and confirm that the paragraphs appear appropriately at various outline levels.

SET THE OUTLINE LEVEL FOR A CUSTOM STYLE

You can also set the entire custom style for a certain outline level. For example,
suppose you have created your own heading styles **Major Head**, **Minor Head**, and
Subhead. You can assign an outline level to each of them so that any paragraphs
formatted with these styles automatically show up appropriately in Outline view.

Change a custom style's outline level:

1   Choose **Format>Style**. The **Style** dialog box opens.

2   Select the style from the **Styles** list, and choose **Modify**.

3   In the **Modify Style** dialog box, choose **Format>Paragraph**.

4   Open the **Outline level** drop-down list; choose the new outline
     level. Refer back to Figure 5.11; it's the exact same dialog box.

  CAUTION: If you created a style based on one of Word's Heading
     styles, you may not be able to set the outline level. The control to do
     so may be dimmed in step 4. If that is the case, go back to the style's
     Modify Style dialog box and change the **Based on** drop-down list
     selection to **Normal**. See Lesson 4 of this section for details.

5   Choose **OK**, and then choose **OK** again.

6   Choose **Close** to close the **Style** dialog box.

Practice Exercise 5-5

Change an Outline Level

1   Start in **05Out4** from the preceding exercise, or open 📁**05Ex5-5** from the **WORDCert\Word B** folder.

2   Save the file as 💾**05Out5**.

3   Change the outline level for the **Title** style to Heading 1 by doing the following:

- Place the insertion point in the **Event Plan** line if it is not already there.

- Choose **Format>Style**. The **Title** style should be selected on the list of styles.

- Choose the **Modify** button.

- In the **Modify Style** dialog box, choose **Format>Paragraph**.

- Open the **Outline level** drop-down list; choose **Level 1**.

- Choose **OK**.

- Choose **OK** again.

- Choose **Apply**. The **Event Plan** line now appears as Level 1 in the outline. (See Figure 5.12.)

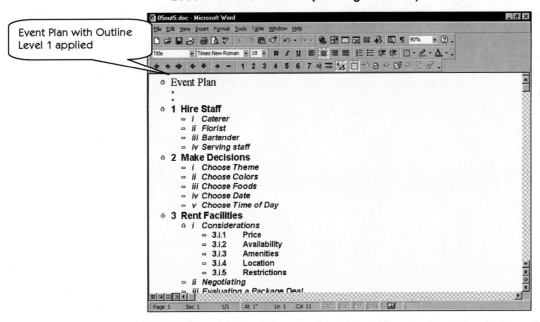

Figure 5.12. The **Event Plan** line appears aligned with other Level 1 lines in the outline, though it retains its **Title** style.

4   Save your work, and close the file.

LESSON 6: MULTI-SECTION DOCUMENTS

As you work with longer documents that contain many pages, you may want to employ some of Word's features that can help you organize and present your work. This lesson touches on two of these features: section breaks and custom headers/footers.

In this lesson, you will learn to:

> Decide when and how to use section breaks

> Insert and remove section breaks in a document

> Set up different headers/footers on odd and even pages

> Carry over headers/footers between sections

You can practice these skills in the numbered steps and exercises throughout this lesson and in the Walk, Run, and Fly exercises at the end of the lesson.

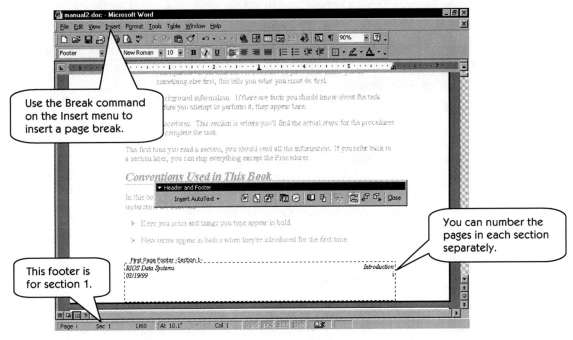

Figure 6.1.   Section breaks allow different document layout settings, such as headers and footers, within the same document.

Create Section Breaks

Before you get started using section breaks, review the following background material that will help you understand them. Then you'll learn to create them in the **Insert a Section Break** section.

ADVANTAGES OF A MULTI-SECTION DOCUMENT

Certain settings in Word affect the entire document. These include page orientation, paper size, margins, header/footer, and number of columns. You can't format individual paragraphs with two different settings for any of these items.

However, it's a fact of life that sometimes people need to create a document with varying numbers of columns, or different margins on some pages, or even different page orientations on some pages. So Word enables you to insert **section breaks** to solve the problem.

By creating a section break, you split your document into two parts, and each part can have its own document-wide settings. So, for example, a letter can have a 2" margin at the top of the first page but a 1" margin at the top of the second. Or a newsletter can have the title appear in a wide, one-column area but the article beneath it in multiple columns. You learned about columns in Lesson 2 of this section.

Another advantage of creating a section break is that you can place different text in the header and footer of each section. For example, the footer in the first section might read "Chapter 1" while the footer in the second might read "Chapter 2." You learned how to create basic headers and footers in **Section A**, but we'll review the basics and go beyond them in this lesson.

BREAK TYPES

There are several kinds of breaks you can create in Word.

- A **line break** (**Shift+Enter**) starts a new line in the same paragraph.
- A **paragraph break** (**Enter**) starts a new paragraph.
- A **column break** (**Ctrl+Shift+Enter**) starts a new column in a multi-column layout.
- A **page break** (**Ctrl+Enter**) starts a new page.

But the most important kind of break in this lesson is the *section break*. A section break divides the document into two sections: one above the break and one below it. A document can have as many sections as you like.

The settings for a section are stored in the break beneath it. The end-of-file marker (the horizontal bar) at the end of the document serves as the end-of-section marker, or "break," for the final section. (It is visible only in Normal view.) You can think of the final section's settings as being stored in the end-of-file marker, the same way the previous section's settings were stored in the section break. (See Figure 6.2.)

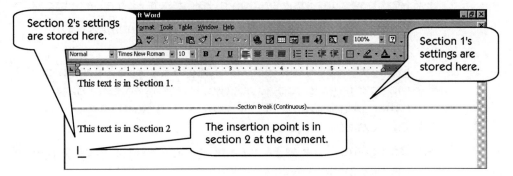

Figure 6.2.   This section break separates the document into two sections, one above and one below.

 NOTE: Figure 6.2 shows a break in Normal view. If you are working in Print Layout view, the break may not be obvious. Switch to Normal view if you want to be sure where the section break is.

If you delete a section break, that section's text becomes part of the next section down. For example, in Figure 6.2, if you were to delete the section break, the entire document would be subject to the settings stored in the end-of-file marker.

INSERT A SECTION BREAK

Insert a section break whenever you want to format part of the document differently from the rest. For example, if you want a different number of columns or different page margins in a certain spot, insert a section break there.

Insert a section break:

1   Position the insertion point where you want the section break to occur.

2   Choose **Insert>Break**. The **Break** dialog box opens. (See Figure 6.3.)

Figure 6.3.   The **Break** dialog box.

3   Select one of the **Section break types**:

- **N**ext page: Inserts a section break that is also a page break
- **Con**t**inuous**: Inserts a section break that continues on the same page
- **E**ven page: Inserts a section break that is also a page break; if the next page is odd-numbered, it inserts an extra page (when printing) so that the new section starts at the top of the next even page
- **O**dd page: Same as **E**ven page, except inserts an extra page if the next page is even-numbered

4   Choose **OK**. The break appears in your document.

As you learned in Lesson 2 of Section B, when you select some text and then change the number of columns, Word inserts section breaks automatically before and after the text. You can work with these as you would any other section break, including deleting them, as you will learn in the following procedure.

DELETE A SECTION BREAK

To delete a break, just delete it as you would any character in a document. That means you can do any of the following to remove it from your document:

- Click on it to select it, and press **Delete**.
- Move the insertion point immediately after it, and press **Backspace**.
- Move the insertion point immediately before it, and press **Delete**.

Practice Exercise 6-1

Work with Section Breaks

1   Start a new document; save it as 🖫**06Sales1**.

2   Press **Enter** about 10 times to create some space. Then type Sales Report , and format it as 26-point, bold, and center-aligned.

3   Press **Enter** twice after **Sales Report**.

4   Choose **I**nsert>**B**reak. The **Break** dialog box appears.

5   Choose **Con**t**inuous**. Then choose **OK**.

 TIP: If you are working in Print Layout view, switch to Normal view so you can see where the section break lies.

6 Beneath the section break, type Introduction in 18-point bold, left-aligned type. The screen should resemble Figure 6.4 at this point.

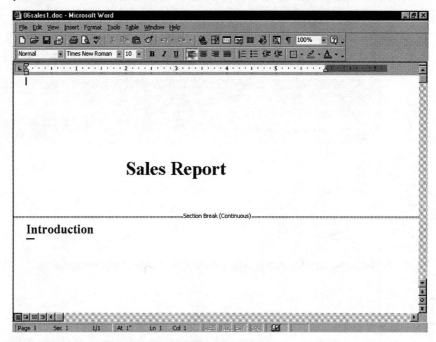

Figure 6.4. Text appears on both sides of the break line.

7 Click on the section break line.

8 Press **Delete**. The section break is deleted.

9 For extra practice, insert a **Next Page** section break to replace it, by doing the following:

• Choose **Insert>Break**. The **Break** dialog box appears.

• Choose **Next Page**. Then choose **OK**.

10 Save your work, and close the document.

Work with Headers and Footers

As you have probably already discovered, headers and footers can help keep the pages of a document organized by placing repeated or incremented data on each page. For example, you might print the company name in the footer (i.e., at the bottom) of each page, and you might include page numbers there too. The following section reviews the basics of headers and footers.

REVIEW: HEADERS AND FOOTERS

Each page has a header and a footer area available for use. You can access it by choosing **View>Header and Footer**. While you are editing the header and footer, the rest of the document is dimmed (unavailable). To return to editing the main document, choose the **Close** button on the Header and Footer toolbar. (See Figure 6.5.)

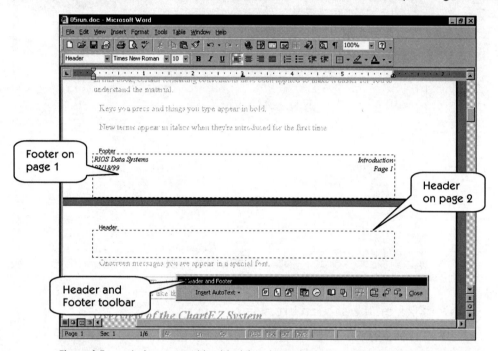

Figure 6.5.   A document with a blank header and a footer consisting of two lines of text.

 TIP: In Print Layout view you can double-click existing header or footer text to quickly enter the header/footer editing mode shown in Figure 6.5. This is a shortcut for choosing **View>Header and Footer**.

 You can use the buttons on the Header and Footer toolbar to insert codes. For example, the **Insert Page Number** button inserts the page number code that will print the correct number on each page of the document.

The other buttons that insert codes are as follows:

Inserts the total number of pages in the document

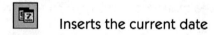

Inserts the current date

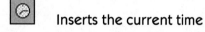

Inserts the current time

 TIP: There is a wide variety of other codes that can be used in the document, both in the header and footer and elsewhere. To access them, choose **Insert>Field**. For instance, you can insert the file name, the author name, the user initials, the date or time the document was last printed, the date or time the document was first created, and so on.

SPECIAL HEADERS/FOOTERS FOR FIRST PAGES OR ODD/EVEN PAGES

You can open the **Page Setup** dialog box (**File>Page Setup**) by choosing the **Page Setup** button on the Header and Footer toolbar. From there, you can choose to use different headers and footers for odd and even pages and a different header and footer for the first page of the document (or section).

Different odd and even headers/footers are useful if you are going to print the document in a two-sided format and bind it into a book or report. In that case, you might always want the page number to be on the outside edge of pages, so you would place its code on the right for odd pages and on the left for even ones.

A different first-page header/footer is useful if your first page is a title page or a cover sheet. Many people choose not to place a header or footer on the first page of a document, because presumably the reader can tell from the title that it is "page 1."

Turn special headers/footers on or off:

1   Position the insertion point in the first section if you have multiple sections defined in the document.

2   Either choose **File>Page Setup** (at any time; you don't have to be working with the header and footer) or choose the **Page Setup** button on the Header and Footer toolbar.

3   Choose the **Layout** tab. (See Figure 6.6.)

4   Select or deselect the **Different odd and even** checkbox.

5   Select or deselect the **Different first page** checkbox.

6   Choose **OK**.

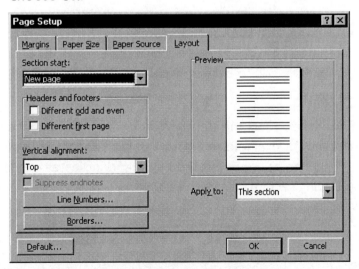

Figure 6.6. Turn on or off special headers and footers here.

After turning on these special headers/footers, you will notice that the header and footer boxes show different names on different pages. For example, Figure 6.7 shows the First Page Footer at the bottom of page 1 and the Even Page Header at the top of page 2.

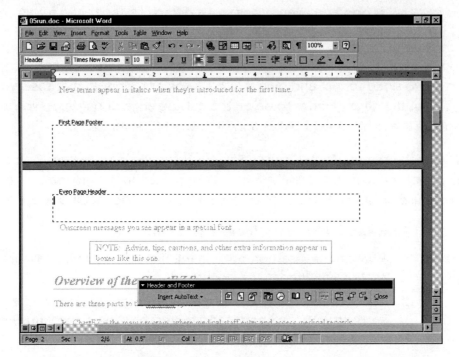

Figure 6.7.   This document is set up for both different odd and even headers/footers and a different first-page header/footer.

MULTI-SECTION HEADERS/FOOTERS

Besides having different headers and footers for the first page and for odd/even pages, you can also have different headers and footers for each section. (Here's where it can get really confusing: Each section can have different odd/even and different first-page headers/footers too!) This can be especially useful if each section has its own title and you want the title to appear in the header or footer.

By default, when you create a section break, all sections use the same header and footer. The first section sets the standard, and then subsequent sections are set to **Same as Previous**. For example, in Figure 6.8, notice that the footer includes **Section 2** in its name. The **Same as Previous** at the right end indicates that the footer is copied from the preceding section.

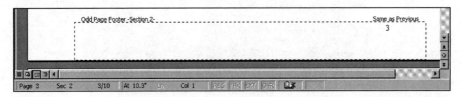

Figure 6.8.   This footer for the odd pages in section 2 is copied from the odd-page footer in section 1.

Turn off the Same As Previous attribute:

1 Position the insertion point in the header or footer of the section you want to work with.

 2 Choose the **Same as Previous** button on the Header and Footer toolbar to toggle the feature off.

You can then edit the header or footer to make it different for the current section.

Practice Exercise 6-2

Work with Headers and Footers

1 Open 📂**06Ex6-2** from the **WORDCert\Word B** folder; save it as 💾**06Poem1**.

2 Create Next Page section breaks between parts 1 and 2 (pages 12 and 13) and between parts 2 and 3 (pages 23 and 24).

3 Turn on separate headers/footers for the first page and for odd/even pages by doing the following:

- Choose **File>Page Setup**, and choose the **Layout** tab.
- Choose the **Different first page** checkbox.
- Choose the **Different odd and even** checkbox.
- Choose **OK**.

4 Place the work's title on the header of the even pages and the author's name on the header of the odd pages:

- Start with the insertion point at the beginning of the file.
- Choose **View>Header and Footer**, displaying the Header and Footer toolbar.

 - Choose the **Show Next** button on the Header and Footer toolbar to move to the second page's header.

- Type The Odyssey in the **Even Page Header - Section 1** box, and format it as bold and italic. (See Figure 6.9.)

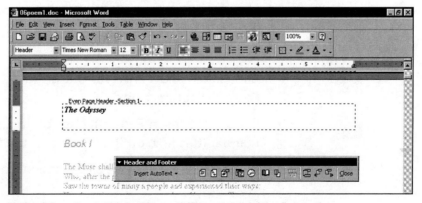

Figure 6.9. Create this header on the even pages of the first section.

- Choose the **Show Next** button again, bringing the **Odd Page Header - Section 1** into view.

- Press **Tab** twice, moving to the second tab stop in the box.

- Type | Homer |; format it as bold and italic. (See Figure 6.10.)

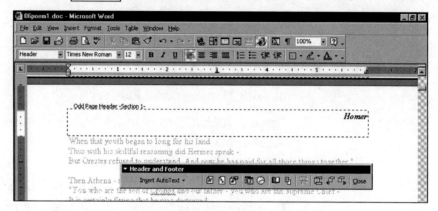

Figure 6.10.   Create this header on the odd pages.

5   Place the page number in the footer of both odd and even pages in section 1, along with the text **Book 1**:

- Choose the **Switch Between Header and Footer** button on the Header and Footer toolbar. You are now looking at the **Odd Page Footer - Section 1**.

- Type | Book I |.

- Press **Tab** twice, moving to the second tab stop.

- Choose the **Insert Page Number** button. The page number appears. (See Figure 6.11.)

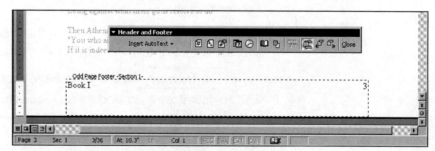

Figure 6.11.   Create this footer on the odd pages.

- Choose the **Show Previous** button to move to the **Even Page Footer - Section 1** box.

- Choose the **Insert Page Number** button, inserting the page number (this time on the left end of the footer).

- Press **Tab** twice, moving to the second tab stop.

- Type | Book I |.

6   Turn off the separate odd and even headers and footers:

- Choose **File>Page Setup**.

- Deselect the **Different odd and even** checkbox.

- Choose **OK**.

7   Set up the footers for sections 2 and 3 to show the appropriate book number (Book II and Book III, respectively):

- Choose the **Show Next** button again, bringing the **Footer - Section 2** box into view.

- Deselect the **Same as Previous** button on the Header and Footer toolbar.

- Change Book I to Book II in the **Footer - Section 2** box.

- Do the same thing for section 3, changing Book II to Book III.

8   Choose **Close**, closing the Header and Footer toolbar.

9   Save your work, and close the file.

A completed example of **06Poem1** is available in the **WORDCert\Word B\Samples** folder on the DDC CD-ROM.

Restart Page Numbering at a Section Break

Wherever there is a page number code (usually in the header or footer), a page number appears. Normally Word numbers all the pages in the document consecutively, regardless of which section they fall into. However, you can set each section's page numbering separately if you like. For example, if you have several chapters in a single document, you might want each chapter to restart the numbering using a scheme like this: 1-1, 1-2, 1-3, and so on in Chapter 1; and 2-1, 2-2, 2-3, etc., in Chapter 2.

To restart the page numbering in a section, use the following procedure.

Restart page numbering in a section:

1   View the section's header or footer (whichever contains or will contain the page number code):

- Choose **View>Header and Footer**.

- Use the **Show Previous** or **Show Next** button to move to the correct section.

- Use the **Switch Between Header and Footer** button to display the header or footer, whichever you need.

2   Choose the **Format Page Number** button on the Header and Footer toolbar. The **Page Number Format** dialog box opens.

3   Choose the **Start at** option button, and enter the page number to start with in this section (for example, 1).

4   Choose **OK**.

If you are numbering each section separately, you will probably want to add some sort of text description to the page number to help the reader understand. For example, in section 2, you might add 2- in front of the page number, so the numbering for the section looks like this: 2-1, 2-2, 2-3, etc.

 TIP: You can insert a field that will automatically print the correct section number in the header or footer if you like. You might use it in conjunction with a page number field when numbering each section separately, like this: {section number} - {page number}. To insert a section field, choose **Insert>Field**. Choose **Numbering from the Categories** list, and choose **Section** from the **Field names** list. Then choose **OK** to insert it.

Practice Exercise 6-3

Restart Page Numbering for a Section

1   Start in the file **06Poem1** from the preceding exercise, or open **06Ex6-3** from the **WORDCert\Word B** folder.

2   Save the file as **06Poem2**.

3   View the footer for section 2, and select the page number field:

- Position the insertion point anywhere within section 2 (that is, anywhere after the Book II heading but before the Book III heading).

- Choose **View>Header and Footer**.

 - Choose the **Switch Between Header and Footer** button to view the footer.

- Click on the page number field to select it. It turns gray.

 4   Choose the **Format Page Number** button.

5   Choose the **Start at** button. The number in its box defaults to 1. Then choose **OK**.

 6   Choose the **Show Next** button.

7   Repeat steps 4 and 5 for the section 3 footer, setting it so that it starts numbering at 1.

8   Choose **Close** to close the header and footer.

9   Save your work, and close the file.

A completed example of **06Poem2** is available in the **WORDCert\Word B\Samples** folder on the DDC CD-ROM.

LESSON 7: DESKTOP PUBLISHING FEATURES

Desktop publishing refers to designing a document to be published, such as a newsletter or a book. Such layouts are often more complex than an ordinary letter or report and require special elements such as text boxes and artwork. Numerous programs are designed specifically for desktop publishing, but many people can accomplish their desktop publishing goals using Word.

In this lesson, you will learn to:

> Place and manipulate pictures and Clip Art

> Insert WordArt

> Draw lines and shapes

> Format graphics

> Control graphic placement

> Place text boxes

> Insert Bullets and Numbering

In the exercises in this lesson, you will become experienced with placing and manipulating a variety of graphic objects.

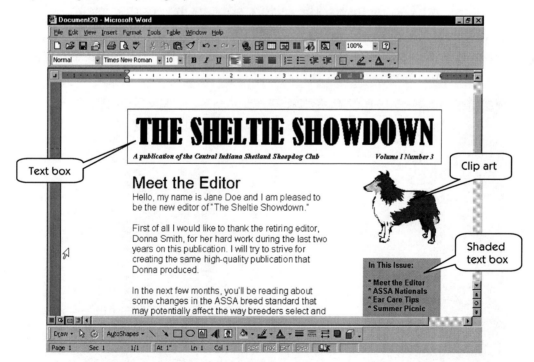

Figure 7.1.   Here's a two-column newsletter created in Word.

Insert a Picture from a File

You can insert any image that you have stored on your computer (or on the network) into your document. For example, you might insert a scanned picture of your CEO into an annual report, or you may include in a presentation an image you downloaded from the Internet.

 NOTE: Images made up of individual dots, such as scanned images, are known as "bitmap" images. One format of bitmap image uses the extension .bmp, but other types of images, such as .jpg, .pcx, and .tif, are also bitmap images.

 CAUTION: If you have downloaded an image from the Internet or scanned an image from a publication, make sure you have the legal right to use that image, or you might violate a copyright and be subject to penalties.

Insert a picture:

1   Open the document you want to place the picture in, and move the insertion point to the spot where it should go.

2   Choose **Insert>Picture>From File**. The **Insert Picture** dialog box opens.

3   Select the picture you want to insert. (See Figure 7.2.)

 NOTE: The Preview window should appear in the right side of the dialog box, as shown in Figure 7.2. If it does not, open the **View** button's drop-down list and choose **Preview**.

4   Choose **Insert**. The picture appears in your document.

After inserting a picture, you can resize, move, copy, and otherwise modify the picture; you will learn how to do all those things later in this lesson, in "Manipulate Graphic Objects" and "Format Graphic Objects."

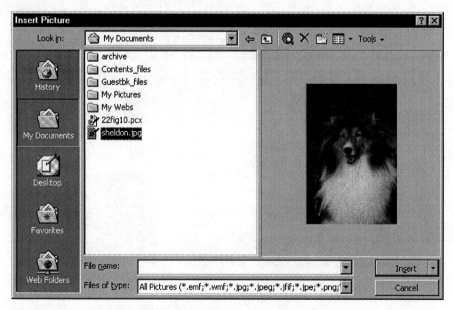

Figure 7.2.   You can choose to insert a picture that is stored on your PC.

Practice Exercise 7-1

Insert a Picture

1 Start a new document, and save it as ⊟**07Photo**.

2 Choose **Insert>Picture>From File**. The **Insert Picture** dialog box opens.

3 Navigate to the **WORDCert\Word B** folder containing the sample files for this class, and choose the .jpg file **07Ex7-1**.

4 Choose **Insert**. The picture appears in your document, as shown in Figure 7.3.

5 Save your work, and close the file.

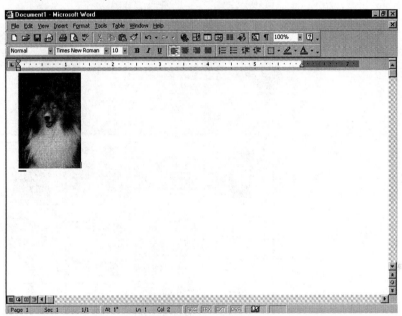

Figure 7.3. The picture inserted in a document.

Insert Clip Art

Clip art is pre-drawn line art that comes with Word (or Office). Hundreds of clip-art images are available on the Word or Office CD, and all are royalty-free, so you can use them as much as you like without violating any copyrights. Hundreds more are available from the Microsoft Web site for free download, as you will learn later in this lesson, in the "Get More Clips from the Internet" section.

The **Clip Gallery** is a convenient mini-application ("applet") that organizes, categorizes, and displays the available clip art, for easy browsing. You can then select a clip-art image and place it in your document.

 NOTE: You can use the Clip Gallery to organize your own artwork, too, such as scanned images. Just import the images to the Clip Gallery to make them available there, as you will learn later in this lesson, in "Add a Scanned Photo to the Clip Gallery."

Locate and insert a clip:

1   Choose **Insert>Picture>Clip Art**. The Clip Gallery opens.

> **NOTE:** The title on the window reads "Insert ClipArt," but you are actually seeing the Clip Gallery. The window's title changes depending on how you open it. You used the **Insert>Picture>ClipArt** command in this case, so that's where its current title comes from.

2   Choose a category from which you want to select a clip. An array of clips in that category appears.

> **NOTE:** You can also browse clips by keyword, as you will learn later in "Work with Clip Keywords."

3   Click on the clip you want to select. A palette of buttons appears beside it. (See Figure 7.4.)

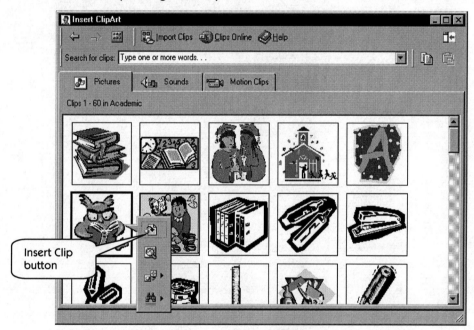

Figure 7.4.   Click the clip, and then choose the **Insert Clip** button.

   4   Choose the **Insert Clip** button. The clip is inserted in your document. The Clip Gallery remains open.

5   Close the Clip Gallery window.

After inserting a clip, you will probably want to move and resize it, and perhaps change its colors or other attributes too. See "Manipulate Graphic Objects" and "Format Graphic Objects" later in this lesson.

MANAGE CLIP CATEGORIES

Many clips have more than one category associated with them. For example, you might see the Owl clip in both the Academic and Animals categories. You might also want to add it to some other category, such as Metaphors. There is also a special category called Favorites in which you can include the clips that you use frequently, for easy access to them.

NOTE: Adding a clip to a category does not remove it from previously assigned categories. A clip could be in every single category if you wanted it to be.

To add a clip to a category, use the following procedure.

Add a clip to a category:

1   In the Clip Gallery, click the clip.

2   Click the **Add Clip to Favorites or Other Category** button, which is the third button on the palette you saw in Figure 7.4.

     A fly-out submenu appears, containing a drop-down list.

3   Open the drop-down list, and choose **Favorites** (or some other category).

4   Click **Add** to add the clip to it. (See Figure 7.5.)

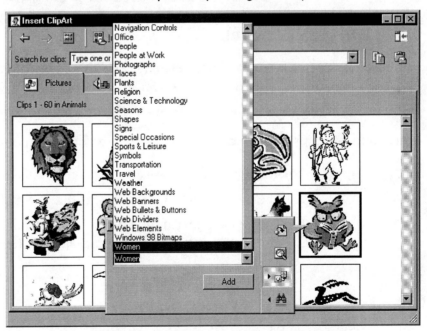

Figure 7.5.   You can add a clip to a category here.

You can also work with a clip's categories through its **Properties** dialog box. From there, you can add a clip to, or remove a clip from, a category.

Manage clip categories with the Clip Properties dialog box:

1   Right-click the clip in the Clip Gallery.

2   Choose **Clip Properties** from the shortcut menu.

3   Choose the **Categories** tab.

4   Place or remove checkmarks next to category names. (See Figure 7.6.)

5   Choose **OK**.

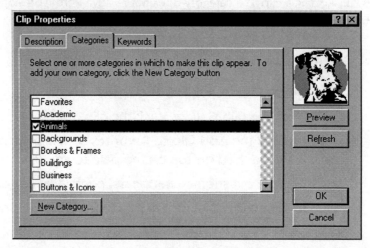

Figure 7.6.   You can manage a clip's categories from its **Clip Properties** box.

WORK WITH CLIP KEYWORDS

Each clip has one or more keywords associated with it. Keywords help describe the clip. For example, the Owl clip you saw earlier has dozens of keywords, including academic, animals, cartoons, nature, birds, fowl, owls, books, and so on.

You can locate clips by keyword instead of by category if you prefer.

Locate clips by keyword:

1   Choose **Insert>Picture>Clip Art**. The Clip Gallery opens.

2   Type a keyword in the **Search for clips** box, and press **Enter**. Clips that contain that keyword appear. (See Figure 7.7.)

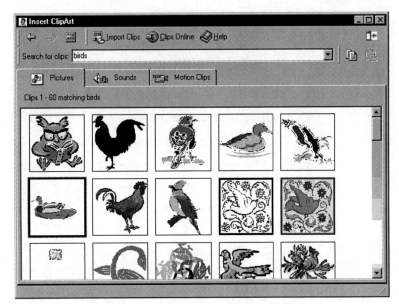

Figure 7.7.   These clips all have the keyword "bird."

3   Click the clip you want to select. A palette of buttons appears.

4   Choose the **Insert Clip** button. The clip is inserted in your document. The Clip Gallery remains open.

5   Close the Clip Gallery window.

To add keywords to a clip, you can use the **Clip Properties** box.

Add clip keywords:

1   Right-click the clip in the Clip Gallery.

2   Choose **Clip Properties**.

3   Click the **Keywords** tab.

4   Choose **New Keyword**.

5   Type the word. (See Figure 7.8.)

6   Click **OK**.

7   Click **OK** to return to the Clip Gallery.

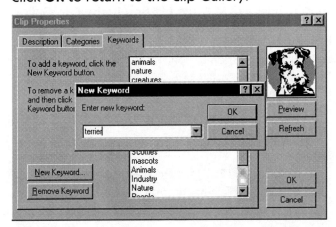

Figure 7.8.   You can add keywords for a clip from the clip's **Clip Properties** dialog box.

Practice Exercise 7-2

Find and Insert a Clip

1   Start a new, blank document; save it as 🖫**07Clip1**.

2   Choose **Insert>Picture>Clip Art**. The Clip Gallery opens.

3   Choose the **Animals** category, and scroll through the list of clips.

4   Scroll to the bottom of the list; choose **Keep Looking**. Another page of clips appears.

5   In the **Search for clips** box, type **dog** and press **Enter**. Only the clips of dogs appear.

6   Find a dog clip that you like, and click on it. Then choose the **Insert Clip** button from the palette that appears.

> **NOTE:** If you see a message that the clip is stored on another disk, insert that disk in your CD-ROM drive and choose **Retry**, or choose **Cancel** and try a different clip if you don't have the CD available.

7   Look at the keywords for the chosen clip by doing the following:

   • Right-click the clip you just chose, and choose **Clip Properties**.

   • Choose the **Categories** tab, and make sure that a checkmark appears in the **Animals** check box.

   • Click the **Keywords** tab; examine the list of keywords for the clip.

   • Choose **OK**.

8   Close the Clip Gallery window.

9   Save your work, and close the file.

Get Clips from the Internet

In addition to the many clips that come on the Office (or Word) CD, you can download clips from the Microsoft Web site, free of charge. This may be useful if you are looking for a specific, unusual image that you can't find in the Clip Gallery.

> **NOTE:** To use the following procedure, you must have an Internet connection available and Internet Explorer Version 5. Connect to the Internet before performing these steps.

Download clip art:

1   Choose **Insert>Picture>Clip Art**. The Clip Gallery opens.

2   Choose the **Clips Online** button. Your Web browser opens.

> **NOTE:** A message may appear before your browser opens explaining that you will be searching on the Web; if so, choose **OK**. If prompted to establish your Internet connection, do so.

3 If a licensing agreement appears, choose **Accept** to accept the licensing agreement for the clip art. The **Clip Gallery Live** Web page appears. (See Figure 7.9.)

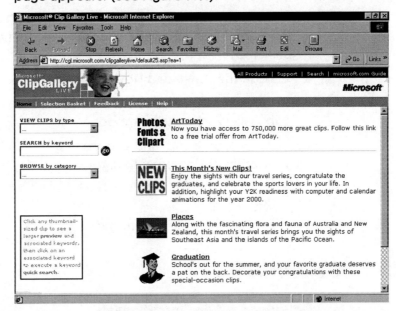

Figure 7.9.   Find and download clips from the **Clip Gallery Live** web page.

4 Type a keyword in the **Search Clips by Keyword** box, and then press **Enter**.

OR

Select a category from the **Browse Clips by Category** drop-down list.

5 Click to place a checkmark under each clip that you want to select. (See Figure 7.10.)

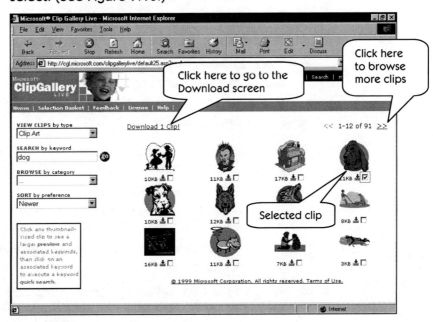

Figure 7.10.   Select the clips you want.

6   Choose the **More (>>)** hyperlink to see more clips of the same type, or enter more keywords or choose more categories, marking each clip that you want.

7   When you are ready to download the selected clips, choose the **Download {x} Clips!** link (where **X** is the number of clips you have selected).

8   Choose the **Download Now!** hyperlink.

9   Wait for the download(s) to take place. The clips appear in the Clip Gallery when they are done.

10 Right-click on a clip, and choose **Clip Properties**. Use the **Clip Properties** dialog box's **Categories** and **Keywords** tabs to add categories and keywords to it, as you learned earlier in this lesson.

11 Close the Clip Gallery window.

Practice Exercise 7-3

Download a Clip from the Web

1   Start a new, blank document; save it as **07Clip2**.

2   Choose **Insert>Picture>Clip Art**. The Clip Gallery opens.

3   Go to the **Clip Gallery Live** by doing the following:

   • Choose the **Clips Online** button. Your Web browser opens. (You may have to click **OK** in a confirmation box first.)

   • If the licensing agreement appears, choose **Accept** to accept the licensing agreement for the clip art. The **Clip Gallery Live** web page appears.

4   Type **dogs** in the **Search by Keyword** box, and then press **Enter**.

5   Place a checkmark under two different pictures of dogs that you like (Click the double right-pointing arrows at the top of the screen to see more) clips), and then click **Download 2 Clips!**.

6   Choose **Download Now!**.

7   When the clips appear in the Clip Gallery, make sure they are properly categorized and then close the Clip Gallery window.

 NOTE: Remember, to categorize a clip, you can right-click the clip, choose **Clip Properties,** and then work with the **Categories** tab. To add a clip to a category, you can also use the **Add Clip to Favorites or Other Category** button on the palette that appears when you click on the clip.

8   Reopen the Clip Gallery (**Insert>Picture>Clip Art**), and locate the new clips by searching for clips by the keyword **dogs**.

9 Insert one of the new clips into your document, then close the Clip Gallery window.

> **NOTE:** Remember, to insert a clip, click on it and then choose the **Insert Clip** button.

10 Save your work, and close the file.

A completed example of **07Clip2** is available in the **WORDCert\Word B\Samples** folder on the DDC CD-ROM.

Add a Scanned Photo to the Clip Gallery

In addition to adding clip art from Microsoft, you can also add your own images to the Clip Gallery. If you use certain images often, it may be easier to have them available in the Clip Gallery than to use the **Insert>Picture>From File** command every time.

Add an image to the Clip Gallery:

1 Choose **Insert>Picture>Clip Art**. The Clip Gallery opens.

2 Choose the **Import Clips** button. The **Add Clip to Clip Gallery** dialog box opens.

3 Locate and select the clip you want (see Figure 7.11).

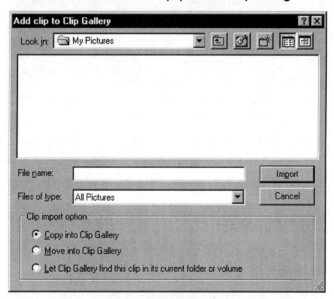

Figure 7.11.   Select the clip that you want to be included in the Clip Gallery.

4 Choose how you want it imported:

- **Copy into Clip Gallery**: Leaves the original in place and makes a copy of it in the folder where clips are stored

- **Move into Clip Gallery**: Moves the original to the folder where clips are stored

- **Let Clip Gallery find this clip in its current folder or volume**: Creates a shortcut to the clip in the Clip Gallery, but does not move or copy the actual clip

5   Choose **Import**. The **Clip Properties** window appears for the clip.

6   Add keywords for the clip, and assign it to categories as needed, and then choose **OK**.

 TIP: If you are importing a scanned photo, make sure you add it to the **Photographs** category, in addition to any other appropriate categories.

7   Close the Clip Gallery window.

Practice Exercise 7-4

Add an Image to the Clip Gallery

1   Start a new, blank document; save it as 🖫**07Clip3**.

2   Choose **Insert>Picture>Clip Art**. The Clip Gallery opens.

3   Choose the **Import Clips** button. The **Add Clip to Clip Gallery** dialog box opens.

4   Select the .jpg file **07Ex7-1** from the **WORDCert\Word B** folder. (This is the same picture you used in Practice Exercise 7.1.)

5   Choose **Copy into Clip Gallery** from the **Clip Import Option** area.

6   Choose **Import**.

7   Type Shetland Sheepdog in the **Description of this clip** box.

8   On the **Categories** tab, select these categories: **Animals, Home & Family,** and **Photographs**.

9   On the **Keywords** tab, add the following keywords for the clip: **Sheltie, Shetland Sheepdog, dog, canine, photograph,** and **pets**.

10   Choose **OK**, closing the **Clip Properties** dialog box.

11   Insert the clip into your document, and then close the Clip Gallery.

12   Save your work, and close the file.

A completed example of **07Clip3** is available in the **WORDCert\Word B\Samples** folder on the DDC CD-ROM.

Draw Lines and Shapes

You can draw your own graphics, one line or shape at a time, using Word's drawing tools. These drawing tools are not terribly sophisticated, and you will not be able to use them to create the kind of high-quality images that you find in the Clip Gallery. Nonetheless, the drawing tools can be useful in constructing simple graphics such as arrows, circles, lines, and so on.

The drawing tools are accessed from the Drawing toolbar. To display it, choose **View>Toolbars>Drawing** or choose the **Drawing** button from the Standard toolbar.

To use a drawing tool, select it and then drag across the workspace to create the line or shape desired. Then, after you have created it, you can use the other tools on the Drawing toolbar to format it further (change its color, its line thickness, and so on).

To resize, move, copy, or delete a drawn shape, see "Manipulate Graphic Objects" later in this lesson.

DRAW A LINE

The simplest shape you can draw is a straight line. Straight lines can be used for a variety of purposes; one of the most common is to draw a connector line between a text box and a picture, pointing out part of the picture, as in Figure 7.12. (You will learn how to create text boxes at the end of this lesson.)

Figure 7.12. Straight lines can be used to connect explanatory text to a figure, among other uses.

Draw a line:

 1 Choose the **Line** button on the Drawing toolbar. The mouse pointer changes to a crosshair.

2 Drag on the workspace where you want the line to appear. When you release the mouse button, the line appears with selection handles at each end. (See Figure 7.13.)

Figure 7.13. A line drawn with the Line tool.

NOTE: You can also create a line with the **Arrow** button on the Drawing toolbar. This creates a line with an arrow at one end.

You can then use the **Arrow Style** button, also on the Drawing toolbar, to modify the arrow's style and choose at which end of the line it appears.

DRAW RECTANGLES AND OVALS

Word's drawing tools can draw two kinds of basic shapes: rectangles and ovals. It can also create other, more complex shapes, but these are AutoShapes, and you will learn about them in the following section.

Draw a rectangle or oval:

1   On the Drawing toolbar, choose the Rectangle or Oval tool.

2   Drag on the workspace where you want the shape to appear. When you release the mouse button, the shape appears with selection handles around it. (See Figure 7.14.)

TIP: To make a perfect square or circle, hold down the **Shift** key as you drag.

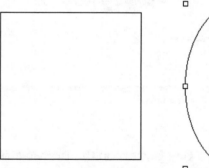 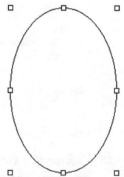

Figure 7.14.   These shapes have been drawn with Word's drawing tools.

DRAW AUTOSHAPES

Word includes a variety of **AutoShapes**, which are more complex shapes such as arrows, starbursts, special lines, and so on. These can be great time-savers; you can simply place a Starburst AutoShape, for example, instead of trying to draw a starburst with individual lines. Figure 7.15 shows some examples of AutoShapes.

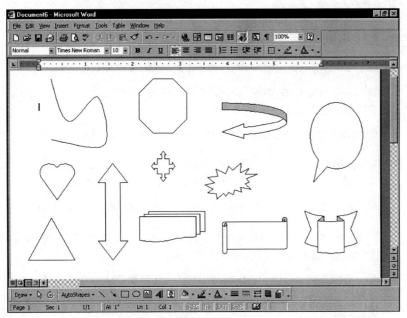

Figure 7.15.   Some of the many AutoShapes you can create with Word.

Draw an AutoShape:

1   On the Drawing toolbar, choose the **AutoShapes** button. A menu opens.

2   Choose a category. A palette of AutoShapes in that category appears. (See Figure 7.16.)

3   Choose the shape you want.

4   Drag on the workspace where you want to place the shape. Release the mouse button when finished.

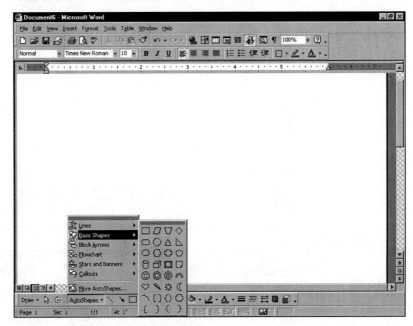

Figure 7.16.   Select an AutoShape to draw.

Practice Exercise 7-5

Draw Lines and Shapes

1 Start a new document; save it as 🖫07Draw1.

2 Display the Drawing toolbar if it does not appear
   (**View>Toolbars>Drawing**).

3 Choose the **Line** button on the Drawing toolbar.

4 Drag across the center of the workspace to create a horizontal
   line approximately 3" long. (Use the ruler to gauge the length.)

5 Choose the **Rectangle** button on the Drawing toolbar.

6 Drag across the workspace to create a rectangle approximately
   1" on all sides, on top of the line.

7 Choose the **AutoShapes** button on the Drawing toolbar. Choose
   Block Arrows and then the up-pointing arrow (third button in
   top row).

8 Drag across the workspace to create an arrow at the right end of
   the line, approximately 3" high and 1" wide.

   When you are finished, your screen should resemble Figure 7.17.

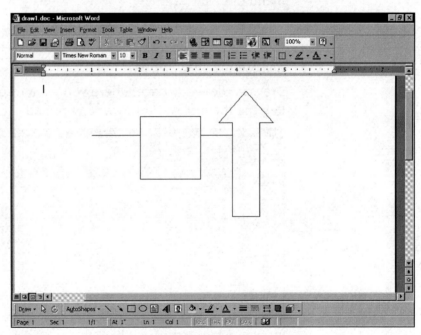

Figure 7.17.   Draw these shapes with the Drawing toolbar's tools.

9 Save your work, and leave the document open for the next
   exercise.

   A completed example of **07Draw1** is available in the
   WORDCert\Word B\Samples folder on the DDC CD-ROM.

Modify a Drawn Shape's Appearance

You aren't stuck with the plain black-and white shapes that Word provides by default. You can change a shape's lines and colors to make it look more interesting. For example, you can change the thickness, color, and style of the line (or the border of the shape), and you can change the color of a shape's interior. You can also apply textures, gradients, patterns, and even pictures to fill a shape.

To change a line or shape, first select it. Then use one of the tools shown in Table 7.1.

Table 7.1: Tools for Modifying a Drawn Shape

Button	Description
	Open this button's list of colors to select a color, or choose More Fill Colors for a larger selection or Fill Effects to choose an effect. (More on effects later.) This is not applicable to lines.
	Open this button's list of colors to select a color, or choose More Line Colors for a larger selection. You can also choose Patterned Lines and then choose a line pattern. When applied to a shape, it affects the shape's outside border.

NOTE: Line patterns don't show up in thin lines very well, but if you use a thick line, you might consider using a line pattern.

Button	Description
	Click this button to open a list of line thicknesses. You can also choose single or double lines. Choose More Lines to open a list of additional line styles. When applied to a shape, line thickness affects the outside border.
	Click this button to open a list of dash styles if you want a dashed, dotted, or otherwise broken-up line. When applied to a shape, dash style affects the outside border.
	Click this button to open a list of arrow styles and placements if you want the selected line to have an arrow. This option is not applicable to shapes.
	Click this button to open a list of shadows that you can apply to lines and shapes. Choose Shadow Settings to open a toolbar containing more shadow controls. Choose No Shadow to turn the shadow off.
	Click this button to open a list of 3-D settings to apply to lines and shapes. Choose 3-D Settings to open a toolbar containing more 3-D controls. Choose No 3-D to turn the 3-D effect off.

WORK WITH FILL EFFECTS

One of the choices on the **Fill Color** button's menu is **Fill Effects**. When you choose that, a **Fill Effects** dialog box appears from which you can select gradients, textures, patterns, or pictures. These effects can be lots of fun, and you may want to experiment with them on your own. For an example, let's look at **Gradient**.

Fill a shape with a gradient:

1   Select the drawn shape.

2   Open the **Fill Color** button's palette, and choose **Fill Effects**.

3   Choose the **Gradient** tab in the **Fill Effects** dialog box.

4   Choose **One Color**, **Two Colors**, or **Preset**.

 NOTE: **One Color** refers to a single color plus either black or white; **Two Colors** refers to two colors you select yourself. **Preset** provides a list of preset color combinations.

5   If you chose **One Color** or **Two Colors**, select the colors you want to use. (See Figure 7.18.) If you chose **Preset**, select the preset color combination.

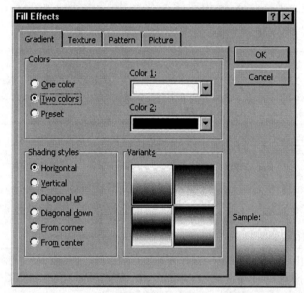

Figure 7.18.   Use the **Color 1** and **Color 2** drop-down lists to choose the colors.

6   Select a shading style and then a variant.

 NOTE: The variants represent different directions in which the colors vary. You can choose **Horizontal** as the shading style, for example, and then choose among the four variants of that style (white to black, black to white, black in the center, and white in the center).

7   Choose **OK**. The effect is applied to the shape.

CHANGE THE PROPORTIONS OF AN AUTOSHAPE

You may have noticed when working with an AutoShape that it has one or more yellow diamonds on it. These diamonds can be dragged to change the shape. Not all AutoShapes have these, but most do.

To modify an AutoShape, simply drag a diamond. A dotted line shows how the shape will be altered. Release the mouse button when you have the shape you want. Figure 7.19 shows a shape being modified.

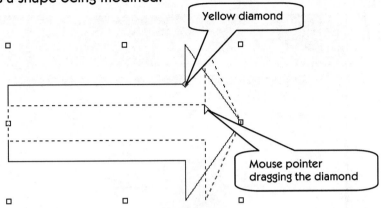

Figure 7.19.   Adjust a shape's proportions by dragging one of its yellow diamonds.

Practice Exercise 7-6

Modify a Shape's Appearance

1   Start in the file **07Draw1** from the preceding exercise, or open 📂**07Ex7-6** from the **WORDCert\Word B** folder. Save the file as 💾**07Draw2**.

2   Select the line, open the **Line Color** button's palette, and choose a medium blue.

3   Open the **Line Style** list, and choose **3 pt**.

4   Select the arrow AutoShape, open the **Fill Color** button's palette, and choose **Fill Effects**.

5   Choose the **Texture** tab in the **Fill Effects** dialog box, and select **White Marble** (the second texture in the second row). Then choose **OK**.

6   Select the rectangle, choose the **3-D** button, and select the second 3-D object in the first row. The rectangle now appears as a 3-D box.

7   Choose the **3-D** button again, and choose **3-D Settings**. The 3-D Settings toolbar appears.

8   Open the **3-D Color** button's palette, and choose a medium red. The "sides" of the rectangle turn red.

9   Open the **Fill Color** button's palette on the Drawing toolbar, and choose a dark red. The front of the rectangle turns dark red.

10 Select the arrow AutoShape, then drag the yellow diamond on the arrow to make it narrower.

Figure 7.20 shows the result of performing the steps in this exercise.

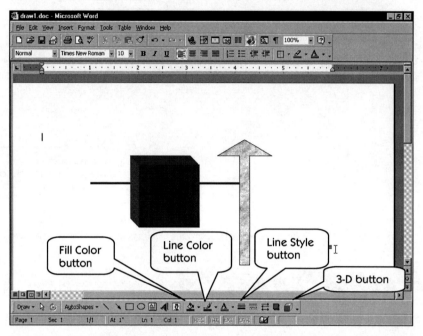

Figure 7.20. The drawn objects from the previous exercise, formatted with the Drawing toolbar's controls.

11 Save your work, and close the file.

Create WordArt

WordArt is a combination of text and graphics. It's text, but it's bent, shaped, colored, and stylized so that it looks like a graphic. Figure 7.21 shows examples of WordArt.

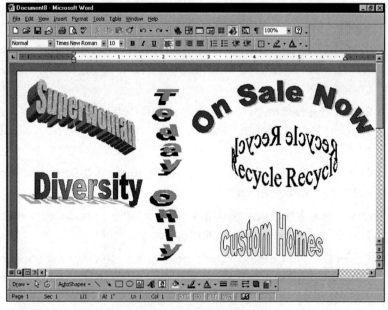

Figure 7.21. A sampling of what you can do with WordArt.

PLACE WORDART

There are two ways to start a new piece of WordArt. You can choose the **WordArt** button on the Drawing toolbar, or you can choose **Insert>Picture>WordArt**. From there, the procedure is the same.

Create WordArt:

1   Choose **Insert>Picture>WordArt**. The **WordArt Gallery** dialog box opens. This shows various styles of WordArt. (See Figure 7.22.)

 NOTE: Don't worry if the WordArt you create at first is not exactly right; you can change almost every aspect of it after creation.

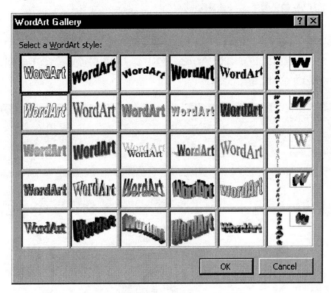

Figure 7.22.   Select a WordArt style to start with.

2   Select a style that is close to what you want, and then choose **OK**. The **Edit WordArt Text** dialog box opens. (See Figure 7.23.)

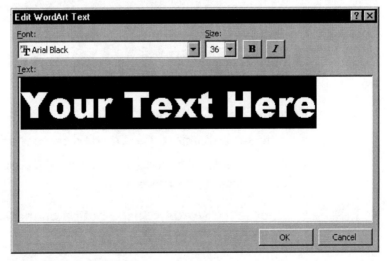

Figure 7.23.   Type the text you want to use here.

3   Type the text that you want to use for the WordArt, and then choose **OK**. The WordArt appears in the document.

After placing some WordArt, you can do any of the following:

- Change the WordArt shape, as you'll learn in the next topic.

- Edit the WordArt text, as you'll learn in the topic after that.

- Delete, move, copy, or resize it (see **Manipulate Graphic Objects** later in this lesson).

- Change the fill or line color, as you did with drawn objects earlier in **Modify a Drawn Shape's Appearance** and **Work with Fill Effects**.

CHANGE THE WORDART SHAPE

The starting shape of the WordArt is only a beginning. You can choose from a palette of many different shapes. For example, Figure 7.24 shows some plain text shaped into several different WordArt shapes.

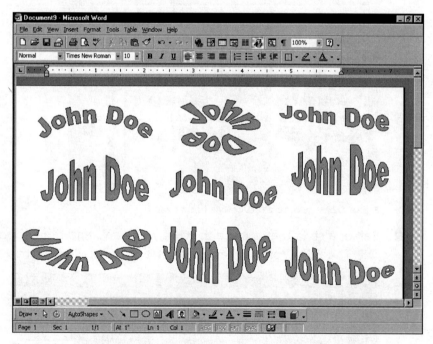

Figure 7.24.   Examples of WordArt shapes.

Change WordArt shape:

1   Select the WordArt. The WordArt toolbar appears.

 NOTE: If the WordArt toolbar does not appear, choose **View>Toolbars>WordArt**.

 2   Choose the **WordArt Shape** button on the WordArt toolbar. A palette of shapes opens.

3 Choose the shape to which you want the WordArt to conform. (See Figure 7.25.)

4 (Optional) To further modify the shape, drag the yellow diamond to change it, as you did in "Change the Proportions of an AutoShape" earlier in this lesson.

5 (Optional) To further change the shape of the WordArt, drag one or more of the side handles around the shape to make it taller, shorter, fatter, or thinner.

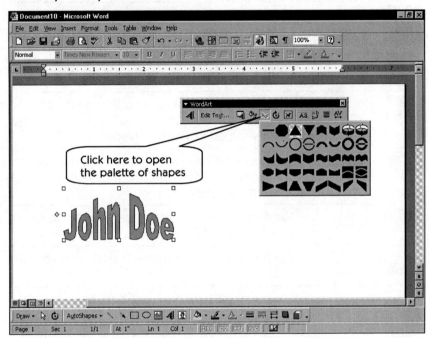

Figure 7.25. Select a shape from the palette of available shapes.

 NOTE: Dragging a corner handle resizes in both dimensions at once, making the shape larger or smaller overall. Dragging a side handle resizes in only one dimension, altering the overall shape of the WordArt.

There are several other ways you can modify the WordArt. Table 7.2 shows some buttons on the WordArt toolbar with which you can experiment.

Table 7.2: WordArt Toolbar Buttons

Button	Description
	Same as the Insert **WordArt** button on the Drawing toolbar; creates a new WordArt
Edit Te_x_t...	Opens the **Edit WordArt Text** dialog box, shown in Figure 7.23
	Reopens the WordArt Gallery for the currently selected WordArt
	Opens the **Format WordArt** dialog box, which you can use to change the fill color (instead of using the Drawing toolbar, if you prefer), the size, and other attributes
	Opens a palette of shapes from which to choose
	Enables you to rotate the WordArt (This is the same as the **Free Rotate** button on the Drawing toolbar, which you will work with later in the chapter.)
	Enables you to control how surrounding text interacts with the WordArt (You will learn about text wrapping for objects later in the chapter.)
	Toggles between letting each letter have its natural height and forcing all of them to be the same
	Toggles between normal horizontal text and a vertical version of it
	Opens a list of alignment settings
	Opens a list of character spacing options (Tight, Loose, etc.) for spacing between letters

EDIT WORDART TEXT

You can't edit WordArt text as you would normal text. Instead, you must revisit the **Edit WordArt Text** dialog box. To redisplay the **Edit WordArt Text** dialog box (Figure 7.23), choose the **Edit Text** button on the WordArt toolbar. Make your changes to the text, and choose **OK**.

Practice Exercise 7-7

Create and Edit WordArt

1 Start with a new, blank document; save it as **07Wrdart**.

2 Display the Drawing toolbar if it does not already appear (**View>Toolbars>Drawing**).

3 Choose **Insert>Picture>WordArt**. The **WordArt Gallery** dialog box opens.

4   Select the fourth style in the bottom row, and then choose **OK**. The **Edit WordArt Text** dialog box opens.

5   Type **On Sale Now**, and choose **OK**.

6   Choose the **WordArt Shape** button on the WordArt toolbar, and choose **Triangle Up** (the up-pointing triangle in the first row).

7   Change the fill color for the front of the WordArt by doing the following:

-   Open the **Fill Color** button's palette (on the Drawing toolbar), and choose **Fill Effects**.

-   In the **Fill Effects** dialog box, on the **Gradient** tab, change Color 1 to a medium green and Color 2 to a dark green.

-   Choose **OK**.

8   Change the 3-D color for the sides of the WordArt by doing the following:

-   Choose the **3-D** button on the Drawing toolbar, and choose **3-D Settings**. The 3-D Settings toolbar appears.

-   Open the **3-D Color** button's palette on the 3-D Settings toolbar, and choose a dark yellow.

-   Close the 3-D Settings toolbar.

9   Choose the **WordArt Character Spacing** button on the WordArt toolbar, and choose **Loose** from the list that appears.
Figure 7.26 shows how your WordArt should look at this point.

Figure 7.26.   The WordArt after applying the formatting specified in Exercise 7-7.

10 Save your work, and close the file.

Manipulate Graphic Objects

So far in this lesson you have learned to insert a wide variety of graphic objects into Word: scanned photos, clip art, drawn lines and shapes, and WordArt. What you may not realize, though, is that they are all manipulated very similarly.

SELECT MORE THAN ONE OBJECT

You have learned that you can select a graphic object by clicking on it. To select more than one object to at once, hold down the **Shift** key as you click on each one.

DELETE AN OBJECT

You can either delete an object or cut it. Deleting it removes it without a trace; cutting it places it on the Clipboard for pasting elsewhere.

Delete an object:

1   Select the object.

2   Press **Delete**.

Cut an object to the Clipboard:

1   Select the object.

   2   Choose **Edit>Cut**, or click the **Cut** button.

> TIP: Remember, a shortcut for the **Cut** command is **Ctrl+X**.

MOVE OR COPY AN OBJECT

To move an object around on the page, drag it where you want it.

Move or copy an object by dragging:

1   Position the mouse pointer over the object (but not over a selection handle).

2   To copy, hold down the **Ctrl** key.

3   Drag the object to a different spot.

To move an object from one page or document to another, use cut-and-paste.

Move or copy an object with the Clipboard:

1   Select the object.

   2   To move, choose **Edit>Cut** or click the **Cut** button.

OR

   To copy, choose **Edit>Copy** or click the **Copy** button.

3   Position the insertion point where you want the object to go. (This can be in a different document or on a different page.)

4   Choose **Edit>Paste**, or click the **Paste** button.

NOTE: By default, drawn objects "float" over the top of the document, so you can drag them anywhere on the page. By default, clip art and WordArt do not; they're treated as text characters, and you can only move them within the text. However, you can control how an object interacts with text by changing its wrapping style. See "Change Text Wrapping Around an Object" later in this lesson.

Preparing for Microsoft Office Specialist Certification

RESIZE AN OBJECT

To resize an object, drag one of its selection handles. Dragging a corner handle resizes in both dimensions at once; dragging a side handle resizes only one dimension.

 TIP: Some objects, like clip art, automatically maintain their proportions when you drag a corner handle, so the image does not get distorted. Other objects, like drawn shapes, do not maintain proportions automatically, but you can hold down the **Shift** key while dragging to force it to do so.

Practice Exercise 7-8

Move, Resize, and Delete Objects

1   Open 📂**07Ex7-8** from the **WORDCert\Word B** folder; save it as 💾**07Draw3**.

2   Drag the box to the top left corner of the page, and drag the arrow to the top right corner.

3   Select the line, and hold down **Ctrl** as you drag it below itself, creating a copy of it.

4   Drag the bottom selection handle for the arrow down about 1", making it taller. (See Figure 7.27.)

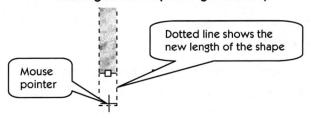

Figure 7.27.   To resize in one direction, drag a side handle (not a corner).

5   Drag the right end of the top line up, tilting it. (See Figure 7.28.)

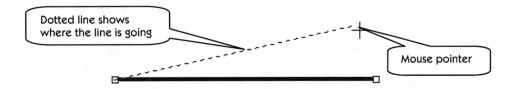

Figure 7.28.   To reposition a line, drag one end of it.

6   Select all the shapes on the page by holding down **Shift** and clicking on each shape.

7   Press **Delete**, deleting all the shapes.

8 Choose **Edit>Undo Clear**, undoing the deletion.

Figure 7.29 shows the completed document.

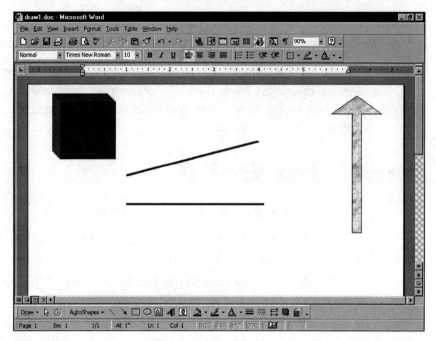

Figure 7.29. The lines and shapes should look like this after you've performed the above steps.

9 Save your work and close the file.

Format Graphic Objects

You have already seen how to format drawn lines, drawn shapes, and WordArt, but you can format other graphic objects in much the same way. This section outlines some common procedures that work with most graphic object types.

CHANGE THE FILL

 You have already learned how to change fill colors for drawn objects, and in the preceding exercise you changed the fill color for some WordArt. But you can also change the fill color for clip art. The fill color for clip art refers to the background color; if you applied a green fill color to a piece of clip art, it would result in a green background, with the rest of the colors unchanged. (See Figure 7.30.)

NOTE: Applying a fill color to a bitmap image, such as a scan, has no effect.

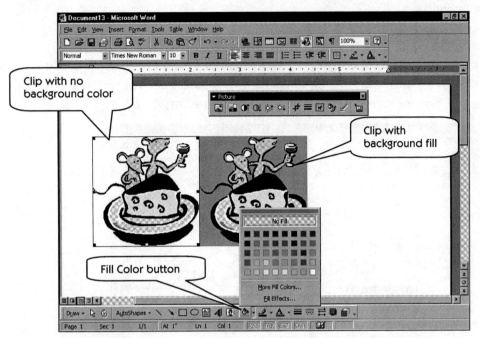

Figure 7.30.   Change a clip's fill color to shade its background.

 NOTE: Changing a clip's fill color changes its background because the background is set to **Transparent**. Some clips do not have a transparent background; with such clips you can use the **Set Transparent Color** button on the Picture toolbar to specify which color in the clip should be transparent. Then, whatever background color you apply to the clip will show through those spots.

CHANGE THE BORDER

 Borders work a little differently depending on the graphic type and its settings. With a drawn line or shape, you apply a border to it with the **Line Style** and **Line Color** buttons, as you have already seen. These tools also work with some styles of WordArt. (Not all styles of WordArt employ a border; when you select a piece of WordArt that doesn't use a border, the **Line Style** and **Line Color** buttons' controls are unavailable.)

These same **Line Style** and **Line Color** buttons work with bitmap images and clip art, too, but not in their default states. By default, these types of graphics have a wrapping style set to **In line with text**; in that state, you cannot apply a border to them as individual objects. You must set the object's wrapping style to one of the other settings in order for the **Line Style** and **Line Color** buttons to become available for the object. You will learn how to set wrapping style later in this lesson, in "Set Text Wrapping Around an Object."

NOTE: When a graphic object is set for <u>I</u>n line with text, you can use the **Border** button from the formatting toolbar (or the **F<u>o</u>rmat>B<u>o</u>rders and Shading** command) to place a border around it.

Figure 7.31 shows some borders around various types of graphics. Notice that for WordArt and drawn shapes, the border clings to the object, but for clip art and bitmap images, the border runs around a rectangular area outside of the image.

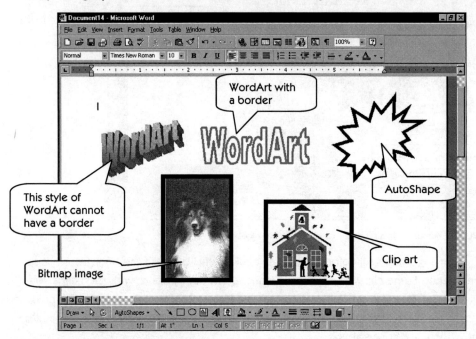

Figure 7.31.   Borders have been applied to each of these graphic objects.

CHANGE IMAGE ATTRIBUTES

Image attributes are applicable to clip art and bitmap images. (You can't use them on WordArt or drawn shapes.) They control the image's appearance, much as the controls on your TV control the picture. The attributes you can set include **Brightness**, **Contrast**, and **Image Type**. Just click on the button you want on the Picture toolbar.

The **Brightness** controls lighten or darken the image overall:

- Increase brightness

- Decrease brightness

The **Contrast** controls lighten the light parts and darken the dark parts:

- More contrast

- Less contrast

The **Image Control** button on the Picture toolbar opens a list of four image types:

- **Automatic**: the image's default; this is normally color
- **Grayscale**: a gray-shaded version of the image, where each color becomes a unique shade of gray
- **Black & White**: an unshaded version, in which all light colors become white and all dark colors become black
- **Watermark**: a semi-transparent, faded version of the image, suitable for use behind text or other objects

Figure 7.32 shows a piece of clip art in each of these image types. You will not notice any difference between Automatic and Grayscale in Figure 7.32 because this book is not in color, but the difference will be obvious on your own screen.

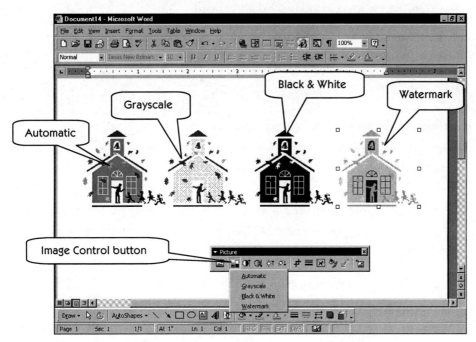

Figure 7.32.   The four image-type settings.

SET TEXT WRAPPING AROUND AN OBJECT

This lesson has referred to text wrapping quite a bit so far, and now it's time to learn more about it.

An object's wrapping setting controls how it interacts with any text on the page. By default, clip art and bitmaps are set for **Inline** wrapping. With **Inline** wrapping, Word treats the image as if it were a big character (e.g., a letter or number) in a sentence, so if that spot to which it is anchored in the sentence changes position (for example, if you add more text in an earlier paragraph), the graphic moves with it. Figure 7.33 illustrates such a situation.

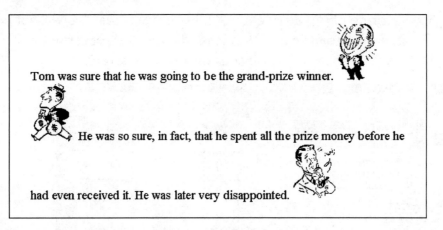

Figure 7.33.   Each graphic belongs in a specific place in the paragraph, so it's appropriate that each graphic is set for **Inline** placement.

Other times it may be more appropriate for a graphic to float freely on the page, so you can position it exactly where you want it. All wrapping settings except **Inline** allow the graphic to float freely.

The difference between the various wrapping settings has to do with the way that the surrounding text interacts with the graphic. You can set the text to wrap around the graphic, or go above and below the graphic, and you can specify how close the text will come to the graphic and whether it will wrap around the graphic itself or around the graphic's rectangular frame. Figure 7.34 shows some examples.

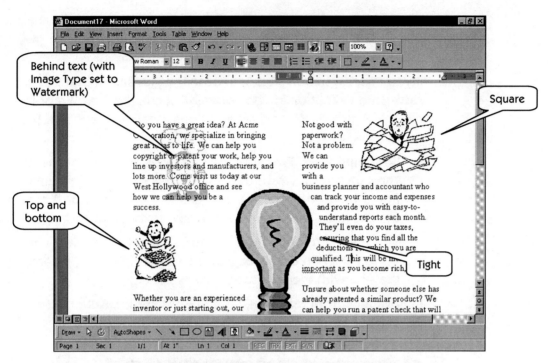

Figure 7.34. Various ways that a graphic can wrap around some text.

Set wrapping for a graphic:

1 Select the graphic.

2 Choose **Format>Picture**. The **Format Picture** dialog box opens.

> **NOTE:** If you are formatting WordArt or a shape instead, you could choose **Format>WordArt** or **Format>AutoShape** instead.

3 Choose the **Layout** tab.

4 Select a wrapping style. (See Figure 7.35.)

5 Choose a Horizontal alignment: **Left**, **Center**, **Right**, or **Other**.

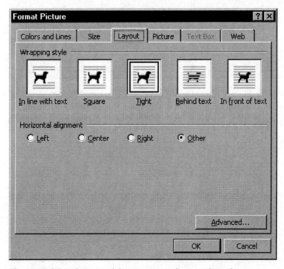

Figure 7.35. Set an object's wrapping options here.

NOTE: Horizontal alignment refers to the way that the text aligns with the image on the left and right. If you choose **Left**, the image will be placed to the left of the text, for example.

6   If you chose **Other** in step 5, choose the **Advanced** button. The **Advanced Layout** dialog box opens. Choose the **Text Wrapping** tab (see Figure 7.36), and set additional wrapping options. Then choose **OK**.

   *   **Wrapping style:** Two additional options are available here: **Through** (which wraps the text around all sides of the image, not just top and bottom); and **Top and Bottom**, which places the image on its own line and wraps text above and below it.

   *   **Wrap text:** Choose where the text should run in relation to the graphic: on both sides, to the left or right only, or only on the side with the largest amount of space.

   *   **Distance from text:** You can set a precise measurement for the buffer of "white space" to appear between the graphic and the text.

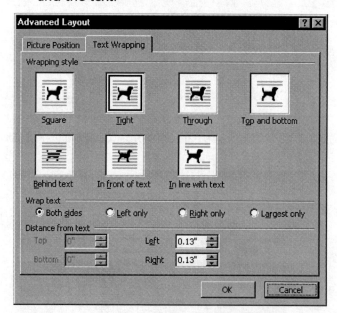

Figure 7.36.   Additional wrapping options are available here.

7   Back in the **Format Picture** dialog box again, choose **OK** to close the dialog box and apply the settings.

An abbreviated set of wrapping commands is available from the Picture toolbar, as shown in Figure 7.37. The **Text Wrapping** button opens a drop-down list containing several kinds of wrapping styles.

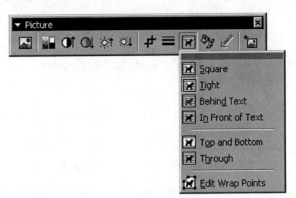

Figure 7.37. Basic wrapping can be set quickly using the Picture toolbar.

 NOTE: How does Word know where the graphic's edges are? Well, with Word-supplied clip art, each graphic has "wrap points" set. You can edit these by choosing **Edit Wrap Points** on the Picture toolbar's **Wrap** button menu. A series of selection handles appears all around the image then, as shown in Figure 7.38, and you can drag each of them in or out individually to alter the way text wraps around the image when its wrapping style is set to <u>T</u>ight.

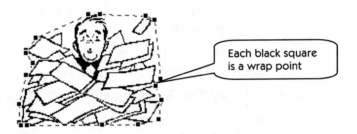

Figure 7.38. You can adjust the wrap points for clip art.

ROTATE OR FLIP AN OBJECT

Rotating and flipping apply only to WordArt and drawn shapes; you cannot rotate or flip a piece of clip art or a bitmap image. You can rotate using a predefined setting, such as 90 degrees to the right or left, or you can use the Free Rotate tool.

Flipping an object creates a mirror image of it. You can flip an object on either its horizontal or its vertical axis.

Flip an object:

1   Select the object to be flipped.

2   Choose **D<u>r</u>aw** on the Drawing toolbar, opening a menu.

3   Choose **Rotate or Fli<u>p</u>**. A submenu appears.

4   Choose **Flip <u>H</u>orizontal** or **Flip <u>V</u>ertical**.

TIP: If you ever need mirror-image text for some reason (for example, for creating an iron-on transfer), the **Flip** command works great for creating it with WordArt.

Rotating an object using one of the Rotate commands rotates it exactly 90 degrees, either to the left or to the right.

Rotate an object by a defined amount:

1   Select the object to be rotated.

2   Choose **Draw** on the Drawing toolbar, opening a menu.

3   Choose **Rotate or Flip**. A submenu appears.

4   Choose **Rotate Left** or **Rotate Right**.

Free Rotate is the most fun of the rotating and flipping commands. With it, you can rotate the object a precise amount that you choose.

Using Free Rotate to rotate an object:

1   Select the object to be rotated.

 2   Choose the **Free Rotate** button on either the Drawing or the WordArt toolbar.

 TIP: You can also use the **Draw** button menu on the Drawing toolbar, choosing **Draw> Rotate or Flip>Free Rotate**, but that takes longer.

3   The selection handles turn into green circles. Drag one of those circles to rotate the object. (See Figure 7.39.)

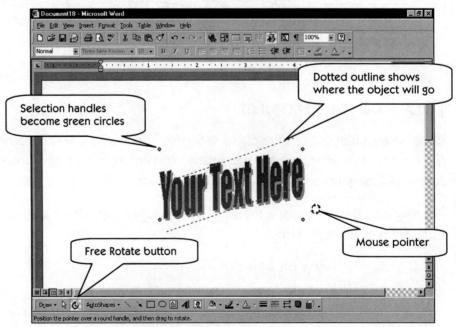

Figure 7.39.   Use **Free Rotate** to rotate an object.

4   Release the mouse button. The object is rotated.

Practice Exercise 7-9

Format a Graphic Object

1   Open 🗁**07Ex7-9** from the **WORDCert\Word B** folder; save it as 💾**07Fmt1**.

2   Set the first image's type to Watermark, and place it behind the first paragraph by doing the following:

- Select the image.

- Choose the **Image Control** button on the Picture toolbar.

- Choose **Watermark** from the list that appears.

- Select the **Text Wrapping** button on the Picture toolbar.

- Choose **Behind Text**.

Figure 7.40 shows the result.

> Do you have a great idea? At Acme Corporation, we specialize in bringing great ideas to life. We can help you copyright or patent your work, help you line up investors and manufacturers, and lots more. Come visit us today at our West Hollywood office and see how we can help you be a success.

Figure 7.40.   The image is set to Watermark and placed behind the text.

3   Set the picture of the man with the papers so that it wraps in a square with the paragraph by doing the following:

- Select the image.

- Select the **Text Wrapping** button on the Picture toolbar.

- Choose **Square**.

4   Add a 1-point border to that same picture, and add a light yellow fill behind the image:

- Select the image.

- Open the **Line Color** button's palette, and choose **Black**.

- Choose the **Line Style** button, and select **1 pt**.
- Open the **Fill Color** button's palette, and choose **Yellow**.

Figure 7.41 shows the result.

Figure 7.41. The image is set to Square wrapping, there is a border, and the image has yellow shading.

5   Change the light bulb's image type to Automatic, and set the text to wrap tightly around it, by doing the following:

- Select the image.
- Select the **Image Control** button on the Picture toolbar.
- Choose **Automatic**.

- Select the **Text Wrapping** button on the Picture toolbar.
- Choose **Tight**.

Figure 7.42 shows the finished document.

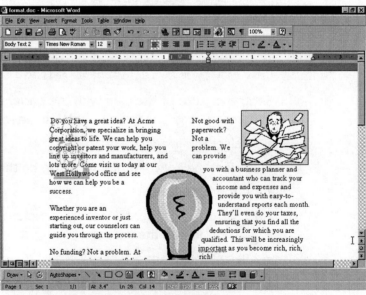

Figure 7.42. Text wraps tightly around the light bulb.

6   Save your work, and close the file.

A completed example of **07Fmt1** is available in the **WORDCert\Word B\Samples** folder on the DDC CD-ROM.

Work with Text Boxes

Text boxes may seem like a very different subject after all the talk of graphics in this lesson, but they are actually very similar. You can think of a text box as a rectangle that is specifically designed to hold text. You can format it in much the same way that you format a drawn shape.

Text boxes are very useful when you need to place some text in a precise spot on a page. With ordinary text, you would need to insert extra blank paragraphs, spaces, or tab stops to place a bit of text where you wanted it, but by placing a text box in the desired spot and typing into it, you can circumvent all that. If you'll turn back to Figure 7.12, you'll see two separate blocks of text. Each is in its own text box (although the borders around the boxes are not visible).

If you have used a page layout program such as PageMaker or Quark XPress, you may be accustomed to laying out text in frames. Instead of typing text directly onto a page, you place a frame and then type the text in it. That way you can easily move the frame around as you add and rearrange different articles and graphics. Word's Text Box feature can be used that way, so that Word can function as a page layout program. Figure 7.43 shows text boxes used to lay out a newsletter.

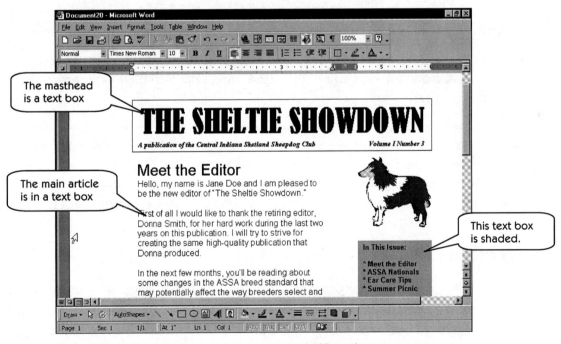

Figure 7.43.   This newsletter layout was constructed with text boxes.

 TIP: If you plan to lay out a page using text boxes, you should turn on the display of text boundaries (i.e., margin lines). To do so, choose **Tools>Options** and choose **Text boundaries** on the **View** tab. To create a multi-column layout like the one shown in Figure 7.43, set up multiple columns (with **Format>Columns**). Then, when you turn on the display of text boundaries, the lines shown will reflect the multiple columns.

PLACE A TEXT BOX

You draw a text box on the document the same way that you draw a shape.

Create a text box:

1   Choose **I**nsert>Te**x**t Box. The mouse pointer turns into a crosshair.

    NOTE: You can also choose the **Text Box** button on the Drawing
    toolbar.

2   Drag on the document to create the text box in the location and
    of the size you want.

3   Type your text in the text box.

MODIFY A TEXT BOX

Text boxes can be moved and resized the same as any graphic object. To move one,
drag it by its middle; to resize it, drag it by its selection handles. To delete it, select it
and press **Delete**.

    CAUTION: If you want to delete a text box, make sure you select the outside border of
    the box before you press **Delete**. If the insertion point is in the text box, and you have
    been typing, pressing **Delete** will merely delete one character of text. To select the text
    box itself, click its border. (In contrast, to move the insertion point inside it, click inside.)

You can also change the border on a text box, change its shading, change the way
regular text wraps around it, and so on, using the same skills you have learned
throughout this chapter.

    TIP: The Text Box toolbar has a button that you might find useful when formatting a text
    box: The **Change Text Direction** button changes where the text in the box appears. By
    default, text appears at the top and runs from left to right, of course, but click this button

    and the text appears at the right and runs from top to bottom. Click it again, and the text
    appears at the left and runs from bottom to top. One more click and you're back to
    normal.

LINK TEXT BOXES

When an article in a text box is longer than will fit on its current page, it needs to wrap
to the next page. You set this up by creating a second text frame on the next page and
then linking the two frames. That way, if you were to make the frame on the first page
smaller, the excess text would float to the second frame.

Link text boxes:

1   Create both text boxes.

2   Click inside the first text box. The Text Box toolbar appears (floating).

3   Choose the **Create Text Box Link** command on the Text Box toolbar.

4   Click inside the second text box. A link is created.

To test a link, type text in the first text box and then resize it so that all the text does not fit. The extra text should appear in the second text box.

To break a link, move the insertion point into the first text box and choose the **Break Forward Link** button. (You cannot break a link "backward").

Practice Exercise 7-10

Work with Text Boxes

1   Start a new document, and save it as ▢07Txtbox.

2   Set up the document by doing the following:

• Display the Drawing toolbar (**V**iew>**T**oolbars>Drawing).

• Switch to Print Layout view (**V**iew>**P**rint Layout).

• Display text boundaries (**T**ools>**O**ptions>View tab>Te**x**t boundaries).

• Set the document for a two-column layout with the **Columns** button on the Standard toolbar.

3   Choose the **Text Box** button on the Drawing toolbar, and draw a text box about 2 1/2" long in the first column. (See Figure 7.44.)

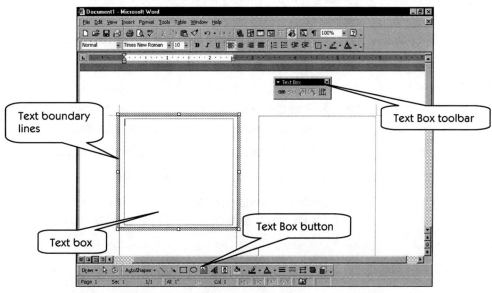

Figure 7.44.   A text box placed in the document.

4 Place text in the text box by doing the following:

- Open the file 📂**07Ex7-10** from the **WORDCert\Word B** folder, and select the entire document (**Ctrl+A**).

- Copy the selected text (**E**dit>**C**opy).

- Switch back to **07Txtbox**; click inside the text box.

- Paste the copied text (**E**dit>**P**aste).

5 Drag the bottom selection handle of the text box down, so that the text box fills the entire first column on the page.

6 Create another text box, this time in the second column of the page.

7 Link the text boxes together, so text flows into the second box, by doing the following:

- Click in the first text box.

- Choose the **Create Text Box Link** button on the Text Box toolbar. (If the toolbar is not visible, choose **V**iew>**T**oolbars>**Text Box** from the menu to select it.)

- Click in the second text box.

8 Add yellow shading to the second text box and remove its border, by doing the following:

- Select the second text box.

- Choose **F**ormat>**Text B**ox.

- On the **Colors and Lines** tab, change the **Fill Color** to **Yellow**.

- On that same tab, change the **Line Color** to **No Line**.

- Choose **OK**.

9 Break the link between the text boxes, and delete the second box, by doing the following:

- Move the insertion point into the first text box.

- Choose the **Break Forward Link** button on the Text Box toolbar.

- Select the second text box. (The border must be selected; don't just move the insertion point into it.)

- Press **Delete**. The second text box disappears.

10 Save your work, and close all open files.

A completed example of **07Txtbox** is available in the **WORDCert\Word B\Samples** folder on the DDC CD-ROM.

Bullets and Numbered Lists

One of the great features in Word is the ability to create automatic numbered or bulleted lists. Gone are the days when you had to laboriously set up hanging indents for numbers or bullets; now Word handles it for you. Figure 7.45. shows sample bulleted and numbered lists.

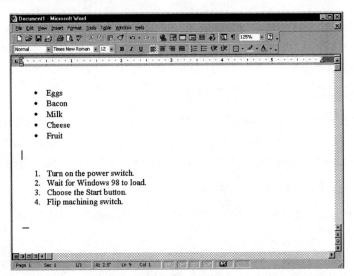

Figure 4.45   Bulleted and numbered lists are a breeze in Word.

TYPE A BULLETED OR NUMBERED LIST

You can type the paragraphs first and then convert them to a bulleted or numbered list, or you can make the list as you type. The following steps show how to make a bulleted or numbered list in the latter way, using automatic bullets or numbering.

Create an automatic bulleted or numbered list

1   Position the insertion point where you want the list to begin.

 or

2   Click either the **Bullets** or **Numbering** button on the Formatting toolbar. A bullet or number appears at the insertion point.

> **TIP:** If you start a paragraph with an asterisk and a tab, Word converts it to a bullet if the **Automatic Bulleted Lists** feature is turned on in the **AutoCorrect** dialog box. (The setting is on the **AutoFormat As You Type** tab.) The same goes for a numbered list; start out with a number and a tab, and Word assumes you want a numbered list item.

3   Type the first paragraph. Press **Enter** when done. A new line with a bullet or number starts automatically.

4   Type the next paragraph. Press **Enter** when done.

5   Repeat step 4 as many times as needed to generate the list.

6   Press **Enter** twice to turn off the automatic bullets or numbering.

Convert Existing Text to Bulleted or Numbered Format

 You can easily make any paragraph(s) into a bulleted or numbered list. Simply select the list and then click the **Bullets** or **Numbering** button on the Formatting toolbar.

Remove Bullets or Numbering

To remove the bullets or the numbering from one or more paragraphs, select the paragraph(s) and then click either the **Bullets** or **Numbering** button on the Formatting toolbar to toggle off the formatting.

GET FANCIER WITH BULLETS AND NUMBERING

You can use the **Bullets and Numbering** dialog box to customize your bullet character or your numbering format. For example, you could use stars instead of dots for the bullets, or you could use Roman numerals for the numbering.

Customize bullets or numbering:

1   Select the paragraphs that should have custom bullets or numbering.

2   Choose **F**o**rmat>Bullets and <u>N</u>umbering**. The **Bullets and Numbering** dialog box opens. See Figure 7.46.

3   Choose the **<u>B</u>ulleted** tab or the **<u>N</u>umbered** tab, depending on which you want.

4   Choose a different bullet or number format from the sample palette shown.

5   Choose **OK**.

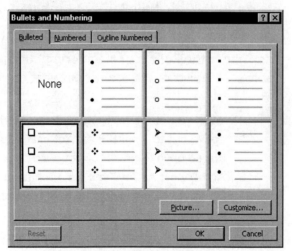

Figure 7.46.   Use this dialog box to choose a different character bullet or numbering style.

 NOTE: Choose the **Cus<u>t</u>omize** button in the **Bullets and Numbering** dialog box to get more customization options. This is not covered in this lesson, but you may want to explore it on your own.

Practice Exercise 7-11

Work with Bullets and Numbering

1   In a new Word document, type the following names, pressing **Enter** after each one:

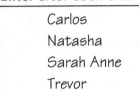

Carlos
Natasha
Sarah Anne
Trevor

2   Select all four paragraphs, and click the **Numbering** button on the Formatting toolbar. The list becomes numbered.

3   Position the insertion point at the end of the last line and press **Enter**. Another numbered line appears.

4   Type Francine.

5   Select all five paragraphs, and click the **Bullets** button on the Formatting toolbar. The list becomes bulleted.

6   Choose **Format>Bullets and Numbering**.

7   Select the second bullet style on the second row, and then choose **OK**. Figure 7.47. shows the document at this point.

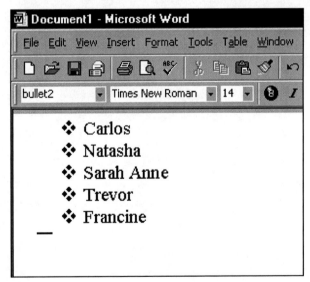

Figure 7.47.   The name list with customized bullets.

8   Click the **Bullets** button again. The list reverts to plain text, with neither bullets nor numbering.

9   Save your work and close the file.

LESSON 1: DEVELOP TEMPLATES

Don't spend time recreating the same basic documents repeatedly. It's often much more efficient to start with a template and customize only the elements that you need to change.

A *template* is a pre-designed starting point. It contains margin settings, styles, and perhaps even sample text or placeholders on which you can base a new document. For example, a newsletter template might contain the newsletter's masthead, the organization's motto, and the editor's name and contact information. Then, each month the editor could start a new document based on that template and paste in the new articles. Other common templates are: company letters, memos, fax cover sheets, and meeting agendas. You can also attach specific AutoText entries, macros, key assignments, and menus to templates.

In this lesson, you will learn to:

> Locate Word templates, workgroup templates, and user templates

> Modify templates   > Add placeholder text

> Add a watermark   > Edit field codes

> Insert a date code   > Attach a template

You will have an opportunity to practice these skills in the Practice Exercises and in the exercises at the end of this lesson.

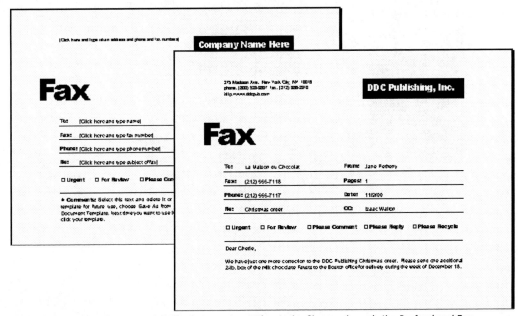

Figure 1.1   Templates can simplify document-creation tasks. Shown above is the Professional Fax template.

Templates and Wizards: A Review

You are probably already familiar with how templates (and their cousins, wizards) work, but let's review quickly.

All documents are based on one template or another. The template tells Word what initial margins to set, which font to use, which styles to include, and so on. When you click the **New Blank Document** button on the Standard toolbar, the new document that's created is based on a template called *Normal* (or *Blank Document*). However, you can base a new document on a different template instead. Microsoft Word offers a variety of templates: Choose **File>New** from the menu bar to display the **New** dialog box and then choose each tab to see the complete array.

Wizards appear along with the templates in the **New** dialog box. A *wizard* is a mini-program that walks you through the process of creating a certain type of document by displaying a series of dialog boxes. The answers you provide (and the settings you adjust) in these dialog boxes establish the form of your final document. For example, if you are creating an agenda, the wizard first asks you which style you want to use. Then you need to include agenda details (such as Date, Time, Title and Location, Headings), key names (meeting called by, facilitator, note taker, timekeeper, attendees, observers, and resource persons), and agenda topics (presenters and the time allotted). You can also specify if you want a form for recording minutes.

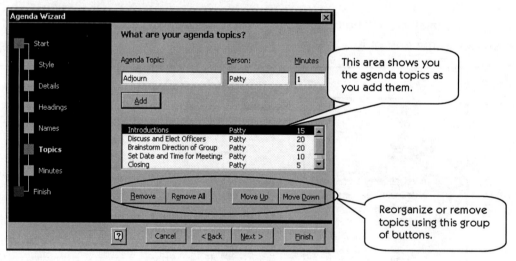

Figure 1.2   The Agenda Wizard is shown above.

Template File Location

Word templates (those that are shipped with Word) are stored by default in a folder either on the hard drive or on a network drive. The first place to look is on your hard drive (C:). The second place to look, if you are accessing workgroup templates, is on the **File Location** tab in the **Options** dialog box (**Tools>Options**)—or you can ask your system administrator. On a stand-alone installation, Word templates are probably in the following location: **C:\Program Files\Microsoft Office\Templates\1033**.

When you use the **New** dialog box to create new documents, you may see many more templates listed than appear when you look at the list of files in the 1033 folder. Where are the other templates? Well, some of them may not be installed yet. Word does not install all templates automatically during setup; it installs only the ones you need as you need them. When you choose a template that has not yet been installed, Word prompts you for your installation CD.

Another feature of templates of which you need to be aware when working with Office 2000 is that *user templates* (that is, the templates you create yourself) are stored in a different location than Word templates. If more than one person is using the same computer and user profiles are defined for each person, your user templates will be in a personalized folder similar to: **C:\Windows\Profiles\[UserName]\Application Data\Microsoft\Templates**. On the other hand, if only one person is using the computer, all user templates will be in the following folder: **C:\Windows\Application Data\Microsoft\Templates**. All templates that appear in the **New** dialog box are stored in this location.

The steps below (and in Practice Exercise 1-1) apply only to modifying an existing Word template—which would automatically be stored in **C:\Program Files\Microsoft Office\Templates\1033**. However, since you are still learning (and most likely not working on your own computer), we will instruct you in this book to save all your modified Word template files in your user template storage folder. Later in this lesson, you'll also learn how to create and modify your own user templates, which will be stored, depending on your setup, in either **C:\Windows\Profiles\[UserName]\Application Data\Microsoft\Templates** or **C:\Windows\ApplicationData\Microsoft\Templates**. In addition, you will learn to organize new templates on new tabs within the **New** dialog box by creating a new folder within the default template file location.

Modify a Word Template

The templates that come with Word can all be modified to fit your needs. For example, suppose you really like the Elegant Letter template, but you need it to begin an additional 1" down on the page to accommodate your company's letterhead—or you simply think the font would be more readable at a 12-point setting. You can make these changes yourself—and you can specify that all future documents based on that template will include these changes.

Modify a Word template:

1   Choose **File>Open** from the menu bar to display the **Open** dialog box.

2   Change the **Look in** folder setting to the location of the default template files, for example: **C:\Program Files\Microsoft Office\Templates\1033**:

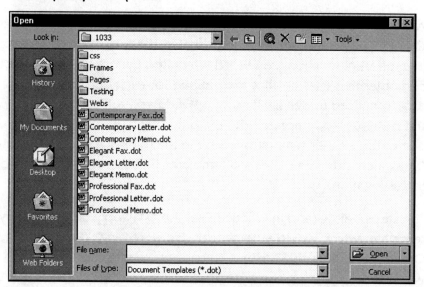

Figure 1.3   The Microsoft Word templates installed on your system.

   TIP: If you plan to modify templates often, you may want to add the 1033 folder to your Favorites list so you can access it quickly from the **Favorites** button on the Places bar in the **Open** dialog box. To do so, choose **Tools>Add to Favorites** from the dialog box toolbar.

3   Choose the template you want to modify.

4   Choose **Open**.

The template opens in a document window.

5   Make formatting and boilerplate text changes to the template as needed. This can include changing margins and/or fonts, adding or removing styles, changing placeholder text, or adding any other formatting that you perform on a regular document.

6   Choose **File>Close** from the menu bar.

A message box appears, asking whether you want to save your changes to the document.

7   Choose **Yes**.

8   Click the **Save as type** arrow, select **Document Templates (*.dot)** and then choose **Save**.

New documents you create with this altered template, which is either in the **General** tab or where you originally found it (depending on your settings), will have these new settings.

Practice Exercise 1-1

Change the Elegant Letter Template and Set a New User Template Location

1   Choose **File>Open** from the menu bar to display the **Open** dialog box.

2   Navigate to the **C:\Program Files\Microsoft Office\ Templates\1033** folder.

3   Choose the **Elegant Letter** template and then choose **Open**.

4   Press **Ctrl+A** to select the entire document. Then click the **Font Size** arrow on the Formatting toolbar and choose **12**.

5   Click anywhere in the document template to deselect the text.

6   Choose **File>Page Setup** from the menu bar to display the **Page Setup** dialog box, and then choose the **Margins** tab if necessary.

7   Set the **Top** margin to 2"; then choose **OK**.

8   Insert text by doing the following:

   •   At the top of the page, click the [CLICK HERE AND TYPE COMPANY NAME] placeholder.

   •   Type: At Your Service for the company name.

   •   In the closing of the letter, click the [Click **here** and type your name] placeholder and type: Julia Alvarez.

   •   Click the [Click **here** and type job title] placeholder and type: President.

- In the footer section of the letter, edit the contact information as shown below:

Street Address	3451 Broadway
City/State	Kalamazoo, MI
Zip/Postal Code	49004
Phone Number	(616) 555-1234
Fax Number	(616) 555-1235

9   Choose **File>Save As** from the menu bar to display the **Save As** dialog box.

10 In the **File name** box, edit the template name to: *01Elegnt*. In the **Save in** box, navigate to your default folder for user templates. *(See page 1-3 for more details.)* Create a new folder named *Personal*. Choose **Save** to save this template in your user-defined template location.

> **NOTE:** If you are unsure of the proper save location for user templates, ask your instructor for assistance.
>
> If you were modifying Word templates on your own computer, you could leave the default name and location of this template in the C:**Program Files\Microsoft Office\Templates\1033** folder.

A completed example of **01Elegnt** is available in the **WORDCert\Word C\Samples\Personal** folder.

Base a New Template on a Word Template

Another way to modify a Word template is to create a new template *based* on an existing one. Some people prefer this method because it prevents alterations to the original template, preserving it for later use.

Create a new template based on a Word template:

1   Choose **File>New** from the menu bar:

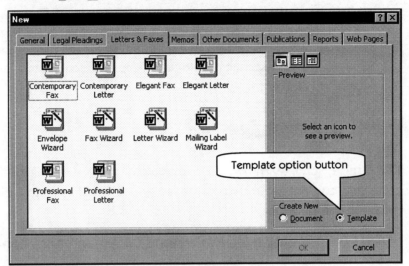

Figure 1.4   Choose **Template** as the type of item to create.

2   Choose **Template** under Create New.

3   Choose the template on which you want to base the new
    template.

4   Choose **OK**.

    A new template window opens.

5   Make formatting and/or text changes to the template as needed.

6   Choose **File>Save** from the menu bar to display the **Save As**
    dialog box.

    The **Save in** location is preset to the default location for user templates.

7   In the **File name** text box, change the template name to
    something unique.

    Notice that the **Save as type** box is grayed out (unavailable) because you
    cannot save a template as anything other than a template.

 8   (Optional) To group your personal templates on tabs in the **New**
    dialog box (see Figure 1.4), you can create a new folder here to
    store those templates. The name of this folder will be the name
    of a new tab in the **New** dialog box.

9   Choose **Save**.

    The template is saved, and will now be available for use from the **New**
    dialog box.

NOTE: The **New** dialog box lists templates that are stored in the folder. You can find and/or change the location of user templates by choosing <u>T</u>ools><u>O</u>ptions from the menu bar to display the **Options** dialog box. Then choose the **File Locations** tab, select **User templates**, and choose <u>M</u>odify to display the **Modify Location** dialog box. In the **Folder <u>n</u>ame** box, you can see the path for user templates; you can then navigate to a new location if you choose.

Practice Exercise 1-2

In this exercise, you'll learn how to create a custom version of the Contemporary Memo template that contains your own name, so you will not have to fill in your name each time you use the template.

Create a New Template Based on Contemporary Memo

1 Choose **<u>F</u>ile><u>N</u>ew** from the menu bar to display the **New** dialog box, and choose the **Memos** tab.

2 Choose **Template** under Create New.

Contemporary Memo

3 Choose the **Contemporary Memo** template.

4 Choose **OK**.

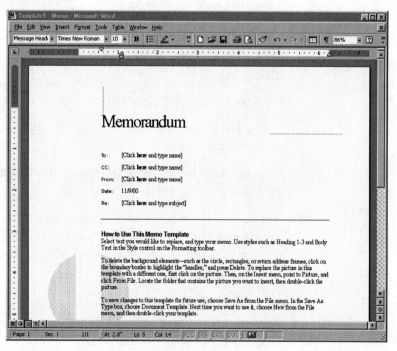

Figure 1.5   Edit this template, and then save it.

Preparing for Microsoft Office Specialist Certification

5 Save the template in the Personal folder (created in Practice Exercise 1-1) as 🖫**01MyMemo**.

- Choose **File>Save As** from the menu bar to display the **Save As** dialog box.

- Click the **Save as type** arrow and select **Document Template (*.dot)**.

- Navigate to and open the Personal folder.

- Type: | 01MyMemo | in the **File name** box; then choose **Save**.

6 Make the following text and paragraph formatting changes:

- Click the **From:** line, the [Click **here** and type name] placeholder.

- Type: | Montgomery Clark |.

- Change the font for the entire template to **12 point Arial** and then change the font for only the *Memorandum* heading to **30 point**.

- Remove the hanging indents on the five routing-information lines.

- Change the tab settings for the routing-information lines to a 1" right tab and 1.5" left tab. Then edit the lines so the colons (:) are right-aligned and the placeholder text is left-aligned.

- Remove the placeholder text in the body of the memo.

7 Save and close the template file.

8 Try out your new memo template by choosing **File>New** from the menu bar. Double-click your new template on the **Personal** tab. Then, close the resulting document without saving changes.

01MyMemo

A completed example of **01MyMemo** is available in the **WORDCert\Word C\Samples\Personal** folder.

Create a New Template

Sometimes you may want to create a template of your own, not based on any existing Word template. For example, suppose you have spent a lot of time setting up a newsletter layout and you want to use the same layout every month. Or maybe you have created 20 or so styles, and you want to group them together in a new template.

There are two ways to create a new template. You can start with a completely blank document (based on the Normal template) and create your customizations, or you can base your new template on a document that already exists.

Create a template from a document:

 1   Start a new, blank document.

OR

    Open an existing document on which you want to base a new template, then delete any text that you do not want to appear as part of the new template.

2   Make any formatting changes needed, so that the document is exactly as you want the template to be.

3   Choose **File>Save As** from the menu bar to display the **Save As** dialog box.

4   Click the **Save as type** arrow and select **Document Template (*.dot)**:

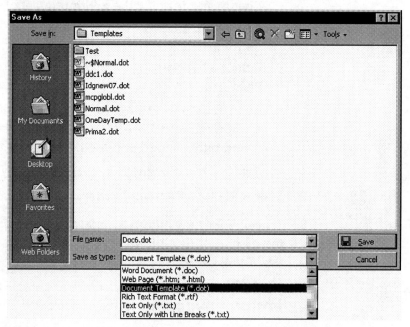

Figure 1.6   Specify the document type as **Document Template (*.dot)**.

The **Save in** location automatically changes to the default folder for user templates.

5   Type a **File name** for the template.

 6   (Optional) To place the new template on a specific tab of the **New** dialog box, either create a new folder here or navigate to one you already created.

7   Choose **Save**.

The file is saved as a new template. You can use it by choosing **File>New** from the menu bar to display the **New** dialog box. If necessary, choose the tab associated with the folder in which you stored the template.

Add Features to Templates

Creating a template is really no more difficult than creating a document. Just keep in mind that everything you place on the template will appear in every document you create with it—so include only suitable items. For example, you would not want to put today's date on a template; instead you would insert a date code to update every time you open the document. You might also want to include a watermark behind the page, or insert your own text placeholders.

In the following topics, you will learn about some Word features that can help you build documents in general, but are especially helpful when used to develop templates.

ADD A WATERMARK

If you have ever used good quality letterhead paper or typing paper, you may have noticed a faint logo on the paper when you held it up to the light. This is known as a *watermark*.

You can use your printer to create faux watermarks on documents. You're probably not going to fool anyone into thinking that your regular paper is high-quality stuff, but a computer-generated watermark serves a different purpose: to print a message. For example, you might use a CONFIDENTIAL watermark on every page of a secret document, as a reminder to employees to keep those printouts safeguarded.

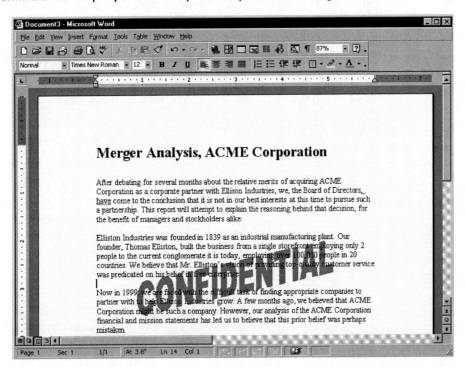

Figure 1.7   This watermark prints as a shaded message behind the regular text on each page.

Watermarks are useful in regular documents, and they are especially nice for templates because you can set them up once and then use them with every document you create using that template. Watermarks can be used in templates to get a message across and to designate specific types of documents. If you are creating a template for a confidential document, you could use the word *Confidential* or the phrase *For Your Eyes Only.* When a document is in development, you could use *Draft, Outline,* or *Rough Copy.* If you need to route the document to multiple people, you could use *Route, En Route,* or *Routing.* You can also use "subliminal messages" or artwork.

You place a watermark on a page while the Header and Footer pane is displayed. You can insert graphics to be used as watermarks anywhere on the page, not just in the header and footer areas. You can use WordArt to generate a text-based piece of art and place it anywhere on the page.

Add a watermark to a template:

1   Open the template for editing, or create a new template.

2   Choose **View>Header and Footer** from the menu bar to display the Header and Footer pane.

3   Insert one of the following as a watermark:

*   WordArt: Choose **Insert>Picture>WordArt** from the menu bar.

*   Picture: Choose **Insert>Picture>Clip Art.**

4   (Optional) After you have added the watermark—whether it is WordArt or a picture—you may want to hide the document text so it is easier for you to position the watermark. On the Header and Footer toolbar, click the **Show/Hide Document Text** button to select it and hide the template text.

5   Move, size, and format the watermark as necessary.

 TIP: You can format the WordArt or image with different colors to make it more or less obvious as a watermark. Also, you may wish to select the **Semitransparent** check box to make the object partially transparent.

6   Close the Header and Footer pane.

The watermark image is displayed behind the template text.

Practice Exercise 1-3

These steps help you create a new template for confidential documents.

Add a WordArt Watermark to a Template

 1 Start a new, blank document.

2 Choose **View>Header and Footer** from the menu bar to display the Header and Footer pane.

3 Create a WordArt watermark by doing the following:

 • Choose **Insert>Picture>WordArt** from the menu bar:

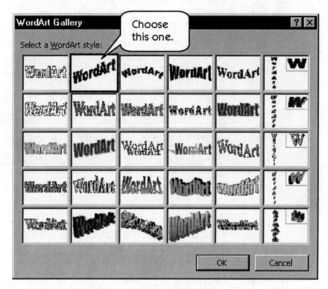

Figure 1.8 Choose simple text for WordArt watermarks.

• Choose the second style in the top row; then choose **OK**.

• In the **Edit WordArt Text** dialog box, type: CONFIDENTIAL and choose **OK**.

The WordArt appears in the document.

4 Drag the WordArt to the center of the document (both vertically and horizontally). Resize the WordArt to fit better within the margins.

5   Change the color of the WordArt to a light color by doing the
     following:

     •   Choose **Format>WordArt** from the menu bar:

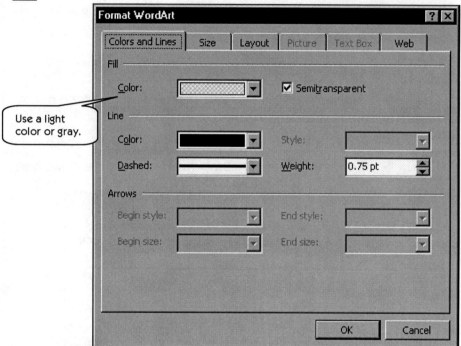

Figure 1.9   To make lighter, less obtrusive WordArt, modify the fill and line colors.

     •   Choose the **Colors and Lines** tab if necessary, click the **Color**
         arrow under **Fill,** and choose a light color.

     •   Select the **Semitransparent** check box.

     These three steps will make the watermark lighter when printed.

     •   Choose **OK**.

6   Close the Header and Footer pane.

7   Save the document as a template in the Personal folder with the
     name 🖫**01Confid** by doing the following:

     •   Choose **File>Save As** from the menu bar to display the **Save
         As** dialog box.

     •   Click the **Save as type** arrow and select **Document
         Template (*.dot).**

     •   Open the Personal folder.

     •   Type: | 01Confid | in the **File name** box; then choose **Save.**

8   Close the new template.

     The file is saved as a new template and will be available on the **Personal** tab
     of the **New** dialog box. A completed example of **01Confid** is available in the
     WORDCert\Word C\Samples\Personal folder.

INSERT AN AUTOMATICALLY UPDATED DATE

If you are working with a document and you are not sure exactly when it will be printed, you may find it useful to insert a date code. Unlike a typed date, a date code is updated automatically based on your computer's built-in clock/calendar. Templates are a prime example of such documents, since you will probably use a template again and again over the course of many days, weeks, and even years.

Insert a date code:

1   Position the insertion point where you want the date code inserted.

2   Choose **Insert>Date and Time** from the menu bar:

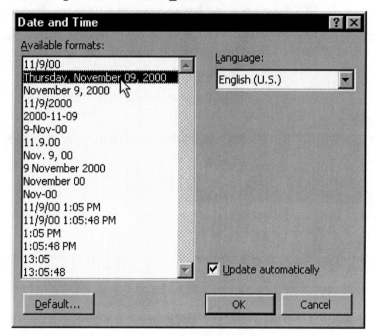

Figure 1.10   Insert a date code with this dialog box.

3   Choose a date format from the **Available formats** list.

4   Select the **Update automatically** check box to update the date each time you create a new document based on this template.

5   Choose **OK**.

Today's date appears in the selected format.

The date that appears looks just like a regularly typed date, so how can you tell it's a date code? Easy—just click it. You see a gray background behind it, indicating that it is a code rather than plain typing.

Practice Exercise 1-4

In these steps, you'll create a template to generate pages for taking notes at meetings.

Add a Date Code to a Template

1   Start a new, blank document.

2   Create a heading by doing the following:

   - Type: Meeting Notes ; then press the **Enter** key four times.

   - Center the *Meeting Notes* text and change the font to **24-point bold**.

3   Insert a code for the current date by doing the following:

   - Place the insertion point on the fourth line in the document and then choose **Insert>Date and Time** from the menu bar to display the **Date and Time** dialog box.

   - Choose the second format from the **Available formats** list. *(See Figure 1.10.)*

   - Select the **Update automatically** check box, if necessary.

   - Choose **OK**.

     The date code is inserted.

4   Select the date, and then format it as **16-point bold** and **centered**.

5   Prepare an area to type the meeting notes by doing the following:

   - Press the **Enter** key a few times after the date, creating some additional lines.

   - Select all the blank lines under the date, and format them as **12-point regular** (not bold) and left-aligned if necessary.

    NOTE: Small details like step 5 can make a big difference when preparing your templates. Doing it once, in step 5, means you don't have to change the font and alignment every time in each document you create.

6 Save the template in the Personal folder as ⊟**01MtgNot** by doing the following:

- Choose **File>Save As** from the menu bar to display the **Save As** dialog box.
- Click the **Save as type** arrow and select **Document Template (*.dot)**.
- Open the Personal folder.
- Type: $\boxed{\text{01MtgNot}}$ in the **File name** box; then choose **Save**.

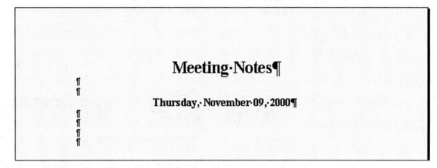

Meeting·Notes¶

Thursday,·November·09,·2000¶

Figure 1.11   The template created in the preceding steps.

7 Leave the template open for use in Practice Exercise 1-5.

A completed example of **01MtgNot** is available in the **WORDCert\Word C\Samples\Personal** folder.

ADD TEXT PLACEHOLDERS

When you worked with the Word letter and memo templates in Practice Exercises 1-1 and 1-2, you used several placeholders to insert boilerplate information, such as [CLICK HERE AND TYPE COMPANY NAME]. You can create placeholders like these for your own templates too.

Once you take a look behind the scenes, you may be surprised how these placeholders are put together.

Explore Word template placeholders:

1 Choose **File>New** from the menu bar to display the **New** dialog box and choose the **Letters & Faxes** tab.

Elegant Letter

2 Choose the **Elegant Letter** template, choose **Template** under Create New, and choose **OK**.

3 Turn the field codes on: choose **Tools>Options** from the menu bar to display the **Options** dialog box and choose the **View** tab if necessary. Select the **Field codes** check box under **Show** and then click **OK**.

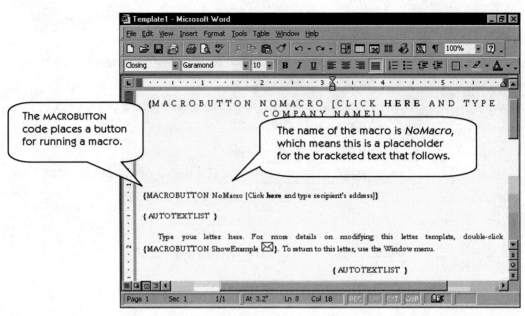

Figure 1.12   Behind every useful template placeholder there is a powerful field code.

   NOTE: The advantage of using fields is that when you click anywhere in the field, the entire block of text is selected. Someone using the template can simply click once and type, rather than being required to select the entire block of text.

4   Turn the field codes off: choose **Tools>Options** again, then choose the **View** tab if necessary. Deselect the **Field codes** check box under **Show** and then click **OK**.

Now that you have seen the mystery behind placeholders, you will learn to create these field codes yourself.

Insert a text placeholder:

1   Open a template to which you want to add placeholder fields.

2   Position the insertion point where you want to insert the placeholder.

3 Choose **Insert>Field** from the menu bar:

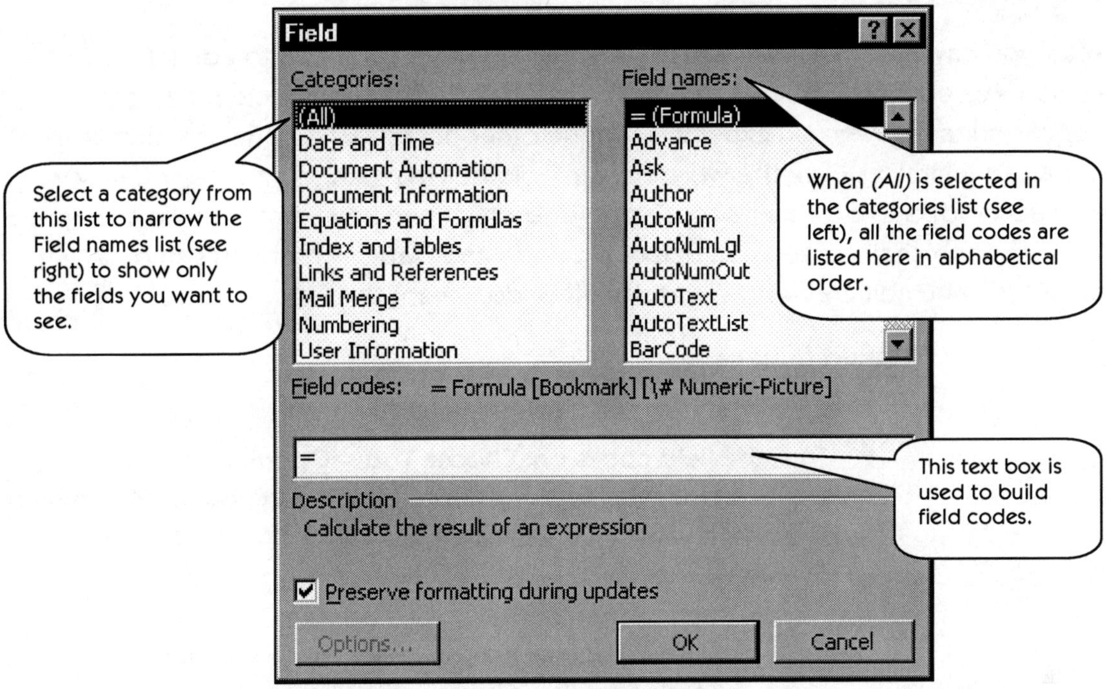

Select a category from this list to narrow the Field names list (see right) to show only the fields you want to see.

When *(All)* is selected in the Categories list (see left), all the field codes are listed here in alphabetical order.

This text box is used to build field codes.

Figure 1.13 Use this dialog box to build your field codes.

4 Find the field name you want to use by doing one of the following:

* If you have an idea of the category to which a particular field name belongs, select a category in the **Categories** list. Then, select the appropriate field from the **Field names** list.

* If you know the name of the field, select **(All)** from the **Categories** list if necessary. Then, select the appropriate field from the **Field names** list.

5 Click after the field name in the text box to continue building your field code. Type a name for the macro, press the **Spacebar**, and then type the placeholder text message in square brackets. For example:

MACROBUTTON Nomacro [Click here and type the description.]

6 (Optional) To further define the behavior of the field code, choose **Options** to add switches (more instructions).

7 Choose **OK**.

The placeholder (field code) appears in your template.

Edit Field Codes

After you have inserted a field code, you may find that you need to edit it for some reason. For example, you may look at the results of a field and decide they don't appear quite the way you expected. On the other hand, you may have noticed that all the Word templates have the word *here* in boldface in placeholders; so you may want all placeholders to be visually consistent for users. When you want to make changes, you have two choices: You can delete the code and start over, or you can display the field code and edit it as you would any other document text.

Edit field codes:

1   Open the document or template you want to edit.

2   Turn the field codes on: Choose **Tools>Options** from the menu bar to display the **Options** dialog box, then choose the **View** tab if necessary. Select the **Field codes** check box under **Show** and choose **OK**.

 TIP: If you want to turn field codes on/off for one field at a time, you can right-click coded text and select **Toggle Field Codes** from the shortcut menu. The keyboard shortcut for this command is **Shift+F9**.

3   Move to the field code you want to edit and click it.

The selected field code is shaded gray.

4   Edit and format the text as you would any other text.

 CAUTION: Be careful not to change field names; edit optional placeholder text only.

5   (Optional) If you understand switches, you can add them at this point.

6   Turn the field codes off once you are finished editing them: Choose **Tools>Options** again and then choose the **View** tab if necessary. Deselect the **Field codes** check box under **Show** and click **OK**.

Practice Exercise 1-5

In these steps, you'll add a placeholder field to the **01MtgNot** template you created earlier.

Add and Edit a Field Code in the Meeting Notes Template

1   The **01MtgNot** template should still be open from Practice Exercise 1-4. If it is not, open it now or open 🗁**01Ex1-5** from the **WORDCert\Word C** folder.

2   Save the open template in the Personal folder as 🖫**01MtgCod**.

3   Insert a placeholder field for the specific meeting by doing the following:

   • Position the insertion point two lines below the date code and choose **Insert>Field** from the menu bar to display the **Field** dialog box.

   • With the **(All)** category selected in the **Categories** list, click the **Field names** list and type: ⬚M⬚ to move to the **MacroButton** field.

   • Click after the MACROBUTTON field name in the text box and finish building the field code as shown:
   MACROBUTTON Nomacro [Click here and type the meeting name.]

   • Choose **OK** to insert the completed field code and placeholder text.

4   Add another field for the meeting location placeholder text by doing the following:

   • Press the **Enter** key and choose **Insert>Field** again.

   • With the **(All)** category still selected in the **Categories** list, move to the **MacroButton** field again.

   • Click after the MACROBUTTON field name in the text box again and finish building the field code as shown:
   MACROBUTTON Nomacro [Click here and type the meeting location.]

   • Choose **OK** again.

5 Edit both of the placeholder field codes to make your template conform to Microsoft's template style:

- Turn the field codes on: Choose **Tools>Options** from the menu bar to display the **Options** dialog box and choose the **View** tab if necessary. Select the **Field codes** check box under **Show** and choose **OK**.

- Select the word *here* inside the first field code and apply the bold font attribute.

- Bold the word *here* inside the second field code.

- Turn the field codes off.

- Move the insertion point off the field codes so nothing is highlighted.

- Compare your template to Figure 1.14, below:

Meeting·Notes¶

¶
¶

Thursday,·November·09,·2000¶

¶
[Click·**here**·and·type·the·meeting·name.]·¶
[Click·**here**·and·type·the·meeting·location.]·¶
¶
¶

Figure 1.14   The **01MtgCod** template after completing steps 1-4.

6 Save and close the template.

A completed example of **01MtgCod** is available in the **WORDCert\Word C\Samples\Personal** folder.

Attach a Template to a Document

When you start a new document based on a template, it automatically has all the formatting of the template. If you start a document and then later decide you want that document to have the same formatting as a different existing template, you can attach the template after the fact.

 NOTE: When you attach a template, the document takes on only the styles of that template; any boilerplate text in the template does not appear. If you want to use the boilerplate text or text placeholders of a certain template, you must start a new document based on the template.

When you attach a different template to a document or template, you decide whether or not you want to update styles automatically. If you choose to update styles, then any text that is formatted using the same styles will change to the styles defined in the attached template. All the styles that the old and the new templates have in common will be updated to reflect the attributes in the attached template. Any text that has been manually formatted (that is, not formatted using a style) will retain its formatting. These changes will become more understandable once you complete Practice Exercise 1-6.

Attach a different template:

1   Switch to or open the document you want to change.

2   Choose **Tools>Templates and Add-Ins** from the menu bar:

Figure 1.15   You can attach a different template from this dialog box.

3   Choose **Attach** to display the **Attach Template** dialog box, which lists all your user templates.

> **NOTE:** If you want to attach one of the Word templates, navigate to the location for the installed Word templates. They may be in the following folder:
> **C:\Program Files\Microsoft Office\Templates\1033.**
> See **Template File Location** at the beginning of this lesson for more information.

4   Navigate to and select the desired template, as necessary.

5   Choose **Open**.

The template pathname is inserted in the **Document template** box in the **Templates and Add-ins** dialog box.

6   Select the **Automatically update document styles** check box to update the styles.

7   Choose **OK**.

Practice Exercise 1-6

Change a Letter's Template

1   Open 📁**01Ex1-6** from the **WORDCert\Word C** folder. Save the document as 💾**01Attach**.

2   View the letter, noticing the document layout.

3   Choose **Tools>Templates and Add-Ins** from the menu bar to display the **Templates and Add-Ins** dialog box.

4   Choose **Attach**.

5   Navigate to the folder where the Word templates are installed. They may be stored in the following folder: **C:\Program Files\Microsoft Office\Templates\1033.**

6   Choose the **Contemporary Letter** template and then choose **Open**.

7   Select the **Automatically update document styles** check box.

8   Choose **OK**.

The styles in the letter are updated to reflect the attributes of the attached Word template, Contemporary Letter. View the letter to see the differences.

9   Save and close the template.

A completed example of **01Attach** is available in the **WORDCert\Word C\Samples** folder.

LESSON 2: WORK WITH LONG DOCUMENTS

When you create documents that are more than a few pages long, you may start encountering special formatting challenges. Perhaps it's an awkward page break that's giving you fits—or a footnote that won't stay anchored at the bottom of the page when you add more text. Whatever the cause of your document headache, Word provides solutions through its advanced formatting features.

In this lesson, you will learn to:

> ➢ Set text flow options

> ➢ Insert cross-references and hyperlinks

> ➢ Sort lists, paragraphs, and tables

> ➢ Build master documents

> ➢ Work with bookmarks

As you are working with these features, you will have an opportunity to apply what you learn in the Practice Exercises and in the exercises at the end of this lesson.

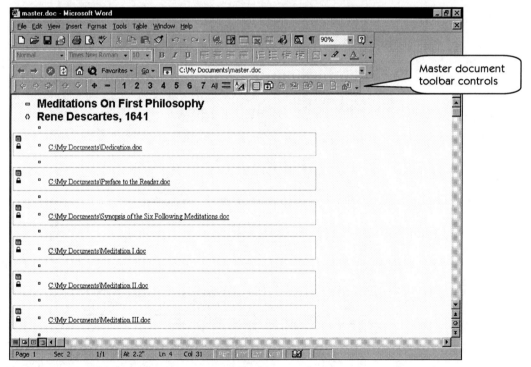

Figure 2.1   Subdocuments linked to the master document.

Line and Page Break Options

As you know, the end of a document or article doesn't always fall where you want it to on the page. You can easily end up with a heading at the bottom of a page while its adjoining text is bumped onto the top of the next page. Fortunately, Word provides several controls that will help you prevent and correct such problems.

These line and page break options are applied to individual paragraphs and are considered paragraph formatting. Except for **Widow/Orphan Control** and **Don't Hyphenate**, you probably will not turn these options on for entire documents. Instead, you'll use them on a case-by-case basis to fix specific problems.

Set text flow options:

1   Select the paragraph(s) you want to affect.

2   Choose **Format>Paragraph** from the menu bar to open the **Paragraph** dialog box. Then choose the **Line and Page Breaks** tab if necessary:

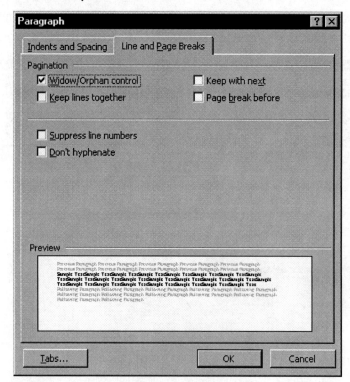

Figure 2.2   Specify text flow options in the **Paragraph** dialog box.

3   Select/deselect check box(es) as needed. See Table 2.1.

4   Choose **OK**.

The following table explains each check box option on the **Line and Page Breaks** tab of the **Paragraph** dialog box:

OPTION	DESCRIPTION
Widow/Orphan control	This option is on by default for all paragraphs. It prevents a single line of a multi-line paragraph from appearing either at the top (widow) or bottom (orphan) of a page. See Figures 2.3 and 2.4.
Keep lines together	Allows you to direct all the lines of a paragraph to stay on the same page. If that means the paragraph has to start at the top of the next page, it will. Compare Figure 2.4 to Figure 2.5.
Keep with next	Forces the selected paragraph to stay on the same page as the paragraph that follows it. It is extremely useful to apply this option to headings; the text paragraph will always follow its heading "paragraph."
Page break before	Forces the paragraph to start on a new page with the help of a manual page break. This option is useful for chapter titles—or when you are creating a document in which each section should begin on a new page.
Suppress line numbers	If you have line numbering turned on, and you *don't* want specific paragraphs to show their line numbers, this option allows you to turn off the line numbers for the selected paragraphs. It is customary for legal exhibits to show line numbers. (See also note, below.)
Don't hyphenate	If you have automatic hyphenation turned on for the entire document but you want to exclude certain paragraphs from it, select this option for those paragraphs. (See also note, below.)

Table 2.1 Set the text flow options options you want in the **Paragraph** dialog box.

 NOTES: To turn on line numbers, choose **File>Page Setup** from the menu bar to display the **Page Setup** dialog box, choose the **Layout** tab, and choose **Line Numbers** to display the **Line Numbers** dialog box. Select the **Add line numbering** check box and define your choices. Choose **OK** twice to close the **Line Numbers** dialog box and the **Page Setup** dialog box.

Automatic hyphenation makes lines come out more evenly by applying hyphenation rules and hyphenating any words that it can. If you are trying to squeeze every word possible onto a page, hyphenation can help. To turn on automatic hyphenation, choose **Tools>Language>Hyphenation** from the menu bar to display the **Hyphenation** dialog box and select the **Automatically hyphenate document** check box.

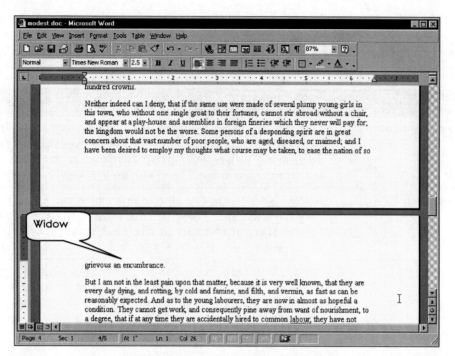

Figure 2.3   When a paragraph breaks so that a single line remains at the top of a page, that single line is called a *widow*. If a single line is at the bottom of a page, it is known as an *orphan*.

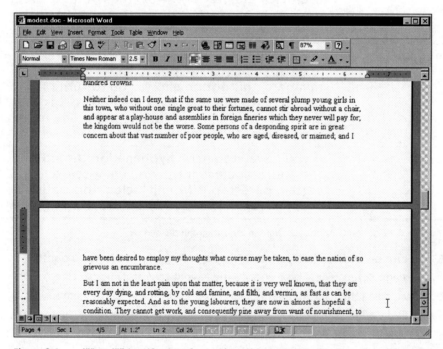

Figure 2.4   When Widow/Orphan Control is enabled, another line from the paragraph moves to the next (or previous) page, so the original line is not alone.

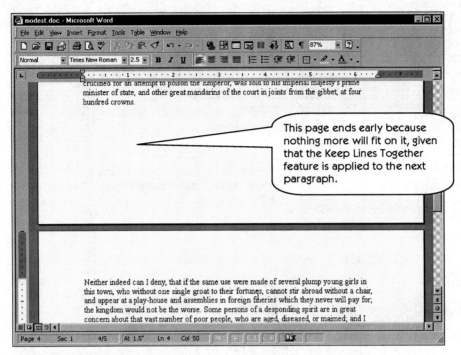

Figure 2.5   When the **Keep Lines Together** feature is on, pages end early.

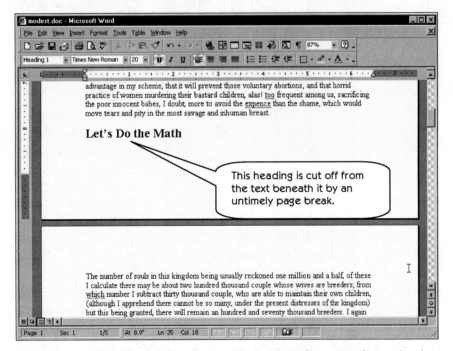

Figure 2.6   This heading isn't "heading" anything because of an automatic page break.

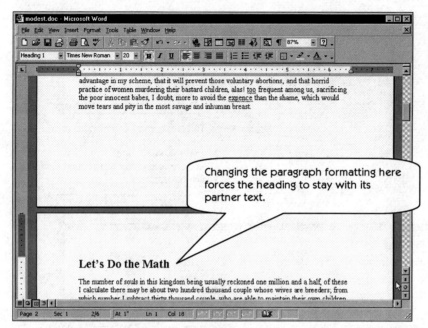

Figure 2.7   The **Keep with Next** feature applied to the heading forces the heading and its following paragraph to stay on the same page.

Practice Exercise 2-1

Set Paragraph Break Options

 1   Open 📂**02Ex2-1** from the **WORDCert\Word C** folder. Save the document as 💾**02Break**.

 TIPS: The text in **02Ex2-1** was acquired from the **Great Books Index** at: **http://www.mirror.org/books/gb.home.html**. You can download free, public-domain text from numerous literary, scientific, and philosophical works in English and in English translation.

Do be careful, however, to verify all downloaded texts with their printed originals before quoting from them. You will often find misspellings and inaccuracies in public-domain texts. In fact, there are some minor errors in the files we will use from the Web site given above. Since we are mainly focusing on layout and advanced features in this book, however, we will usually not go back to correct such errors.

 2   Choose **View>Print Layout.**

3   Select the last paragraph on page 1, *Effects of external conditions....*

4   Choose **Format>Paragraph** from the menu bar to display the **Paragraph** dialog box and choose the **Line and Page Breaks** tab.

5 Select the **Keep lines together** check box and then choose **OK**.

The heading and paragraph move to the next page.

6 Move to the middle of page 3 and select the *Introduction* heading.

7 Choose **Format>Paragraph** again.

8 Select the **Page break before** check box, and then choose **OK**.

Now the Introduction starts on its own page.

 9 Save and close the document.

A completed example of **⊟02Break** is available in the **WORDCert\Word C\Samples** folder.

Sort Information

If you have used Microsoft Excel or Microsoft Access, you have probably sorted lists before—either alphabetically, numerically, or by some other criterion. You can also sort in Word. It is important to note that, although the command for sorting is on the **Table** menu in Word, you do not have to use a table to sort; Word can sort text in lists and regular paragraphs too.

SORT INFORMATION

A Word table works a lot like an Excel spreadsheet with regard to sorting. To sort information, whether it is in a table or not, use the following steps.

Sort a list, paragraph, or table:

1 Select the list or paragraphs you want to sort.

OR

Move the insertion point into the table to sort.

 2 Choose **Table>Sort** from the menu bar:

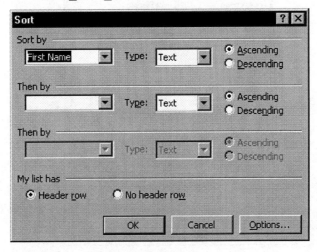

Figure 2.8 Set your sort criteria here.

3 Choose **Header row** under **My list has** if you are sorting either a list or a table—and if that object contains headings in its top row.

OR

Choose **No header row**, if necessary.

4 Click the **Sort by** arrow and choose the list or table column you want to sort, if necessary.

NOTES: If you are sorting paragraphs, the **Sort by** setting defaults to *Paragraphs.*

If you chose **Header row** in step 3, the list/table headings are listed in the **Sort by** box. If you chose **No header row**, designations like *Column 1, Column 2,* and so on appear in the list.

5 Click the **Type** arrow and specify the data type to sort, if necessary: *Text, Number,* or *Date.*

6 Choose one of the following sort orders: **Ascending** (A-Z or 0-9) or **Descending** (Z-A or 9-0).

7 (Optional) To perform multi-level sorts: choose additional fields from the **Then by** boxes, and repeat steps 4-6 for each criterion.

8 Choose **OK** to perform the sort.

TIP: If you are not happy with the sort results, remember the **Edit>Undo** menu command. The keyboard shortcut for the Undo command is **Ctrl+Z**.

SORT A DELIMITED, MULTI-COLUMN LIST

As mentioned above, you can sort data that appears in a list rather than in a table. *Delimited lists* are lists in the form of multiple columns, separated using one consistent character—such as a Tab, comma, or hyphen. The figure below shows a list of names as tab-delimited text (top) and comma-delimited text (bottom).

Title	First Name	Last Name
Mrs.	Anne	Michaels
Dr.	Barry	Kurtswiler
Dr.	Benjamin	Miller
Miss	Cynthia	Brady
Mr.	Frederick	Haddix
Ms.	Judy	Braswell
Mr.	Tom	Jones

Title, First Name, Last Name
Mrs., Anne, Michaels
Dr., Barry, Kurtswiler
Dr., Benjamin, Miller
Miss, Cynthia, Brady
Mr., Frederick, Haddix
Ms., Judy, Braswell
Mr., Tom, Jones

Figure 2.9   In this example, delimiters are used to separate titles, first names, and last names.

Preparing for Microsoft Office Specialist Certification

NOTE: Sometimes tab-delimited lists are referred to as *tabular columns*.

To sort a tabbed list, Word needs to know which character separates the columns. In the top of Figure 2.9, that character is a Tab. You can also work with data where the columns are separated by commas, as in the bottom of Figure 2.9. (The latter is common in exported data from a database program.) You tell Word which character to use in the **Sort Options** dialog box.

Sort a delimited list:

1   Select the entire list (all "paragraphs" to include).

2   Choose **Table>Sort** from the menu bar to display the **Sort Text** dialog box.

3   Choose **Options**.

The **Sort Options** dialog box appears.

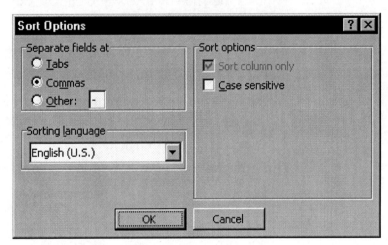

Figure 2.10   The **Sort Options** dialog box

4   Verify that the correct delimiter character is chosen under **Separate fields at**.

 TIP: Does the **Separate fields at** section of the dialog box look familiar? It should—remember the **Convert Text To Table** dialog box? You'll see it again in Practice Exercise 2-2.

5   Choose **OK**.

6   Finish specifying your sort criteria as desired.

7   Choose **OK** to perform the sort.

Practice Exercise 2-2

Sort a Table, Paragraph, or List

1   Open 📁**02Ex2-2** from the **WORDCert\Word C** folder. Save the document as 💾**02TbSort**.

2   Sort the table by date and location by doing the following:

   • Move the insertion point into the table at the bottom of the document.

   • Choose **Table>Sort** from the menu bar to display the **Sort** dialog box.

   • Choose **No Header row** under **My list has**, if necessary.

   • Click the **Sort by** arrow and choose **Column 1**.

   Notice the **Type** list changes to *Date* automatically.

   • Click the **Then by** arrow and choose **Column 3**.

   • Choose **OK**.

   The list is now sorted by date and then by location.

3   Sort the list by doing the following:

   • Move to the beginning of the document and select all the "paragraphs" that end with question marks.

   • Choose **Table>Sort** again.

   • Verify the following settings in the **Sort Text** dialog box:

Sort by	Paragraphs
T**y**pe	Text
sort order	**A**scending
My list has	No header ro**w**

   • Choose **OK**.

   The paragraphs are now sorted alphabetically.

4   Create and sort a delimited list by doing the following:

   • Select the table you sorted in step 2.

   • Choose **Table>Con**v**ert>Ta**b**le to Text** from the menu bar to display the **Convert Table To Text** dialog box.

   • Choose **OK** to accept the default separator (**Tabs**) and convert the table to text.

   • Choose **Table>Sort** once more.

   • Open the **Sort by** list and choose **Field 2**.

   The **Type** list setting changes to *Text* automatically.

- Open the **Then by** list and choose **Field 4**.

The **Type** list setting changes to *Date* automatically.

- Choose **OK**.

The delimited list is now sorted by the day of the week and then by time.

 5 Save and close the document.

A completed example of **02TbSort** is available in the **WORDCert\Word C\Samples** folder.

Work with Bookmarks

Bookmarks help you mark specific locations in a document. Although they can be used in any document, bookmarks are especially useful in long documents where you often find yourself scrolling through many pages to find what you need.

For example, in a document with several main headings, you could bookmark each heading. Then you could move quickly to any heading by using the bookmark.

Bookmarks are hidden, so they do not display on your printouts. Also, they do not display on-screen unless you specify that they do so in the **Options** dialog box.

Another reason to define bookmarks is that they can be integrated with other, advanced Word features. For example, you can create a hyperlink (as you'll learn later in this lesson) to jump to a bookmark in the same document—or even in a separate document. You use bookmarks and hyperlinks frequently when building Web pages. Bookmarks are also used when creating cross-references.

CREATE BOOKMARKS

You can create a bookmark anywhere. You can bookmark text, a graphic, an imported object, or any other element in a document.

Insert a bookmark:

1 Select the text you want to bookmark.

OR

Position the insertion point where you want to insert the bookmark.

NOTE: If you bookmark selected text and later move that text, the bookmark will move along with it.

2   Choose **Insert>Bookmark** from the menu bar:

Figure 2.11   Define bookmarks using this dialog box.

3   Type a **Bookmark name**.

NOTE: The bookmark name cannot include symbols or spaces.

4   Choose **Add**.

The bookmark is inserted and the dialog box closes.

USE BOOKMARKS

There are several ways to use bookmarks. The most common use for them is as reminders. Bookmarks allow you to "flag" items (e.g., words, statistics, quotations) in the drafting process of long documents so that you can return to them directly—after verifying facts or figures, for example. In such situations, bookmarks are used in conjunction with the **Go To** command.

Go to a bookmark:

1   Choose **Edit>Go To** from the menu bar:

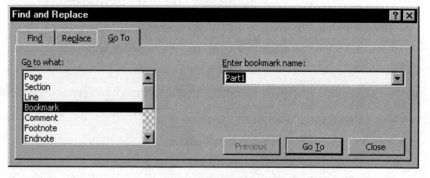

Figure 2.12   The **Go** To tab is preselected in the **Find and Replace** dialog box.

TIP: The shortcut for the Go To command is **Ctrl+G**.

2 Select **Bookmark** in the **Go to what** list.

3 Click the **Enter bookmark name** arrow if you have inserted multiple bookmarks; then select the bookmark you want to go to.

4 Choose **Go To**.

The insertion point moves to the location of the bookmark in the document.

 5 Choose **Close**.

VIEW BOOKMARKS

To view a list of the bookmarks in your document, choose **Insert>Bookmark** from the menu bar to display the **Bookmark** dialog box. From this dialog box, you can browse, sort, add to, delete, or go to the bookmarks in the list. Bookmarks can be sorted by **Name** or **Location**.

If you want to display the bookmarks themselves in your document, you can use the **View** tab on the **Options** dialog box (**Tools>Options**).

Display/hide bookmarks in a document:

1 Choose **Tools>Options** from the menu bar to display the **Options** dialog box and choose the **View** tab if necessary:

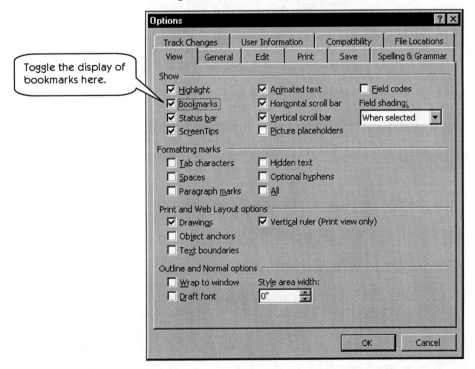

Figure 2.13   Show bookmarks by selecting the **Bookmarks** check box.

2 Select/deselect the **Bookmarks** check box under **Show** as desired.

3 Choose **OK**.

If text (e.g., a word or phrase) was selected when the bookmark was inserted, bookmarks are denoted by heavy square brackets at the beginning and end of the bookmarked text. If text was not selected when the bookmark was defined, the bookmark is a heavy I-beam symbol:

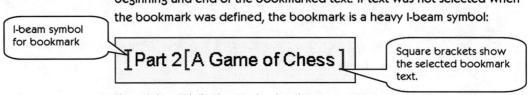

Figure 2.14   This line has two bookmarks.

DELETE BOOKMARKS

Once you have inserted a bookmark, you cannot move it. You can, however, delete or replace it. So if you have made a mistake in a bookmark's placement, there is no need to panic.

 NOTE: You cannot rename a bookmark, but the name is not significant to the bookmark's operation; it is just for your own reference. For example, you could theoretically have a bookmark called *Bottom* that takes you to the top of a document.

Delete a bookmark:

1 Choose **Insert>Bookmark** from the menu bar:

Figure 2.15   Choose the bookmark you want to delete.

2 Select the name of the bookmark you want to delete.

3 Choose **Delete**.

4 Repeat steps 2 and 3 as needed to delete other bookmarks.

5 Choose **Close**.

Practice Exercise 2-3

Create and Use Bookmarks

1   Open 📂**02Ex2-3** from the **WORDCert\Word C** folder. Save the document as 💾**02BkMrk**.

2   Position the insertion point right before *Part 1* and choose **Insert>Bookmark** from the menu bar to display the **Bookmark** dialog box.

3   Type ⬚Part1⬚ in the **Bookmark name** box and choose **Add**.

4   Move to *Part 2* and select the whole line.

5   Choose **Insert>Bookmark** again.

6   Type ⬚Part2⬚ in the **Bookmark name** box, and choose **Add**.

7   Create bookmarks for Parts 3-5, alternating between selecting the text and positioning the insertion point before the section heading.

8   Move to your bookmarks by doing the following:

   • Choose **Edit>Go To** from the menu bar to display the **Go To** tab of the **Find and Replace** dialog box.

   • Select **Bookmark** in the **Go to what** list.

   • Select **Part1** from the **Enter bookmark name** list.

   • Choose **Go To**, and then choose **Close**.

   The insertion point is now at the Part 1 heading.

   • Choose **Edit>Go To** again and move to all of the bookmarks you created, noticing which ones select text and which simply stop at the bookmark location.

9   Save and close the document.

   A completed example of 💾**02BkMrk** is available in the **WORDCert\Word C\Samples** folder.

Work with Cross-References

Cross-references are useful when you need to refer to a certain heading, illustration, or other object in a document but you are not sure which page the referenced object will appear on in the completed document.

For example, suppose you are writing a report. You want to refer readers to an illustration, but its page number will change later as you continue to revise the report. The solution is to create a cross-reference to that illustration. Word can then update the page number automatically if (or when) the page numbering changes.

CREATE CROSS-REFERENCES

To create a cross-reference, place the insertion point where you want the reference to appear. For example, if you want a reference to appear on page 1 that says: *See the summary on page [number]*, you would place the insertion point on page 1, right after the word *page* and a space:

See·the·summary·on·page·¶

Figure 2.16 Include any spaces and/or punctuation that is necessary before inserting your cross-reference.

Insert a cross-reference:

TIP: You can create a bookmark for the object you want to cross-reference. This step is not necessary, however, if you are cross-referencing a numbered object. To reference one of those items, you must instead make sure that object numbering is turned on *before* you start this procedure. See Lesson 3 for more information.

1 Type the introductory text for the cross-reference (such as *For more information, see*), including any necessary spaces and/or punctuation.

2 Position the insertion point where you wish to place the cross reference, and then choose **Insert>Cross-reference** from the menu bar:

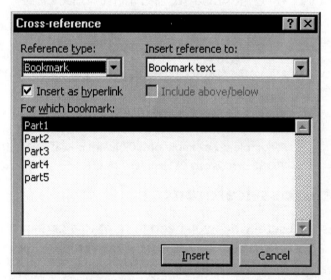

Figure 2.17 Create cross-references here by specifying "what" (**Reference type**) and "how" (**Insert reference to**).

3 Choose the **Reference type** you want (Heading, Figure, Table, etc.).

Preparing for Microsoft Office Specialist Certification

TIP: If you created a bookmark before step 1, choose **Bookmark** from the **Reference type** list.

4 Choose the form you want the reference to take from the **Insert reference to** list:

OPTION	DESCRIPTION
[Object] text	Inserts the actual text of the bookmark, table title, caption, or whatever you chose in step 3.
Page number	Inserts the page number on which the referenced item falls. In most cases, you will choose this option.
[Object] number	Inserts the paragraph number on which the referenced item falls.
Above/below	Inserts either the word *above* or *below*, depending on where the referenced item appears in relation to its cross-reference.

Table 2.2   In this table, [Object] is replaced by an object type, such as *Paragraph* or *Bookmark.*

5 (Optional) Select/deselect the check boxes as desired:

- **Include above/below**   Inserts either the word *above* or *below* if the referenced item appears on the same page as its cross-reference; inserts the words *on page* when the referenced item falls on another page.

- **Insert as hyperlink**   Enables the ability to jump to the referenced object/text.

6 Choose **Insert**.

The dialog box remains displayed (albeit inactive) so you can move through the document and insert more cross-references.

7 Format cross-reference text and insert any closing punctuation as desired.

8 Choose **Close** when you are finished inserting cross-references.

As you can tell by the many choices in the steps above, the cross-referencing feature is extremely powerful and flexible. You can cross-reference many kinds of text and graphics in your document and you can express that reference in a variety of ways.

REFERENCE	EXAMPLE (REFERENCE IN BOLD)
[Object] text	See **Operating the Drill Press**.
Page number, with **Include above/below** selected	See the diagram on page **12**.
Heading number	See section **12-3** of the State Regulations.
Above/below	See the steps **above** to learn how to do it.

Table 2.3   Examples of cross-references.

USE A CROSS-REFERENCE ON-SCREEN

Cross-references serve two purposes. First, they ensure accuracy in your final document. Second, cross-references can serve as hyperlinks that allow you to navigate through your document quickly.

To use this feature, you must select the **Insert as hyperlink** check box when you insert the cross-reference (see step 5 in the previous procedure). To use a cross-reference as a hyperlink, simply point at the link with the mouse so that the mouse pointer turns into a pointing hand, and then click the link. A ScreenTip identifies the link when the hand pointer appears. The Web toolbar appears after you click the link, allowing easy access to its commands.

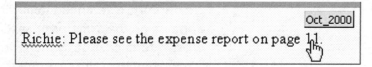

Oct_2000

Richie: Please see the expense report on page 11.

Figure 2.18   To use a cross-reference as a hyperlink, click it. Above is a hyperlink to a bookmark, which is named in the ScreenTip.

 NOTE: A cross-reference is only one of several types of links a document can have. You'll learn more about them later in this lesson.

DELETE A CROSS-REFERENCE

To delete a cross-reference, remove it as you would any other text. Simply select it and press Delete.

 NOTE: If the cross-reference is also a hyperlink (see above), it may be difficult to select directly. You can't click it; to do so moves you to the linked location. Instead, you must position the insertion point to one side of the cross-reference, and then hold down **Shift** and use the right or left arrow key to extend the selection.

Practice Exercise 2-4

Work with Cross-References

1   Open 🗁 **02BkMrk**, which you created in Practice Exercise 2-3, or open 🗁 **02Ex2-4** from the **WORDCert\Word C** folder. Save the open document as 💾 **02XRef**.

2   Create a bookmark for the final line in Part 3 by doing the following:

- Choose **Edit>Go To** from the menu bar to display the **Go To** tab in the **Find and Replace** dialog box. Select **Bookmark** in the **Go to what** list. Select **Part4** from the **Enter bookmark name** list. Choose **Go To**, and then choose **Close**.

- Position the insertion point at the end of the final line of text, *burning*, above the Part 4 heading.

- Choose **Insert>Bookmark** from the menu bar to display the **Bookmark** dialog box.

- Type: End3 in the **Bookmark name** box.

- Choose **Add**.

3   Move to the beginning of the document and insert a cross-reference by doing the following:

- Add two blank lines at the beginning of the document. On the first line, type the following text with the Normal style applied:

  The exam will cover Part 3, on pages

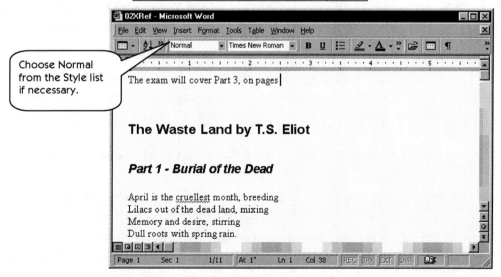

Figure 2.19   This is how **02XRef** should appear at this point in the Practice Exercise.

- Type a space, and then choose **Insert>Cross-reference** from the menu bar to display the **Cross-reference** dialog box.

- Select **Heading** in the **Reference type** list. Select **Part 3 - The Fire Sermon** in the **For which heading** list.

- Select **Page number** in the **Insert reference to** list, then choose **Insert**.

- Click the document window to reactivate it. Type a space, then type: through and another space.

- Reactivate the **Cross-reference** dialog box to insert the next cross-reference.

- Select **Bookmark** in the **Reference type** list. Select **Page number** in the **Insert reference to** list. Select **End3** from the **For which bookmark** list.

- Choose **Insert**, and then choose **Close**.

- Type a period to end the sentence:

The exam will cover Part 3, on pages 5 through 8.

4 Use cross-references and the Web toolbar by doing the following:

- Point to and then click the page 5 reference.

The following ScreenTip appears: Current Document. The insertion point automatically moves to the beginning of *Part 3 – The Fire Sermon* on page 5 and the Web toolbar appears.

- Look at the Web toolbar and notice that the **Address** box displays the complete document pathname.

- Click the **Back** button on the Web toolbar to return to the cross-reference at the beginning of the document.

- Point to and then click the page 8 reference.

A ScreenTip appears for the bookmark you created in step 2: End3. The insertion point automatically moves to the end of Part 3 on page 8.

- Click the **Back** button again.

5 Delete the cross-reference for page 8 by selecting its reference and pressing the **Delete** key.

6 Reverse your last action (deleting the cross-reference) by choosing **Edit>Undo Clear** from the menu bar.

7 Save the document, but leave it open for use in Practice Exercise 2-5.

A completed example of **02XRef** is available in the **WORDCert\Word C\Samples** folder.

Use Hyperlinks

When you think of *hyperlinks*, you probably think of links on Web pages. Hyperlinks have a much broader application than just the Internet, however. For example, in the preceding exercise, you saw one type of hyperlink at work when you clicked a cross-reference to move to referenced text within the same document.

A *hyperlink* is a link to any of a wide variety of locations—from a Web site halfway around the world to locations within single or multiple Word document(s), a workbook range in Excel, an Access database object, a single PowerPoint slide, or an e-mail address. Click a hyperlink and go somewhere!

INSERT A HYPERLINK

Because of Word 2000's AutoFormat feature, all Internet and network paths are automatically formatted as hyperlinks—with blue text and an underline. You could click that address in the template (or a document you base on the template) and open a window to compose an e-mail message. Now, wasn't that easy?

If you want to add a link to an object that is not on the Internet or a network, you have to go through the process manually: choose **Insert>Hyperlink** from the menu bar to display the **Insert Hyperlink** dialog box. Then choose the item you want to link—a location in another document or Web page, a location in the current document, a new document, or an e-mail address.

Link to a location in the same document:

1 Create a bookmark for the hyperlink source if the location is not at the beginning of the document, a heading, or an existing bookmark.

2 Position the insertion point where you want to place the hyperlink.

OR

(Recommended) Select the text you want to convert to a hyperlink.

  3 Choose **Insert>Hyperlink** from the menu bar.

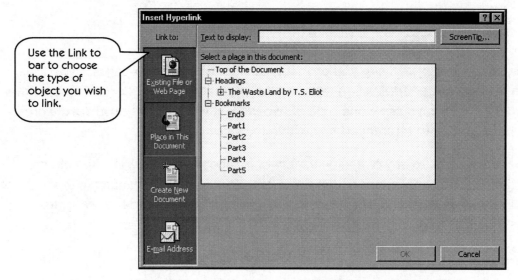

Use the Link to bar to choose the type of object you wish to link.

Figure 2.20   Reminder: Minus signs collapse lists; plus signs expand them.

    TIP: The keyboard shortcut for the **Insert Hyperlink** command is **Ctrl+K**.

4   Click the **Place in This Document** button on the Link to bar.

5   Choose the location to which you want to link in the **Select a place in this document** list (e.g., Top of the Document, Headings, Bookmarks).

6   Type or edit the hyperlink text as you wish it to appear in the document in the **Text to display** box. If you selected text in step 2, skip to step 7.

The new hyperlink text entered in the step above appears where you positioned the insertion point in step 2.

7   (Optional) To display a ScreenTip when the mouse pointer rests on the link, choose **ScreenTip**, type the ScreenTip text, and then choose **OK**.

    NOTE: If you do not specify ScreenTip text, Word provides it for you automatically. For a link within the same document, Word uses either the bookmark's name or the phrase *Current Document* for links to the Top of the Document or Headings.

8   Choose **OK**.

Preparing for Microsoft Office Specialist Certification

Link to another document or a Web page:

1   Position the insertion point where you want to place
    the hyperlink.

    OR

    (Recommended) Select the text you want to convert to a
    hyperlink.

2   Choose **Insert>Hyperlink** from the menu bar:

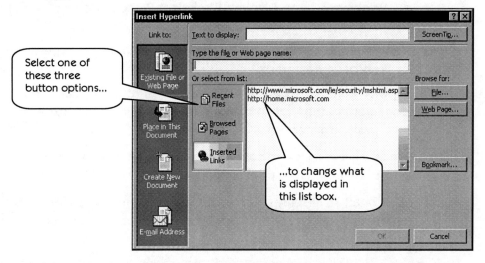

Figure 2.21   Use the buttons beneath **Browse for** to find a file, Web page, or bookmark
that isn't displayed in the list box.

3   Choose the **Existing File or Web Page** button on the Link to bar.

4   Choose one of the following button options to the left of the list
    box to locate and select the document or Web page to which
    you want to link:

    •   **Recent Files**   Displays a list of files you have worked with
                              recently.

    •   **Browsed Pages**   Shows a list of recently viewed Web pages.

    •   **Inserted Links**   Displays a list of the most recent links you
                              have added to this file or typed in your Web
                              browser's **Address** box.

5 (Optional) To browse in order to locate and select the document, Web page, or bookmark to which you want to link, choose one of the following buttons:

- **File**   Displays the **Link to File** dialog box, which functions like the **Open** and **Save As** dialog boxes.

- **Web Page**   Launches your Internet browser (e.g., Internet Explorer).

- **Bookmark**   Displays the **Select Place in Document** dialog box. Compare with Figure 2.20.

6 Verify the file pathname or the Web page URL in the **Type the file or Web page name** box.

7 Type or edit the hyperlink text as you wish it to appear in the document in the **Text to display** box. If you selected text in step 1, skip to step 8.

    The new hyperlink text entered in the step above appears where you positioned the insertion point in step 1.

8 (Optional) To display a ScreenTip when the mouse pointer rests on the link: choose **ScreenTip**, type the ScreenTip text, and then choose **OK**.

    NOTE: If you do not specify ScreenTip text, Word provides it for you automatically. For a link within the same document, Word uses either the bookmark's name or the phrase *Current Document* for links to the Top of the Document or Headings. For a file, Word uses its pathname. For a Web page, Word displays its URL.

9 Choose **OK**.

EDIT A HYPERLINK

To edit a hyperlink, open the dialog box for it and make your changes. You can change anything about it: the description, the address (or file name), and the ScreenTip.

Edit a link:

1 Move the insertion point within the hyperlink (or select it), and then choose **Insert>Hyperlink** from the menu bar to display the **Edit Hyperlink** dialog box.

    OR

    Right-click the hyperlink and choose **Hyperlink>Edit Hyperlink** from the shortcut menu.

    The controls available in the **Edit Hyperlink** dialog box are the same as the ones you saw in the **Insert Hyperlink** dialog box.

2 Make any changes as desired and choose **OK**.

USE AND VIEW HYPERLINKS

To use a hyperlink...just click it. If the link is to another location in the same document or to any Word document, you move directly to that linked object. If the link is to a document created in another program, that program opens. If the link is to a Web page, your Web browser (e.g., Internet Explorer) opens and you are prompted to connect to the Internet. If the link is to an e-mail address, your message browser (e.g., Outlook Express) opens, with the address entered in the **To** box.

You can view the path or address to the linked object without actually jumping to it, however. To do so, right-click the hyperlink and choose **Toggle Field Codes**. This displays the link code, as shown below. Right-click the link code and choose **Toggle Field Codes** again to redisplay the hyperlink.

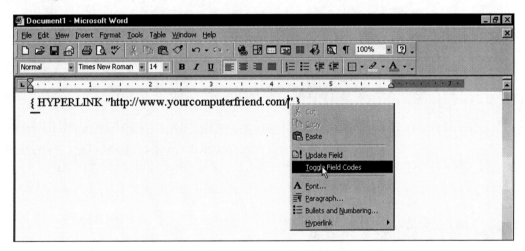

Figure 2.22   View the field code (the path or address behind the link) by right-clicking and choosing **Toggle Field Codes**.

REMOVE HYPERLINKS

When people say they need to remove hyperlinks from a document, you will often find that they can mean two very different things, each having a very different effect on your documents. You can either revert a hyperlink to regular, unformatted text—or you can delete the hyperlink altogether. If someone tells you to remove a hyperlink, ask him or her to be more specific.

As with most commands in Word, both "removal" activities have multiple methods for execution. Pick the methods that fit your style of editing.

Revert a hyperlink to text:

The link text is converted to regular text in your document.

- Position the insertion point at the end of the hyperlink and press the **Backspace** key.

  OR

- Right-click the hyperlink and choose **Hyperlink>Remove Hyperlink** from the shortcut menu.

  OR

- Display the **Edit Hyperlink** dialog box (see **Edit a hyperlink**, above), then choose **Remove Link**.

Delete a hyperlink:

Link text is deleted from your document.

- Select the hyperlink and press the **Delete** key.

  TIP: Remember that, to select a hyperlink, you can't click it directly. You must extend the selection to include it.

  OR

- Right-click the hyperlink, choose **Hyperlink>Select Hyperlink** from the shortcut menu, and then press either the **Delete** or **Backspace** key.

Practice Exercise 2-5

Create and Manage Hyperlinks

1   Open ☐**02XRef**, which you created in Practice Exercise 2-4, or open ☐**02Ex2-5** from the **WORDCert\Word C** folder. Save the open document as ☐**02Hyper**.

2   Select *Part 3* in the first line of text.

3   Choose **Insert>Hyperlink** from the menu bar to display the **Insert Hyperlink** dialog box.

   TIP: The keyboard shortcut for the **Insert Hyperlink** command is **Ctrl+K**.

4   Click the **Place in This Document** button on the Link to bar.

⊞   5   Click the plus sign next to *Bookmarks* in the **Select a place in this document** list to expand the bookmark list, if necessary. Select *Part 3* from the list, and then choose **OK**.

   Part 3 is formatted as a hyperlink.

Preparing for Microsoft Office Specialist Certification

6 On a new line, right under the first one, type the following text with the Normal style applied:

> See the Great Books Index on the Web for more poems by T.S. Eliot.

7 Select *Great Books Index*, and then choose **Insert>Hyperlink** again.

8 Click the **Existing File or Web Page** button on the Link to bar.

9 Type: http://books.mirror.org/gb.home.html in the **Type the file or Web page name** box.

10 Choose **OK**.

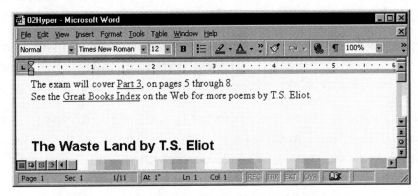

Figure 2.23   The two links you just created should appear as shown here.

11 Insert another hyperlink to a Web page: Select *T.S. Eliot* at the end of the second line, choose **Insert>Hyperlink** once again, and click the **Existing File or Web Page** button if necessary. Type: http://web.missouri.edu/~tselist/tse.html in the **Type the file or Web page name** box. Then choose **OK**.

12 View the ScreenTips for all three of your new hyperlinks. Then click each link to test it.

NOTE: If any confirmation boxes appear, move past them with **OK**, **Yes**, **Connect**, or whatever is required.

13 Disconnect from the Internet, if necessary.

TIP: Remember that, when the Web toolbar is displayed, you can use the **Back** button to return to your last location (i.e., the beginning of the document).

14 Change the ScreenTip for <u>T.S. Eliot</u> by doing the following:

- Right-click the hyperlink and choose **Hyperlink>Edit Hyperlink** from the shortcut menu to display the **Edit Hyperlink** dialog box.

- Choose **ScreenTip**.

- Type: $\boxed{\text{TSE: The Web Site}}$, and then choose **OK** twice.

- View your new ScreenTip.

15 Revert a hyperlink to text: Position the insertion point at the end of <u>T.S. Eliot</u>, before the period, and press the **Backspace** key.

16 Save and close the document.

A completed example of ⊟**02Hyper** is available in the **WORDCert\Word C\Samples** folder.

Work with a Master Document

If you have ever tried to create a very long document in a word processor, you know that it can be a cumbersome process. If your computer is not powerful, working with a large document can slow down your word processor's performance.

One solution to this problem is to break the document into separate files and then tie them all together with a master document. For example, if you were writing The Great American Novel, you could compose each chapter in a separate document file. Later, you could create a master document to link them together. From within the master document, you could then generate a table of contents and an index.

You can create a master document in one of two ways: you can build one from scratch, or you can convert an existing document to a master document.

START A MASTER DOCUMENT

To create a master document, it's best to start in Outline view. From there, you can do one of the following:

- **Split a large document into several subdocuments**

  You can either create a new document or open an existing one, converting parts of it into subdocuments. Each of the subdocuments is saved under a unique name; the original document becomes the master document.

- **Build a master document from existing pieces**

  You can start a new, blank document and add existing documents to it as subdocuments.

NOTE: In previous versions of Microsoft Word, Outline and Master Document were separate views. In Word 2000, their best features have been combined in Outline view.

SPLIT A DOCUMENT INTO SUBDOCUMENTS

Suppose you have to write a book and you know that you want to create subdocuments for each chapter. If you're able to plan ahead, you can start with an outline and create subdocuments right from there. If, on the other hand, you're writing a book and you have no idea what form it will take (or perhaps you aren't really known for your organizational skills), you can just as easily split your existing file into subdocuments later.

Create subdocuments from a single document:

1 Start a new, blank document.

OR

Open the file containing whatever text you might have completed for the project.

 NOTE: If you are working in an existing document, make sure that you are using Word's built-in heading styles to designate your headings. If you have not been using them, go back and apply them now.

2 Switch to Outline view.

3 Type a project outline if you are working with a new, blank document.

 TIP: Press **Tab** to demote a heading line; press **Shift+Tab** to promote one.

4 Select all the text that you want to include in the first subdocument. For example, this might be a Chapter 1 heading and all the text beneath it.

 TIP: To select all the text under a heading quickly, click the hollow plus sign to the left of the heading.

5 Click the **Create Subdocument** button on the Outlining toolbar.

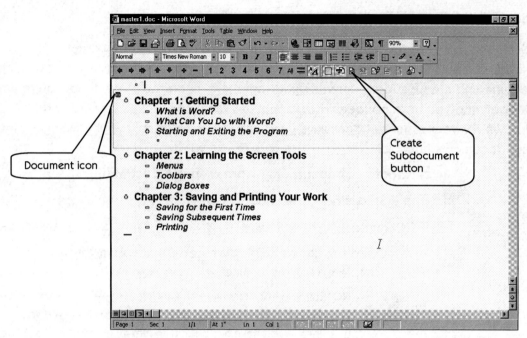

Figure 2.24   The Chapter 1 heading and the text underneath it is now a subdocument.

The selected text appears with a gray box around it and a document icon in the top-left corner, indicating that it is now a subdocument.

6   Repeat steps 4 and 5 to create more subdocuments as needed.

 7   Save and close the document.

When you save, each of the subdocuments is saved separately with a name that Word assigns automatically. For example, when saving the file shown above, Word assigned the name *Chapter 1* to the first subdocument. Word names subdocuments using the text at the highest heading level, up to the first punctuation mark.

INSERT DOCUMENTS INTO A MASTER DOCUMENT

In the preceding topic, you took a single document and broke it into subdocuments. In this section, you'll do the opposite: take several independent documents and tie them together.

Create a master document (insert subdocuments):

1   Start a new, blank document.

OR

Position the insertion point in the outline of the document where you want to insert the subdocument.

 2   Switch to Outline view.

 3   Click the **Insert Subdocument** button on the Outlining toolbar to display the **Insert Subdocument** dialog box.

4   Select the document you want to insert as a subdocument, and choose **Open**.

5   Repeat steps 3 and 4 to insert more subdocuments as needed.

 6   Save and close the document.

Each subdocument is resaved to its original location.

Practice Exercise 2-6

Create a Master Document

 1   Open 📂**02Ex2-6** from the **WORDCert\Word C** folder. Save the document as 💾**02Mastr1**.

 TIP: To make it easier to find the master document and its subdocuments, you may wish to create a new folder for them within your default save location. Use the **Create New Folder** button in the **Save As** dialog box.

 2   Switch to Outline view.

 3   Click the **Show Heading 1** button on the Outlining toolbar to reduce the document view to just the level 1 headings.

 4   Click the plus sign next to *Dedication*.

 5   Click the **Create Subdocument** button on the Outlining toolbar.

A gray box appears around the *Dedication* heading and a document icon is in the top-left corner, indicating that it is a subdocument.

6   Click the plus sign next to *Preface to the Reader*.

 7   Click the **Create Subdocument** button again.

8   Continue creating subdocuments for the remaining headings as shown below:

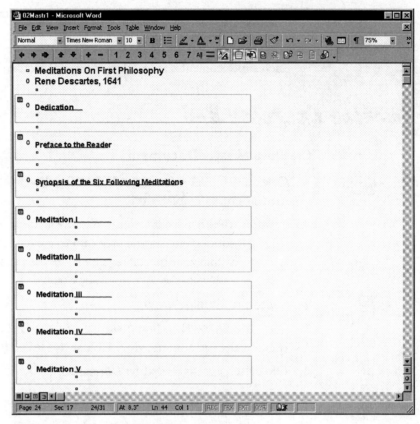

Figure 2.25   Compare your work with this illustration.

 9   Save and close the master document.

A completed example of 🖫**02Mastr1** (and its subdocuments) is available in the **WORDCert\Word C\Samples\Master Docs** folder.

USE DIFFERENT MASTER DOCUMENT VIEWS

You can work on subdocuments in separate Word files or within the master document itself. Further, you are not confined to Outline view; you can work in any view.

You can expand or collapse the document outline in Outline view, just as you would any regular outline.

You can switch to another view (such as Print Layout) to see how the document will look when printed.

If you want to see the outline of your document without the sub-document indicators, you can toggle Master Document view on or off.

After you have closed and re-opened the master document file, when you expand subdocuments, they are displayed in Outline heading mode. When you collapse subdocuments, they are displayed as hyperlinks, as shown below. You can then click a pathname hyperlink to work on the linked document in its own window.

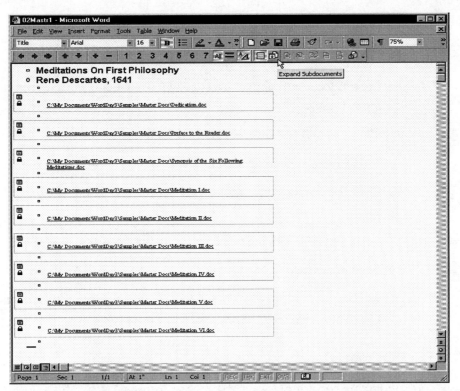

Figure 2.26   This is the same document you saw in Figure 2.25, except that Master Document view is on and subdocuments have been collapsed. Note also that the **Expand Subdocuments** button selected above toggles with the **Collapse Subdocuments** button.

Practice Exercise 2-7

Change the Master Document View

1 Open ☐**02Mastr1**, which you created in Practice Exercise 2-6, or open ☐**02Ex2-7** from the **WORDCert\Word C** folder. Save the open document as ☐**02Mastr2**.

2 Click the **Expand Subdocuments** button to display the subdocuments in the Outline heading view.

3 Click the **Show All Headings** button to display all the text in the subdocuments.

4 Switch to Print Layout view.

5 Scroll through the document.

The document looks like a normal document in every way.

6 Switch back to Outline view.

7 Return to the beginning of the document and click the **Master Document View** button on the Outlining toolbar to deselect it.

Master Document view is off; notice that the gray lines delineating sections are replaced by continuous section break markers.

8 Click the **Collapse Subdocuments** button to deselect it.

The subdocuments appear again as hyperlinks. Continuous section breaks are still visible.

9 Click the **Expand Subdocuments** button.

The subdocument headings return with section breaks between them.

10 Click the **Master Document View** button to select it again.

Word redisplays gray boxes around each section; you're back in Master Document view with the headings for the subdocuments displayed.

11 Save and close the document.

A completed example of 🖫**02Mastr2** (and its subdocuments) is available in the **WORDCert\Word C\Samples\Master Docs** folder.

EDIT A MASTER DOCUMENT

You can edit subdocuments separately, as if they were "regular" Word files. Indeed, they *are* regular Word files in almost every way; the only thing that distinguishes them is that they are called for in a master document. You can also edit subdocuments from within the master document in any view.

BUTTON	NAME	DESCRIPTION
	Remove Subdocument	Converts the selected subdocument to regular text within the master document. Select the subdocument and click this button.
	Merge Subdocument	Combines two or more selected subdocuments into a single one. Select the subdocuments you want to merge together and click this button.
	Split Subdocument	Splits a subdocument into two separate ones at the position of the insertion point. Position the insertion point where you want the new subdocument to begin, and then click this button.
	Lock Document	Locks the subdocument or the master document so they cannot be edited. Position the insertion point in the subdocument or at the top of the master document, and then click this button.

Table 2.4   Advanced editing tools for master documents.

Practice Exercise 2-8

Advanced Editing for Master Documents

 1 Open 📁**02Mastr2**, which you created in Practice Exercise 2-7, or open 📁**02Ex2-8** from the **WORDCert\Word C** folder. Save the open document as 💾**02Mastr3**.

 2 Click the **Expand Subdocuments** button on the Outlining toolbar.

 3 Select the *Preface to the Reader* subdocument and click the **Remove Subdocument** button to revert to normal text.

 4 Select the first two Meditation subdocuments, *Meditation I* and *Meditation II*, and click the **Merge Subdocument** button to combine these two documents into one.

 TIP: You cannot select the subdocuments by clicking the hollow plus signs. To enable the Merge feature for the next step, you must select the subdocuments by dragging.

 5 Select the *Meditation II* heading and click the **Split Subdocument** button to separate the subdocuments again.

 6 Position the insertion point at the beginning of the document and click the **Lock Document** button to protect the document from alteration.

7 Choose **OK** to save changes to the master document.

Notice the title bar now displays *(Read-Only)* after the document name.

 8 Save and close the document.

A completed example of 💾**02Mastr3** (and its subdocuments) is available in the **WORDCert\Word C\Samples\Master Docs** folder.

LESSON 3: PUBLISHING FEATURES

Sometimes, when you create long documents, you need special layout elements: footnotes or endnotes to clarify document text, numbered captions so you can refer readers to inserted figures, tables or equations, and a table of contents or an index for easy reference. Word provides numerous features for building these elements.

In this lesson, you will learn to:

> Use footnotes and endnotes

> Insert numbered figure and table captions

> Insert numbered headings

> Build a table of contents or a table of figures

> Create and modify an index

Your documents will be more thorough and comprehensive once you've mastered these advanced Word features.

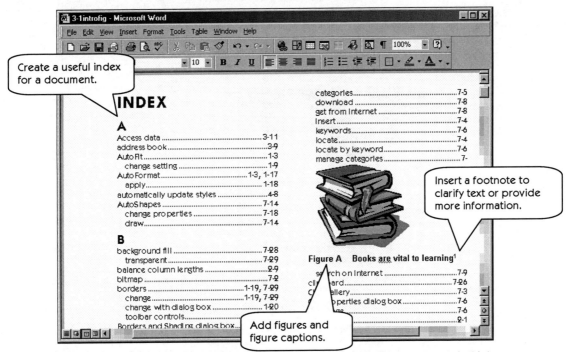

Figure 3.1   An index is one of the many advanced features you will learn to create in this lesson.

Use Footnotes and Endnotes

Notes provide a way for an author to give you supplemental information without interrupting the main flow of the text. Footnotes and endnotes fulfill essentially the same purpose, except that **footnotes** appear at the bottom of the same page as the citation while all **endnotes** appear together at the end of the document no matter where the citation is located within the text. Footnotes and endnotes are used most extensively in textbooks and scholarly texts.

CREATE FOOTNOTES AND ENDNOTES

To insert a footnote or endnote, select the text to note and then choose **Insert>Footnote** from the menu bar to display the **Footnote and Endnote** dialog box. From this dialog box, you will specify if you wish to insert a footnote or endnote.

Insert a note:

 TIP: The keyboard shortcut to insert an footnote is **Ctrl+Alt+F**. The keyboard shortcut to insert an endnote is **Ctrl+Alt+D**. If you use either keyboard shortcut, skip to step 7.

  1   Switch to Print Layout view.

2   Select the text to which you want to attach a note.

3   Choose **Insert>Footnote** from the menu bar:

Figure 3.2   Specify if you want to create a footnote or endnote in this dialog box.

4   Choose **Footnote** or **Endnote** as desired.

5   Choose the Numbering option you want to use:

- **AutoNumber**   Numbers footnotes/endnotes automatically, starting with 1. This is the default setting.

- **Custom mark**   Specify a standard keyboard character for a footnote, such as an asterisk (*).

- **Symbol**   Choose a symbol for your custom mark, such as: † ‡ §.

6   Choose **OK**.

A note pane displays at the bottom of your page (or document) with the cursor ready.

7   Type the note text as desired.

 8   Close the note pane.

OR

Press **F6** to leave the note pane open and return to the document.

CUSTOMIZE FOOTNOTES AND ENDNOTES

In Figure 3.2, above, you may have noticed that there is an **Options** button in the **Footnote and Endnote** dialog box. Choose this button to display the **Note Options** dialog box, from which you can specify footnote or endnote behavior for the document as a whole.

Set note options:

1   Choose **Insert>Footnote** from the menu bar to display the **Footnote and Endnote** dialog box.

2   Choose **Options**:

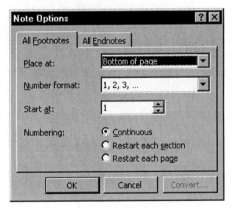

Figure 3.3   Set global note options in this dialog box.

3   (Optional) Choose the **All Endnotes** tab to set endnote options.

4   Click the **Place at** arrow and select note placement.

5   Choose a **Number format**.

6   (Optional) Choose a number to **Start at** if you do not want to start note numbering with the default setting (e.g., 1, a, A, i, I).

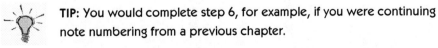 TIP: You would complete step 6, for example, if you were continuing note numbering from a previous chapter.

7   Choose a Numbering option from the following: **Continuous**, **Restart each section**, or **Restart each page**. Choose **OK**.

VIEW FOOTNOTES AND ENDNOTES

Footnotes and endnotes appear as they will print when you view the document in Print Layout view. In other views, you can view note text by hovering the mouse pointer over the note's reference mark or the text to which the note is attached:

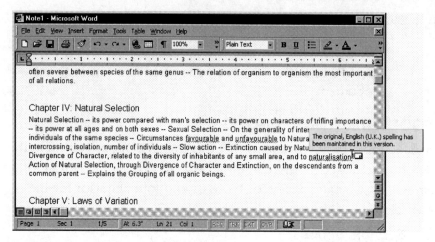

Figure 3.4   Note text appears in a ScreenTip when you hover the mouse pointer on a note
                      reference mark.

TIP: To jump quickly between the note reference mark and the note itself—or vice versa—
double-click the reference mark.

EDIT AND DELETE FOOTNOTES AND ENDNOTES

You may have instances where you need to edit a footnote or endnote, or delete one altogether.

Edit note:

1   Find the note reference mark for the footnote/endnote you want to edit.

2   Double-click the reference to move to the note text.

3   Edit the footnote/endnote text as desired.

Delete note:

1   Find the note reference mark for the footnote/endnote you want to delete.

2   Position the insertion point to the left of the note reference mark and press the **Delete** key to select it.

3   Press the **Delete** key again to delete the reference mark and the footnote/endnote.

Practice Exercise 3-1

Work with Footnotes

1   Open 🗁**03Ex3-1** from the **WORDCert\Word C** folder. Save the document as 🖫**03Foot**.

2   Switch to Print Layout view if necessary.

3   Insert a footnote by doing the following:

- Double-click the word **Favoured** in the heading paragraph to select it.

- Choose **Insert>Footnote** from the menu bar to display the **Footnote and Endnote** dialog box.

- Verify that **Footnote** is selected in the Insert section and that **AutoNumber** is selected in the Numbering section.

- Choose **Options** to change the footnote format.

- Choose **a, b, c, ...** from the **Number format** list, and then choose **OK**.

- Choose **OK** again.

Though you cannot see it now, a footnote reference mark (*a*) was inserted at the end of the selected text before the insertion point jumped to the footnote pane.

- Type the following footnote text next to the reference letter:

> The author's original spelling has not been changed in this edition.

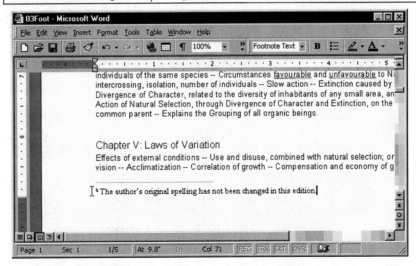

Figure 3.5   The footnote pane appears at the bottom of the page. Page 1 is shown here (note the status bar).

4   Move to the footnote reference mark in the document by double-clicking the reference mark next to the note you just typed, *a*.

The cursor returns to a location after the word you selected in step 3, *Favoured*.

5 View the footnote ScreenTip by pointing to the reference mark or the word itself.

The footnote text appears in a ScreenTip. Notice, however, that the reference mark is closer to the word *Races*. This is because the space after *Favoured* was selected when you inserted the footnote.

6 Delete the footnote by doing the following:

- Press the **Delete** key twice.

The reference mark is selected and then deleted.

- Scroll to the bottom of the page to verify that the footnote itself is also deleted.

7 Insert a new footnote by doing the following:

- Select the word *Favoured*, but do not include the following space.
- Choose **Insert>Footnote** again.
- Choose **Options**.
- Choose **1, 2, 3, ...** from the **Number format** list, and choose **OK**.
- Choose **OK** again.
- Type the following footnote text:

The author's original spelling has not been changed in this edition.

8 Move to the footnote reference mark in the document.

The display moves back to the original word you chose.

9 View the footnote ScreenTip. Point to the reference mark (*1*) in the text.

The footnote text appears in a ScreenTip. Notice now that the reference mark is closer to the word *Favoured*; this is because you did not select the space after it when you inserted the footnote.

10 Save and close the document.

A completed example of 🖫**03Foot** is available in the **WORDCert\Word C\Samples** folder.

Create Numbered Captions

Technical reports and textbooks often have many illustrations and tables, which are usually numbered sequentially for the reader's convenience.

If you number the instances of a certain type of object (e.g., figures, tables, equations) manually, and then you add another object midway through the document, you must manually renumber each caption from that point forward. This could be a cumbersome process if you have a lot of labeled graphic objects. If you create numbered captions in Word 2000, however, Word tracks the numbering for you and renumbers objects if necessary.

Word has three default caption labels (*Figure*, *Table*, and *Equation*), but there is no limit to the number of custom label types you can add. Labels for each object type are numbered independently. For example, suppose you have a figure, a table, another table, and then another figure; caption labels would appear in order as follows: Figure 1, Table 1, Table 2, Figure 2.

As with most Word 2000 features, captions can be customized in a variety of ways. You can, for example, change the start number and/or the number formatting.

Insert a caption:

1   Position the insertion point where you want to place a caption.

OR

To create a caption for an existing figure, table, or equation, select the object.

 NOTE: Selecting the object in the step above allows you to position the caption as desired. The caption is not attached to the object, however. If you move the object, the caption will *not* move with it automatically.

2   Choose **Insert>Caption** from the menu bar:

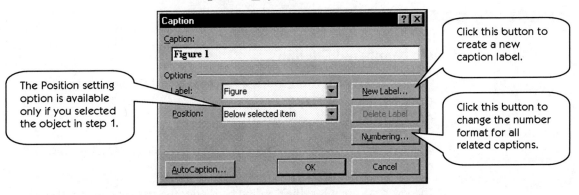

The Position setting option is available only if you selected the object in step 1.

Click this button to create a new caption label.

Click this button to change the number format for all related captions.

Figure 3.6   Specify the settings for the caption to insert.

3   Choose a **Label** type from the list if necessary.

TIP: You can create a new label type by choosing **New Label** and specifying a name for it.

4 (Optional) Click the **Position** arrow and choose the desired caption position from the list if you do not want to use the default setting (e.g., *Below selected item* for figures or *Above selected item* for tables and equations).

5 (Optional) To change the number format, choose **Numbering**, select a numbering **Format** from the list, and then choose **OK**.

6 Type any **Caption** text as desired and choose **OK**.

OR

Choose **OK** to insert the caption label and return to the document, where you can then type any caption text as desired.

7 Format and edit the caption text as desired.

When you look at a caption in the on-screen document, it appears to be normal text. If you click the caption number, however, the number turns gray. Why? You guessed it—because the caption number is actually...a field code. If you insert another object (and caption) of the same type, Word automatically updates all existing caption numbers.

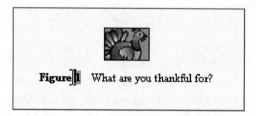

Figure 3.7   A caption includes a field that tracks and updates caption label numbers.

 NOTE: Remember, you can toggle field codes if you want a firsthand look behind the caption (review Lesson 1 of Section C: Edit field codes). You will see a code like this: { *SEQ Figure * ARABIC* }. Translation: A sequential number with the label *Figure* formatted in Arabic numerals lives here.

Practice Exercise 3-2

Create Numbered Captions

 1 Open 📂**03Ex3-2** from the **WORDCert\Word C** folder. Save the document as 💾**03Captn**.

2 Select the figure under the first question.

3 Choose **Insert>Caption** from the menu bar to display the **Caption** dialog box.

The insertion point is in the **Caption** box, after the default caption label (*Figure 1*).

4 Insert a single space in the **Caption** box, and then type:
How many triangles? .

5 Choose **OK**.

The insertion point appears at the end of the caption text.

6 Select the table under question 2 and choose **Insert>Caption**.

7 Insert a space in the **Caption** box and then type:
Fill in the next number .

8 Choose **Table** from the **Label** list and then choose **OK**.

The insertion point is above the table, next to the table caption.

9 Add a caption for the figure under question 3 that reads:
How many rectangles?

 TIP: Remember to verify the **Label** setting.

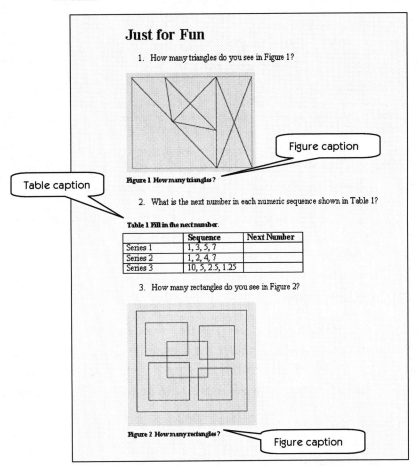

Figure 3.8   Your **03Captn** document after steps 1-9 are completed.

A completed example of **03Captn** is available in the
WORDCert\Word C\Samples folder on the DDC CD-ROM.

Create Numbered Headings

If you are creating a technical report, you may want to number the section headings.
Doing so can help readers quickly refer to specific portions of the document. For
example, government regulations often use numbered headings so citizens (and law-
enforcement officers) can refer to a specific law or rule (e.g., 1.45.2b or 9-IV-ii).

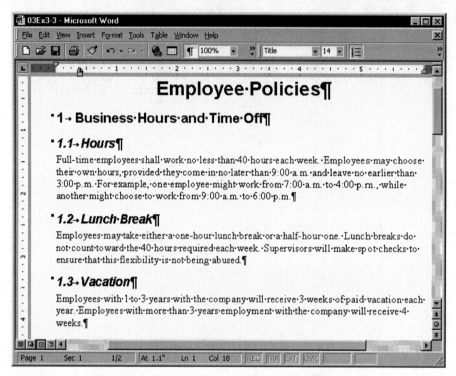

Figure 3.9   Numbered headings can make it easy to refer to a specific section quickly.

If you use Word's built-in heading styles, you will find that they are already set up for
heading numbering. If you use custom heading styles, you must enable the numbering
feature.

APPLY HEADING NUMBERING

Word's heading styles (Heading 1, Heading 2, etc.) are preset to work with heading
numbering. Word automatically recognizes the hierarchy of its headings; so, if you have
a heading numbered *5* formatted with the Heading 1 style and a heading beneath it
formatted with the Heading 2 style, the subordinate heading will automatically be
numbered 5.1.

Preparing for Microsoft Office Specialist Certification

Turn on heading numbering:

1 Select all the headings you want to number.

 TIP: It may be easier to select the headings if you are in Outline view .

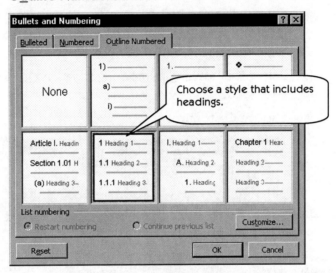

2 Choose **Format>Bullets and Numbering** from the menu bar to display the **Bullets and Numbering** dialog box. Choose the **Outline Numbered** tab:

Figure 3.10 Define numbered headings from the **Outline Numbered** tab.

3 Select a numbering style that has headings, such as the one shown above.

 CAUTION: If you choose a numbering style that does not include *Heading 1, Heading 2,* and so on, every paragraph is numbered—rather than just the heading paragraphs.

4 Choose **OK**.

Numbering is applied to all the headings you selected in step 1. (See Figure 3.9.)

CUSTOMIZE OUTLINE NUMBERING

Although Word has predefined styles for outline numbering that you can use to number your headings, there may be an instance where you need to customize the numbering.

Customize outline numbering:

1   Select all the headings you want to number.

2   Choose **Format>Bullets and Numbering** from the menu bar to display the **Bullets and Numbering** dialog box, and then choose the **Outline Numbered** tab.

3   Select the heading numbering style that is closest to the format you need.

4   Choose **Customize**:

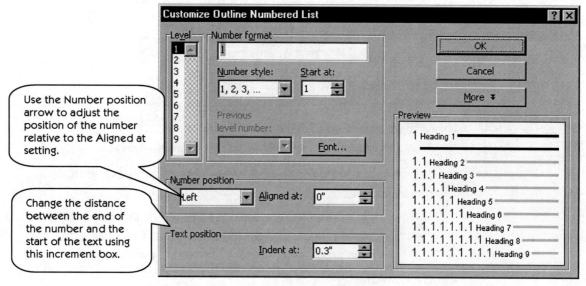

Figure 3.11   Advanced options are available if you choose **More**.

5   Choose the outline **Level** you want to change.

6   Choose the **Number style** you want to use.

7   Change any of the other dialog box options as desired, including the **Font** and the **Start at** setting.

8   Choose **OK**.

Practice Exercise 3-3

Number Headings

1 Open 03Ex3-3 from the **WORDCert\Word C** folder. Save the document as **03Number**.

2 Switch to Outline view, and display only the level 2 headings.

3 Select everything in the document—except for the title, *Employee Policies*.

4 Choose **Format>Bullets and Numbering** from the menu bar to display the **Bullets and Numbering** dialog box, then choose the **Outline Numbered** tab.

5 Select the second numbering style in the second row. (Refer back to Figure 3.10.)

6 Choose **Customize** to display the **Customize Outline Numbered List** dialog box.

7 Choose **2** from the **Level** list to customize the number for Level 2 headings.

8 Choose **A, B, C, …** from the **Number style** list.

9 Choose **OK**:

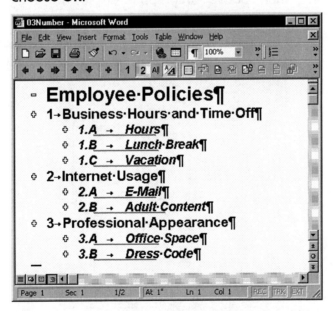

Figure 3.12 Level 1 uses Arabic numbers; Level 2 adds capital letters.

10 Review the document changes in Print Layout view.

11 Save and close the document.

A completed example of **03Number** is available in the **WORDCert\Word C\Samples** folder on the DDC CD-ROM.

MODIFY HEADING LEVELS FOR STYLES

When you wish to use custom styles in documents that call for heading numbers, you simply need to: 1.) identify the custom style as a heading, and 2.) specify which built-in Word heading level the custom style corresponds with.

You can also change the heading levels for the built-in Word styles used in the active document. Suppose, for example, that you want to create a new style called *Chapter Title*, which you want to be equivalent to a standard Level 1 heading. You could make Word's built-in Heading 1 style into Level 2, the Heading 2 style into Level 3, and so on.

Set a style's heading level:

1 Create the new style if needed.

2 Choose **Format>Style** from the menu bar to display the **Style** dialog box.

3 Click the **List** arrow, and then select **User-defined styles**.

4 In the **Styles** list, select the name of the custom style to which you want to assign a heading level.

5 Choose **Modify** to display the **Modify Style** dialog box.

6 Choose **Format** to display a menu of all the items you can change; then choose **Paragraph** to display the **Paragraph** dialog box.

7 Click the **Outline level** arrow and then choose the built-in Word heading level with which your custom style corresponds:

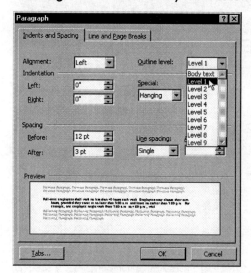

Figure 3.13   Change the heading style's paragraph formatting.

8 Choose **OK** twice.

9 Choose **Close**.

Practice Exercise 3-4

Create a New Heading Style

1 Start a new, blank document.

2 Type: Overview and press **Enter**. Format the new text as 18-point bold and bright red.

3 Create a new style for this heading based on the selected text by typing: ChapterTitle in the **Style** box on the Formatting toolbar and pressing **Enter**:

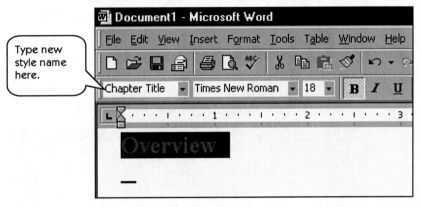

Figure 3.14   Create a new style by naming the formatting you just applied.

4 Choose **Format>Style** from the menu bar to display the **Style** dialog box.

5 Click the **List** arrow, and then select **User-defined styles**.

6 Select **Chapter Title** in the **Styles** list, if necessary.

7 Choose **Modify** to display the **Modify Style** dialog box.

8 Choose **Format** to display a menu of all the items you can change; then choose **Paragraph** to display the **Paragraph** dialog box.

9 Click the **Outline level** arrow. Then choose **Level 1** to specify the built-in Word heading level your custom style corresponds with.

10 Choose **OK** twice, then choose **Close**.

11 Save the document as 🖫**03Chapt**, then close it.

A completed example of 🖫**03Chapt** is available in the **WORDCert\Word C\Samples** folder on the DDC CD-ROM.

Create a Table of Contents

If your document has more than 10 pages, a table of contents could be very useful for your readers to help them locate the material they need quickly.

Word builds tables of contents based on the same heading levels you saw in the preceding topic. Similarly, Word's built-in headings have table of contents levels pre-applied (Level 1 for Heading 1, and so on). The procedure for applying table of contents levels to custom styles is the same as for applying heading levels.

Create a table of contents:

1   Position the insertion point where you want to place the table of contents in the document. (It customarily appears at the beginning of the document or after the title pages.)

 TIP: You will probably want to place a table of contents on its own page with a heading (e.g., *Contents, Table of Contents, Chapters*).

2   Choose **Insert>Index and Tables** to display the **Index and Tables** dialog box. Then choose the **Table of Contents** tab:

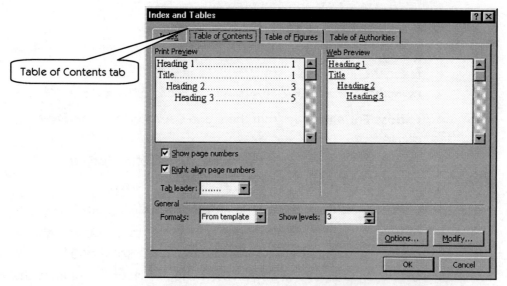

Table of Contents tab

Figure 3.15   The **Print Preview** box shows how the table of contents will look when printed; the **Web Preview** box shows how the table of contents will look when it is saved as a Web page and viewed in a Web browser.

3   (Optional) Deselect the **Right align page numbers** check box.

4   (Optional) Choose a **Tab leader** character if you do not like the default periods (...   .).

 NOTE: As a reminder, a *tab leader* is a series of characters that guides the reader's eyes across the page. Typical leader characters are periods (.......),dashes (-----), or lines (____), but you may opt not to use one at all.

5   (Optional) Click the **Formats** arrow under General to choose a built-in table of contents format.

 NOTE: The default **Formats** setting is **From template**, which uses the attached template's styles for table of contents entries, but you can also choose from among several other built-in table of contents formats or create a custom format, as you will see in the following pages.

6   Change the number of heading levels that show in the **Show levels** box if you do not want to use the default setting, 3.

7   Choose **OK**.

In Word 2000, the entries in a table of contents are hyperlinks to the named headings. You can click a table of contents entry and move to that heading in the document.

You can create a table of contents in a master document to tie all the subdocuments together. Just make sure all subdocuments are expanded. Review Lesson 2 of this section, **Work with a Master Document**.

Practice Exercise 3-5

Generate a Table of Contents

1   Open ⌒**03Number**, which you created in Practice Exercise 3-3, or open ⌒**03Ex3-5** from the **WORDCert\Word C** folder. Save the open document as ⊟**03TOC1**.

2   Position the insertion point at the beginning of the document to place the table of contents there, and press **Ctrl+Enter** to create a new page. Return to the beginning of the document, type: Table of Contents , and press **Enter**.

3   Choose **Insert>Index and Tables** from the menu bar to display the **Index and Tables** dialog box. Choose the **Table of Contents** tab if necessary.

4   Choose **Classic** from the **Formats** list.

The Classic table of content format is displayed in the **Print Preview** and **Web Preview** boxes.

5   Choose .... (periods) from the **Tab leader** list.

A dot leader is added to the table of contents in the **Print Preview** box.

6   Choose **OK**.

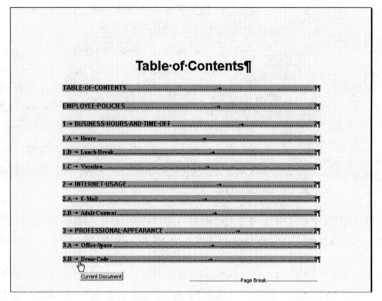

Figure 3.16   Your **03TOC1** table of contents.

7   Save and close the document.

A completed example of ▢**03TOC1** is available in the
WORDCert\Word C\Samples folder on the DDC CD-ROM.

SET TABLE OF CONTENTS OPTIONS

As with most high-tech things, Word 2000 features are only useful if they can be fitted
to your specific purposes and needs. Accordingly, you can customize the appearance
of your table of contents. The two major elements you can change are: 1.) which styles
are included, and 2.) how the various heading levels are formatted.

Choose Styles to Include

If you use custom heading styles, you will need to set the options for your table of
contents to include them. Similarly, if you don't want to include all the default heading
levels in your table of contents, you will need to exclude them.

Specify table-of-contents styles:

1   Select the existing table of contents that you want to replace, or
position the insertion point where you want to insert a new table
of contents.

2   Choose **Insert>Index and Tables** from the menu bar to display the
Index and Tables dialog box. Choose the **Table of Contents** tab if
necessary.

3 Choose **Options**:

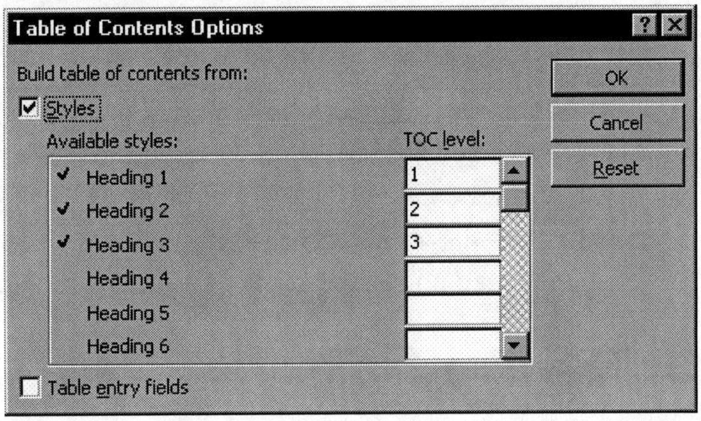

Figure 3.17   Choose the styles to include by specifying a table of contents (TOC) level.

4 Type a **TOC level** number in the box next to each style you want to include in the table of contents and/or remove the number corresponding to any style you don't want to use.

5 Choose **OK**.

6 Continue setting up the table of contents as desired from the **Index and Tables** dialog box.

OR

Choose **OK**.

Change the Table of Contents Format

You have already seen a few built-in table of contents formats in the **Formats** list in the **Index and Tables** dialog box. You can take even more control of your table of contents by formatting each level's style individually.

Modify formatting for a table-of-contents style:

1 Select the existing table of contents that you want to replace, or position the insertion point where you want to insert a new table of contents.

2 Choose **Insert>Index and Tables** from the menu bar to display the **Index and Tables** dialog box. Choose the **Table of Contents** tab if necessary.

3 Choose **Modify** to display the **Style** dialog box.

4 Choose the table-of-contents style you want to modify from the **Styles** list.

5 Choose **Modify** to display the **Modify Style** dialog box.

6 Choose **Format** to display a menu of all the items you can change, and make style changes as needed.

7 Choose **OK** twice.

8   Repeat steps 4-7 modify additional styles as needed.

OR

Choose **Close**.

9   Continue setting up the table of contents as desired from the **Index and Tables** dialog box.

10 Choose **OK**.

11 (Optional) Choose **OK** again to confirm the replacement if you selected an existing table of contents in step 1.

Practice Exercise 3-6

Please refer back to Figure 3.16 and notice the table-of-contents style format on TABLE OF CONTENTS and EMPLOYEE POLICIES. Both items are formatted with the Title style, which Word sets to Level 1 by default. This exercise excludes them, and also sets the formatting of the Level 1 table-of-contents style.

Create a Custom Table of Contents

1   Open 📂**03TOC1**, which you created in Practice Exercise 3-5, or open 📂**03Ex3-6** from the **WORDCert\Word C** folder. Save the open document as 💾**03TOC2**.

2   Select the table of contents.

3   Choose **Insert>Index and Tables** from the menu bar to display the **Index and Tables** dialog box. Choose the **Table of Contents** tab if necessary.

4   Choose **Options** to display the **Table of Contents Options** dialog box (see Figure 3.17).

5   In the **Available styles** list, move to the Title style and delete the number for the **TOC level**, then choose **OK**.

6   Choose **Modify** to display the **Style** dialog box.

7   Select **TOC 1** from the **Styles** list and then choose **Modify**.

8   Choose **Format**, and choose **Font** to display the **Font** dialog box. Set the font to regular 12-point Arial Black and choose **OK**.

9   Choose **OK**, choose **Close**, and then choose **OK** again.

10 Choose **OK** to confirm the replacement.

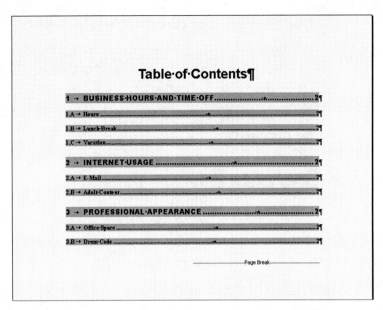

Figure 3.18   The table of contents is more concise with the Title style removed.

 11 Save and close the document.

A completed example of 🖫**03TOC2** is available in the **WORDCert\Word C\Samples** folder on the DDC CD-ROM.

Congratulations on completing your first table of contents and modifying the original table of contents to create a second one! Doesn't that feel good? Here's your chance to gloat: look back at Figures 3.16 and 3.18. Aren't they wonderful, aren't they—wait a minute. Do you see anything wrong with these pictures? Why do they say everything is on page 2?! Whoops! We're missing one very important step.

Since you probably don't want Word to include the page(s) in the table of contents when the program is paginating for the table itself (i.e., you want page 1 to be the first page *after* the table of contents), you *must* insert a section break after the table of contents instead of a regular page break. The page numbering must also be adjusted so that the new section's numbering starts on page 1. Next time you can remember to do this from the beginning, but for now we'll explore how to fix the problem after the fact.

UPDATE A TABLE OF CONTENTS

Tables of contents do their work using field codes. When you make a change to a document containing a table of contents, that table of contents does not update automatically. Instead, you must instruct it to do so.

Updating is more efficient than regenerating the entire TOC *if* the only thing that has changed are the headings and their corresponding page numbers. If, on the other hand, you need to change the TOC's formatting—or change which headings are included in the table of contents—you must regenerate it.

Update a table of contents (field codes):

1   Right-click the table of contents and choose **Update Field** from
    the shortcut menu to display the **Update Table of Contents** dialog
    box.

2   Choose **Update entire table**.

3   Choose **OK**.

Practice Exercise 3-7

In this exercise, you'll practice restarting the page numbering so that the table of
contents' own page is not included in the numbering. You will also update the table of
contents to reflect the modified page numbers.

Update a Table of Contents

1   Open 📂**03TOC2**, which you created in Practice Exercise 3-6, or
    open 📂**03Ex3-7** from the **WORDCert\Word C** folder. Save the
    open document as 💾**03TOC3**.

2   Replace the page break after the table of contents with a section
    break, which also starts a new page.

       TIPS: Choose **Insert>Break** from the menu bar to display the **Break**
                   dialog box.

                   To view the page break, switch to Normal view.

3   Insert a page break before the last two first level headings: *2
    Internet Usage* and *3 Professional Appearance*.

4   Position the insertion point in the second section (i.e., below the
    section break).

5   Choose **Insert>Page Numbers** from the menu bar to display the
    Page Numbers dialog box.

6   Choose **Format** to display the **Page Number Format** dialog box.

7   Choose **Start at** under Page numbering, and then choose **OK** to
    accept the default **Start at** setting (1).

8   Choose **OK** again.

9   Return to the beginning of the document. Right-click the table of
    contents, and then choose **Update Field** from the shortcut menu
    to display the **Update Table of Contents** dialog box.

10 Choose **Update entire table** and choose **OK**.

       TIP: If you only want to update the page numbers of the
                   table of contents, choose **Update page numbers only**.

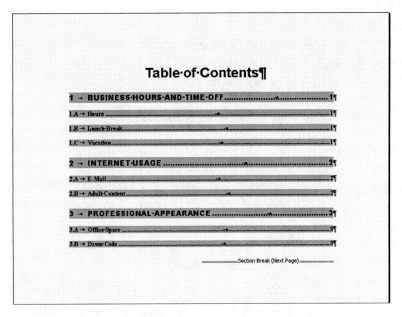

Figure 3.19   The page numbers change to reflect the new page numbering.

    11 Save and close the document.

Create a Table of Figures

A table of figures is similar to a table of contents, except that a table of figures lists numbered object captions rather than text headings. In fact, the only difference you'll find on their respective tabs in the **Index and Tables** dialog box is that, where **Table of Content**s asks for you to specify the number of heading levels to display (**Show levels**), **Table of Figures** asks for the label you wish to display and whether or not you wish to include that label and each caption number. Most documents do not have a table of figures, however. The table of figures is a specialized creature used mainly in technical publications that contain numerous illustrations.

Since tables of figures are generated based on numbered object captions, you must first create automatically numbered captions for each type of object using the method you learned earlier in this lesson.

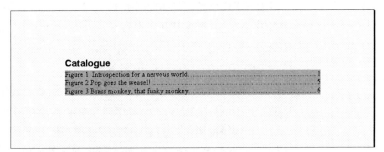

Figure 3.20   Table of figures.

As you can see from Figure 3.20, tables of figures by default include the following: object caption label, caption number, caption text, and the object's page number. Tables of figures are also modified (style options and formatting) and updated in the same manner as tables of contents.

Create a table of figures:

1   Insert all the numbered captions for your document.

2   Position the insertion point where you want to place the table of figures in the document. (It customarily appears after the table of contents and/or introduction, or as an appendix.)

   TIP: You will probably want to place a table of figures on its own page with a heading (e.g., *Figures, Table of Figures, Illustrations, Tables, Charts*).

3   Choose **Insert>Index and Tables** from the menu bar to display the **Index and Tables** dialog box. Choose the **Table of Figures** tab if necessary:

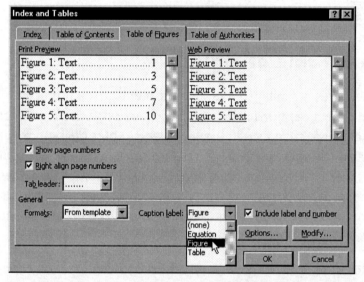

Figure 3.21   The **Table of Figures** tab looks and works like the **Table of Contents** tab, including the **Options** and **Modify** buttons.

4   Set the table of figures options as desired: **Show page numbers, Right align page numbers,** and **Tab leader.**

5   (Optional) Click the **Formats** arrow under **General** to choose a built-in table of figures format.

   NOTE: As with the table of contents, the default **Formats** setting is **From template,** which uses the template's styles for table of figures entries, but you can also choose from among several other formats.

6   Choose a **Caption label** (e.g., Figure, Table, Equation, *custom*), if necessary.

7   (Optional) Deselect the **Include label and number** check box to display only the caption text and the object page number.

8   Choose **OK**.

Practice Exercise 3-8

Create a Table of Figures

1   Open 🗁**03Captn**, which you created in Practice Exercise 3-2, or open 🗁**03Ex3-8** from the **WORDCert\Word C** folder. Save the open document as 💾**03TOF**.

2   Move the insertion point to the bottom of the document and add a page break (**Ctrl+Enter**).

3   Apply the Heading 1 style to the following new heading:
    Table of Figures .

4   Choose **Insert>Index and Tables** from the menu bar to display the **Index and Tables** dialog box, and then choose the **Table of Figures** tab.

5   Choose **OK**.

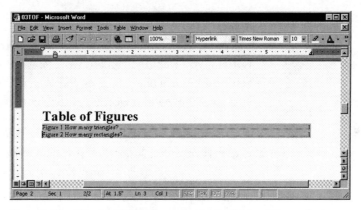

Figure 3.22   This short table demonstrates the Table of Figures feature.

6   Save and close the document.

A completed example of 💾**03TOF** is available in the **WORDCert\Word C\Samples** folder.

Create Indexes

An index is an alphabetical listing of all key terms and/or topics in a document, along with the page number(s) on which the reader can find these terms discussed.

The first time people create an index, their first reaction is usually: *Wow, what a lot of work!* And suddenly they gain a new appreciation for the intense effort that goes into indexing procedure manuals, textbooks, and reference books.

There are two steps to building an index: 1.) marking the words to index, and 2.) generating the index itself. The latter is fast and easy. Guess which one is the energy-drainer and time-evaporator! Marking terms for indexing, above all else, has to be done intelligently, with a lot of thought and care for making the index as usable as possible.

There are some shortcuts for marking index entries, but they can result in an inferior-quality index if they are not used with common sense and good judgment. This lesson teaches both the manual (time-consuming) and the automated (less reliable) methods so you can judge the results for yourself.

MARK INDEX ENTRIES MANUALLY

This is the best method for marking index entries if index quality is your primary concern.

Mark a word or phrase for indexing:

1   Select the word or phrase to index.

2   Choose **Insert>Index and Tables** from the menu bar to display the **Index and Tables** dialog box, then choose the **Index** tab if necessary.

3   Choose **Mark Entry**.

4   (Optional) Edit index entry as desired in the **Main entry** box.

   NOTE: If you want the marked word(s) to be a subentry under some other main heading, type the main entry in the **Main entry** box and copy the marked word(s) to the **Subentry** box.

5   Choose one of the following **Options** as desired:

   • **Cross-reference**   Selected term is a synonym for another term. Then type the other term in the box.

   • **Current page**   Refers to the page on which the selected text appears. This is the default setting.

   • **Page range**   Refers to a range of pages delineated by a bookmark you have created. Choose the bookmark from the Bookmark list.

6   Choose **Mark**.

   TIP: It may be necessary for you to move the dialog box so that you can locate subsequent words you wish to mark.

7   Select another word or phrase to mark, and then click the **Mark Index Entry** dialog box.

   The newly marked word(s) appear in the **Main entry** box.

8   Repeat steps 4-7 to mark all words for the index. Then choose **Close**.

Although you can mark index entries as you work on each chapter in a book (or other multi-document product), you will want to wait until you create the master document that ties all the chapters together before you generate the index.

You may have noticed that, when you mark index entries, Word automatically turns on the Show/Hide ¶ feature. To hide these symbols, click the **Show/Hide ¶** button on the Standard toolbar to deselect it.

Once the index codes are inserted in the document, you can edit them on the screen like regular text.

Practice Exercise 3-9

Mark Index Entries Manually

1 Open 🗁**03Ex3-9** from the **WORDCert\Word C** folder. Save the document as 💾**03Indx1**.

2 Select the heading, *Starting the MedReport Server*.

3 Choose **Insert>Index and Tables** from the menu bar to display the **Index and Tables** dialog box, and then choose the **Index** tab if necessary.

4 Choose **Mark Entry** to display the **Mark Index Entry** dialog box.

5 Choose **Mark**.

6 Add a main entry and subentry index item by doing the following:
   - Edit the text in the **Main entry** box to read: *MedReport Server*.
   - Type: Starting in the **Subentry** box.
   - Choose **Mark** to create a second index entry.

7 Add another main entry and subentry index item as shown: Server:Start .

8 Choose **Close**.

9 Edit the last two new index codes on-screen to read as follows:

   { XE "MedReport Server:start" } { XE "server:start" }

10 Save and close the document.

   A completed example of 💾**03Indx1** is available in the **WORDCert\Word C\Samples** folder.

MARK INDEX ENTRIES AUTOMATICALLY (AUTOMARK)

To mark index entries automatically, you must first create an AutoMark file (i.e., concordance file). An **AutoMark file** is a file that lists all the terms or topics you want to mark. Word then marks each instance of each of those words automatically for you.

If you are thinking, *Wait a minute, won't that index too much?*, you are on the right track! For example, if the term *MedReport* appears in a document 80 times and you include that word in the concordance file, each of those 80 instances will be indexed. That's why AutoMarking may not be the best choice for most situations.

Create a Concordance File

A **concordance file** is a standard two-column table. In the first column, type the document text to locate. In the second column, type its index entry. Subentries are created in the second column using colons (:). For example, in the first column, you might type *Starting the MedReport Server*, and in the second column *MedReport:start*.

Develop a concordance file:

1   Start a new, blank document.

2   Create a two-column table.

3   Enter the document text to index in the first column.

4   Enter the wording to appear in the index in the second column.

 TIP: To isolate one instance of a particular word or phrase for AutoMark indexing, include some of the words around the term/phrase in the first column. For example, to index the phrase *so that the file server can run a backup program*—but not any other phrases in the document that might include the word *backup*—you could include that entire phrase in the first column of the concordance table and then just *backup* in the second column.

5   Continue entering pairs of words or phrases, using as many rows as needed, until you have listed all the words you want to index.

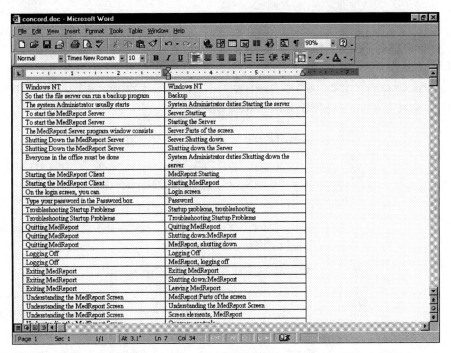

Windows NT	Windows NT
So that the file server can run a backup program	Backup
The system Administrator usually starts	System Administrator duties:Starting the server
To start the MedReport Server	Server:Starting
To start the MedReport Server	Starting the Server
The MedReport Server program window consists	Server:Parts of the screen
Shutting Down the MedReport Server	Server:Shutting down
Shutting Down the MedReport Server	Shutting down the Server
Everyone in the office must be done	System Administrator duties:Shutting down the server
Starting the MedReport Client	MedReport:Starting
Starting the MedReport Client	Starting MedReport
On the login screen, you can	Login screen
Type your password in the Password box.	Password
Troubleshooting Startup Problems	Startup problems, troubleshooting
Troubleshooting Startup Problems	Troubleshooting Startup Problems
Quitting MedReport	Quitting MedReport
Quitting MedReport	Shutting down:MedReport
Quitting MedReport	MedReport, shutting down
Logging Off	Logging Off
Logging Off	MedReport, logging off
Exiting MedReport	Exiting MedReport
Exiting MedReport	Shutting down:MedReport
Exiting MedReport	Leaving MedReport
Understanding the MedReport Screen	MedReport:Parts of the screen
Understanding the MedReport Screen	Understanding the MedReport Screen
Understanding the MedReport Screen	Screen elements, MedReport

Figure 3.25 A concordance, or AutoMark, file lists terms to index and the phrasing for their index entries.

 6 Save and close the document.

Use AutoMarking

When your concordance file is complete, you must attach it to your document to create automatic index entries.

Index with AutoMark:

1 Open the document you want to index.

2 Choose **Insert>Index and Tables** from the menu bar to display the **Index and Tables** dialog box, and then choose the **Index** tab if necessary.

3 Choose **AutoMark** to display the **Open Index AutoMark File** dialog box.

4 Select the concordance file.

5 Choose **Open**.

The number of entries AutoMarked appears in the status bar.

Practice Exercise 3-10

A concordance file has been provided in this Practice Exercise to save you time. It's the same file that is shown in Figure 3.25.

AutoMark with a Concordance File

1   Open 📂**03Ex3-10a** from the **WORDCert\Word C** folder. Save the document as 💾**03Concrd**.

2   Examine the entries on the list. Notice that a single phrase in the right column may be repeated several times so it can be indexed in different ways. See Figure 3.25.

3   Close the **03Concrd** document.

4   Open 📂**03Indx1**, which you created in Practice Exercise 3-9, or open 📂**03Ex3-10b** from the **WORDCert\Word C** folder. Save the open document as 💾**03Indx2**.

5   Choose **Insert>Index and Tables** from the menu bar to display the **Index and Tables** dialog box, and then choose the **Index** tab if necessary.

6   Choose **AutoMark** to display the **Open Index AutoMark File** dialog box.

7   Select the **03Concrd** document, and then choose **Open**.

   37 index entries are marked.

8   Scroll through the document to see some of the AutoMark index entries.

9   Save and close the document.

   Completed examples of 💾**03Concrd** and 💾**03Indx2** are available in the **WORDCert\Word C\Samples** folder on the DDC CD-ROM.

GENERATE THE INDEX

As stated earlier, marking index entries is the bulk of the work in creating an index. The actual index-generation process is quick and easy.

Generate an index:

1   Verify that all index entries are marked as desired.

 NOTE: You can use manual marking, AutoMark, or a combination of the two.

2   Position the insertion point where you want to place the index. (It customarily appears at the end of the document.)

TIP: You will probably want to place an index on its own page with a heading (e.g., *Index, References, Topics*).

3 Choose **Insert>Index and Tables** from the menu bar to display the **Index and Tables** dialog box, and then choose the **Index** tab if necessary:

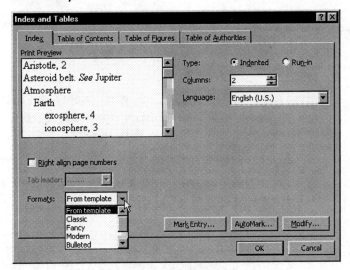

Figure 3.26 The **Index** tab is similar to the other tabs you have seen in the **Index and Tables** dialog box, including the **Print Preview** box and the **Modify** button.

4 (Optional) Click the **Formats** arrow to choose a built-in index format.

 NOTE: The default **Formats** setting is **From template**, which uses the attached template's styles for index entries, but you can also choose from among several other built-in index formats or create a custom format as you will see in the following steps.

5 Set the index options as desired: **Right align page numbers** and **Tab leader**.

AND/OR

To move all subentries into one "paragraph" with all their main entries, choose **Run-in** next to Type.

6 Change the number of **Columns** for your index page(s) if you do not want to use the default setting, 2.

7 Choose **OK**.

As you examine your index, you will probably find lots of ways to improve it by adding more accurate or appropriate words, varied terminology (synonyms), and cross-references. All of this adds thoroughness and helps your readers. To update your index after adding more entries, simply select the index and repeat steps 3 and 7 in the procedure above.

One key to a good index is to list each important concept under every synonym that might occur to your readers when they are looking for information on a given topic. For example, if you are indexing the heading *Quitting MedReport,* you might index it under the following terms: *quit, shut down, exit,* and *log off.* As you can imagine, such thoroughness is a very time-consuming task for you but very helpful to readers.

Practice Exercise 3-11

Generate an Index

1   Open 📂**03Indx2,** which you created in Practice Exercise 3-10, or open 📂**03Ex3-11** from the **WORDCert\Word C** folder. Save the open document as 💾**03Indx3.**

2   Insert a page break at the end of the document.

3   Press the **Enter** key, press the **Up** arrow key; then center and format the following index heading in 18-point bold: Index . Position the insertion point on the blank line beneath the heading line.

4   Choose **Insert>Index and Tables** from the menu bar to display the **Index and Tables** dialog box. Choose the **Index** tab if necessary.

5   Choose **Modern** from the **Formats** list.

6   Choose **OK.**

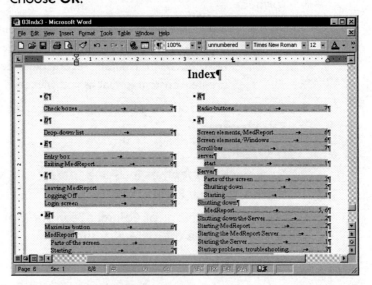

Figure 3.27   Your **03Indx3** document.

7   Save and close the document.

A completed example of 💾**03Indx3** is available in the **WORDCert\Word C\Samples** folder on the DDC CD-ROM.

LESSON 4: SHARE DATA WITH OTHERS

Several people may collaborate to create a business report, a procedure manual, a manuscript for publication, a Web site, or even a group term paper. This lesson shows you how to work with comments, manage revisions, and protect documents when more than one person is involved in a document's creation. Since it's not always clear who changed what or which version of a multiple-draft document is the most recent, Word's group-editing features help you keep your project organized.

In this lesson, you will learn to:

➢ Attach non-printing comments

➢ Save multiple versions of a document

➢ Track document changes

➢ Protect a document from alteration

With the help of Word 2000's group-editing features, your group projects—whatever final form they take—will fall together without your group falling apart!

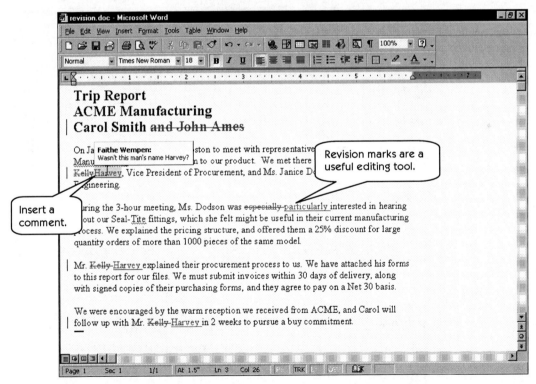

Figure 4.1   Revisions and comments can make sense of changes from multiple sources.

Use Comments

When more than one person reviews a document (such as a book manuscript or a business report), one reviewer may want to include a non-printing comment that discusses a particular aspect. For example, a sales representative might question a particular sales figure in a table, or an editor might request that the author rephrase a sentence or verify a statistic. Such queries, obviously, should not be part of the main document. A comment provides a handy, out-of-the-way place to store such notes.

ADD COMMENTS

When you can select text in step 1, take care not to select any more than two or three words. Otherwise, as other people add comments (some in response to yours) the comments may become unnavigable to reviewers.

Insert a comment:

1 Position the insertion point at the beginning of the sentence (or next to the word) you want to comment on.

 OR

 Select the word(s) you want to comment on.

2 Choose **Insert>Comment** from the menu bar:

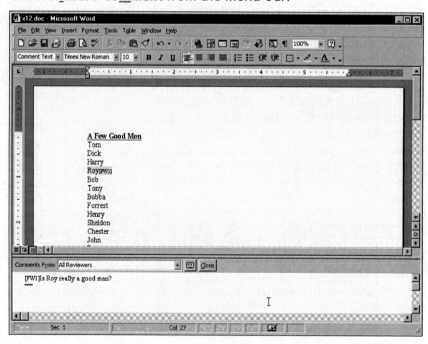

Figure 4.2 Your initials and a comment number appear in brackets beside the comment while the word next to the insertion point is highlighted.

3 Type your comment.

4 Close the Comments pane.

VIEW COMMENTS

You can view a comment by pointing the mouse pointer at the highlighted text. When the mouse pointer is in the correct position, a note icon (📝) appears next to the I beam, indicating that you can now view the comment. The comment pops up in a ScreenTip:

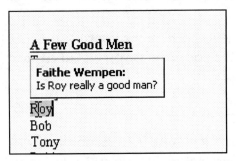

Figure 4.3   To view comment text, point at the highlighted text or the comment mark.

If you have multiple comments in a document, you may find it more convenient to use the Reviewing toolbar to move between comments. To display the toolbar, choose **View>Toolbars>Reviewing** from the menu bar or right-click a toolbar and choose **Reviewing** from the shortcut menu. Then use the **Previous Comment** and **Next Comment** buttons to move quickly from comment to comment. This toolbar is also useful when inserting, editing, and deleting comments.

Figure 4.4   The Reviewing toolbar helps you manage comments.

You can also view the comments in the Comments pane, of course. Doing so may become necessary (albeit somewhat confusing) if multiple reviewers "stack" comments. There are three ways to redisplay the Comments pane:

*   Choose **View>Comments** from the menu bar.
*   Click the **Edit Comment** button on the Reviewing toolbar.
*   Double-click a comment mark in the document text.

When you move to another comment within the Comments pane, the document view jumps correspondingly to show the associated text on the screen.

EDIT COMMENT

To edit a comment, reopen the Comments pane and type your changes there.

Edit a comment:

 1 Choose **View>Comments** from the menu bar to display the Comments pane.

2 Click the Comments pane to position the insertion point as desired, and then edit the comment as you would any text.

 3 Close the Comments pane.

DELETE COMMENT

If you are the last person to review a document, it may be your responsibility to delete the comments so the document can be finalized. Before you do so, however, make certain *everyone* working on the project has that same understanding.

There are three main ways to delete comments:

- Select the comment mark, and then press the **Delete** key.

   TIP: The fastest way to select a comment is to use the **Previous Comment** and **Next Comment** buttons on the Reviewing toolbar.

 - Select the text to which the comment is attached, and then click the **Delete Comment** button on the Reviewing toolbar.

- Right-click the text to which the comment is attached, and choose **Delete Comment** from the shortcut menu:

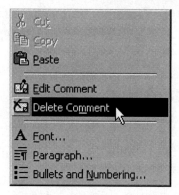

Figure 4.5   Delete a comment using a shortcut menu.

Please note also that if you delete the text a comment is attached to, the comment is deleted automatically.

Practice Exercise 4-1

Work with Comments

 1 Open ☐04Ex4-1 from the **WORDCert\Word C** folder. Save the document as ☐04Men1.

2 Double-click *Mickey* to select it.

 3 Choose **Insert>Comment** from the menu bar to display the Comments pane.

4 Type: ☐Wasn't he one of the Monkees?☐ in the Comments pane.

 5 Close the Comments pane.

6 Point at *Mickey* to display the comment in a ScreenTip.

 7 Right-click *Mickey* and choose **Edit Comment** from the shortcut menu.

8 Change the comment in the Comments pane to: *He was one of the Monkees.*

 9 Close the Comments pane.

 10 Point at *Mickey* to display the revised comment in a ScreenTip.

 11 Right-click *Mickey* and choose **Delete Comment** from the shortcut menu.

 12 Save and close the document.

ADD COMMENTS TO DOCUMENT PROPERTIES

If you have general comments to make about the document, there are two places you might put them:

- At the beginning of the document.
- In the document's **Properties** dialog box.

If you have general comments about the document that need to be seen by each reviewer (but not necessarily addressed), it is best to place them at the beginning of the document. Such comments might include notes about the document formatting or ideas about document organization.

On the other hand, suppose you have information that doesn't need to be seen by each reviewer, but which you nevertheless want to include. Those comments should be added to document properties. For example, you might want to list the "genealogy" of a document, or you may need to record the names of all files graphics were imported from before you send the document to a service bureau for final output.

Add comments to document properties:

1   Choose **File>Properties** from the menu bar to display the document's **Properties** dialog box. If necessary, choose the **Summary** tab.

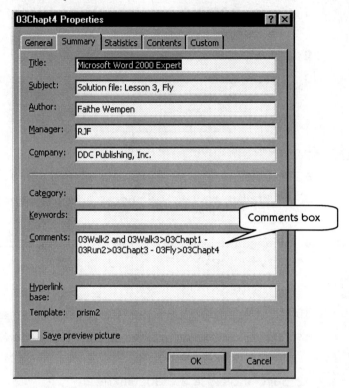

Figure 4.6   The genealogy of your **03Chapt4** document from Lesson 3.

2   Type your comments as desired in the **Comments** box.

3   Choose **OK**.

Who sees the properties? Often most people don't. As you learn to create more complex documents, however, you will find that **Properties** dialog boxes are valuable organization tools. For example, when you point to a file name in Windows Explorer, if that document has a complete properties sheet, you can see what is in the document without opening it. Any comments inserted in the **Properties** dialog box appear here too.

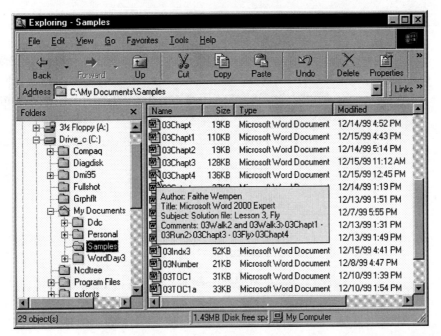

Figure 4.7   Windows Explorer: A ScreenTip appears when you point to the **03Chapt4** file in the **Samples** folder. Remember also that there is a **Properties** button on the Standard Buttons toolbar.

The same can be said for documents placed on the desktop:

Figure 4.8   Point to the **03Chapt4** file on the desktop.

You can also set up a document so that its properties print along with the document automatically. Choose **Tools>Options** from the menu bar to display the **Options** dialog box and choose the **Print** tab. Select the **Document properties** check box under Include with document, and choose **OK**.

Practice Exercise 4-2

Add Comments to Document Properties

1   Open 📂**04Men1**, which you created in Practice Exercise 4-1, or open 📂**04Ex4-2** from the **WORDCert\Word C** folder. Save the open document as 💾**04Men2**.

2   Choose **File>Properties** from the menu bar to display the document's **Properties** dialog box. Then choose the **Summary** tab if necessary.

NOTE: Word inserts the document author's name in the properties sheet by consulting the stored user name. To change the user name, choose **Tools>Options** from the menu bar to display the **Options** dialog box and choose the **User Information** tab.

3   Type the name of your class and its duration in the **Comments** box, for example:

> Word 2000 Microsoft Office Specialist Expert review
> Fall 2000

4   Choose **OK**.

5   Save and close the document.

A completed example of 🖫**04Men2** is available in the **WORDCert\Word C\Samples** folder on the DDC CD-ROM.

Work with Multiple Document Versions

When several people are working on the same document, things can get extremely confusing—and sometimes (it has to be said) things can go extremely wrong. For example, let's say that four people are working on a document and one of these people...say, accidentally deletes half the document. Or, suppose several reviewers didn't follow Comments etiquette and the document has several layers of overlapping Comments highlighting, leading the final reviewer to accidentally delete a comment with some good rewrite suggestions. With version management, you can get back to an earlier version, even after someone has made and saved changes.

SAVE A VERSION

Version management is not enabled by default because it tends to make files rather large. Once you enable this feature, however, you can save a version at any time (using the **Save Version** button 🖫 on the Reviewing toolbar, for example)—or you can set the feature up to save a new version each time the document is closed.

Save multiple versions:

1   Open the document you want to save multiple versions of.

2   Choose **File>Versions** from the menu bar to display the **Versions in [File Name]** dialog box.

3   (Optional) Select the **Automatically save a version on close** check box to save versions automatically each time you close the file.

4 Choose **S**ave Now:

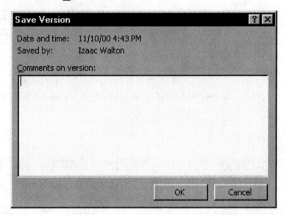

Figure 4.9   Type any comments about the saved version here.

5 Type comments on the version as desired to help distinguish this version from any others.

6 Choose **OK**.

OPEN A SAVED VERSION

When you open a file, its most recent version opens by default. You can use the following procedure to open a version other than the latest one.

Open a saved version:

1 Open the document.

2 Choose **File**>**Versions** from the menu bar:

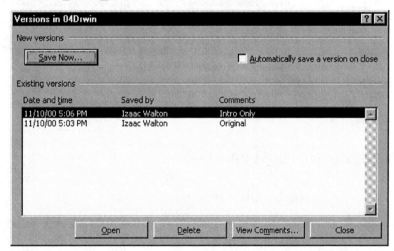

Figure 4.10   Select the version you want to open and then choose **Open**.

3 Select the version you want from the **Existing versions** list.

NOTES: You can also delete versions from the list by selecting the version, choosing **Delete**, and then choosing **Yes** to confirm the deletion.

If a comment is too long to view in the **Version in [File Name]** dialog box, click the **View Comments** button to see the entire comment.

4 Choose **Open**:

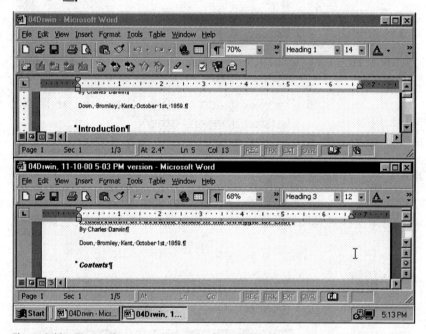

Figure 4.11   The version opens in a new window, allowing you to view both versions.

 5 Choose **File>Save** from the menu bar to create a document from the saved version.

OR

 Close the document without saving it.

Practice Exercise 4-3

Work with Versions

 1 Open 📂**04Ex4-3** from the **WORDCert\Word C** folder. Save the document as 💾**04Drwin**.

 2 Choose **File>Versions** from the menu bar to display the **Versions in 04Drwin** dialog box.

3 Choose **Save Now** to display the **Save Version** dialog box.

4 Type: Original and choose **OK**.

5 Delete the entire *Contents* section of the document, leaving only the Introduction (which currently starts on page 3).

6 Choose **F̲ile**>**V̲ersions** again, and choose **S̲ave Now**.

7 Type: Intro Only and choose **OK**.

8 Choose **F̲ile**>**V̲ersions** again.

9 Choose the original version from the **Existing versions** list.

10 Choose **O̲pen**.

This version opens in a separate window, allowing you to view both versions (see Figure 4.11).

11 Close both documents without saving changes.

A completed example of 04Drwin (with its two saved versions included) is available in the **WORDCert\Word C\Samples** folder on the DDC CD-ROM.

Edit Documents On-Screen

When you turn on Track Changes, all edits are displayed in a different color for each reviewer so you can clearly identify who changed what.

NOTE: It is possible that your computer may be set up in such a way that all reviewer changes appear in the same color; however, this is not the default.

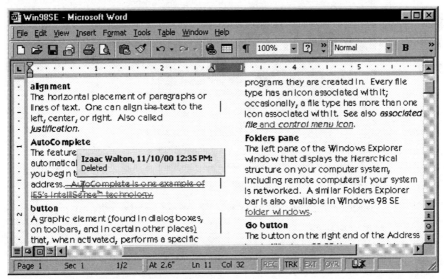

Figure 4.12   Additions are underlined in the reviewer's color, while deletions appear in the reviewer's color in strikethrough.

When you point to a revision with the mouse, a ScreenTip appears, indicating who made the revision and when. This feature is especially helpful when more than one person has edited a document.

NOTE: Word knows that a different person is editing a document by consulting the stored user profile. To change the profile, choose **Tools>Options** from the menu bar to display the **Options** dialog box and then choose the **User Information** tab.

TRACK CHANGES

If you want to track revisions, you must turn Track Changes on. Any edits you make after the feature is enabled appear as revision marks.

This feature can also be turned off and on temporarily if you want to insert edits that do not need to be reviewed by others in your editing group. Simply double-click the TRK indicator on the status bar to select it or deselect it as desired. Similarly, the **Track Changes** button on the Reviewing toolbar can also be selected or deselected as desired; indeed, when you select the toolbar button, the status bar indicator is selected automatically—and vice versa. People often temporarily disable this feature to change document formatting.

Toggle revision tracking:

1   Choose **Tools>Track Changes>Highlight Changes** from the menu bar.

    OR

 Choose the **Track Changes** button on the Reviewing toolbar.

    OR

 Double-click the **TRK** button on the Status Bar.

    The **Highlight Changes** dialog box appears.

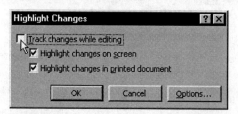

Figure 4.13   Turn on revision tracking here.

2   Select/deselect the **Track changes while editing** check box as desired.

3 Select/deselect the other two check boxes in the dialog box as desired:

- **Highlight changes on screen**: Determines whether revision marks will appear on-screen as you work.

  Deselect this feature if there are numerous reviewers and you want to work on a "clean copy," taking all previous edits into account. All changes on-screen are placed in regular text as if they had already been approved.

- **Highlight changes in printed document**: Determines whether revision marks will appear on your printouts.

  Deselect this feature if you prefer to work from a clean hard copy rather than a clean "electronic" one. All changes in the printed document are placed in regular text as if they had already been approved.

4 Choose **OK**.

By default, each person's revisions show up in a different color. You can select "signature colors" for all your revisions, however. You can set one color for all the text you author and another for all the text you mark for deletion. All edits, whether they display on-screen or not (e.g., text formatting when Track Changes is enabled), are "marked" by an outside-border line in the margin. Choose **Options** in the **Highlight Changes** dialog box (see Figure 4.14) to change any default settings for Track Changes:

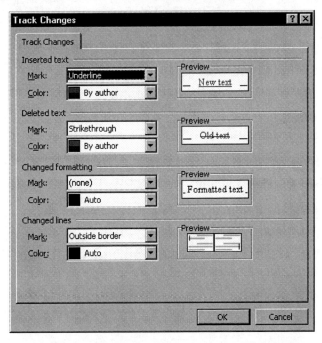

Figure 4.14   Customize your revision tracking here if desired.

Practice Exercise 4-4

Track Revisions

1   Open 📂**04Ex4-4** from the **WORDCert\Word C** folder. Save the document as 💾**04Revis**.

2   Choose **Tools>Track Changes>Highlight Changes** from the menu bar to display the **Track Changes** dialog box.

3   Select the **Track changes while editing** check box. Choose **OK**.

4   Make the revisions shown below:

> **Trip Report: ACME Manufacturing**
> **Carol Smith and John Ames**
>
> On January ~~89~~, ~~John Ames and I~~we traveled to Boston to meet with representatives of ACME Manufacturing to introduce them to our product line. We met with James Kelly, Vice President of Procurement, and Janice Dodson, Vice President of Engineering.
>
> During the ~~3~~three-hour meeting, Ms. Dodson was especially interested in hearing about our Seal-Tite fittings, which she thought might be useful in ~~their~~ ACME's current manufacturing process.
>
> We explained the pricing structure, and offered ACME a 25% discount for large-quantity orders of more than 1,000 pieces of the same model.
>
> Mr. Kelly described ~~their~~ ACME's procurement process to us. ~~I~~We have attached his forms to this report for our files. We must submit invoices within 30 days of delivery, along with signed copies of their purchasing forms; they agree to pay on a Net 30 basis.
>
> We were encouraged by the warm reception we received in Boston from ACME. ~~I~~Carol will follow up with Mr. Kelly in ~~2~~two weeks to pursue a buy commitment.

Figure 4.15   Make these changes to your **04Revis** document.

5   Save and close the document.

ACCEPT OR REJECT REVISIONS

There are three common ways to accept or reject revisions. You can use the Reviewing toolbar, the **Accept or Reject Changes** dialog box, or the shortcut menu (right-click).

The advantage of the shortcut-menu method is that you can use it quickly; you do not have to display a toolbar or open a dialog box to accept or reject changes. This method is often the most convenient when you have only one or two edits to approve or reject.

Simply right-click the edit and specify if you wish to accept or reject it.

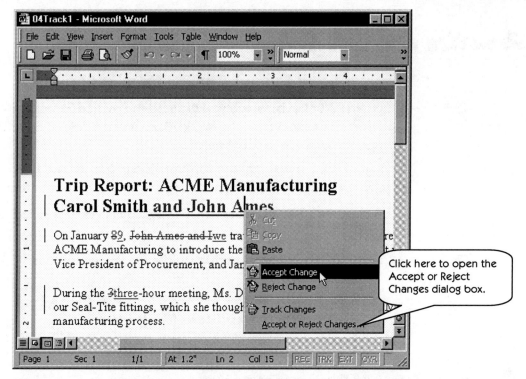

Figure 4.16   If you find have more edits than you anticipated, you can also open the **Accept or Reject Changes** dialog box from the shortcut menu.

The Reviewing Toolbar

You saw the Reviewing toolbar earlier in this chapter, when you learned about the Comments feature (see Figure 4.4). This same toolbar also contains buttons for finding and accepting or rejecting changes:

BUTTON	NAME	DESCRIPTION
	Track Changes	Toggles on/off the use of revision marks. Deselect it to make a revision that does not show on-screen; select it again to continue tracking revisions.
	Previous Change	Moves back to the previous revision (i.e., the first one prior to the insertion point's current location).
	Next Change	Moves forward to the next revision (i.e., the first one after the insertion point's current location).
	Accept Change	Removes the revision marks for the current change and accepts the revision as regular text in the document.
	Reject Change	Removes the revision marks for the current change and rejects the revision.

Table 4.1: The Reviewing toolbar

Practice Exercise 4-5

Accept or Reject Changes (Shortcut Menu and Toolbar)

1. Open 🗁**04Revis**, which you created in Practice Exercise 4-4, or open 🗁**04Ex4-5** from the **WORDCert\Word C** folder. Save the open document as 💾**04Track1**.

2. Right-click the text marked for insertion in the second line, ...*and John Ames*. Choose **Accept Change** from the shortcut menu.

   The revision marks disappear for the change; John's name is added to the byline.

3. Click the **Next Change** button on the Reviewing toolbar.

    TIP: If the Reviewing toolbar is not visible, choose **View>Toolbars>Reviewing** from the menu bar.

   The next change is highlighted—the deletion of *8*.

4. Click the **Reject Change** button.

   The change is rejected; the *8* is no longer marked for deletion.

5. Repeat steps 3 and 4 to reject the next edit.

6. Click the **Next Change** button; then click the **Accept Change** button to accept the deletion of *John Ames and I*.

7. Repeat step 6 to accept the next edit.

   There are no more changes marked through the first paragraph.

8. Save and close the document.

    NOTE: You will finish accepting/rejecting changes using the **Accept or Reject Changes** dialog box in Practice Exercise 4-6.

   A completed example of 💾**04Track1** is available in the **WORDCert\Word C\Samples** folder on the DDC CD.

Use the Accept or Reject Changes Dialog Box

Some people prefer the **Accept or Reject Changes** dialog box to the shortcut menu and toolbar methods because the dialog box provides additional capabilities, and therefore people may feel they have more control. For example, you can use it to accept or reject all the changes in the document at once.

CAUTION: Accepting or rejecting all the changes at once may produce unexpected results. It is always wise—whether you are group editing or working on a personal document—to review all changes before choosing either of these options.

Accept or reject changes (dialog box):

1 Choose **Tools>Track Changes>Accept or Reject Changes** from the menu bar to display the **Accept or Reject Changes** dialog box.

2 Choose **Find** to move to the first change.

Figure 4.17   Changes are labeled with the reviewer's full name and the document review date.

3 Choose **Accept** or **Reject**.

Word moves to the next change automatically.

 4 (Optional) To postpone a change so that you may consider it further, choose **Find** again.

5 Repeat steps 3-5 until all changes have been accepted or rejected as desired.

6 Choose **OK**.

7 Choose **Close**.

Practice Exercise 4-6

Accept or Reject Changes (Dialog Box)

 1 Open 📂**04Track1**, which you created in Practice Exercise 4-5, or open 📂**04Ex4-6** from the **WORDCert\Word C** folder. Save the open document as 💾**04Track2**.

2 Position the insertion point at the beginning of the document if necessary.

3 Choose **Tools>Track Changes>Accept or Reject Changes** from the menu bar to display the **Accept or Reject Changes** dialog box.

4 Choose **Find**.

The strikethrough text, *3*, is selected.

5 Choose **Reject**.

The next change, *three*, is selected.

6   Choose **Reject** again.

The next change, *their*, is selected.

7   Choose **Accept**.

8   Choose **Accept All** to accept all the remaining revisions.

A message verifies that you want to accept all remaining revisions without reviewing them.

9   Choose **Yes**.

10   Choose **Close**.

 11   Save and close the document.

A completed example of 🖫**04Track2** is available in the **WORDCert\Word C\Samples** folder on the DDC CD-ROM.

Protect Document

Using revision marks is one way to make sure that no one alters your document without your knowledge and consent—provided that each person keeps Track Changes on the entire time he/she is reviewing the text.

Protecting a document offers a stronger defense against unauthorized changes, however, as it blocks people from making any changes at all. You might want to do this, for example, if you were posting personnel policies on a network and you wanted everyone to be able to read, but not modify, them.

On the other hand, if you are involved in a group project, using these options will probably not go over well with your coworkers who may (with reason) feel that you do not trust them. Your work partners may be merely confused by the unavailability of options; they might be annoyed because they are not able to get assigned work done; or they may get downright angry. Carefully evaluate whom you really need to "protect" your document from before using these options. To avoid misunderstandings, always let people know ahead of time if you have enabled any of these features.

There are three ways to protect a document:

• **Protect for Tracked Changes:** Any changes made appear in Track Changes, which is password protected. The status bar indicator is locked on and the **Track Changes**, **Accept Change**, and **Reject Change** buttons on the Reviewing toolbar are unavailable to users who open a file with this option selected.

• **Protect for Comments:** Users can only add comments. Screen elements are the same as for the option above, but only comments are inserted as Tracked Changes.

• **Protect for Forms:** Users can add comments only in form fields or unprotected sections, which you specify on a case-by-case basis. The entire Reviewing toolbar is unavailable—as are most of the **Edit**, **Insert**, and **Format** menu items.

You can protect a document either with or without a password. Unless a password is assigned, however, Protect Document is a very weak form of security; anyone can turn the protection off by choosing **Tools>Unprotect Document** from the menu bar.

Protect a document:

1   Choose **Tools>Protect Document** from the menu bar:

Figure 4.18   Choose how you want the document protected, and specify a password.

2   Choose a document protection level: **Tracked changes, Comments,** or **Forms.**

 TIP: You can choose **Forms** even if you don't have form features in your document. The option would then forbid all changes.

3   Type a **Password.**

 NOTE: Passwords are case sensitive and can be any combination of letters, numbers, spaces, and symbols—up to 15 characters.

4   Choose **OK.**

The **Confirm Password** dialog box displays.

5   Retype the password, and choose **OK.**

Unprotect a document:

1   Choose **Tools>Unprotect Document** from the menu bar to display the **Unprotect Document** dialog box.

2   Type your **Password.**

3   Choose **OK.**

Practice Exercise 4-7

Protect and Unprotect a Document

1   Open 📁**04Track2**, which you created in Practice Exercise 4-6, or open 📁**04Ex4-7** from the **WORDCert\Word C** folder. Save the open document as 💾**04Protct**.

2   Password-protect the document by doing the following:

- Choose **Tools>Protect Document** from the menu bar to display the **Protect Document** dialog box.

- Choose **Tracked changes**, if necessary.

- Type a password (of your choice—but don't forget it!) in the **Password** box. Choose **OK**.

- Retype the password when prompted, and choose **OK** again.

3   Change the meeting date in the first paragraph to *January 10*.

4   Change *3-hour meeting* back to *three-hour meeting* in paragraph 2.

5   Choose **Tools>Track Changes>Accept or Reject Changes** from the menu bar to display the **Accept or Reject Changes** dialog box.

The **Accept**, **Reject**, **Accept All**, and **Reject All** buttons are unavailable.

6   Choose **Close**.

7   Choose **Tools>Unprotect Document** from the menu bar.

8   Type the **Password**, and choose **OK**.

9   Accept both new revisions using the shortcut-menu method.

10 Save and close the document.

A completed example of 💾**04Protct** is available in the **WORDCert\Word C\Samples** folder on the DDC CD-ROM.

LESSON 5: MICROSOFT OFFICE DATA SHARING

Word 2000 is a powerful program by itself, but when you combine its capabilities with those of the other Microsoft Office 2000 suite programs, it becomes an amazing tool. For example, you may need to create a report that includes number specifications (Access or Excel), charts representing numerical summaries (Excel or Microsoft Graph), and a workflow chart (PowerPoint). Since the Office programs are specialized, take advantage of each program's capabilities and then link (or insert) the finished product into your final Word report.

In this lesson, you will learn to:

> Create links between Office files

> Embed data from Office programs

> Import data into charts

> Maintain linked files

> Work with Excel worksheets and charts in Word

> Create Word charts with Microsoft Graph

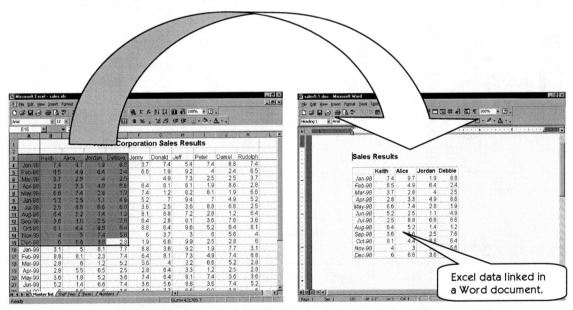

Figure 5.1   Linking data from other programs enhances your Word documents.

Connect Data Files

There are two ways to "connect" data files from different programs: linking and embedding. These two methods are different in two main respects: where the object is stored and how that object is updated once it is placed in the destination file.

In this context, an **object** is any piece of data–from a single character to an entire data file–that is placed in another data file. For example, if you copy a few cells from Excel and paste them into a Word document, that group of pasted cells is considered an object.

Linking can be considered a special kind of Paste procedure that maintains a connection between the source file and the destination file. In a regular Paste procedure, when you paste a chart from Excel into a Word document, the Word copy does not change when you edit the original Excel chart. When you use Link, however, the linked object in the destination file reflects any changes made to the source *file*; you can update linked objects because a connection is maintained between the two files and the object technically does not become a part of the destination file.

Embedding, on the other hand, establishes the object as part of its destination file but maintains a connection with the source *program* only. For example, if you embed a Paint picture in a Word document, you can double-click that picture at any time to open the image into Paint for editing.

	Link	Embed
Paste Special option	**Paste link**	**Paste**
Data stored	Source file	Destination file
Update	Automatic	N/A
Advantages	Ability to enter numerous and/or frequent edits in source file Automatic update in destination file	Ability to enter minor and/or infrequent edits quickly in destination file It is not necessary to keep the source file in the same location
Disadvantage	Must keep source file in same location to maintain links	Cannot transfer edits from destination file to source file

Table 5.1   Linking vs. embedding

When you link, you create a connection between the source file and the destination file. When you embed, you create a connection between the destination file and the source file's program.

Share Data

How do you know which procedure to use when you're working with multiple programs? It all depends on the needs of your document, and the kinds of edits you are likely to make in the future.

Feature	Data-sharing capability
copy and paste	Copy data from one program to another; no edits are expected.
drag-and-drop editing	Copy or move data quickly from one program to another; no edits are expected.
hyperlink	Allows users to jump to data available in another program via hyperlink text or a graphic.
link	Paste data into another program, keeping that data current if the source file is edited.
embed	Paste data into another program, editing that data from the destination file only.

Table 5.2   How do you want to connect to your documents?

Link Data

You may have heard the term **OLE** before; it stands for **Object Linking and Embedding**, a variation on copy-and-paste. OLE is the process by which a link is maintained between one document and another.

There are two ways to link objects in Word 2000: Paste Special and Insert Object. Use Paste Special to link only a portion of a file; use Insert Object to link an entire file. For example, if you need to use project-costs data in an Excel worksheet, use Paste Special. If you need to link an entire Paint graphics file, use Insert Object.

To edit linked data, you have two choices: open the source program and source file and edit it, or double-click the linked object to start the source program and open the source file. Once again, all edits to a linked source file are mirrored in the destination file.

LINK A PART OF A FILE

When you link data with Paste Special, you must open two programs—the source program and the destination program. While Paste Special can be used to paste the entire file, it is most often used to paste partial files.

To store the information as an icon in the destination file, select the **Display as Icon** check box and change the icon and/or icon caption as desired. Once this icon is inserted in the destination file, you can reposition it. This option, which is actually a fast method of inserting a graphic hyperlink, is useful if you don't have much room to display the full contents of the linked data. The user double-clicks the icon to display the linked object in its source program. All link icons are anchored automatically.

Link data (Paste Special):

1   Start the source program.

 2   Select and copy the data you want to link.

3   Switch back to Word, the destination program.

4   Position the insertion point where you want to place the data.

5   Choose **Edit>Paste Special** from the menu bar:

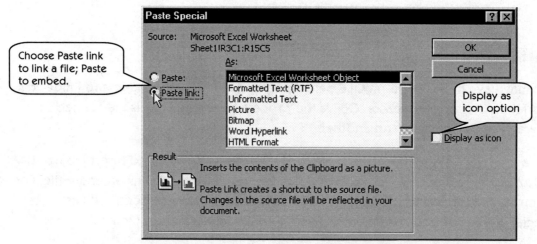

Figure 5.2   Specify if you want to link (**Paste link**) or embed (**Paste**) data.

6   Choose **Paste link**.

7   Select the file type that ends with *Object* from the **As** box (e.g., to paste from Excel, select **Microsoft Excel Worksheet Object**).

 NOTE: If you do not see any choices in step 5 that end in *Object*, you cannot embed the type of data that you have selected. You are trying to embed data from a program that does not fully support OLE (Object Linking and Embedding).

8   Choose **OK**.

The linked data appears in your Word document but does not become part of the destination file. The linked object can be updated when the source file is updated.

Practice Exercise 5-1

Link Data (Paste Special)

1   Create a new, blank document. Save the document as 🖫**05Sales1**.

2   Type the following heading with the Heading 1 style applied: Sales Results . Then insert a blank line beneath the heading.

3   Start Microsoft Excel and then open 📂**05Ex5-1** from the **WORDCert\Word C** folder.

4   Select the range A3:E15 and choose **Edit>Copy** from the menu bar.

5   Switch back to **05Sales1** in Word.

6   Choose **Edit>Paste Special** from the menu bar to display the **Paste Special** dialog box.

7   Choose **Paste link**.

8   Select **Microsoft Excel Worksheet Object** from the **As** box.

9   Choose **OK**.

Sales Results

	Keith	Alice	Jordan	Debbie
Jan-01	7.4	9.7	1.9	8.8
Feb-01	6.5	4.9	6.4	2.4
Mar-01	3.7	2.8	4	2.5
Apr-01	2.8	3.3	4.9	8.6
May-01	6.6	7.4	2.8	1.9
Jun-01	5.2	2.5	1.1	4.9
Jul-01	2.5	8.8	6.6	6.6
Aug-01	6.4	5.2	1.4	1.2
Sep-01	3.6	3.6	2.5	7.6
Oct-01	8.1	4.4	8.8	6.4
Nov-01	4	3	7.4	5.6
Dec-01	6	6.6	3.6	2.8

Figure 5.3   Excel data linked to a Word document.

10 Save and close **05Sales1**.

11 Close **05Ex5-1** but do not save changes.

LINK AN ENTIRE FILE AS AN OBJECT

Word's Insert Object command allows you to link a large file—an Access database, an Excel worksheet, or a PowerPoint presentation—but does not require you to open the source file.

Link data (Insert Object):

1   Start Word, the destination program.

2   Position the insertion point where you want to place the data file.

3   Choose **Insert>Object** from the menu bar to display the **Object** dialog box and then choose the **Create from File** tab:

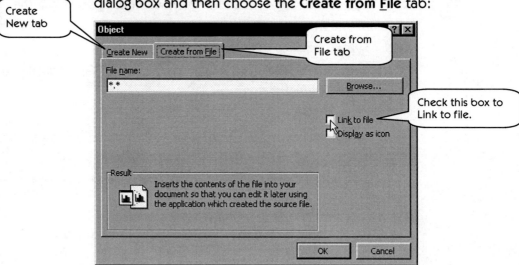

Figure 5.4   Inserts and links the file so you can edit it later using the source program.

4   Do one of the following:

   •   Type the complete path and **File name** of the file to link.

   •   Choose **Browse** to display the **Browse** dialog box. Locate and select the file to link, and then choose **Insert**.

5   Select the **Link to file** check box.

6   Choose **OK**.

   The linked data appears in your Word document but does not become part of the destination file. The linked object can be updated when the source file is updated.

Practice Exercise 5-2

Link Data (Insert Object)

1 Open ⊡**05Ex5-2** from the **WORDCert\Word C** folder. Save the document as ⊟**05Link1**.

2 Position the insertion point on the second line, beneath the first question.

3 Choose **Insert>Object** from the menu bar to display the **Object** dialog box, and then choose the **Create from File** tab.

4 Choose **Browse** to display the **Browse** dialog box.

5 Locate and select the bitmap file named ⊡**05PicA** in the **WORDCert\Word C** folder, and choose **Insert**.

6 Select the **Link to file** check box.

7 Choose **OK**.

8 Position the insertion point on the second line, beneath the second question.

9 Repeat steps 3-7 to insert the ⊡**05PicB** bitmap file from the **WORDCert\Word C** folder:

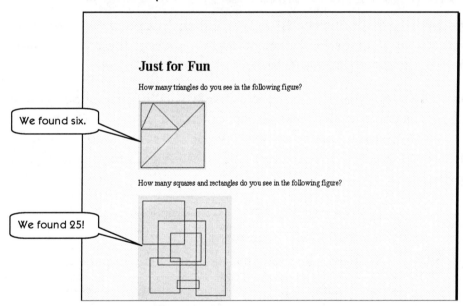

Figure 5.5 Your **05Link1** document after pasting links to the two pictures.

10 Save and close the document.

Embed Data

As noted in Table 5.1, the two advantages of embedding data are the fact that 1.) you have the ability to enter minor and/or infrequent edits quickly directly in destination file, and 2.) it is not necessary to keep the source file in the same location.

Keeping in mind that the difference between linking and embedding lies mainly in the object's location and how that object is updated once it is inserted, it becomes apparent why embedding has the advantages it does. Embedding establishes the object as part of the destination file but maintains a connection with the source *program* only; it loses all connections with the source file.

To edit an embedded object, simply double-click it to display the source program's editing tools. You are then able to modify a *copy* of the original source file. For example, if you embed a range of Excel cells in Word and then double-click the object, Excel "restarts" within the Word window (that is, its menu bar and toolbars reappear), allowing you to edit the cells. Once you embed objects, it no longer matters what workbook they were originally a part of; those particular cells now belong only to the destination file.

EMBED DATA FROM AN EXISTING FILE

Depending on your specific needs, you can either: 1.) embed data from a source file, or 2.) create a new, embedded element directly in Word. These options are the same as those you saw when linking: Paste Special and Insert Object.

In a quarterly sales report, for example, you may want to include portions of an Excel worksheet that contains all your sales data organized by region. On the other hand, you may also wish to include a new, small region in a specialized section of your report that highlights the quarterly sales there and provides goals for the next quarter and/or fiscal year.

Embed existing data (Paste Special):

1   Start the source program.

2   Select and copy the data you want to embed.

3   Switch back to Word, the destination program.

4   Position the insertion point where you want to place the data.

5   Choose **Edit>Paste Special** from the menu bar to display the **Paste Special** dialog box (see Figure 5.2).

6   Choose **Paste**, if necessary.

7   Select the file type that ends with *Object* from the **As** box (e.g., to paste from Excel, select **Microsoft Excel Worksheet Object**).

Preparing for Microsoft Office Specialist Certification

NOTE: If you do not see any choices in step 7 that end in *Object*, you cannot embed the type of data that you have selected. You are trying to embed data from a program that does not fully support OLE (Object Linking and Embedding).

8 Choose **OK**.

The embedded data appears in your Word document and becomes a part of the destination file. The embedded object is no longer connected to the source document; any changes are not reflected in the source file.

Edit an embedded object:

1 Double-click the embedded object to display the source program's tools within the Word window.

2 Edit the embedded data as desired.

3 Click away from the embedded data to hide the source program's tools.

Practice Exercise 5-3

In this exercise, you will embed the same cells that you linked in Practice Exercise 5-1. You will then compare the results.

Embed Existing Data (Paste Special)

 1 Open 📂**05Sales1**, which you created in Practice Exercise 5-1, or open 📂**05Ex5-3** from the **WORDCert\Word C** folder. Save the open document as 💾**05Sales2**.

 2 Position the insertion point at the end of the document.

 3 Start Microsoft Excel and reopen 📂**05Ex5-1** from the **WORDCert\Word C** folder.

 NOTE: You are instructed to reopen the Excel worksheet from Practice Exercise 5-1 in the step above because the data file you are using is linked to that file.

 4 Copy the range A3:E15.

5 Embed Excel data in your Word document by doing the following:

- Switch back to **05Sales2** in Word.

- Insert another blank line at the end of the document.

- Choose **Edit>Paste Special** from the menu bar to display the **Paste Special** dialog box.

- Choose **Paste**, if necessary.

- Select **Microsoft Excel Worksheet Object** from the **As** box.

- Choose **OK**.

6 Edit embedded Excel data in your Word document:

- Double-click the embedded Excel object to display the source program's tools.

- Change the value in Keith's *Jan-01* sales to *4.5*; change Keith's *Feb-01* sales to *5.2*.

- Click away from the Excel worksheet object to hide Excel's program tools.

7 Compare the linked object with the embedded object by doing the following:

- Notice the value for Keith in *Jan-01* and *Feb-01*.

- Scroll down to see the embedded object and notice the same values:

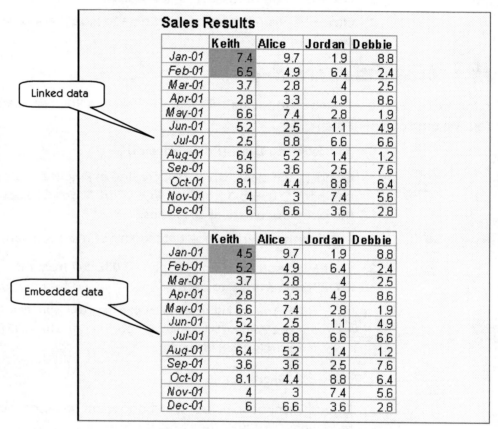

Figure 5.6 There is no visible difference between the linked and embedded data in your **05Sales2** document. The changes made in step 5 have been highlighted in this illustration.

8 Save and close **05Sales2**.

9 Close **05Ex5-1** but do not save changes.

EMBED A NEW OBJECT

To create and embed a new object in Word—for example, a new Paint (bitmap) picture or a simple worksheet—use this procedure, which works much like the Insert Object command you saw earlier in this lesson. When you embed a new object, you are not required to open the source file.

Embed a new object (Insert Object):

1　Start Word, the destination program.

2　Position the insertion point where you want to place the new object.

3　Choose **Insert>Object** from the menu bar to display the **Object** dialog box. Then choose the **Create New** tab if necessary.

4　Select the desired new **Object type** from the list.

5　Choose **OK**.

The program for creating the object appears within your Word window. The window below appears if you selected **Bitmap Image** in step 4:

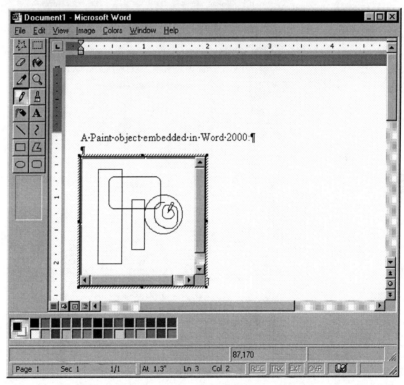

Figure 5.7　Note the following Paint program elements in the shared Word program window: menu items, tools, color palette, and small workspace. The title bar, status bar, and main workspace are still Word's.

6　Create the new embedded object as desired.

7　Click away from the embedded object's workspace to hide its program tools.

Practice Exercise 5-4

Embed a New Object (Insert Object)

1 Create a new, blank document. Save the document as 🖫**05Paint**.

2 Type the following text and then insert two blank lines:

> Double-click the following image to edit it in Paint, which opens into Word 2000.

3 Choose **Insert>Object** from the menu bar to display the **Object** dialog box. Choose the **Create New** tab if necessary.

4 Select **Bitmap Image** from the **Object type** list; then choose **OK**.

5 Draw and format a simple picture using AutoShapes and the color palette:

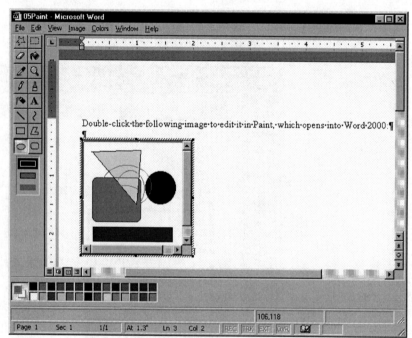

Figure 5.8   Use the Paint tools to draw your object.

6 Click away from the picture to hide the Paint program's tools.

7 Double-click the picture to redisplay Paint's tools.

8 Edit the picture as desired, and then hide the Paint program's tools again.

9 Save and close the document.

Work with Links

If you are generating a Word document for traditional or Web publication, you should verify that your links are up to date. From the **Links** dialog box, you can update links, specify an update method, open or change source files, and/or break the links.

UPDATE LINK

While links are updated automatically whenever you reopen your destination document, you may also choose to update links manually.

Update links manually:

1   Open the destination file to update.

2   Choose **Edit>Links** from the menu bar:

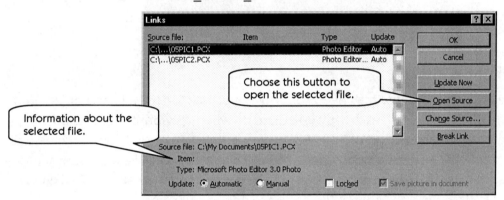

Figure 5.9   Manage your links using the **Links** dialog box.

3   Select the link to update from the **Source file** list; then choose **Update Now**.

4   Choose **OK**.

If you have a linked file that is edited continually but you only want the link updated at specified intervals, you can change the link's Update setting. The link can only be updated manually once you have changed this setting.

Change a link's Update properties:

1   Choose **Edit>Links** from the menu bar to display the **Links** dialog box.

2   Select the link you want to change from the **Source file** list.

3   Select **Automatic** or **Manual**, as desired, next to Update.

4   (Optional) To block all link updates, select the **Locked** check box.

5   Choose **OK**.

BREAK LINK

You may accidentally break a link by moving or deleting a linked source file. When you break a link, the linked object becomes a normal object in the document, as if you had placed it there using the copy-and-paste procedure. You may also have an instance when you know you want to break a link but keep the linked data in place because you are going to delete the source file.

Break a link:

1   Choose **Edit>Links** from the menu bar to display the **Links** dialog box.

2   Select the link you want to break from the **Source file** list.

3   Choose **Break Link**.

4   Choose **Yes** to confirm that you want to break the selected link.

5   Choose **Close**.

    The object remains in the document.

CHANGE SOURCE FILE

There are many reasons you may need to change a source file for a linked object, but most of them occur when files are group-edited or when the source file is used extensively over a long period of time. For example, links are often broken accidentally when a source file is renamed or moved. You will also find that links that were set for manual update but that have not been maintained also need their source files changed from time to time when the source file has been edited regularly.

Keep in mind, however, that this procedure works only for source files of the same size. In other words, if your new source file is larger or smaller than the current linked object, simply break the old link and then link the new source file.

Reconnect links:

1   Choose **Edit>Links** from the menu bar to display the **Links** dialog box.

2   Select the link you want to update from the **Source file** list.

3   Choose **Change Source** to display the **Change source** dialog box.

4   Locate and select the new source file.

5   Choose **Open**.

    The link is updated in the **Links** dialog box.

6   Choose **OK**.

Practice Exercise 5-5

Manage Links

1   Open 📁**05Sales2**, which you created in Practice Exercise 5-3, or open 📁**05Ex5-5** from the **WORDCert\Word C** folder. Save the open document as 💾**05Sales3**.

2   Start Microsoft Excel, open 📁**05Ex5-1** from the **WORDCert\Word C** folder, and save the Excel workbook as 💾**05SaleA**.

> **NOTE:** You are instructed to reopen the Excel workbook from Practice Exercise 5-1 in the step above because the data file you are using is linked to that file.

3   In Excel, change Debbie's *Jan-01* sales figure to *1.1*.

4   Switch back to **05Sales3** in Word:

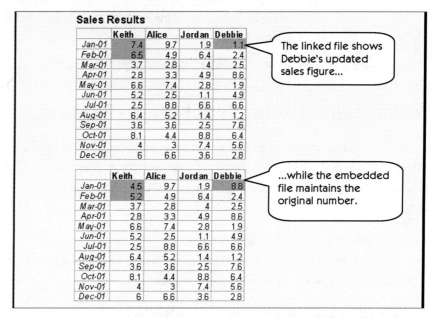

Figure 5.10   The linked table (the one on top) is updated automatically. The changes made in Practice Exercise 5-3 and in step 3 above have been highlighted in this illustration.

5   Choose **Edit>Links** from the menu bar to display the **Links** dialog box.

6   Choose **Change Source** to display the **Change source** dialog box.

7   Locate and select **05SaleA**. Choose **Open**.

The **Source file** is updated in the Links dialog box.

8   Choose **OK**.

9   Choose **Edit>Links** again, choose **Manual** next to Update, and
    then choose **OK**.

10 Switch back to **05SaleA** in Excel, and then make the following
    changes:

Jordan	Apr-01	9.4
	May-01	8.2
Alice	Mar-01	3.2
	Nov-01	2.9

11 Switch back to **05Sales3** in Word, and notice that the linked
    table is not updated.

12 Choose **Edit>Links** again, choose **Update Now**. Choose **OK**.

    The linked table is updated.

13 Choose **Edit>Links** once again, choose **Break Link**, and choose
    Yes to confirm that you want to break the selected link.

    The **Edit>Links** command is no longer available because there are no links
    available in the document.

14 Save and close **05Sales3** and **05SaleA**.

Data-Sharing with Excel Worksheets

So far in this lesson, you have learned how to insert data from an Office program into
Microsoft Word 2000 using linking and embedding. The skills you've learned apply to
almost any program, including non-Microsoft programs such as WordPerfect and
Lotus 1-2-3.

But wait—there's more! Since Microsoft Excel is by far the most popular program used
in conjunction with Word, Microsoft provides several tools designed specifically to
make importing worksheet data even easier.

EMBED AN EXCEL WORKSHEET (TOOLBAR)

Word provides a toolbar-button equivalent to the **Insert>Object** menu bar command—
the **Insert Microsoft Excel Worksheet** button on the Standard toolbar. This button
works just like Word's **Insert Table** button: Click the button, and then drag across the
drop-down palette to choose the number of columns and rows to create.

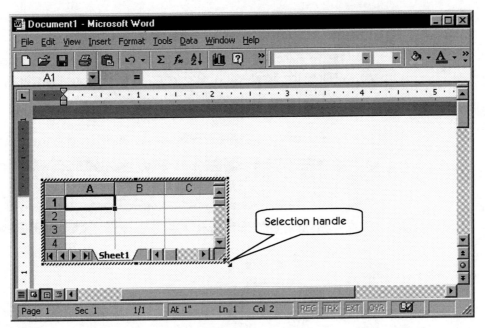

Figure 5.11   Drag a selection handle to enlarge or reduce the Excel workspace window.

When you embed an Excel worksheet using this method, Excel appears "in miniature," as it did when you edited embedded objects earlier in this lesson. The Excel menu bar, toolbars, and the Formula bar appear along with a small Excel workspace window inside Word's main window. The Excel window contains independent scroll bars for worksheet navigation. You can size the Excel workspace by dragging any of its eight selection handles.

Embed an Excel worksheet (toolbar):

1   Position the insertion point where you want to place the Excel data.

2   Click the **Insert Microsoft Excel Worksheet** button on the Standard toolbar.

3   Drag the mouse across the drop-down palette to select the number of columns and rows you want in your spreadsheet. Click once the spreadsheet reaches the desired size:

Figure 5.12   Specify the size of the embedded Excel spreadsheet.

NOTE: Microsoft uses the terms *worksheet* and *spreadsheet* interchangeably here. Try not to let this confuse you.

4   Enter data into the cells and format the worksheet as desired, using the Excel menus and toolbar buttons.

 TIP: To make the worksheet easier to work with, you might want to enlarge the Excel workspace window (by dragging the selection handles) while entering data. You can reduce the window once you are finished, so that only the cells containing data are visible.

5   Click away from the Excel worksheet to hide its program tools:

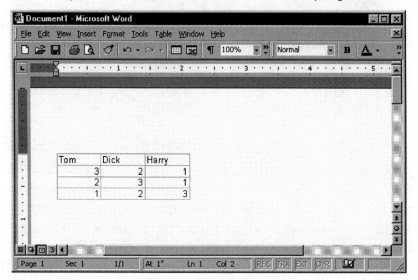

Figure 5.13   Word's menu and toolbars reappear.

Even though the Excel data looks like a table in Figure 5.13, you cannot edit it as you would a Word table; you must double-click it to redisplay Excel's program tools.

To delete an embedded Excel object, simply click it to select it (the eight selection handles alone appear) and press the **Delete** key.

CONVERT AN EXCEL WORKSHEET TO A WORD TABLE (COPY AND PASTE)

While Excel has the best tools for performing calculations on tabular data, Word has the best tools for formatting that data. If you have data in an embedded Excel worksheet, you can make use of both programs' talents.

The copy-and-paste procedure below also allows you to convert from a separate Excel worksheet into a Word table. Just select the appropriate cells in step 2.

Format Excel data in Word (Copy and Paste):

1   (Optional) To format an embedded Excel worksheet, double-click the worksheet to activate the Excel controls.

2   Select the cells to format.

 3   Choose **Edit>Copy** from the menu bar.

4   Switch to the destination file in Word, if necessary.

5   Position the insertion point where you want to place the Word table.

6   Choose **Edit>Paste**.

> **TIP:** If you copied from an embedded Excel worksheet that you now no longer need, select the worksheet object and delete it.

7   Format the table as desired, using Word menus and toolbars.

Practice Exercise 5-6

Work with Embedded Excel Cells

1   Create a new, blank document. Save the document as 🖫**05Embed1**.

2   Click the **Insert Microsoft Excel Worksheet** button on the Standard toolbar and drag the mouse pointer across the palette to create a 4 X 5 Spreadsheet.

3   Drag the bottom-right selection handle to increase the size of the Excel workspace window so that columns A through H and nine rows are visible.

4   Type data into the cells, as shown below:

	A	B	C	D	E	F	G	H
1		Spring	Summer	Fall	Winter			
2	Barbie	65	45	34	22			
3	Ken	52	38	50	44			
4	Skipper	49	77	81	25			
5								
6								
7								
8								
9								

Sheet1

Figure 5.14   Enter the data shown above.

5   Resize the Excel workspace window so that only the range containing data appears, A1:E4.

6   Return to Word and save the document.

7   Redisplay Excel's program tools.

8   Select the range A1:E4 and choose **Edit>Copy** from the menu bar.

9   Return to Word once again. Click beneath the embedded object and insert two blank lines.

10 Choose **Edit>Paste** to paste the copied data as a Word table.

 TIP: The Word table can now be formatted as desired.

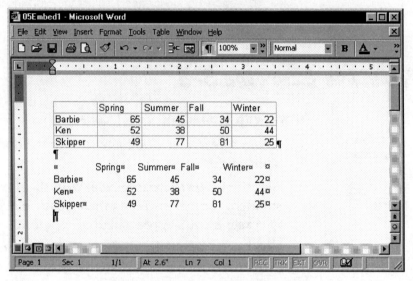

Figure 5.15   The embedded object you created in steps 2-4 is at the top of the document; its Word table copy appears beneath it.

 11 Save and close the document.

Work with Charts

As with other imported data, there are three main ways of working with Excel charts in Word: you can copy it, link it, or embed it. To copy an Excel chart, simply use the cut-and-paste method. To link or embed it, use the Paste Special procedure you learned earlier in this lesson.

Just as you were able to create an Excel worksheet directly in Word with the help of the **Insert Microsoft Excel Worksheet** button on the Standard toolbar, you can also create a new chart directly in Word 2000 using Word's own charting tools.

EMBED A NEW EXCEL CHART

The chart you create using the Insert Object feature provides placeholder data, which you can later replace with your own.

As with any other embedded object, you can double-click the chart to redisplay the editing tools at any time. Drag the selection handles to resize the Excel chart workspace window.

Embed a new Excel chart (Insert Object):

1 Position the insertion point where you want to place the chart.

2 Choose **Insert>Object** from the menu bar to display the **Object** dialog box. Choose the **Create New** tab if necessary.

3 Choose **Microsoft Excel Chart**, and then choose **OK**.

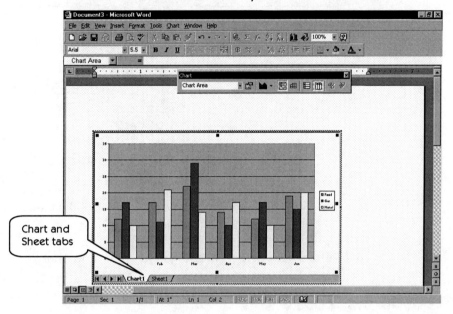

Chart and Sheet tabs

Figure 5.16 A chart appears in the Excel workspace window with placeholder data.

4 Choose the **Sheet1** tab, at the bottom of the window, to switch to the Excel worksheet upon which the chart is based:

	A	B	C	D	E	F	G	H
1		Food	Gas	Motel				
2	Jan	12	17	10				
3	Feb	17	11	21				
4	Mar	22	29	14				
5	Apr	14	10	17				
6	May	12	17	10				
7	Jun	19	15	20				
8								
9								
10								
11								
12								
13								
14								
15								
16								
17								

Chart1 \ **Sheet1** /

Figure 5.17 Worksheet placeholder data.

5 Delete the worksheet placeholder data and replace it with your own data.

6 Choose the **Chart1** tab.

7 Edit and format the chart as desired, using the Excel menus and the Chart toolbar buttons:

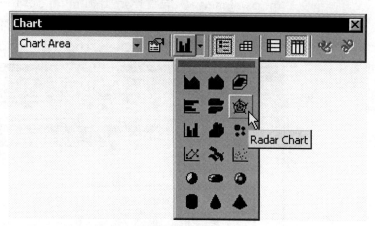

Figure 5.18   Select a different chart type, if desired.

 TIP: ScreenTips are available for all of the tools on the Chart toolbar (**View>Toolbars>Chart**).

8 Return to Word by clicking away from the chart.

Practice Exercise 5-7

Create an Embedded Excel Chart (Insert Object)

 1 Open ⌂**05Embed1**, which you created in Practice Exercise 5-6, or open ⌂**05Ex5-7** from the **WORDCert\Word C** folder. Save the open document as ⌂**05Embed2**.

 2 Select the entire Word table (the one on the bottom) and choose **Edit>Copy** from the menu bar.

3 Position the insertion point at the end of the document, and insert one blank line.

4 Choose **Insert>Object** from the menu bar to display the **Object** dialog box, then choose the **Create New** tab if necessary.

5 Select **Microsoft Excel Chart** from the **Object type** list, then choose **OK**.

6 Choose the **Sheet1** tab in the Excel workspace window, and clear the placeholder data from all cells.

 7 Select cell A1 and then choose **Edit>Paste** from the menu bar to paste the copied table data into the worksheet.

8 Choose the **Chart1** tab.

Notice that the data does not fit properly in the Excel chart.

9 Right-click the Excel chart workspace background and choose **Source Data** from the shortcut menu:

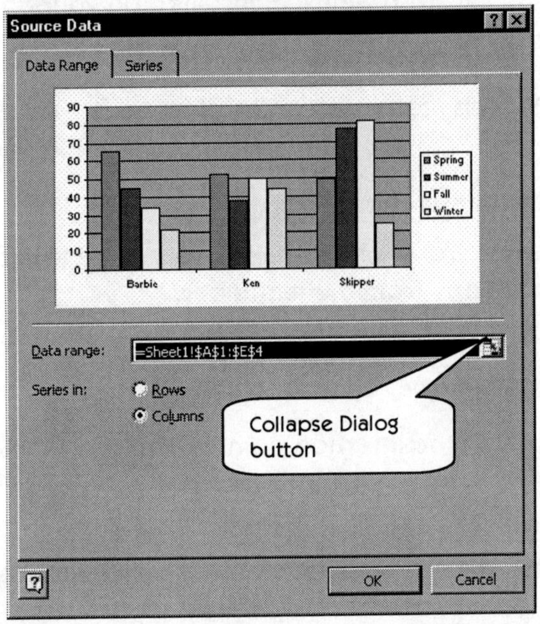

Figure 5.19 When you change the cells that are reflected in the chart, you must also change the source data reference.

10 Change the value in the **Data range** box to the following:

=Sheet1!$A$1:$E$4

NOTE: The exclamation mark (!) is a separator between the sheet name and the range address. The dollar signs ($) denote absolute references (i.e., references that don't change when formulas are moved to other locations).

TIP: If you didn't know the data range to type in step 10, you could select it by doing the following: Click the **Collapse Dialog** button next to the **Data range** box and then select the cells directly on the worksheet.

11 Choose **OK**.

12 Return to Word.

13 Save and close the document.

A completed example of **05Embed2** is available in the **WORDCert\Word C\Samples** folder on the DDC CD-ROM.

CREATE A NEW CHART IN WORD

Word comes with its own simple chart-making program, called **Microsoft Graph**. This program is built into all the Office programs that do not have Excel. If your charting needs are simple, or if you do not have Excel installed on your computer, you can use this program to create a chart.

The chart you create using this feature provides placeholder data, which you can later replace with your own.

Create a new chart:

1   To use Word table data for your chart, select it and choose **Edit>Copy** from the menu bar.

    OR

    Create a new, blank document.

2   Position the insertion point where you want to place the new chart.

3   Choose **Insert>Picture>Chart** from the menu bar:

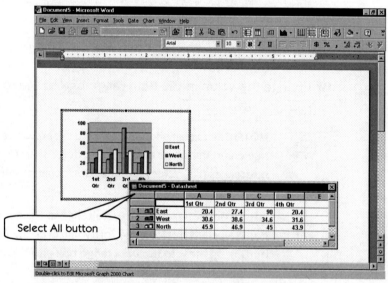

Figure 5.20   A chart appears with a datasheet floating in a separate window. The datasheet contains the values shown in the chart.

4   Do one of the following:

    •   If you copied Word table data in step 1, select the entire datasheet (by clicking the **Select All** button) and then choose **Edit>Paste** from the menu bar.

        OR

    •   Clear the entire datasheet and enter your data, including heading and row labels.

5   Return to Word.

6   (Optional) Drag the selection handles to resize the chart.

7   (Optional) To reformat an area of the object, make sure you are in chart view and then right-click the area and choose **F_ormat>[Object]** from the shortcut menu.

 NOTE: The name of the shortcut menu command in step 7 varies; for example, when you right-click a data series (a bar), the command is **F_ormat>Data _Series**.

IMPORT DATA INTO CHARTS

You can also use Microsoft Graph to import data from text files and Office and non-Office applications. If you have Microsoft Excel 2000 on your computer, you can choose that application in step 3, below, instead.

File extension	File type
.txt, .csv	Text file (delimited)
.wks, .wk1	Lotus 1-2-3
.xls	Microsoft Excel 2000 worksheet or workbook
.xlw	Microsoft Excel 4.0 workbook
.xlc	Microsoft Excel 4.0 (or earlier) chart

Table 5.3   Import these file types into Microsoft Graph.

Import chart data (text file):

 1   Create a new, blank document.

2   Choose **_Insert>_Object** from the menu bar to display the **Object** dialog box; then choose the **_Create New** tab if necessary. *(See Figure 5.4.)*

3   Select **Microsoft Graph 2000 Chart** from the **_Object type** list, and then choose **OK**.

4   Replace the placeholder text by doing the following:

•   Select the entire datasheet (click the **Select All** button).

 •   Choose **_Edit>_Import File** from the menu bar to display the **Import File** dialog box.

•   Click the **Files of _type** arrow and select **Text Files**.

 •   Select the text file to import and choose **_Open** to display the Text Import Wizard.

•   Choose **Next>** twice to accept all the default settings, then choose **_Finish**.

5   Edit imported chart as desired.

Position an Object

After you insert an object—no matter what type of object—you may find it's necessary to force it to stay in place. This is referred to as **anchoring** the object.

Anchor an object:

1   Select the object you need to lock in place.

2   Choose **F̲ormat>[Object]** from the menu bar to display the **Format [Object]** dialog box.

> **NOTE:** The name of the submenu command (and dialog box) in step 2 varies; for example, when you right-click a picture, the command is **F̲ormat>Pi̲cture**.

3   Choose the **Layout** tab if necessary.

4   Choose **A̲dvanced** to display the **Advanced Layout** dialog box, and then choose the **Picture Position** tab.

5   Choose **L̲ock anchor** under **Options**, and then choose **OK**.

6   Choose **OK** again.

Now your object will stay where you placed it.

Practice Exercise 5-8

Create a Chart in Word

1   Open 📂**05Ex5-8** from the **WORDCert\Word C** folder. Save the document as 💾**05Chart1**.

2   Select the entire table and choose **E̲dit>C̲opy** from the menu bar.

3   Position the insertion point on the second blank line beneath the Word table.

4   Choose **I̲nsert>Pi̲cture>Ch̲art** from the menu bar.

5   Replace the placeholder text by doing the following:

   • Select the entire datasheet (click the **Select All** button):

The Select All button

📊 05Chart1.doc - Datasheet					☒
	A	B	C	D	E
	1st Qtr	2nd Qtr	3rd Qtr	4th Qtr	
1 📊 East	20.4	27.4	90	20.4	
2 📊 West	30.6	38.6	34.6	31.6	
3 📊 North	45.9	46.9	45	43.9	
4					

Figure 5.21   Select the entire datasheet.

   • Choose **E̲dit>P̲aste** from the menu bar.

The chart placeholder data is replaced with your copied data.

6   Return to Word.

7   Click the new chart to select it.

8   Drag the middle-right selection handle to the right, enlarging the chart workspace window to display all of the data labels on the horizontal axis (Spring, Summer, Fall, and Winter):

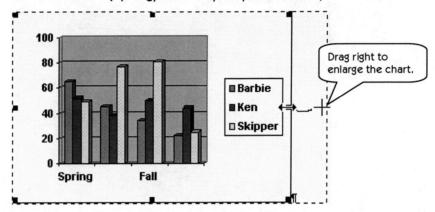

Figure 5.22   Enlarge the chart frame as shown here.

   9   Save and close the document.

A completed example of 🖫05Chart1 is available in the WORDCert\Word C\Samples folder on the DDC CD-ROM.

Index of Microsoft Office Specialist Objectives

About the CD

Inside the back cover of this book, you'll find a CD-ROM that contains:

- **DDC Testing Center software** that provides realistic experience of an actual Microsoft Office Specialist exam.
- **Practice files** that you'll use to complete the exercises in this book. Read the **How to Use the Practice Files** section at the front of the book before beginning the exercises in this book.
- Sample exercise solutions that let you check your work. Read the **How to Use the Sample Exercise Solutions** section at the front of the book.
- **Walk, Run,** and **Fly** challenge exercises for each lesson.
- **Final Exercises** to test the skills you learn at the end of each section.
- **Four bonus lessons** covering advanced Word features.
- **Summaries** of all the lessons.
- **Appendices** covering basic Windows skills, ways to get help in Office, keyboard shortcuts for common tasks, and a glossary of Microsoft Office 2000 terms.
- Adobe® Acrobat Reader® 4.0.

Installing the DDC Testing Center

FOR WINDOWS 95/98, WINDOWS NT 4.0, WINDOWS 2000/XP

1. Exit out of all applications before you begin the installation process.
2. Insert the DDC CD into your CD-ROM Drive.
3. From the Desktop, click on the **Start** button, and then click on **Run**.
4. At the command line, type **D:\DDCtest\SETUP** where **D** is the letter of your CD-ROM Drive, press **Enter**.
5. Setup will now initialize. Follow the onscreen instructions.
6. When your setup is finished, click on **Start/Programs/DDC Testing>DDC Testing Center**.

   After the program loads, the Main Menu appears.